# MINDFUL FINANCE

Text and Image Composition Copyright © 2022-24 Dr Esther J. Cole
First Published 2024.

All rights reserved. No part of this publication may be reproduced, distributed, or transmitted in any form or by any means, including photocopying, recording, or other electronic or mechanical methods, without the prior written permission of the publisher, except in the case of brief quotations embodied in critical review and certain other non-commercial uses permitted in copyright law.

ISBN: 9781805170693 (eBook)
ISBN: 9781803528205 (Hardcover)
ISBN: 9781803528199 (Softcover)

This book was written, designed and edited by Dr Esther J. Cole. The views and opinions expressed in this book are the author's own and do not necessarily reflect the view of any organisation, group or individual mentioned therein.

The author is not a regulated financial advisor. All content is of a general nature and does not address the circumstances of a particular individual or entity. The content is for informational purposes only and does not constitute medical, legal, tax, investment, financial or other advice. Nothing contained constitutes a solicitation, recommendation, endorsement, or offer by the author or any third party to buy or sell any securities or other financial instruments in this or in any other jurisdiction.

Scripture quotations marked (NIV) are taken from the Holy Bible, New International Version®, NIV®. Copyright © 1973, 1978, 1984, 2011 by Biblica, Inc.™ Used by permission of Zondervan. All rights reserved worldwide. www.zondervan.com The "NIV" and "New International Version" are trademarks registered in the United States Patent and Trademark Office by Biblica, Inc.™

Scripture quotations marked (NLT) are taken from the Holy Bible, New Living Translation, copyright ©1996, 2004, 2015 by Tyndale House Foundation. Used by permission of Tyndale House Publishers, Carol Stream, Illinois 60188. All rights reserved.

Scripture quotations marked (ESV) are from The ESV® Bible (The Holy Bible, English Standard Version®), © 2001 by Crossway, a publishing ministry of Good News Publishers. Used by permission. All rights reserved.

Images, unless otherwise specified, are provided by Canva.com and are covered by Canva's Free Content license.

First printing edition 2024.

Publisher: Independent Publishing Network
Printer and Distributer: IngramSpark

Email: WesternSpiralArt@yahoo.com
Website: www.instagram.com/mindful_finance_uk

# Mindful Finance

*How To Be Successful With Money*

**DR ESTHER J. COLE**

Independent Publishing Network

*This book is dedicated to my parents, Alan and Brenda Cole,
and to my family who invested in me as I grew up.*

*It's also dedicated to my Pastors, Luke and Emma Bryant,
and to my Liverpool One Church family
who invested in me and encouraged me as an adult.*

*This book is for anyone who dreams of one day
becoming who they were created to be.*

# Mindful Finance:
## How to be successful with money

### DR ESTHER J. COLE

# CONTENTS

*Dedication*   iv

Foreword   1

Preface   2

Introduction   10

## PART 1: GET YOUR FINANCIAL HOUSE IN ORDER

**1**   Chapter 1: Build A Firm Foundation   39

**2**   Chapter 2: The Four Walls   101

**3**   Chapter 3: Roof of Protection   143

**4**   Chapter 4: Possessions and Debt   161

**5**   Chapter 5: Family   211

**6**   Chapter 6: Generosity   245

## PART 2: JOURNEY TO FINANCIAL SUCCESS

| 7 | Chapter 7: Make Your Garden Grow | 285 |
| 8 | Chapter 8: Roadmap To Your Financial Future | 333 |
| 9 | Chapter 9: A Brief History of Money | 387 |
| 10 | Chapter 10: Ways To Invest | 403 |
| 11 | Chapter 11: Resources | 451 |

| References | 474 |
| Glossary (Phrasebook) | 502 |

| *About The Author* | 506 |

# Foreword

# Preface

I'm so excited that you've decided to pick up a book about finance! We're about to have a conversation about money. Money can be one of the most challenging, mystifying, complicated, and potentially stressful areas of life that we have to navigate as adults. But it doesn't have to be that way. You may even discover that talking about money can be exciting and interesting. It can even be *fun*!

Picking up this book is the first step in mastering a topic that hardly anyone learns about at school. You may remember some money tips from parents, friends, family, TV shows, university or your employer. But you could just as easily have not. And there's no guarantee the advice was any good to start with.

If you were brought up having conversations about money, where talking about finance was as easy as asking, *"How was your day?"* then you were extremely lucky. I'm sure that this book can still help you on your personal development journey. I hope that it will help you realise if you're on track and change course if not.

I'm sure that you can already tell that I'm passionate about personal finance. But I never started out that way. You can get excited about it too!

I'd like to see more financial education everywhere, for people of all ages and circumstances. I believe everyone should have the opportunity to learn how money works and how to take control of their finances. There's so much wisdom available to put into practice. And if we practice, we can get better at it!

The basics of personal finance shouldn't be a mystery. And yet for many of us, it seems like nobody is talking about it, at least not in a positive way. We don't stop learning just because we've left school. That's why I've written this book. I want everyone to have the opportunity to enter the conversation and improve their financial health and wellbeing.

You probably want to see my credentials for writing a book called *'Mindful Finance: How To Be Successful With Money.'* Well, I'm not a millionaire investor, finance guru or money expert, though I've learnt a lot from people who are. Mine is not exactly a *rags-to-riches* success story. I'm still on the journey too.

I feel like I'm in the process of becoming who I was created to be. I'm probably a lot like you. I'm someone who used to be disorganised with money. Then I had a wake-up call and decided to get my financial house in order. It's changed the way I see the world and how I understand my place in it. Even now, I'd say I'm a work in progress and I probably always will be.

I think I had a relatively *normal* upbringing. My sister Liz and I were blessed with a loving family who encouraged us to develop a love of learning. We were probably a middle-income family (as a kid you don't think to ask your parents how much they make and whether it's above or below average). Both my parents were the first in their family to go to university and that's where they first met.

I worked hard at school, got the grades and became a doctor. But that didn't mean that I had it all together. I had money coming in but I didn't know what to do with it. Being disorganised with money is easy, especially when you don't know any other way.

Just like the natural state of a field or garden is for weeds to grow, organising our lives takes intentional actions, energy, self-discipline and hard work. Though some people are naturally gifted at managing money, I wasn't one of them. However, I discovered that becoming successful with money is something that you can learn and get better at. Over time, it's possible to radically change the direction of your life.

*Mindful Finance* is about paying attention to where we are in our money situation. It means making deliberate choices every day because the little things we do regularly have far-reaching consequences. Some decisions may not feel so great in the here and now. However, they'll set us up for a better future ahead. Making sacrifices and putting off immediate pleasure may even go against what culture tells us to do. But we don't have to listen to those voices.

That's what I've learnt and I'd like to pass it on to you.

We all have our own unique story to tell. But there are lots of things that make us similar. There's usually a moment on our journey when we get a wake-up call. We go with the flow for as long as we can and then something happens to make us realise that it isn't working. We need to make a change.

Perhaps you find money difficult to manage or you just want to get better at it. Maybe you've never thought about it before. Talking about money may make you feel tense or embarrassed, or maybe you just don't talk about money at all. If any of these things sound familiar, it's okay. You sound like me when I first started adult life. Money came and went, slipping through my fingers like sand. If I had money to spare, I couldn't tell you where it went.

Unfortunately, that's what *normal* looks like in the developed nations. In relatively high-income countries like the UK and USA, we still struggle with money while nearly half of the world lives on less than $5.50 a day.[1] It's estimated that around 60% of Americans are living paycheque to paycheque.[2] Later in this book, we'll look at why that happens and how we can live differently. You don't have to be *average*. You can become *extraordinary*.

I was living in a state of unawareness, doing life on autopilot, wondering why other people seemed to have it all together. I was doing the best I could with the resources and knowledge I had at that time. I did what I thought was right, what felt right, but I always had the sneaking suspicion that I might be missing something. Turns out I had a huge blind spot.

*'How do other people manage their money? Is there a different way to do things?'* The answer turned out to be, yes!

In 2014, I joined Liverpool One Church and heard people talking about money for the first time. They were talking about things like financial stewardship (taking care of the money you've been entrusted to manage), budgeting and generosity. I listened, but I only applied some of it. That's why I ended up where I ended up. But first, I'll take you back to the beginning. Feel free to skip ahead if you want.

I don't remember my family talking about money much, except when we couldn't afford something. I just watched what my parents did. My dad budgeted in his head and collected things like books and guitars. So I grew up in a very interesting but cluttered house. What we experience as children becomes our version of *normal* as well. We absorb and inherit the habits, attitudes and culture of those around us. We inherit a lot more from our family than just our genes.

Grandma started my savings habit for me when I was a child by putting a pound a week into my money box (which I spent on sweets). I knew that my grandparents' generation hated debt and credit cards, but it wasn't too long before I got them anyway. Debt is *normal* when you're going off to uni, right?

The only money lesson I remember from school was being taught how to write a cheque (a relic that some of you will probably never even see!). As a teenager, especially one who was encouraged to study most of the time, I was quite sheltered from real-world responsibilities. I didn't get a part-time job until my late teens when I used my savings to buy a computer of my own.

When I got to university I lived off my student loan and took out more loans to cover my tuition fees. I did some travelling and took out a private loan (just in case). I also had help from my parents, money gifts that I immediately spent. I'm sorry to say I have no idea where the money went. When money came in, I spent it. That's the pattern I took into my working life. It's all I knew.

I'm not sure exactly how much debt I had. I thought of it as a black hole without a defined size or mass. It was just something huge that I carried around, sucking everything in, so it didn't seem to matter how much debt I had. Visualising it in this way helped me cope. One day, I was sure *'Future Me'* would somehow be earning enough to be able to escape the event horizon and pay the debt off. Well, one day we become the version of ourselves that has to tackle our problems head-on.

I managed to get through 6 years at medical school and I accumulated at least £30,000 in student loan debt. Of course, looking back, this isn't much compared to some of today's uni students who could have more than double that amount. But my debt accumulation journey didn't stop there.

I started full-time work as a doctor at age 24. I bought everything with a credit card and tried to pay it off each month, but sometimes it would take two or three. I needed a car, so I took out a car loan. When the car insurance came due I'd put that on a credit card for reward points (for some reason that bill always came as a surprise). My black hole of debt was probably about £45,000 but I can't tell you for sure. I didn't want to pay attention.

Eventually, I started to pay down my debts. But it took years of slow progress. I tried to live a modest lifestyle, but as you get older there are more things to spend money on. I had a vague idea that being debt-free would be a good place to be. But I didn't have a plan for how to get there. Nearly 8 years went by and I still had a £20,000 student loan left. Some people told me not to worry about it because I was on a *normal* trajectory for the millennial generation.

By the age of 30, I can honestly say that I'd never seen a budget before. It was just something I kind of did in my head because that's what I'd seen other people do. I never stopped to evaluate. I thought I was doing just fine... until I wasn't.

Like many other people drifting through life, there comes a point where a crisis hits and you have no choice but to wake up and stare reality in the face. It may not be pleasant at the time, but the lessons you learn can be invaluable. It's usually better to learn from others and avoid having to go through this pain yourself. I've heard it said that many years of experience can be condensed down to a few hours in a self-help book. That's why I'm telling you about my experiences, so you can hopefully avoid learning the lessons the hard way.

In my early 30s, I'd changed my career from being a salaried doctor (where I got a regular paycheque each month) to doing contract work (where some months my income can go to zero). In retrospect, I *really* should have been paying attention to my finances. But I wasn't. Then, one month, my paycheque got delayed. So I ran out of money. Only then did I realise I didn't have any money to pay my rent or bills.

It came as a big surprise. I hadn't realised I was so close to the edge. For the first time, I felt the fear of not having enough. I imagined myself homeless, having to give up my flat and moving in with my wise and frugal grandma. I was embarrassed, overwhelmed and more than a little terrified.

*'Wait a minute, how did I get here? Why don't I have any savings? Why didn't I see this coming? I've done 6 years at uni. I'm a young professional adult with a doctor's title. Why am I borrowing money from my parents in my 30s to pay my rent? This isn't right! Something has to change!'*

I did have a pot of money at some point, but I didn't call it an emergency fund. I hadn't decided in advance what an emergency was. So I dipped into it for all sorts of things and it eventually disappeared.

This was my *'I've had it!'* moment when I knew things couldn't stay this way. I had to ask myself how I'd got into this situation and how I could make sure I never got there again.

In this book, I'm going to share with you some of the things I learned in the process of changing the direction of my life and taking control of my finances. I've already mentioned how money can affect any and every area of our lives. For me, it was a spiritual journey too. The journey to get financially stable was also a journey of faith.

Anyone can find themselves in financial difficulty. Storms can show up at any time, especially when we don't see them coming. Life events can happen, usually all at once. Sometimes paycheques just get delayed or a financial need pops up. But there are lots of things we can do to prepare, to put a cushion between us and life.

It's not just about surviving. We can make decisions that see us thrive. We can become successful with money. We can set financial goals, to go beyond just struggling and getting by. During my research (my curious and panic-stricken internet searches to work out how to get out of the mess I was in), I found many people who have done it and I believe it's possible for you too.

There's something powerful about the story of a person who overcame and achieved that can inspire you to follow in their footsteps. I'm not just talking about me, specifically, though I hope my story does inspire you. There are lots of stories of people who have turned their lives around. While these can sometimes look like cheesy testimonials from someone trying to sell you something, they can also be the thing that makes you believe you can do it too, so keep an open mind!

As I said before, I hope that one day everyone can be part of this conversation about money. Personal finance education is more accessible now than ever before. We can teach kids this stuff. We can teach ourselves. Why is it important? Because it makes life a lot less stressful! We can become financially resilient. Personal finance can be fun! The earlier we start, the more time we have for our money to grow and make a powerful impact on the world.

There are many resources available – videos, blogs, podcasts, books, eBooks, and courses. Some of them are freely available on the internet. Yet I only discovered them when I ran out of money and started searching for a better way to live.

I believe anyone can learn money skills, no matter their income level. However, the key to lasting behaviour change is to be able to apply this knowledge every day. We can develop new thought patterns, positive habits and routines that will last a lifetime. Thankfully, there are resources to help you with that too. You can also help spread the word and invite others to join the conversation.

One brief word of warning. As I'm sure you're aware, you can also find a lot of rubbish advice and misinformation on the internet. Unfortunately, there are always people looking to take advantage of the lone traveller, a mysterious stranger or a sleazy salesman trying to tempt you off the well-beaten track with a shortcut to riches or magic potion to heal all your ailments.

As you start your journey, you'll become a target for crooks. The internet algorithms will send them in your direction. You'll be interrupted by clickbait adverts, scammers and bots disguised as people you trust. So beware!

Be careful not to fall for a *too-good-to-be-true, get-rich-quick* scheme. If someone is promising you great rewards for minimal effort, or telling you that you can have it all right now – don't listen. If someone is promising you a super-rich lifestyle *'if you just follow this simple strategy'* – sorry, but that's usually not the case. Remember, a genuine content creator will never give you their WhatsApp number. Make sure you don't get scammed!

Becoming successful with money can take a lifetime to master. There are tools to help you achieve your goals along the way and enjoy the process. You'll find that we're all pretty much in the process of becoming, working on ourselves to unlock our potential. There are positive voices out there, people who want to help you win. This will help offset the negative voices (including our own!) and people who want to prey on our naivety.

Whether it's education, motivation or learning from the example of others, I recommend finding a community of like-minded people who can journey together with you. You can encourage each other as you work towards your goals. Your aim may be financial freedom or saving for a holiday. It could be using a budget regularly, or saving £10 a week. Success is going to look different for each of us.

Often we can use our own experiences to help others and turn our pain into purpose. You'll find that most people writing self-help books usually have a backstory. There will be some sort of difficulty or struggle they've overcome. Life looks very different on the other side. Often, they've been transformed, with new insights to pass on.

Now I feel like I'm one of *those* people, writing one of *those* books. So, if *Mindful Finance* resonates with you, perhaps you can pass this book on to someone else. Perhaps one day you can share your own story to help someone rewrite theirs.

I'm not a finance expert, but I've been in a pit of debt and found my way out again. As Jim Rohn once said, you can't change your destination overnight, but you can change your direction.

I didn't pay attention to my money and ended up spending all I had. I came to the realisation that you have to be in control of your own finances before you can help someone else with theirs. It's hard to bless others financially without the means to do so. That's when I discovered how important mindful finance can be. It means paying attention to our money situation even if the reality is painful and we'd rather bury our heads in the sand.

In January 2018, I started my first budget. I made a commitment to a process that I've seen work for others. Of course, it eventually worked for me too. This book has a whole chapter looking at ways to pay off debt, if that's your priority.

But I'll also cover everything else besides, which is why the book is unapologetically long. Learning how to pay off debt is only one part of the story.

*Mindful Finance* means paying attention to where our money is going and exploring how money makes us feel. It means understanding why we do what we do when it comes to our spending and saving habits. Our thoughts underpin our behaviour. Changing these thoughts isn't easy, but we can let go of some and try to hold on to new ones.

On this journey, I got to know myself. Then I could start the process of changing things for the better. And yes, it was a kind of healing too.

We can't always control our external circumstances, but we can decide to make some changes in ourselves. It might be a change of outlook, a new attitude, removing a bad habit and replacing it with a positive one, getting around the right people and learning some new skills.

What we change on the inside might just overflow outwards and help us to make the external world around us a little better.

I have a quote on my wall that says, 'It's not how many goals you reach but how many lives you touch.' I need to remind myself of this often as I'm one of those annoying hyper-achievers. As I said, this is a book that's about more than just money. Money touches every single aspect of our lives.

I want this book to be a letter to my previous self, maybe 10 or 15 years ago. I remember clearly the struggles I faced as a young adult, transitioning from being a university student to getting my first job. If that's you now, then this book is written especially with you in mind. Of course, I hope this book will help many people at different ages and life stages. We're all on a journey and we can all get better at managing money.

I hope that you find this book full of wisdom. It contains signposts to the knowledge and education that can get you started on your journey. For those of you already well on your way, I hope that you'll find a cheerleader and companion to help you know that you're on track and spur you on.

As I've said before, I'm not a financial adviser. You'll have to find a regulated professional if you want specific help and advice, someone who can look into your personal circumstances. I'm not a financial coach either, so if you want to get help with changing your behaviours and habits then that might be a worthwhile investment too.

All I am is a fellow traveller, still learning and applying what I'm discovering. I'd like to pass these things on to you: timeless principles, knowledge, behavioural finance and budgeting tips. I'm still in the early stages of my journey but I know I'm moving in the right direction. I want to encourage you to believe that it's possible to take control of your finances and turn things around.

As this world of personal finance education opens up to you, you'll probably feel like you've entered a new country, hearing another language for the first time.

Don't let that put you off. When I started, I needed to know the basics. I needed to know what a budget was and go from there.

But as I grew in confidence (and I hope you will too) I started to learn some of the language and terminology, the weird words finance people use. You can think of this book as your travel guide to the world of personal finance. I've put a handy glossary of terms at the back which might feel like a phrase book at times.

I'm based in the UK, so I'm addressing a mainly UK audience. But I'm mindful that you could be reading this book from anywhere in the world. There are so many wonderful resources out there, mainly from the UK, Europe, North America and Australia, that need to be adapted depending on what country you're living in. You'll have to do your own research to make sure this information still applies to you.

The main differences I've noticed are the types of retirement accounts available. Sometimes the same words have completely different meanings. Sometimes the same type of thing has a different name. You'll also hear student loan debt talked about differently in the USA compared to the UK. But a lot of the same information will apply to everyone.

Wherever you are on your journey – still thinking of getting started one day, just setting out, or well along the path towards financial freedom – I hope this book is a useful guide to becoming *mindful* of your finances and *successful* with your money.

I hope it encourages you to give, save and spend with intentionality, to maximise your positive impact on the world and build a firm financial foundation, so that you can feel a sense of peace, bless those you love and support the causes you care about.

Thank you in advance for taking the time to read this book. You don't have to read all of it in one go. But I'm sure there will be something in here that will help you at some point, perhaps just when you need it the most.

So, let's get started!

# Introduction

**How To Read *Mindful Finance***

This book is split into two parts. I hope that it will give you two distinct frameworks for how to visualise your *Mindful Finance* journey.

In Part 1, I'm going to take you through a series of chapters that help you *'Get Your Financial House In Order.'* We're going to use the analogy of building your financial house from the foundation up – walls, roof, everything! Even if you don't own a house in real life, I hope you're going to enjoy designing your dream financial house.

Part 2 of the book will guide you on your *Journey to Financial Success.'* This will include chapters on building wealth (*Chapter 7: Make Your Garden Grow*), setting goals (*Chapter 8: Roadmap to your Financial Future*) and investing (*Chapter 10: Ways to Invest*).

Like any travel guide, this isn't a book that you can expect to finish in a day. So I don't recommend you try! It took me a year and a half to write it and many more months to edit it! So I don't want you to feel disappointed if your progress feels slow. *Mindful Finance* is a journey of self-discovery, so you can take your time.

If you want to, you can use *Mindful Finance* as a workbook to help you through each phase of your wealth-building journey. Whether you're doing your first budget, paying off consumer debt, saving for an emergency or learning about insurance, I'll talk you through it, step by step.

If you're not there yet in real life, you can still travel ahead in the book to see what could come up in the future. You can read on and build knowledge to inspire you to keep going. You can use *Mindful Finance* as a reference book and dip in and out of topics that interest you.

Perhaps you'd like to invest one day but don't know how to go about it. Maybe you'd like to understand how goal-setting works, but retirement feels like a distant dream. Well, reading ahead may give you the encouragement and motivation you need to get the solid foundations in place. Getting a glimpse of a better tomorrow can show you why it's so important to do the groundwork today. You'll understand what all the hard work is for and why it's so worthwhile.

Now, I know this introduction might seem a bit long. Feel free to skip ahead or return to it again when you're ready. Still, I think it's important to set the scene. I want you to get the most out of this book.

I want this book to be useful to you without being overwhelming. There's a lot of information to process and even more to discover on your own. After all, this is only meant to be an introductory guide! I hope you can use *Mindful Finance* in the way that suits you best, depending on where you're at on your journey.

I decided to write this book with lots of references (mostly websites and YouTube videos) telling you where I got my ideas from and who inspires me. If you don't think of yourself as an academic person or a big reader, try not to let that put you off. I'm the sort of person who likes to know where facts come from so that I can check them. I know some of my readers will be fact-checkers like me. So I've deliberately put in lots of links, resources and signposts for people who want to go and learn more about a topic by themselves.

Unfortunately, there isn't an easy way to link to internet sources in a paper book or eBook. So you may need to use a search engine or do a YouTube search to find a particular video or website I mention. Hopefully, you can find all the resources you need. They may become dated, but new ones will undoubtedly take their place.

Thank you in advance to all of the content creators mentioned in my book. This is my way of suggesting people *'Share, Like and Subscribe'* to your content. I hope I've quoted you in a way that is respectful and represents your views fairly. I hope many of my readers feel inspired to go and look at your work for themselves. I hope that you get some extra traffic to your websites and that a new audience will be introduced to you.

So, dear reader, don't forget to *'Like'* and *'Subscribe'* to any content creators that you enjoy. You'll find that the YouTube algorithm will start recommending other finance videos that you might like based on your viewing history which is how I discovered these channels in the first place.

Do email me to let me know if there are any broken links or websites that are no longer available. I'll try to update future editions.

I've tried to keep things simple. But if there's something you still find confusing or you'd like to get in touch to share your ideas, I'd be happy for the conversation to continue beyond the pages of this book. Feel free to contact me and I'll do my best to reply!

You can email me at:
**WesternSpiralArt@yahoo.com**

There's also my Instagram accounts:
**www.instagram.com/western_spiral_art/**
**www.instagram.com/mindful_finance_UK/**

> *'Nothing is worth more than this day. You cannot relive yesterday. Tomorrow is still beyond your reach.'*
> ~ JOHANN WOLFGANG VON GOETHE

## Mindfulness and Lifestyle Medicine

The title of this book introduces several big ideas and topics that we'll explore in detail: *mindfulness, success* and *money*. But what do these things mean?

*'Mindfulness'* means different things to different people. I use the term *'mindfulness'* in this book quite loosely to mean being aware of ourselves in the present moment. It's a proven way to improve our health and wellbeing, part of stress management and building resilience.

I love the above quote by Goethe. We can't change the past. The future may feel far off. It may seem obvious, but we only exist in the present moment. So we need to keep ourselves grounded in the here and now.

I've recently become interested in *Lifestyle Medicine* and decided to re-write my book with some insights I've learnt from the *British Society of Lifestyle Medicine* (BSLM) Conference 2023 and beyond.

Dr David Unwin, a GP based in Southport, is renowned for achieving significant remission rates in many of his patients with Type 2 diabetes using a low-carb diet approach. He said during his closing remarks, *"Each of us has a range of different futures. But the future you experience depends very much on the choices you make every day. And Lifestyle choices can help give you the future you're hoping for."*

Mindfulness is a key part of personal development and healthy behaviour change. If we aren't aware of our actions and why we do what we do, it's hard to put healthy habits in place or stop the things that are bad for us. This applies to every area of our life, including personal finance.

Though money isn't explicitly mentioned, it can affect each of the 6 Pillars of Lifestyle Medicine.[3] These are:

1. Mental wellbeing
2. Minimising harmful substances (like smoking and alcohol)
3. Healthy relationships
4. Healthy eating
5. Sleep
6. Physical activity

Lifestyle Medicine overlaps with the *NHS's **5 Steps To Mental Wellbeing***: [4]

1. Connecting with other people
2. Being physically active
3. Learning new skills
4. Giving to others (generosity)
5. Paying attention to the present moment (*mindfulness*)

There are many ways to practice mindfulness. Perhaps it's through yoga or meditation, identifying our thoughts and feelings as they arise, watching them drift past like clouds. It could mean being aware of our current situation, the position of our body in the physical world, focusing on our breathing, giving us a sense of grounding. You'll find apps and YouTube videos that can help you with your mindfulness practice – yoga, body scan meditations, sleep wind-downs etc. You can explore and see what works for you.

Perhaps it's going for a walk, paying attention to nature, connecting with the world around us – the greens of the forest, or blues of the ocean. In Lifestyle Medicine, these are sometimes called *'green prescriptions'* and *'blue prescriptions.'* You might even have come across the term *'forest bathing.'*

There's evidence that spending time in nature is good for us. It reduces stress, strengthens our bodies, reconnects us to each other and allows us the time and space to think in our otherwise busy lives. But we've got to look after nature too, so we have to be mindful of environmental issues and planetary health. Later on, you'll see how this relates to how we use our money and resources.

Mindfulness could be doing art or painting, colouring-in, or some other creative task, letting our right brain become active and give us a sense of flow, whilst silencing the left brain's incessant analysing and commentary, even if it's just for a few minutes. It could be journaling or self-reflection. It could be deciding to live with intentionality rather than just drifting through life.

Mindfulness helps us stay connected to the present moment. This creates a place of stillness, an anchor point from which we can gain a new perspective. We can't change the past, but we can still learn from it. We can stop worrying about the future and thinking up worst-case scenarios. We can stop rushing around, striving and being busy. Instead, we can take note of where we are, make a new goal, one with the end in mind, and devise a strategy to get there.

Everyone seems to be talking about mindfulness. Don't worry. I was sceptical too. Then one day I experienced a time of great stress and uncertainty. Mindfulness helped. Eventually, I discovered Dr Giles P. Croft talking about *'Innate Health'* and the 3 principles of **Mind, Consciousness and Thought** developed by people like Sydney Banks and Richard Carlson. You'll find some of those ideas in this book too.

## What is *Mindful Finance*?

There are many ways to think about *'Mindful Finance.'* It could be being aware of where we're at on our path towards financial independence. It could be noticing our spending habits, asking how our decisions today affect our future, the people around us, and our planet (*sustainability*). It could be creating a spending plan, setting a goal and moving towards it with intentionality through our daily habits. All these things require us to be mindful of our finances and aware of our relationship with money.

While mindful finance or *'financial fitness'* isn't one of the 6 pillars of Lifestyle Medicine, the topic of money – including affordability and wealth inequality – comes up again and again when we look at the different domains of health and wellbeing. Money, health and wellbeing are connected. Perhaps our money habits can be seen a lifestyle issue too.

Just like lifestyle and fitness coaches exist for our health, finance coaches exist for our wealth. But this is often an expense that may be unaffordable to a lot of people. Or perhaps it's just not cost effective, especially when we're starting out on our wealth-building journey.

GPs in the UK can refer their patients to get practical support as part of social prescribing, covering topics such as money, debt, housing or legal issues.[5] There's also a suggestion that employers in the USA should offer financial wellness programmes that encourage people to save for retirement along with making better lifestyle choices.[6]

But the majority of us go it alone and don't know who to ask for help. We may not even realise that we need help or that support is available. There's no equivalent to the UK government's healthy eating campaign, encouraging us to eat at least 5 portions of a variety of fruit and vegetables every day, for our financial health. As adults, we're pretty much expected to get on with it.

Can we get financially healthier too? What are the simple steps we can take to improve our financial wellbeing? That's why I want to point you in the direction of the content creators I mention in this book who have created free content so that anyone can go and educate themselves.

Firstly, what do financial struggles look like? Money issues can affect any and every area of our lives. Did you know that money fights and money problems are a leading cause of relationship strain and divorce in the UK and USA? When we haven't got control of our finances it can lead to anxiety and depression. Things like healthy food and gym memberships cost money. The lack of money can leave us feeling stressed and worried. It affects our mental wellbeing and ability to sleep at night, it can cause chronic stress which contributes to physical disease.

What's more, you don't need to have a low income to experience financial strain. You can have a high-income job and still have no money. For many of us, it's not the amount of money we have coming in each month that's the issue. It's knowing how to manage the money we have. It's doing the best we can with what we've got. This is called *'financial stewardship.'*

Improving our financial health can help other areas of our life as well. After all, developing healthy habits in one area of our life can spill over to other areas.

Clearly, we don't all get to start from the same position in life. There are all sorts of inequalities in our society and around the world. There's the divide between rich and poor. There are ethnicity barriers and marginalised groups who may struggle to access healthcare and opportunities available to other people. There's homelessness or poor housing. There's prejudice, discrimination and racism. There's violent crime, war, refugees, modern slavery and human trafficking.

The climate crisis and global warming disproportionately affects the poorest people around the world. These are big system problems which often leave people feeling powerless to improve their situation. The fight to right these wrongs is called *'Social Justice.'*

Lifestyle Medicine recognises that there are *Socioeconomic Determinants of Health.*[7] That's a scientific way of saying that being poor is associated with poorer health. There are lots of reasons why this may be. Unfortunately, more money isn't the answer. It doesn't change the underlying reasons why someone ended up in poverty in the first place.

People who are born into poverty often have the odds stacked against them. There is a growing body of research into adverse childhood experiences (known as 'ACEs'). These are potentially traumatic events, such as experiencing or witnessing violence, abuse, or neglect at home or in their community. More ACEs increases the risk of childhood trauma and is associated with greater risk of poverty in adult life.

ACEs can affect the way people process emotion. It can lead to addiction and substance misuse, criminality, negative habits and dysfunctional coping strategies. ACEs and poverty also make people targets for modern slavery and human trafficking.

ACEs can be passed on to the next generation too. Though it's not easy, the generational poverty cycle can be broken. We'll talk about this more in *Chapter 5: Family*.

When it comes to poverty in the UK, people who live in deprived areas are more likely to struggle to access healthy food, green spaces, and safe places to live, work and exercise. Housing can be overcrowded or unsuitable. The air is more polluted which is associated with more respiratory illnesses. Crime rates are higher.

They may have less support during those crucial years of early childhood development and miss out on educational opportunities later in life. There are higher rates of teenage pregnancy. They are more likely to smoke, drink alcohol and misuse substances. These all contribute to worse health outcomes and keep people trapped in poverty.

Many of the health issues we face today have arisen because our modern lifestyles have changed faster than our bodies can evolve. We live sedentary lifestyles (we don't move as much). We often have high-stress jobs or situations. We've become socially isolated and technology-dependent (we've lost our sense of community). And the cheapest food to access just happens to be ultra-processed and packed with chemicals, sugar or artificial sweeteners. Unfortunately, these lifestyle issues can affect us all, no matter our income level.

Whereas poverty in the Victorian era often looked like malnourished and emaciated people on the verge of starvation, in the USA and UK today we have a childhood and adult obesity crisis which is associated with multiple chronic diseases in later life. It's not the quantity of food that matters, but the quality. We can be overweight, but still lack essential vitamins and nutrients. We might be living longer, but we're not living healthier for longer.

The reason why I'm talking so much about Lifestyle Medicine in this introduction isn't just because I'm a doctor and I want you to live a happier and healthier life (of course I want that for you too). It's because **what we do with our money is a lifestyle choice** too. I want to show you that the choices we make today matter for our future.

I hope I can be sensitive to everyone reading this book, whether you have a higher-than-average income or are on a low fixed income, whether you live in an affluent country or a developing nation. I believe we can all learn how to manage money better and live well on less. And it's okay to ask for help.

One of the criticisms of Lifestyle Medicine – it applies to the personal development industry and I'm sure it will be a criticism of *Mindful Finance* as well – is that it seems to place the burden of lifestyle change on the individual.

In the same way that some people see chronic health issues as the deserved consequence of an unhealthy lifestyle, it's easy to fall into the trap of thinking that poor people deserve to be poor or broke people are in debt as a consequence of their actions. It's important to acknowledge that there are both individual factors and society factors. Sometimes we need the system to change as well.

Inequality and social injustice are complex issues that contribute to poverty in developed countries like the UK and global poverty around the world. Of course, we need real large-scale interventions from governments, charities and NGOs to address them. But there are still things we can do on an individual level, like campaigning for change, raising awareness and building strong community networks.

In reality, we need both - to educate and empower individuals to make changes on a personal level, as well as helping to make our broken world better, tackling the issues that make poverty and social injustice possible. That's why I get excited about personal finance. Taking control of our finances gives us the opportunity to impact the world in a positive way. We can use our time, talents and resources to help other people. We'll talk about this in *Chapter 6: Generosity*.

Anyone can find themselves in poverty or debt. There are all sorts of reasons why we can end up there. But that doesn't mean we need to stay there. We need to believe that change is possible. I fell into the trap of thinking someone would come and rescue me. I was subconsciously waiting for a change in my circumstances rather than doing the hard work myself.

That's why I want to acknowledge that it may feel like the odds are stacked against you. It may be challenging. There may be lots of things you have to overcome. But you can do it, even if it takes a long time.

I want to give you a toolkit to equip you and help you. We need to empower ourselves and others to make some changes. It won't be easy. But you can overcome the things that keep you stuck. There is always something we can do. What we need most is *hope*.

Throughout this book, you'll find plenty of opportunities to stop, breathe and ask yourself questions. I want you to notice where you are, explore what you're thinking and feeling, and ask yourself where those thoughts might have originated from.

Mindfulness is often put in the same category as relaxation. I can't promise that you'll find this book relaxing. You might find it challenging or even unsettling at times. But I hope that you will also find it inspiring and encouraging. Having an open conversation about money, perhaps for the first time, and learning to apply some of these foundational principles should eventually give you a sense of financial peace.

We often live our lives in a state of busy unawareness, experiencing an expectation gap, the disappointment of our reality not turning out how we imagined it would. We may feel stressed and burnt out. We can find ourselves living with the unintended consequences of not paying attention, making mistakes or drifting off in the wrong direction. If we're not careful, we can allow other people to make decisions for us and we can find ourselves far from where we want to be.

Mindfulness also means being aware of where there is a problem and knowing when to ask for help. Some negative emotions might be a warning sign that something is up and we need to take action. If you don't have financial peace – if you feel like you've lost control, if you're anxious and worried about the future – maybe it's time to start by looking at what's causing those thoughts and feelings.

### What To Do In A Debt Crisis

You may have picked up this book because you're facing a debt crisis. Maybe you're feeling overwhelmed, struggling to pay your basic outgoings or have more than a year's income in debt. It's sometimes called a spiral as it's almost impossible to dig yourself out on your own. The more you struggle, the deeper you sink. But help is available.

Unfortunately, it also means that this book isn't for you right now. Hopefully, it will be in future. But right now, you might need a different sort of help.

For my UK readers, I've found a helpful article from the *'Money Saving Expert'* website that tells you what to do if you're facing a debt crisis or debt spiral: [8]

www.moneysavingexpert.com/loans/debt-help-plan/

It's a great place to start if you have overwhelming debt. Feel free to pass this website on to anyone you know who needs help.

This website has information on how to recognise if you might be experiencing a debt crisis. It has links to different charities and organisations that can give you help and advice, such as *StepChange, National Debtline, Citizens Advice* and *Christians Against Poverty*. They have specialist advice and programmes that can help you.

The first step of *Mindful Finance* is knowing where you are right now. If you're in the middle of a debt crisis where things are spiralling out of control I encourage you to recognise it and ask for help. You may feel terrified, ashamed or beyond hope. But bankruptcy isn't always inevitable and there are services available to help you. I encourage you to take action and let someone know you're experiencing difficulty.

It's important to take a debt spiral seriously. Money issues can affect every area of our lives, including our physical and mental health, faith, relationships, emotions and wellbeing.

It's okay to ask for help. It's okay to open up and talk to people about your money struggles. Don't go through this alone and isolated. Try to start a conversation with someone you trust and join a supportive community if you can.

> *'Success is a daily thing, success is determined by your daily agenda...*
> *Do not take the agenda that someone else has mapped out for your life.'*
> ~ JOHN C. MAXWELL

## What Does It Mean To Be *Successful*?

You'll find dictionary definitions of *'success'* as achieving, accomplishing or attaining. Perhaps it's a goal, aim or purpose. It might be something you're trying hard to complete, such as a task, project or physical challenge. Perhaps it's wealth, respect or fame, status or admiration from your peers.

Most of these are worldly views of success, focusing on external appearances or things valued highly by our society and culture.

These definitions don't take into account that you can be apparently *'successful'* in one area of your life, but sadly lacking in others – a life out of balance. There have been many rich and famous people who are unhappy and unfulfilled, who appear to have it all and yet lack some of the most important things. There are things that money can't buy, such as gratitude, joy and happiness, community, peace (freedom from anxiety despite our external circumstances) and a sense of purpose.

So what does it *really* mean to be successful? Why strive for it? Is it even right to strive? What goals are we meant to be achieving anyway? Is it possible for someone to be truly successful in every area of their lives?

When we look at our values, beliefs and priorities, then we're looking at things from a *spiritual perspective*. It may be our sense of who we are (our *identity*), why we're here and what makes life worth living (our *purpose* and *calling*). The answer will be different for each of us.

One of my favourite definitions of success comes from author and speaker, John C. Maxwell. One day I came across a speech he gave about his definition of success. He talks about this in his book *'Today Matters.'*[9]

In summary, he says that most people think of success as a distant destination, a dream or a place that they can arrive at one day with a clearly defined endpoint. Instead, he defines success as a process or a journey. The very fact that you are moving in the direction of your goal means that you are being *successful* every day and you achieve this by setting a daily agenda.

I've been trying to apply this to the writing process of this book. I've been taking a little bit of time to regularly write and edit, to reflect and gather any content that I come across. You'll see what progress I made by tracking the dates on my references. Some days I'd write loads. Then maybe there would be a few weeks where I stopped writing, where life happened and I had to focus on my job in the hospital or some other deadline. But at what point did I become a successful writer?

When from my A levels, university degrees, jobs and post-graduate exams did I become a successful doctor? When on my mindful finance journey did I become successful with money? I'm sure you can ask yourself similar questions. Have you ever thought about *your* definition of success?

In the first part of my book, we'll talk about some of the daily habits and disciplines that can help you to become successful with money. You may find that this discipline spills over into other areas of your life, such as your career, health, wellbeing, relationships and spiritual life.

Remember that success is a process. We may not reach our personal finance goals for another 30 years. We will never be perfect. However, by reading a book like *Mindful Finance* or accessing the resources contained within this book – guess what – you're already on your way to becoming successful with money, at least by John C. Maxwell's definition.

> *'Success is knowing your purpose in life, growing to reach your maximum potential, and sowing seeds that benefit others.'*
> ~ JOHN C. MAXWELL

Another of my favourite motivational speakers is Zig Ziglar who famously said, *'If you aim at nothing, you will hit it every time.'* He's someone else who believed that being successful involves making goals and working towards them.

> 'Success is measured by some of the things you have that money will buy, but all of the things that money won't buy. See, money will buy you a house but it won't buy you a home, it'll buy you a companion but won't buy you a friend, it'll buy you a good time but won't buy you peace of mind, it'll buy you a bed but won't buy you a good night's sleep. The more of the things you have that money won't buy will enable you to get more of the things that money will buy and that's a fact.'
>
> ~ ZIG ZIGLAR

I also love listening to Jim Rohn. So much of the imagery you'll find in *Chapter 7: Make Your Garden Grow* comes from him. He teaches the laws of sowing and reaping, daily routines and habits. It may be as simple as eating an apple a day, which leads to walking around the block, and other good habits.

There's something about building good habits and routines that can boost your confidence and self-esteem in a way that makes you want to do more of it. It may seem overwhelming at the moment to even think about starting. But once you get some momentum going, you'll see that you're making progress and it will spur you on.

> 'The greatest step toward success is self-confidence. The greatest builder of self-confidence is self-esteem, and self-esteem comes from doing the daily things you know you should do. Your self-esteem will start to soar when you make some critical decisions – decisions to walk a new road, to start a new direction, to start a new discipline.'
>
> ~ JIM ROHN

Another message of my book, something I've discovered from speakers such as Tony Robbins, Craig Groeschel and others, is that as you strive towards your destination it helps if you learn to love the process. If success is a journey, then you might as well enjoy yourself along the way!

The process of behaviour change, intentionally putting new habits in place and getting rid of unhelpful ones, can lead to positive emotions. It's possible to find happiness despite the hardship and satisfaction despite the struggle.

Setting goals and starting new habits can help develop your character. Jim Rohn often said it's not what you get that matters, but who you become. We're all in the process of becoming. His protégé, Tony Robbins, teaches a similar principle:

*'I always tell people if you want to know the secret to happiness, I can give it to you in one word: Progress. Progress equals happiness. That's because reaching a goal is satisfying, but only temporarily. There are levels of making it in life and whatever you think 'making it' is, when you get there, you'll see there's another level [...] I don't care what it is you've achieved, and the reason is because life is not about achieving the goals, life is about who you become in pursuit of those goals.'*

~ TONY ROBBINS

I've also heard it said that to stay motivated and work towards a goal you need to have a *why*. There has to be a sense of purpose, a reason (often bigger than ourselves) to explain why it matters to us. Often the *why* is not just for us, but for the people we love and causes we care about. Often it's because we want to help someone, serve someone or be there for someone that we need to take care of ourselves first. Our health, wealth and wellbeing aren't just for us. They can make other people's lives better too.

It doesn't usually feel good to sacrifice now for greater gain later. So we need to trick our brains into delaying gratification. I'm sure you've seen the experiments with the kids and sweets where the parents leave the room and see what happens. Well, we all have an inner kid who wants it *now!* Part of growing up is learning to be the adult who says, *"No."*

When it comes to being successful with our finances, we all have a different *why*. For me, it was never wanting to be in a situation again where I have to borrow money from my family to pay the bills. I wanted to be generous and a blessing to others. Instead, I found myself broke and powerless. I decided to turn that situation around.

For Tony Robbins, it was his experience of lack and hunger when he was growing up that made him vow to feed a billion people. That was his way of turning his pain into purpose.

Your *why* doesn't need to be as ambitious. We've all got things that motivate us. Perhaps it's wanting to protect someone vulnerable. Maybe it's helping someone else deal with the same thing we struggled with and overcame. Maybe we want to build a better future for our family and loved ones.

As you read through *Mindful Finance* I want you to ask yourself *'What is my reason why?'* When it comes to any goal, in any area of your life, you can ask yourself *'Why does it matter to me?'* Knowing your *why* will help you to stick to the process, to go after your goal over years and decades, and not to give up when obstacles come your way.

Whether we have a goal to pay our bills this month, become a millionaire, find financial freedom, be able to retire one day, be generous, or just know that we have enough, you have to admit that money is important. We all need money to live. Money gives us options and opportunities. And oftentimes the pursuit of money can become all-consuming. So how do we find balance?

So let's go there and start the conversation.

## Money: Is It Important?

We've already talked a little bit about why money is important for the basic essentials of life, health and wellbeing. But our relationship with money is complicated. We might love it, hate it or avoid talking about it completely.

Let's just say what you're all probably thinking. Who *actually* enjoys talking about money? Do you find it easy or difficult? Who hears the "B" word (for *budget*) and wants to run a mile? Does the phrase *'we need to talk about our finances'* just make your heart sink?

For some people, the mention of money may trigger some painful memories. You may have grown up in a household that went silent whenever money was mentioned. Perhaps it was a taboo subject or forbidden. It may have been a word that sparked anger, arguments or resentment. It may have caused fear and worry of debt collectors and bailiffs who could turn up at the door at any time. At school, you may have been aware that you didn't have what other people had and may even have been bullied for it.

Even the wealthiest families can struggle to talk to their kids about money. It may feel awkward or embarrassing, something secret and private, that's just for grown-ups. But kids can still sense what's going on. We often learn and pick up money habits and attitudes from our parents.

We'll look at how to talk about money with your family and kids in *Chapter 5: Family*. Hopefully by becoming aware of negative money thoughts and attitudes, likely picked up in childhood, you can start doing some work to change them. It's possible to change your own life and your family tree for the better.

If nobody talked to you about money growing up, I hope this book will give you the confidence to start to talk to children about money in a way they'll understand, that will set them up for the future. The Ramsey Solutions book *'Smart Money Smart Kids'* may be a useful place to start.[10]

Explaining money management to kids is something we can learn and get better at. Getting them started with good money habits at an early age can set them up to win. I'm not a parent yet, so I'll let the experts guide you.

What I want to do in this book is for us to have one of those over-the-dinner-table conversations about money, one that's positive and constructive. I want you to focus on what you *can* do now, not what you wish you'd done in the past. We've all got an opportunity to get better at managing money, to build a better future for ourselves and our loved ones.

It's important not to do the journey alone. If you're married, it's highly recommended that you talk to your spouse about money. You need to make sure you're doing life together, dreaming together, moving in the same direction. I want this to be a book that brings you closer. Perhaps you can read it with your spouse, chapter by chapter, asking each other reflective questions and seeing where the points of friction are.

If you're single, perhaps you can read this book with an accountability partner or group of friends. There are lots of online communities you can join where you can ask questions, gain wisdom and journey together, encouraging each other and sharing advice.

## What Is Money Anyway?

*'Money'* is simply what we can use to buy things. For people interested in learning more about the concept of money and the topic of *'macroeconomics,'* I've written an optional section just for you, *Chapter 9: A Brief History of Money*. This will set you up for *Chapter 10: Ways To Invest*.

Money is an example of an *asset* – something useful or valuable. There are lots of things I thought I knew about money which turned out to be wrong. I assumed that money was backed by gold – it isn't! What we have is something called a *'fiat currency'* – paper money, not backed by anything. I also assumed that money holds its value – it doesn't! That's because of *inflation* where things tend to get more expensive over time. Inflation slowly eats away at the buying power of our money.

Money works because we believe in it. Banks work because we believe in them. If we lose trust in these things, society would fall apart. Sometimes it does and there's a big shake-up. There have been many times in history when people have lost confidence in the ability of money to buy things and banks to keep our money safe. We'll talk about this later, as well.

We'll also look at the future of money, things you might have heard of, including digital currencies, cryptocurrencies and NFTs (non-fungible tokens). Who knows what money will look like in future!

Remember, while *'past performance is no guarantee of future results,'* as all the investment advisors warn us, we can still learn a lot from history. Things tend to work in cycles and the past is all we have to go on.

> *'The real measure of your wealth, is how much you would be worth if you lost all your money.'*
> ~ ANON.

## Material Wealth vs. Spiritual Wealth

A big part of the conversation about money is looking at the difference between *'material wealth' and 'spiritual wealth'*. This is the distinction between storing up physical possessions, like money, piles of gold and treasure, versus the things that money can't buy. Some things we just can't put a price on, things like our relationships, quality time, peace of mind, happiness, health and wellbeing.

Though money can be put towards developing some of these things (like gym memberships, travelling to nice places, sharing experiences, meals and gifts with people we love) sometimes the best things in life are free. Remember what Zig Ziglar said before? Money can *'buy you a bed but won't buy you a good night's sleep.'*

It's hard to define spiritual wealth, but I think it can include a sort of inner contentment with what we already have, valuing important things in life that money can't buy. Aristotle's version of happiness is called *'eudaimonia'* and can be translated as *'flourishing.'* It's the idea of living well, being fruitful, growing and progressing in all the different areas of our lives. You don't need to have a lot of money to be wealthy in a spiritual sense. You just need enough.[11]

Remember how we redefined what success looks like? Well, we can also redefine the world's definition of *'wealth.'* A great place to look at this is in John Mark Comer's book, *'The Ruthless Elimination of Hurry.'*[12] Spiritual wealth may look like living an unhurried life. Sometimes we think that successful people need to be busy, but Comer says being too busy and hurrying can destroy your sense of wellbeing.

In the same way that people sometimes find their work taking over their lives, striving for money and riches, because they think this will fulfil them, Comer suggests people should consume less and share more. It's okay to be wealthy but it's better to get there slowly. This will help eliminate a lot of the stress and hurry from our lives.

You can be spiritually wealthy in every area of your life. You can be wealthy in your relationship with yourself, your sense of self-worth, understanding yourself and honouring your boundaries, being kind to yourself and allowing yourself to get the rest you need. Mindfulness techniques and counselling may help you with these things.

You can be wealthy in your relationships, finding community and people to serve. You can find a sense of purpose. It could be through a career, volunteering or helping others. It could be found in spirituality or religion, finding a relationship with God, a sense of connection with the universe and understanding of our place in it.

> *'True wealth is not measured in money or status or power. It is measured in the legacy we leave behind for those we love and those we inspire.'*
> ~ CESAR CHAVEZ

When it comes to material wealth, there's also a difference between having *actual wealth* and *looking rich*. I've heard lots of finance podcasts talking about how genuinely wealthy people often hide their wealth and keep it a secret. They don't feel the need to drive a flashy car, wear designer clothes or have collectable watches, although, of course, they could buy them if they wanted to.

It's the people who spend money trying to appear rich who often go broke. They pursue wealth the wrong way, trying to buy their way there, faking it for social media, rather than saving or investing over decades (which isn't nearly as glamorous). They often buy luxury items on credit cards, a lifestyle funded by monthly payments, trying to keep up with the Joneses (or more recently, the Kardashians). It's like putting on a show, trying to look the way they imagine a rich person should look.

As I've said before, part of *Mindful Finance* is being aware of what money means to us and exploring why it's important to us. And it is important! We need it to put food on the table and keep a roof over our heads. Life with no money at all can be awful. Talking about these things will help you determine your financial goals.

> *'I think everybody should get rich and famous and do everything they ever dreamed of so they can see that it's not the answer.'*
> ~ JIM CARREY

There are many things to be grateful for that you can't put a price on. I've heard several millionaires and entrepreneurs interviewed say that it's *gratitude* that has kept them grounded, that gives them satisfaction and perspective. It could be as simple as saying thank you for three things when you wake up or before you go to bed. It could change the way you see the world as you'll start to notice more things to be grateful for.

Ultimately, when people are at the end of their lives, it isn't their money and material possessions that they want around them, but their loved ones. The legacy we leave behind can be more than just our stuff. It's the impact we've had on people, the values we've passed on, the memories and experiences we've shared, our wisdom and what we've done to help others.

You may have heard it said that your *net worth* should not determine your *self-worth*. I want to remind you that you are more valuable than your valuables. While I hope that you find *Mindful Finance* to be a practical book about money and building wealth, I hope that it also helps you see that money isn't everything.

I'd love for you to be a millionaire and retire comfortably. And yes, this book can point you in the right direction to get there. But I want the overarching message of this book to be that you can be *successful* without needing a lot of money, and you can be *wealthy* without needing to *be rich*.

It's okay to be wealthy. You don't need to apologise to anyone for achieving material wealth (so long as you didn't do anything illegal or immoral to get it). But you can also stop chasing, striving and comparing your wealth with others. You can become spiritually wealthy along the way to building material wealth. This will help you use your material wealth wisely so that it becomes a blessing rather than a burden.

> *'Tell them to use their money to do good.*
> *They should be rich in good works and generous to those in need,*
> *always being ready to share with others.'*
> ~ 1 Timothy 6:18, New Living Translation (NLT)

## Money And Faith

As a Christian myself, I've spent the last few years studying and reflecting on what the Bible says about money. I'm naturally drawn to Christian speakers and content creators because their values resonate with mine and help shape my thoughts. There are a multitude of other faiths and beliefs, all with their unique perspectives on money and wealth. While you may not be a Christian, I hope that you will still find some timeless wisdom in this book that will apply to your current situation.

I'm also mindful that sometimes there are different interpretations among the different Christian traditions. I hope that this book helps to open up a constructive conversation between us so that we can be united in our core beliefs. I hope that we can keep our disagreements to the sidelines and respectfully agree to disagree. Both life and faith are a journey that we've got to travel by ourselves. But sometimes people can walk alongside us for part of the way. There's a lot we can learn from each other.

Though the Bible was written a long time ago, it has a lot to say about money. Money was as much of a challenge then, thousands of years ago, as it is now. One example is Jesus' teachings on how to use money responsibly and wisely, without becoming corrupted by the love of it. This is another way of defining *'financial stewardship.'* There are other types of stewardship too, including how to look after the environment and other resources.

> *'A man's true wealth hereafter is the good he has done to his fellowmen'*
> ~ MAHATMA GANDHI

It's not easy to balance *spiritual wealth* with *material wealth*. Accumulating money can cause us to lose perspective. Another way that people try to keep balance is through *generosity*. This means living in a giving way, open-handed and open-hearted. It helps us to loosen our grip on stuff, so we can own it without it owning us.

I'm so passionate about generosity that I've dedicated a whole chapter to it, *Chapter 6: Generosity*. Generosity also goes beyond money and material possessions. You'll hear people say that you can be generous with your *time, talents and treasures*.

Generosity is often a path to spiritual wealth and paradoxically can lead us to material wealth as well. Many entrepreneurs and millionaires say that acts of generosity have been part of their wealth-building journey by changing the way they work. They're better bosses and leaders. Generosity can benefit all areas of our life. It changes our hearts and helps us become better people.

Giving to bless others is called *philanthropy*, which in Greek means to *'love your fellow man.'* It isn't just something millionaires and wealthy people do. We can all find opportunities to give and help people, no matter how much money we have.

> *'The purpose of life is to discover your gift;*
> *the work of life is to develop it;*
> *and the meaning of life is to give your gift away.'*
> ~ DAVID VISCOTT

## Money And Mindset

We're nearly at the end of this introduction. After talking so much about spiritual wealth, yes, we're going to be talking about growing material wealth – real-world things that people put a value on, like money, real estate, the stock market and gold. Some of you may already be feeling uncomfortable at the idea of building up material possessions. Perhaps you've been told that wealthy people are evil or it's not good to be materialistic.

That's okay. I get uncomfortable sometimes too. That's why money mindset matters.

By now, it should be obvious that I think spiritual wealth is important. I believe that if you're taking care of your mental health and wellbeing along the way, then you're going to be better prepared to manage the responsibility of material wealth when it eventually comes. The burden of responsibility can be a heavy one and we need to be prepared to handle it.

It's the discipline and mindset you develop in the process of reaching your goal that will help you carry the weight when your blessing eventually comes. Lots of good things in life come with responsibility attached. Think of children or a promotion at work!

We have a responsibility to be good stewards of what has been placed into our hands.

Sometimes our mindset can be set by the standards of the society we live in. We can look at what other people have and become envious. We get jealous, wishing we were in their position or situation, but we don't see the sacrifices they made to get there. We look at someone's beautiful garden, wishing ours looked like theirs, but we ignore the hours of work, weeding and watering that went into it. The grass will always look greenest where it's watered – so maybe we need to go do some watering of our own!

Social media has a lot to answer for. It took the comparison game to another level, showing a reel of someone's best moments, a snapshot of someone's destination without showing you what they went through to get there. That's why mindset is so important when it comes to money. Sometimes we have to rewire our thinking.

Having the right mindset when it comes to money will help us find financial peace instead of becoming enslaved to debt. It'll help us escape the rat race, jump off the conveyor belt, and stop the never-ending pursuit of stuff, materialism and consumerism. Without the right mindset, we will never be satisfied. It will never feel like enough. If we think more money will solve our problems, we will always be asking for more. You'll hear it said that money just makes us become more of what we already are. Money mindset matters.

> 'This wise man observed that wealth is a tool of freedom.
> But the pursuit of wealth is the way to slavery.'
> ~ FRANK HERBERT

There are 3 main mindsets that you're likely to come across when it comes to wealth. I want to talk about them briefly so you'll understand where I'm coming from. Every content creator has a bias and I want to tell you about mine. We'll talk more about mindset in *Chapter 5: Family*. Sometimes our mindset is inherited or influenced by the people we hang around with. It can also be transformed and renewed. These are:

1. *Poverty (or scarcity) Mindset*
2. *Prosperity Mindset*
3. *Abundance (or growth) Mindset*

In a *Poverty Mindset* people think about the world from a place of lack and scarcity. They may feel like a victim, that the world is stacked against them, that life is unfair and there isn't enough to go around. They can behave in ways that compensate for the belief that things will run out, like hoarding, storing or gathering. They may think that it's good to be poor because it's humble or holy. They sometimes believe that rich people are evil and built their wealth by taking advantage of others.

This is a common mindset to have in society, especially for people who grew up with social deprivation, who are caught in cycles of poverty. Unfortunately, a poverty mindset can keep people poor and takes away any hope that things can change for the better. This mindset is like a lead weight to anyone trying to build wealth for the first time in a generation or community.

Then there's the **Prosperity Mindset**. Christians may refer to it as the *Prosperity Gospel*. This is the view that blessings come from good behaviour and being poor is a punishment for bad behaviour. It's especially common for some religious groups to develop this mindset, believing that you can become wealthy by being a good and moral person. Some religions call this karma.

The Pharisees in the Bible are sometimes given as an example of a prosperity mindset, where riches were shown off as a sign of divine favour. In this mindset, it's believed that blessings can be earned, for example, by giving money to charity to show how righteous you are. It's easy to fall into this mindset.

Some churches are criticised for teaching that you will be rewarded for your giving and blessed if you give money to the church. But as I'll talk about later, I don't feel that these are necessarily examples of prosperity mindset. They may be prime examples of an **Abundance Mindset** in action.

In this third way of thinking, there is more than enough to go around. But to activate that abundance, you must first sow. You can plant a seed of potential – for example, by acts of generosity or by investing – so that it can grow, multiply and bear fruit. Giving to others can cause a ripple effect, helping others to become fruitful too and pass on the blessing. Blessings may return to you one day through this abundance cycle.

When it comes to the abundance mindset, you may still be blessed, but not because you've earned it through being a good and moral person. You are blessed because you've put in the effort, sown a seed, paid it forward. Through your actions you can set in motion a series of events that results in a harvest. We'll talk about the laws of sowing and reaping in *Chapter 7: Make Your Garden Grow*.

The downside to this is that it works in reverse too – we have to be careful not to plant seeds of jealousy, gossip, criticism, negativity and all those unhelpful things that can multiply and come against us. It's a battle of the mind. Anyone can overcome this inner battle, but it won't be easy.

I would like everyone to have the opportunity to grow as a person and unlock their potential. It's possible to move from a poverty mindset to a growth mindset, in the same way that it's possible (but not easy) to break from generational cycles of poverty.

I believe we all have a unique purpose, hidden away as a seed inside us. Good habits can be stacked (or hacked) and eventually bear fruit. We can sow into others and celebrate their wins, just as other people have sown into us. It may look to the casual observer like we're being blessed for our good deeds. But on closer inspection, you'll notice the heart behind the abundance mindset is different. As Pastor Luke Bryant puts it, "We give to give, not to get."

My mindful finance journey led me from a *poverty mindset* to an *abundance mindset* even before I knew what these words meant. Whatever your personal beliefs, I wish this book to be encouraging, uplifting and full of hope.

I want this book to be my way of sowing into you, giving you some of the tools and resources that helped me on my journey. I hope that you will grow, flourish and start planting some seeds of your own – generosity seeds, investment seeds, sowing into others with wisdom and knowledge – so that this can be your legacy too.

This is the abundance cycle at work.

**Time to Reflect:**

Thank you for taking the time to read this preface and introduction. Hopefully you've got to know me a little better as your guide. I feel like we've taken some time to mentally prepare, pack our bags, and equip ourselves for the adventure ahead.

I've given you an overview of some of the places we're going to visit. I hope you're excited! Or maybe you're a bit nervous. There will be some challenges up ahead, of course. I hope that we can have some fun too. Most of all, I hope that you'll get to know yourself better as we walk along and talk about money.

Before we set off on our journey, I want you to have a think through some questions. *What does success mean to you and why do you want to be successful with money?* Maybe write it down and you can revisit this again a few chapters from now.

I hope that throughout this book your mindset will shift away from a place of lack to one of abundance. Your *why* will most likely change as *you* do.

**This is what success means to me...**




**I want to be successful with money because...**

Design your dream house

*Get your financial house in order*

# PART 1: GET YOUR FINANCIAL HOUSE IN ORDER

*'Money is only a tool. It will take you wherever you wish, but it will not replace you as the driver.'*
~ AYN RAND

In this section of the book, I'm going to give you a toolkit for how to be successful with money. If you haven't read the preface and introduction yet, I suggest you go back and read them. I share why I'm writing this book and explain what I think mindful finance is. We also talked about the importance of having a *why,* a reason for going on this journey of self-development. I want you to reflect on your relationship with money and what success means for you.

Over the next 6 chapters, I want to give you some mindful finance techniques that will help you build wealth with intentionality. It's going to be a sort of visualisation, imagery to help you understand and remember. As you *get your house in order,* I'm going to use the metaphor of a house to help you build your finances the right way.

Along the way, there will be some questions for you to answer and some challenges to complete. Feel free to go at your own pace. Some of this may seem familiar or basic. But it could just as easily be completely new to you. Don't worry. Take your time. Building wealth, just like building a house, is a process.

When someone builds a house the correct way, they start with a firm foundation and then build on top of it, brick by brick. A house doesn't build itself. It takes careful planning, time, massive action and effort. But when it's finished it can provide shelter and protection. It can be a store of value, filled with possessions we love. A house can become a home, somewhere we can spend time with family and share hospitality with others. A physical house may represent *material wealth*, but when it becomes a home it represents *spiritual wealth*.

You'll have heard the saying *'Money can't buy you happiness.'* But it's hard to be happy when you don't have the basics covered. Earning money is not the purpose of life, but money can help us reach our goals and fulfil our purpose. It's hard to help others financially without the money to do so. Money is a tool. It's not innately good or bad. It allows us to build the life we want.

> *'A man who both spends and saves money*
> *is the happiest man, because he has both enjoyments.'*
> ~ SAMUEL JOHNSON

Just like a building, we want our wealth to last over the years. That means we need a financial plan.

A house has to be designed in advance. It needs to be structurally sound and fit for purpose. It needs to be the right size with the right number of rooms. The building work needs to keep to budget to make sure there's enough money to complete it. There's a schedule to make sure it's finished in the right time frame.

Before breaking ground, there has to be an architect's blueprint and a strategy to follow. Building a house properly takes time. You've got to have the right tools and materials. Well, the same is also true of our finances.

We're all at different stages of our mindful finance journey. These are the different stages of building wealth. If you're just getting started, then perhaps you're designing your financial house from scratch. You're starting with the foundation and building from the ground up.

If you've been on this journey for a while, then you may already have built a financial house. But perhaps it needs some renovation work.

> *'You don't have to see the whole staircase,*
> *just take the first step.'*
> ~ MARTIN LUTHER KING, JR.

There may be structures that need fixing, a leaky roof, or foundation problems causing cracks to appear.

Building wealth, like building a house, needs to be done in the right order. You wouldn't build your roof before you've put your walls up, right? You wouldn't put in your sofa until you've built the floor!

When I first started adult life, I didn't have a clear picture in my mind of what my financial house would look like. I thought I was building on solid ground, but my foundations were shaky, and they washed away with the first storm.

Like lots of people, I was doing *financial DIY* without a clue. It's easy to pick up soundbites on the internet, or advice and wise sayings from relatives (which may or may not be true).

DIY is absolutely fine, but you have to make sure you *really* know what you're doing. You need a blueprint, a roadmap, a game plan, a financial plan, or whatever you want to call it.

Having a financial plan tells you exactly what to do, so you can complete each important step before moving on to the next. You may have come across Dave Ramsey's *'7 Baby Steps.'* [13] You might have heard of the Money Guy Show's *'Financial Order of Operations.'* [14] These are great examples of financial plans from content creators in the USA. I encourage you to go and explore these tools for yourself later on. They're my inspiration for creating this house model of wealth-building and I'll refer back to them every now and again.

> *'It is thrifty to prepare today for the wants of tomorrow'*
> ~ *AESOP*

\* \* \*

### *How To Build A House*

Our house is going to be built in stages, which we'll explore in detail:

1. **The Foundation** – good money habits, like having a spending plan, creating margin (living on less than you make), regular budget meetings to know you're on track, becoming mindful of where your money is going. Keeping more money than you spend is the key to building wealth.
2. **The Four Walls** – these are the essential things we need to live: food and clothes, shelter (somewhere to live), utilities (keeping the lights on and water running), and transportation (to get to work).
3. **The Roof** – a rainy day fund, insurance policies (life insurance, car insurance, home insurance, income protection), to protect you against the storms of life
4. **Possessions and Debt** – things we furnish our house with, the extra things we enjoy in life, assets (things we own that have value) and liabilities (like debt and borrowing)
5. **Family** - fun, experiences, legacy, generational wealth, wills and estate planning
6. **Generosity** – showing hospitality, opening our home to others, giving gifts, serving others, helping people in need and organisations we care about

You'll have noticed that there's absolutely nothing here about investing or retirement accounts. Sorry to disappoint you, but I'm saving all that fun stuff for Part 2 of the book.

There's some important groundwork to do before we can think about maximising our wealth-building and building our investment portfolio. We can't grow our financial garden until time is right. It's important to get our financial house in order first.

It doesn't matter how well your garden is growing when there isn't a roof to protect what you've already built. That's why most experts recommend that you pay off your high-interest debt and have a 3- to 6-month emergency fund in place before you start investing.

As I said before, it's a journey. So don't rush the process. You'll thank yourself later that you took the time to build a strong financial foundation.

*'Money amassed either serves us or rules us'*
~ HORACE

When it comes down to it, being successful with money isn't about having great big piles of money heaped up. It's our daily habits and choices: what we buy (or don't buy), what we save (or don't save), and what we give (or don't give). *Mindful Finance* is what we believe, think and feel about money, and ultimately what we believe, think and feel about *ourselves*.

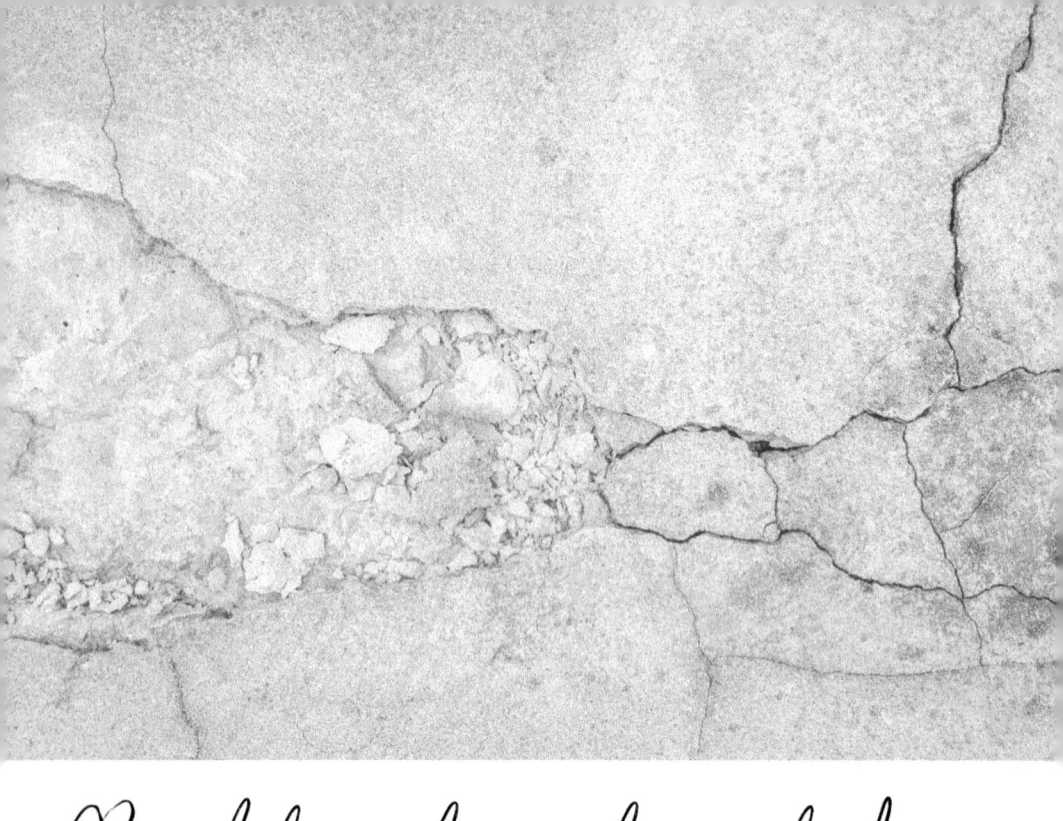

Build a firm foundation

| 1 |

# Chapter 1: Build A Firm Foundation

You've probably heard it said that you need to build a house on a firm foundation, one of stone or concrete. There's an old Bible story where Jesus talks about a man who built his house on the sand. It was washed away as soon as the first storm came. But the house built on solid rock stood firm.

While Jesus was originally talking about faith, the same is true of our wealth-building. Storms always come to test us in life. We might think we've built a pretty sturdy house until there's a change in our circumstances, a life event or some other challenge that stress-tests what we've built.

That's what happened to me when I discovered I was living paycheque to paycheque with no emergency fund. I was walking on a knife-edge and it didn't take much to make me fall off.

You might have heard the fable of *'The Three Little Pigs.'* When the Big Bad Wolf comes, it's the sturdy house made of bricks that we want to be in. It's the quickly-built flimsy house of straw or sticks that get blown away. We can't control when the wolf will come. So how we build matters.

The same is true of our finances. If our foundation is strong, then we can stand firm when the challenges of life inevitably arise.

I already mentioned in the introduction what to do if you're in a spiralling debt crisis. You feel like you're building your financial house on quicksand. You may not have a big income shovel to dig your way out.

When you're deep in debt and you can't afford to pay the interest, the harder you struggle without help, the deeper you may find yourself sinking.

It's in these situations that you may need help from a debt service or charity to come to the rescue. They can help pull you out and get you back on a firmer footing.

If that's where you're at right now, if you're working with a service to pay off your debt, then I still want you to build a strong financial foundation. It's okay to ask for help, but you also need to be ready when the time comes to go it alone again so you don't drift back into the pit.

The foundational principle behind becoming successful with money is developing **good money habits**. Habits are repeated patterns and routines which eventually become second nature. Of course, it's not as simple as just deciding to start. And yet in some ways, it is. The trick is to keep going.

So, what are these good money habits? I'll try and break them down so they don't feel too overwhelming.

Remember, as Jim Rohn said, *'Your health plan starts with the apple a day.'* The same is true for your finances. Start somewhere small. Tiny habits stack up over time. So maybe start with one or two new things and go from there.

When you're starting at the beginning, building a foundation, you're preparing the ground to carry the weight of what you're going to build. It's laying the groundwork, taking control of your finances rather than letting your finances control you. It's waking up and getting organised. It's knowing your numbers. In essence, it's *Mindful Finance*.

## Reflection Questions:

Here are some questions to see how mindful you are of your finances right now. Don't worry if you don't know the answers. When I first started I didn't know the answers either. But you soon will.

- *Who does the finances in my household?*
- *Do I even think about money day to day?*
- *How much do I get paid (or pay myself) every week / fortnight / month?*
- *How much do I need to live on each month?*
- *If my income stopped, how long could I go before I run out of money?*

## Living With Margin

*'Financial peace isn't the acquisition of stuff.*
*It's learning to live on less than you make,*
*so you can give money back and have money to invest.*
*You can't win until you do this.'*
~ DAVE RAMSEY

Would it surprise you to learn that up until my early 30s, I didn't know how much I got paid or how much I needed to live on? I just bought stuff on a credit card each month, discovered money in my bank account and used it to pay off the bills. Sometimes I was able to save a little.

Sometimes I'd be surprised by a big predictable expense, like my car insurance or Christmas (that just happened to come around every year). So I'd stick that on the credit card too. After all, I was getting reward points and that's free money, right?

One day I got a £5000 tax refund. That was a good day. Soon afterwards I got an unexpected £2000 student loan bill. Not such a good day as I didn't have the £5000 anymore. These shouldn't have been surprises. But I wasn't paying attention. The money just disappeared.

If this sounds familiar, you're in good company. A survey by CNBC showed that more than half of Americans are living paycheque to paycheque and that 70% of people feel stressed about their finances.[15] When you spend everything you have each month, it's impossible to save money. Your emotions are all over the place. You're living a life without any margin.

I've heard it said that our income is our most powerful wealth-building tool. So how do we make sure we're harnessing that power?

**The answer is** *'margin.'* You can think of margin as creating room to breathe, having extra resources, freeing up spare time or money. When it comes to our finances, it means making sure we have more coming in than going out. It means not spending everything we make.

I first heard about the concept of margin from Pastor Craig Groeschel in a 4-part sermon series called *'Margin.'*[16] He quotes from Dr Richard Swenson's book, *'Margin: Restoring Emotional, Physical, Financial, and Time Reserves to Overloaded Lives.'*[17] He defines **margin** like this:

*"Margin is the amount available beyond what is necessary. It's the difference between what you have and what you need."* [18]

We need to create margin in all areas of our life for our wellbeing, not just financially. It's not only possible to have enough but also to have more than enough. That's living with margin. It's having an abundance mindset. We can reset our vantage point to recognise what is surplus or extra. We can find contentment with what we already have. We can start building wealth, brick by brick.

Being mindful of our finances helps us create margin by making sure we're paying attention to where all our money is going, every last penny. Like most good habits, it's a simple idea. If it's so easy to do, why don't we do it? Jim Rohn says that's because it's also easy *not* to do it. Forming a new habit and not giving up takes effort and intentional action. But it's potentially life-changing if you can master this foundational skill.

Over our lifetime we will have a stream of income flowing through our hands. It could add up to millions of dollars or pounds over the years. So, how do we make sure we're keeping some of it to build our wealth, rather than letting it slip through our fingers? Are we saving some of it into buckets or reservoirs to water our financial garden with?

There comes a point on your mindful finance journey where you realise that the responsibility is yours. Nobody cares about your money or your life as much as you do. So it's time to start paying attention. There's nobody coming to the rescue. You don't need to rely on a change in your external circumstances or a sudden pay rise. Often it's not an income problem, though you may need to go get yourself a bigger shovel. Apart from that, you can start right now using the resources you already have.

It turns out we're the CEO of our own life. You may have heard motivational speakers asking, "If you were paying *yourself* to manage your own money, would you fire *you*?" I hope the answer is no! If it's yes, then it's time to do some training! Let's focus on some basic things you can do to take control of your finances.

**The equation to build margin is:**
**Margin** = your **income** minus your **expenses**

Ultimately, if you spend as much as you earn, you're left with zero. You don't have any bricks to build with. What's more, if you spend more than you make, you're *actually* going backwards! This is how most people drift or fall into debt, by spending more money than they have.

If you live in the Western world, then you're probably living in a culture that values *stuff*. We buy things to make us feel better. The adverts even tell us that we deserve it, that it'll make us happy, that we'll be a better person if we just own that thing, get that service, treat ourselves to that luxury. It should be clear to you by now that part of this mindful finance journey is resetting our expectations, asking ourselves what we really *need* rather than demanding everything we *want*. It's about having gratitude for what we already have.

This isn't the only reason why we can get into debt. Sometimes it's a life event, like a divorce, job loss or unexpected emergency. It could be a cost of living increase: our rent or mortgage payment goes up, bills cost more and prices go up. Perhaps we made an unwise decision and took out debt we couldn't afford to pay back, or even co-signed on someone else's loan.

Creating margin is the key to building your financial future. It's the bricks and mortar of your financial house and the seeds to make your garden grow. It's the same behaviour that helps us get out of debt and also save for the future. It's learning to live on less than we make.

To create margin, we either need to increase our income or lower our expenses – preferably both! So, there are 3 steps to creating margin that we'll look at separately:

- **Step 1: Understand Your Income**
- **Step 2: Maximise Your Income**
- **Step 3: Control Your Expenses**

Then, once we've created some margin, we'll look at how to put it to use and build wealth.

## Step 1: Understand Your income

*'Never spend your money before you have it'*
~ THOMAS JEFFERSON

Income is a tricky topic to talk about because you'll all be reading this from a different perspective. We all need an income to live. For a season, debt may be part of the story, for example, if you're investing in yourself through education or trying to grow a business. It's possible to live on very little. I know people who have done voluntary work and been given free food and accommodation in return. I also have friends who can't work due to health reasons.

We already reflected a little in the introduction on global issues of poverty and social injustice. Income is complicated and varies greatly depending on where you live, your health and social circumstances. While I want to acknowledge the income inequality in our world, that isn't the main focus of this chapter. Instead, I want to help you understand and become aware of your own income situation.

In the UK, if you're a student, your income might be a student loan, apprenticeship, part-time job or a gift from family. If you can't work for whatever reason, it could be your benefits payment, insurance or emergency fund, a subsidy or charitable donation. If you're working as an employee, it could be a paycheque that's paid weekly, fortnightly or monthly. If you're running a business, then you might not get paid until a contract is complete, so your pay can vary from month to month. If you're retired, it could be your investments, workplace pension, state pension, annuity, or even a side business.

Step 1 is understanding your income. Knowing what you've got coming in each month is vital. Checking that it's the right amount is just as important. If our income is our most powerful wealth-building tool, then we've got to understand how to use it properly just like with any other power tool.

Knowing how much you're earning is essential for you to calculate how much you can afford to spend each month. It sounds straightforward, but knowing your income might not be as easy as you think. A trap that I've seen a few people fall into, including myself, is thinking that just because there is money arriving into your bank account then that must be your income. Well, not exactly! It's easy to get caught out.

You will probably have tax to pay, pension contributions, student loan repayments, salary sacrifice schemes, payroll giving etc. Unfortunately, HMRC here in the UK has been known to get their numbers a bit mixed up at times. Your tax code may be wrong in either direction. Sometimes they give and sometimes they take away. What you think of as your income might not belong to you at all. So you need to check your numbers.

Some people, like Robert Kiyosaki, suggest that we should all run our finances like a business, even if we don't have one. Business owners keep a profit and loss statement. They need to know how much is coming in from sales and how much is going out as expenses. The difference between the two is their profit. Then they need to pay tax on this. Only then can a business owner see what they have earned and decide to pay themselves an income.

The same sort of thing applies when you're an employee with a paycheque. There will be your *gross income* (before tax) paid to you by your employer. Then there'll be payments to make before you ever see that income, such as your income tax and national insurance contributions (in the UK). Only then will your *net income* be paid into your bank account.

Remember, there's no guarantee that the numbers will be correct. That's why you need to check them. Did you keep a record of what hours you worked and check your timesheet? Were you paid correctly for the hours you worked? Did you do some overtime or extra shifts? There may also be expenses, allowances or benefits that you can claim too. Is your tax code right? *Why couldn't it be more straightforward!?*

It gets even more complicated if you have a variable income, meaning you get paid different amounts each month. You may find yourself in this position especially if you do freelance work, irregular hours, contract work or run a business. In this case, you might want to set up a *hill and valley account,* an *emergency fund* or a *sinking fund,* where you can save money in the busy seasons to pay out when you're going through a dry spell. It's like storing up your harvest to get you through the winter.

If this applies to you and you don't yet have any money in reserve, it's definitely something to think about. I've done contract work for a few years now and experienced several months without work, including editing this book in the spring and summer of 2023, and again in 2024! You might not want to think about it, but it can and does happen! I think I've just about got used to it now.

Having an extra big emergency fund or some money set aside brings not only peace but also means you can choose what work to say "Yes" to. It means you can apply for jobs without appearing desperate or stressed, which can put employers off. It may seem like a far-off dream to have extra money set aside like that. But there will be a time in the wealth-building process when this can become your focus.

## Mindful Finance Challenge 1

Okay, it's time to do the first *Mindful Finance Challenge.* I'm going to call the first part *'Understand Your Payslip.'* You can skip ahead if this doesn't apply to you. You can come back and do this later (I know how annoying it can be when an author gives you homework!). If you're an employee with a payslip to hand, then I want you to take a moment to really look at it.

Ultimately, I want to help you avoid the situation I got into where I was emergency taxed at 40% for a whole year and didn't even realise it! Or the time when I missed my student loan payments for a whole year and ended up with a hefty bill. Getting to know your payslip will help you to avoid these sorts of surprises.

If you live in the UK, there are websites that can help you get to know your payslip, such as this one provided by *The Money & Pensions Service:* [19]

www.moneyhelper.org.uk/en/work/employment/
understanding-your-payslip

Anyone who is paid a salary in the UK should have a tax code. The first part is a number which refers to your tax-free allowance. The letters afterwards can mean all sorts of different things that effect the amount of tax you pay. Unfortunately, it's not uncommon for your tax code to be wrong. So make sure you check!

If you notice a discrepancy, there are a couple of things you can do. You can ring up HMRC (HM Revenue & Customs) to inform them but expect to be on hold for a while. Or you can update your details on the UK government website. This automatically adjusts your tax code going forward. The second way usually works well. Only once have I had a letter back asking for proof of my income because my numbers changed so drastically.[20]

www.gov.uk/check-income-tax-current-year

If you do a tax return, you should eventually end up paying the right amount of tax for that year. But it's better to be paying the right amount of tax at the beginning of the year. Nobody wants the government to be holding onto money that belongs to them, money that could be put to work building your financial house.

This is a common topic talked about on the American podcasts I listen to. You'll hear people in the USA talking about tax credits and allowances, withholdings allowances and deductions. In the USA, the IRS (International Revenue Service) have powers of enforcement, including sending you to prison if you don't pay your taxes. So it's important to prioritise paying your tax over paying off your other debts.

If you do an internet search for *'understand your payslip'* and whatever country you live in, you'll find plenty of resources and pictures that talk you through each element of your payslip. You'll see the hours you've worked, and how much income tax and national insurance you've paid. You'll see any pension contributions from you or your employer. If you're making student loan payments, those should be on there too.

Ultimately, your payslip will tell you your *gross income* (before tax and other deductions) and *net income* (the amount you receive after all those other payments have been made).

If you want to go even further, you can also have a go at calculating how much you earn in a year.

Of course, this will be different if you run a business. But for anyone receiving a salary from an employer, you can work this out from your payslips.

Each month's payslip often has a total of the income you've received so far during the financial year. So you can get an idea of how much income you've paid each year from the total on your March payslip.

You can also use the government's income tax website from earlier to make sure that your payslips match what the government thinks you've earned or are going to earn. This is especially important if you have several jobs or sources of income. Each one will probably have a different tax code. They can sometimes put you on a second job tax code or an emergency tax code. So watch out!

Knowing how much you've earned in a year is important, especially if you have to do a self-assessment tax return. It also means you can use online income tax calculators to check that you're paying the right amount of tax.

## How Much Tax Should I Be Paying?

Income tax depends on how much you earn and where you live (it's different in Scotland, for example). The allowances and tax brackets can change each year which is why I've deliberately not mentioned them. So here's a link to the UK government website so that you can check the latest numbers:[21]

www.gov.uk/income-tax-rates

In the UK, unless you are a very high earner, you'll probably have a personal allowance where the first portion of your income is tax-free. After that, you'll usually pay a percentage of tax depending on how much you earn. There are ways to take advantage of tax relief and legally lower your tax bill, such as paying into a pension and through charitable giving. These are ways that the government encourages good behaviour, incentivising us to save for the future and give to good causes. You should do your research, or you can speak to a financial advisor or tax preparer for advice if you need it.

Another way to check that you've paid the right amount of tax is to use a free *income tax calculator*. There are lots of these online and I like to use different ones for different reasons. Some of them show a breakdown of the different rates of income tax you pay. Some calculators show what happens to your tax bill if you pay into a pension. Some will let you include student loan payments, other allowances and deductions too.

I like to use these calculators to help me know that I'm paying the right amount of tax, so I know how much money to set aside and make sure I'm not due a big bill or refund.

I've included some of my favourite online calculators on the next page so you can plug in some numbers and see how they work.

## Reflection Questions:

- *Do you know where your income is coming from?*
- *Do you know whether you were paid correctly?*
- *Do you know how much you have coming in each month?*
- *Do you know how much you made in the last year or financial year?*
- *How much are you on track to make this year?*
- *Are you paying the right amount of tax?*

# Income Tax Calculators (UK)

## How much tax should you be paying?

**01** — **Which? Income Tax Calculator**
Simple to use, calculates the income tax and National Insurance you'll pay in each financial year. Doesn't include pension contributions.

**02** — **Which? Pension Relief Calculator**
Simple to use, calculates how much tax relief you can get on your pension contributions in a given tax year.

**03** — **MoneySavingExpert Calculator**
Tries to include everything and has advanced options. But I find the monthly pension calculation confusing. I prefer the other calculators.

**04** — **Listen To The Taxman**
I like how this calculator gives a breakdown of income tax by tax band making it useful to plan your pension tax reliefs and charitable giving. Not as simple as Which? but makes more sense to me than MSE.

The links to these different income tax calculators can be found in the Resources Chapter

## Step 2. Maximise Your Income

*'You don't get paid for the hour.
You get paid for the value you bring to the hour.'
~ Jim Rohn*

Just a reminder of our margin equation:
**Margin** = your **income** minus your **expenses**

Let's continue with the income side of the equation. If you want to create more margin, it may be necessary to increase your income, even if it's just for a short time. You might need to do this if you've got a financial goal, like paying off your high-interest debt or saving for a wedding, emergency fund or house deposit.

It may be necessary to aim to increase your income gradually over time as things tend to get more expensive due to inflation. Also, life tends to get more complicated and more expensive as you get older. Getting married, getting a mortgage, having kids, and increasing your lifestyle all cost money. Sound familiar?

This is a huge topic. You'll find lots of motivational speakers and coaches talking about how to develop your career, find purpose and add value in the workplace. In the Resources Chapter, I've put some links to people who can help you find a career and purpose. There's Ken Coleman, who is a career coach in the USA and part of the Ramsey Solutions team. My other favourite speaker is Pastor Rick Warren, author of *'The Purpose Driven Life.'*

It's important to remember that your personal value and worth are not the same as your value to the marketplace. But your value in the marketplace is something that you can develop and grow.

One of the best investments you can make is in yourself, by up-skilling, re-training, life-long learning and personal development. In this way, you can add more value through the work you do. Jim Rohn always says, *'Work harder on yourself than on your job.'* He tells his audience to *'take the classes, do the courses, burn the midnight oil.'* You can work harder and you can also work smarter. He also says there's a difference between a job and a career.

The highest-paying jobs are usually ones that bring the most value to other people, jobs where you aren't easy to replace, which can't be automated or replicated (and yes, robots, machines and A.I. will continue to take over human jobs). These are usually jobs that need specialist skills, knowledge and experience.

It may mean that in 20 or 30 years, the job or business field you choose to work in could look very different. It may not even exist at all! We need to prepare for that change and make sure the work we choose to do is still needed in the future.

If you want to grow your income in the short-term, the easiest thing to do is look at your situation right now. Are there opportunities to build more income as a household? Can you free up any spare time? Can you sell some stuff you don't use anymore? Could you work some overtime? How about weekends? In the USA, it's common for people to take on second jobs. It's not as easy in the UK, but there may still be opportunities if you think creatively.

If you have a short-term goal, such as paying down debt or saving for something special, you may need to work harder at your job or take on some extra work for a time. It's amazing what focus our minds and bodies can achieve when we do something for a short time, around 18 to 24 months. It can be hard to sustain beyond that, so we need to find a healthy balance and ease off the accelerator once the goal is achieved.

So if you want to increase your income over the long-term then what you need is a *career*. You may need to start with an entry-level job. But there are often opportunities for promotions and personal development along the way. You may need to do courses or post-graduate exams. You may need to level up and take on more responsibility. Perhaps a leadership or management role. Typically, the more value you can add, the more you will get paid.

It's a strange thing, but studies have shown that you can earn more if you switch jobs every so often.[22] It's not clear how exactly this pay increase works. It might be that you've got more chances to negotiate better pay. There may be competition between rival companies to attract employees. Or maybe you just get a better idea of your value in the marketplace.

It's the people who stick at a job for decades who may find that they miss out on opportunities for a pay rise or promotion. So maybe you need to ask yourself *'am I getting paid the right amount for the work I'm already doing?'*

You may be doing the day job that moves you in the direction of your dream job. You might not enjoy your job right now, but it may be the stepping stone that moves you closer to where you want to be. Sometimes we need to stick at it and sometimes we need to make a change. You could even get a pay rise along the way.

Did you know that if you want to earn more money, you can ask?

Of course, you have to ask your boss nicely for a pay rise. There are ways to do it tactfully with a better chance of success. I've heard people like Ken Coleman give tips on how to ask your boss for a pay rise the right way.[23] It's good to do your research and find out what other people in the industry get paid for a similar career to yours.

I was re-writing this chapter in June 2023. Looking back at what I wrote in February 2022 all seems very cheery and upbeat. I wrote:

*"Sometimes more responsibility isn't the answer. It depends on your specific circumstances; what you love to do, what you're good at and how you're wired. It could be a change of attitude, making sure we turn up on time, work while we're at work, always think what value you can add, go the extra mile – these things really do make a difference."*

The reality is that workplace stress and burnout are common. I've worked for the NHS since 2011 and I've seen first-hand the effect of workforce pressures, increasing workload and staff shortages. This can result in something called *'moral injury'* where we wish we could do the job better but there simply aren't the resources. We don't have the time or energy to do the job the way we think it should be done.

Employees can end up going the extra mile, working longer than they're meant to, missing breaks and learning opportunities, doing more with little or no reward or recognition.

It's not just the NHS. Many people are feeling workplace pressure, even if they're working from home. There's a suggestion that remote working makes it more difficult for people to take sick leave.[24] Stress-management, resilience training, wellbeing in the workplace – these things are becoming commonplace because the need is so great. The income side of the equation is just one part of the story.

2023 also saw a *'cost of living crisis'* after the COVID-19 Pandemic as inflation in the UK soared to its highest level in 30 years. We've seen strike action from employees demanding higher wages through their trade unions. Sometimes you can't ask politely for a pay rise. It becomes a battle where there's power in unity. When morale is low and workplaces are coming increasingly under strain, going the extra mile at work and having a good attitude can only get you so far. Workers are increasingly looking to industrial action for their wage increases.

There's also been talk for the last few years of a possible recession. These usually come with job losses as companies can no longer afford to have as many employees in an economic downturn. We didn't have mass unemployment during the COVID-19 pandemic because of furlough schemes for businesses. So if a recession comes, it'll be important to hold on to any kind of job. The usual rules no longer apply.

So there are ways you can work differently. Work smarter, not harder. One way to protect yourself from loss of income is to diversify your income streams. Some people choose to create a portfolio career, where they no longer have to rely on one job for their income. They may decide to start a business on the side, known as a *'side-hustle.'*

On the next page, I've listed some of the ways people make money on the side, or even as a full-time gig. There are plenty of blogs or websites to give you ideas.[25] There are YouTube tutorials that show you what to do which I've linked to in the Resources Chapter.

# Side-Hustle Ideas

## Having an extra job on the side is normal

Online product business:
- Etsy (handmade gifts / digital downloads)
- T-shirts / merchandise / eBooks and self-publishing
- Sell your photography or digital products
- Sell stuff on Amazon, eBay, Vinted, online market places

Network Marketing / Multi-level Marketing

Online opportunities:
- Monetise your YouTube channel
- Become a social media influencer
- Start a podcast or blog, affiliate marketing
- Design online teaching courses / tutoring / virtual assistant

Gig Economy / App-based jobs:
- Drivers / Food delivery
- Rent out a room or your house on Airbnb
- Be a freelancer / provide a service
- House sitting / pet sitting / dog walking

There are lots of creative ideas you can try. You could become a landlord or start a business. Who could you help or serve?

Work no longer looks like a job for life. Work isn't necessarily 9 to 5. People are deciding to work differently and technology is a big part of making this happen. You may have a health issue which means you can't work in the traditional sense. You may just have a passion you want to pursue. I encourage you to think creatively about the different ways you can add value to others.

You might be able to monetise your hobby, or you may just decide to start a business for fun and see what happens. Some people enjoy working unsociable hours. You might be able to take the skills from your day job and do consulting work. You might decide to be your own boss and become a freelancer. You could do contract work instead of having a traditional job with a salary. You can do these things alongside your full-time or part-time job. If it takes off, it might even become your full-time job.

If you think of your career as a business, even if you don't have one yet, it may open up some options for you. It's very rare for people to give up work entirely, even when they retire. So doing a side-hustle may end up being something you enjoy more than your day job. Many people have created their dream career this way.

## Step 3. Control Your Expenses

*'A budget gives you freedom.*
*It gives you permission to spend.*
*It gives you permission to do the things that you value.'*
~ RACHEL CRUZE

Here's the margin equation again:
**Margin** = your **income** minus your **expenses**

The other side of the margin equation is controlling our expenses. It doesn't sound like we should be able to find freedom by putting limits on something. But there are many examples where having a boundary can lead to freedom and peace within those limits. It's like working hard at work, then not bringing it home with you so that you can find rest for your soul. It's like putting stones around a campfire to stop it from spreading out of control so that it's useful and not destructive. It's like a parent saying *"No"* to a child to protect them, keeping them away from things that will hurt them so that they're able to play in safety. I'm sure you can think of other examples.

Whether it's a diet plan, a relationship goal, or any other area of our lives, putting limits on something can give us the freedom to do whatever we want within that boundary. It takes self-control. It's one of the hardest things to do, to say *"No"* now so that we can say *"Yes"* later. This one habit is a real game-changer. It's absolutely foundation if you want to win with money, especially if you have combined your finances with someone else.

> *'If we command our wealth, we shall be rich and free.
> If our wealth commands us, we are poor indeed.'*
> ~ EDMUND BURKE

Can you believe we've gone so far into this book and barely even mentioned the "B" word yet? Well, it's time to talk about the *budget*! It shouldn't be something that fills you with dread. It should liberate you! If you learn to think about it differently, then a budget actually gives you *permission* to spend. Some people prefer to call it a *spending plan* because it's less terrifying. So that's what I'm going to call it for the most part.

Often people feel guilty for over-spending, in the same way that they feel guilty for over-eating or over-sleeping. Putting a boundary in place with a spending plan helps you to see where the limits are. You have the freedom to buy whatever you want, as long as it's within the limits of your spending plan. We can still get it wrong sometimes, and that's okay. Instead of feeling guilty, we adjust the plan and go again next month.

There may be a reason why you couldn't stick to the plan. Mindful finance involves asking yourself why. Perhaps your spending categories were unrealistic. Maybe you need to re-adjust them because you spend more on fuel or food than you realised. Perhaps you've got TV or entertainment subscriptions you rarely use or maybe eating out is more expensive than you realised.

Maybe you need to cut back on some things so that you can prioritise others. Maybe there's a cheaper way to have fun. If you're an impulse buyer, maybe you need to have some *'fun money'* to allow you to satisfy that urge to splurge so that you don't blow the whole thing. Is this a wake-up call that your income doesn't match your spending?

Developing good money habits is a similar process to taking control of other areas of your life. If you've decided to start a healthy eating plan, then it's important to do *mindful eating.* Some people plan and track what they eat. There are apps, like *'My Fitness Pal'* to help you do that.[26] If you want to get up at a certain time, you've got to set an alarm clock the night before, or in my case, two alarm clocks.

When it comes to a spending plan, you've got to do the same. You've got to plan out in advance what your spending is going to look like, usually at the beginning of the month. Then you've got to track your spending to make sure you're staying on course.

If you already use a budget – then, congratulations! Keep it up! Hopefully there are some tips here to help you get better at what you're already doing and make it fun.

If you don't have a spending plan at the moment, don't worry. If you've never used a budgeting app, spreadsheet or even thought about money, you're not alone. That's where I used to be too. But you don't have to stay there. Mindful finance involves paying attention to where your money is going. It means telling it where to go, rather than wondering where it went. That's what we're going to do in this chapter.

Before we go deeper into this, I want to ask you if you combine your finances with someone else? If so, I want you to make sure you're reading this book together. There's lots of advice out there to suggest that if you're married, then you should be doing your finances together. Working together means you can align yourselves in the same direction and accelerate your way towards a common goal.

If you're single or living with a partner, but not married, then it's recommended that you keep your spending separate for now. Legally, spiritually and ethically, it just seems to work out better if you don't tie yourself to a person you're not married to. It may be more expensive in the short term, but you can avoid getting into some messy situations whenever there's a dispute or separation.

You hear anecdotes: she leaves him and drives off in the car that he's making payments on; he won't leave the house that's in both their names after the breakup etc. Keeping your finances separate avoids these sorts of horror stories.

## Your Spending Habits

Before we look at how to make a spending plan, I want you to have a good think about how you're naturally wired. If you're a couple, then there's usually someone who takes a greater interest in the finances. If you're single, then perhaps you're not interested right now, but you can become interested, which is what happened to me.

We've all got different personality types. Some people like details, while other people like the bigger picture. Some people like to spend money, while other people like to save it because of the feeling of security it gives. Some people are free spirits and like to go off on adventures, whilst other people are nerdy and prefer a nice spreadsheet. Often it's the nerd who is the saver and the free spirit who is the spender, but not always. Do you recognise which one you are?

When you've got some spare time, I want you to have a go at Dave Ramsey's *'Nerd or Free Spirit Quiz.'*[27] This is a fun way to help you get to know yourself. It'll also help you when talking about personal finance with friends, family or a life-partner. You may be able to recognise some of their behaviours and values too. You might start to understand why you do what you do and understand why you sometimes clash. After all, opposites often attract. Meanwhile, behaviours and values are often passed on through the generations so being aware of how you're wired can help you as a parent too.

If you're a free spirit paired with a nerd, then maybe you'll start to see their focus on numbers as a blessing rather than something annoying and frustrating. It may help you rein in your spending. If they're a saver too, then you might be able to work towards a common savings goal. If you're the nerd, then maybe you can be less stingy and loosen up the purse-strings a bit. Spending a bit more can be a compromise that keeps your free spirit partner happy.

If you're both free spirits, then good luck with that! You might need to unlock some undiscovered nerdiness or you might both end up spending uncontrollably forever! Of course, I'm joking, but only sort of. Understanding how we're wired is important. Then we can decide if we need to embrace it or make a change.

It's tempting to let all the finances in a partnership be done by one person, the one who has been labelled *'good at finance.'* We learn a lot about money from our families. Perhaps you've grown up in a household where it was the woman's responsibility to manage the finances and the man's responsibility to bring home the income. Perhaps it was the other way round and managing money was seen as the man's job. This can make the death of a spouse even more tragic if the person left behind doesn't know where the accounts are and how to manage money on their own.

I've heard lots of experts say that if you're combining finances, both of you should be involved. It's difficult to have a healthy relationship when one person is carrying all the responsibility for financial decisions or controlling how much the other person spends. It needs to be a team effort. Creating a spending plan needs to be like a contract, agreed by both of you. Some people even choose to sign the bottom of their budget like a legal contract!

Having integrity and being open with each other about your finances is called *'financial fidelity.'* It means not keeping secrets, especially when it comes to spending. Remember, personal finance is a behaviour thing, not just a maths thing. It's not just what you know, but what you do. This will save you lots of relationship strife. It's important to have open conversations about money in advance, even if they're difficult ones, rather than having arguments every time the money runs out.

If you're single, then it's good to have a way to stay accountable. Some people like to have an accountability partner, a mentor or coach, someone a little way ahead on the journey who can guide them and make sure they're sticking to the plan.

For me, it's the process of recording my spending on a spreadsheet that keeps me accountable. I know that *Future Me* can look back and see where my money is going today, and I want her to be proud of me. There are lots of ways to hold ourselves accountable.

It's good to join a community as well. Many of the content creators I mention in this book have a community of followers that has grown up around them online. Sometimes they even meet up in person. Maybe you can get on social media or have a conversation with people you know. You can make some friends, find a mentor, or sit down with a couple who are already successful with money. Learn from them, encourage each other, grow and keep going.

## Reflection Questions:

- *Are you naturally a saver or a spender? Are you a nerd or a free spirit?*
- *Perhaps you've got elements of both or you can see yourself changing from one to the other.*
- *Can you see how these can be a strength and a weakness?*
- *Can you think of ways to work together with your spouse to complement each other?*
- *Are there things you would like to change about yourself?*
- *Are there compromises you can make to bring balance?*
- *Think about what matters to you and why*

MINDFUL FINANCE — 63

*Make a spending plan*

# Budgeting Basics

## How to use a monthly budget

**01** **Calculate your monthly income**
-> that's your net income, after taxes, the money you pay yourself each month to live on

**02** **Track last month's spending**
-> how much did you spend previously and can you divide it into categories?

**03** **Direct next month's spending**
-> pre-decide before the month begins what you want to spend in each category

**04** **Check your spending**
-> have regular budget meetings to check your progress, maybe once a week

**05** **Adjust your budget categories**
-> did you over- or under-spend in a certain category? Were your targets realistic? Adjust your spending categories for next month.

**06** **Repeat**
-> it usually takes around 3 months to get the hang of living on a budget, so don't give up!

## Mindful Finance Challenge: 2 - Make a Spending Plan

It's time for another *Mindful Finance Challenge* - that's two challenges in one chapter! It's time to get practical. I hope you feel like you're gaining confidence in the fundamental skills of personal finance. This may seem basic, but it's foundational. Let's look at how to plan our spending before the month begins... yes, it's the dreaded "B" word again... we're going to look at different ways to budget! So what does a budget look like?

Just like me at age 31, you may have never seen a budget before. You may have found a budgeting app. You might even have used a spreadsheet or pen and paper. If you're already a budgeting pro, then feel free to skip this section, though I'm sure you'll still find ways to improve on what you're already doing. For everyone else, this one thing has the power to change your life for the better!

Doing a budget can be a nuisance. It takes time and effort. You'll have to crunch some numbers and track your spending. But it may just give you the sense of control and the peace of mind you've been longing for! The good news is that it usually gets easier with practice. It becomes just another habit.

A budget is a spending plan. It's usually a monthly spending plan because that's how both we and our bills are often paid. Budgets help us divide our spending into categories. Some of these are things that we have little control over (*non-discretionary* spending covers our *essential needs*, like our utility bills, house payments, insurance, car payments etc.) while other categories allow more freedom and choice (*discretionary spending* includes our *optional wants*, like eating out, luxury purchases and entertainment).

Before I started budgeting I always used to feel embarrassed and overwhelmed when financial planners asked me basic questions, like how much I earned and how much I spent each month. I just didn't have the answers. It still took me a long time to get to the place where

I was mentally ready to start living on a budget. I thought it would be restrictive and difficult, but it did get easier. The benefits for me were so extreme because I'd been so disorganised for years. Even if I didn't stick to the plan, I was so much better off just because I'd tried to control my spending, even if I wasn't doing it perfectly.

I wish someone had come alongside me earlier and said, "Hey, this is what a budget might look like for you and this is how you use it." It's okay if you're new to this. It may still all feel a bit overwhelming. You may have some of the same emotions I did, like guilt, shame, and overwhelm. Putting your numbers all down on paper is the first step towards taking responsibility and changing your life.

> 'A budget is telling your money where to go,
> instead of wondering where it went.'
> ~ JOHN C. MAXWELL

To create a budget, we're going to follow a 6-step process:

1. **Calculate your monthly income**
2. **Track last month's spending**
3. **Direct next month's spending**
4. **Check your spending**
5. **Adjust your budget categories**
6. **Repeat**

## 1. Calculate Your Monthly Income

The first thing you need to know is your monthly income. If you run a business, you get to decide what proportion of your profits to take as an income. If you get a regular paycheque each month and still aren't sure what your income is, you might need to do *Mindful Finance Challenge 1* over again.

Even if you're a student or not working, you'll still need an income number. If your income number isn't enough to cover your expenses, maybe this is the wake-up call you need to get some help from a debt charity or adviser. Maybe it's time to take a hard look at how you can increase your income or cut your spending.

If you're married and combining finances, you'll want to know your total household income – that means knowing what both of you have coming in.

If you're paid weekly or fortnightly, you may still choose to do your budget monthly. The key will be knowing what bills are due on what day of the month. You may need to save up a month's worth of money in advance to make sure you're not getting behind with payments.

For simplicity, we're going to look at what a budget for a single person without kids or pets could look like. If you combine finances or have dependants, you'll have a different income number and may have to add extra budget categories. You need to adapt your budget to fit your personal circumstances.

## 2. Track Last Month's Spending

*'The basic thing with frugality is:*
*IF YOU CAN'T AFFORD IT, DON'T BUY IT'*
*~ HARKEN HEADERS*

You can get an idea of how to budget by looking at what you spent last month. This could go one of two ways. Either you're on track and this will form the basis of next month's budget. Or it could be the wake-up call and you need to make some drastic changes! We're going to divide our spending into categories. Some budgeting apps and banking apps even let you divide your spending into categories as you go.

To do this part of the exercise you're going to need to look at last month's bank statement. You may have a paper bank statement or online banking. Either way, you need to be able to track your spending.

# SPENDING PLAN :

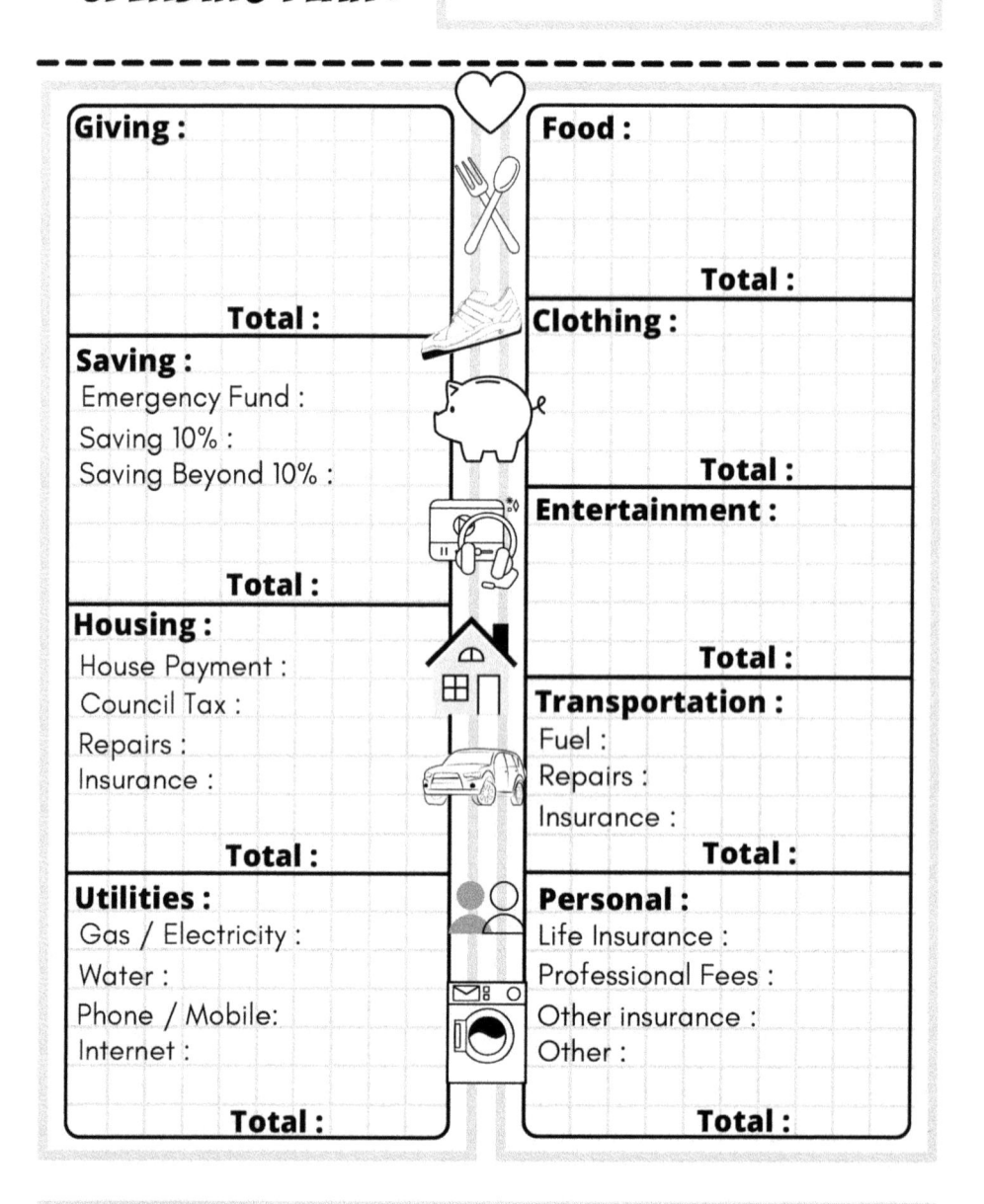

**Giving :**

Total :

**Saving :**
Emergency Fund :
Saving 10% :
Saving Beyond 10% :

Total :

**Housing :**
House Payment :
Council Tax :
Repairs :
Insurance :

Total :

**Utilities :**
Gas / Electricity :
Water :
Phone / Mobile:
Internet :

Total :

**Food :**

Total :

**Clothing :**

Total :

**Entertainment :**

Total :

**Transportation :**
Fuel :
Repairs :
Insurance :

Total :

**Personal :**
Life Insurance :
Professional Fees :
Other insurance :
Other :

Total :

## INCOME :

## OUTGOINGS :

On the other page, I've put a copy of my budget template to give you an idea of how you can divide your spending into categories. We'll look at some of these categories later in the book. These usually include things like giving, saving, housing, utilities and bills, food, clothing, entertainment, transport, insurance and other fees.

You'll notice I put *Giving* first and *Saving* second in their own distinct categories. You'll see why later on. So get a paper and pen, a spreadsheet or use your banking app, to see just how much you spent in each category last month.

## Reflection Questions:

- *Were you surprised by how much you spent in each category?*
- *Was there any margin (money left over) last month?*
- *Did you spend everything? Where could you save money?*
- *Are there any obvious patterns in your spending? Perhaps it's eating out, buying expensive coffees every day or TV subscriptions. Maybe it's impulse buying on the internet or clothes shopping. Again, were any of these spending habits a surprise to you?*
- *Are there any big fixed costs that you have no choice over, like your housing or car payments?*
- *Is what you spent last month more your monthly income?*

## SPENDING PLAN :

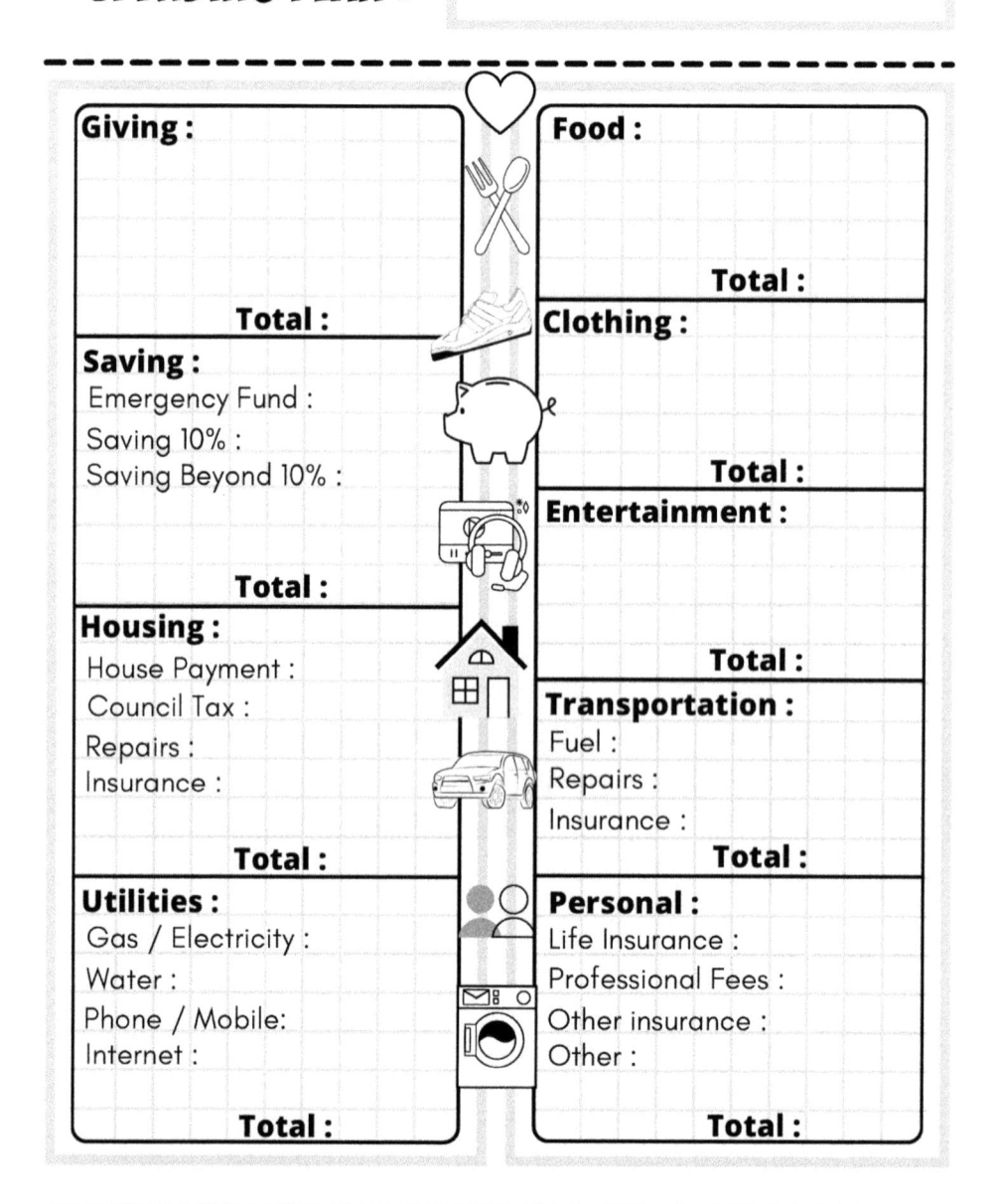

**Giving :**


Total :

**Saving :**
Emergency Fund :
Saving 10% :
Saving Beyond 10% :


Total :

**Housing :**
House Payment :
Council Tax :
Repairs :
Insurance :


Total :

**Utilities :**
Gas / Electricity :
Water :
Phone / Mobile:
Internet :


Total :

**Food :**


Total :

**Clothing :**


Total :

**Entertainment :**


Total :

**Transportation :**
Fuel :
Repairs :
Insurance :


Total :

**Personal :**
Life Insurance :
Professional Fees :
Other insurance :
Other :


Total :

## INCOME :

## OUTGOINGS :

## 3. Direct Next Month's Spending

*'We must consult our means rather than our wishes'*
~ GEORGE WASHINGTON

Next, you're going to create your budget, a spending plan for next month. That means you're not only tracking your spending, but you get to tell your money where to go. It means you're deciding in advance how much you're going to spend in each category.

It's got to be realistic too, remember! If you commute for your job, then you need to make sure you're putting the right amount to cover your fuel costs and car repairs. It's not going to be easy to suddenly cut your food bill in half. We get used to a certain kind of lifestyle. So sometimes you might need to make some steady changes so you can adapt gradually. That said, sometimes we just need to *rip the plaster off* and say, *"No more eating out for a few months!"* Remember, you can do pretty much anything for a short time.

So let's go through the basic budget template.

You can email me if you'd like a digital copy of the budget template to print off at home and use again. You can also find budget templates online if you search for them or buy them from places like Etsy as a digital download. You could also upgrade to a spreadsheet or budgeting app. For this next exercise, a pen and paper are all you'll need.

Let's start by looking at the difference between *discretionary* and *non-discretionary spending*.

Some of our budget items are compulsory. These are also called *non-discretionary*. We have to pay them. We don't get to choose whether we pay our council tax bill or not (or we'd get into trouble!). We have to make our house payments (or we get evicted or we default on our mortgage and lose our house). We have to pay our car payment (or it gets repossessed).

Other categories allow more choice. These are our *discretionary* spending. We can choose between luxury brands or budget brands.

There's a difference between what we need and what we want. For example, there's a difference between eating packet ramen noodles and eating at a Michelin-starred restaurant. It's the difference between shopping at Aldi or Waitrose. There's a difference between buying a uniform for work and buying a new outfit for a party that we may never wear again.

You'll also notice that some bills are paid monthly, whilst others may get paid quarterly (every 3 months) or annually. It's a good idea to keep an eye on when each bill is due. This is where the *sinking fund* comes in. A sinking fund is a pot of money that you can use to cover *expected* payments, like Christmas presents or your car insurance. Instead of paying the bill each month, you can pay yourself a payment into the sinking fund. Then you'll have the money ready when the payment is due.

Sinking funds are great because they stop those big annual expenses from suddenly creeping up on you. We get so used to the idea of paying monthly payments to companies and credit cards, we can actually pay ourselves payments too! Then you can earn interest on your savings, rather than paying interest to a credit card company!

You can also use a sinking fund approach if you're saving towards a particular goal, such as a wedding, holiday or paying down a lump sum debt. I personally like to keep my sinking fund for bills in a separate account from my other savings, so I don't accidentally spend the money on something else!

\* \* \*

## 4. Check Your Spending

*'A budget tells us what we can't afford,*
*but it doesn't keep us from buying it'*
~ WILLIAM FEATHER

What we're creating is something called a zero-based budget. That means your **income** (what you've got coming in) should equal your **expenses** (what you've got going out) to reach **zero**. It means that every penny is being accounted for.

So you've tracked last month's spending and made a spending plan. Now what? Well, you've got to track this month's spending too to make sure you're staying on track.

I like to have a budget meeting with myself once a week. If you've combined finances, you need to be tracking your spending together, communicating so there are no nasty surprises.

Some people choose to have a joint bank account. They may also have a personal account with some fun money that they don't need to talk to their spouse about. Some couples decide to ask each other's permission if they're buying something over a particular amount, say £50 or $100. In these cases, the budget is like a written contract between you. You can work together and hold each other accountable.

Some people use the *'Envelope System.'* This is where they convert a discretionary spending category like food, clothes or entertainment, into cash. Once the cash is gone, it's gone – no more spending.

There are lots of different ways to track your spending. I like to use my debit card and record every item on a spreadsheet. Some people use a budgeting app or banking app. Mindful spending means knowing when you need to ease up. It might mean skipping the restaurant and eating at home instead, making packed lunches instead of buying food at work etc. Cutting spending in one category means you have more to spend elsewhere. If you're way off course, don't worry. Just make sure you realise and try again next month.

## 5. Adjust Your Budget Categories

It's only when you start living on a budget that you realise just how much you're spending in particular areas. I've heard it said that getting the hang of budgeting can take 3 months or more to get it right. So don't be hard on yourself if you're new to this!

Every month we have a chance to reset the budget categories and start again. Some months there will be birthdays and parties, weddings or other financial commitments. At other times, we may find ourselves with a bit more breathing space. The key is that you always need to be mindful, adjusting and adapting.

If you spend a little too much one day, don't worry. Just try to spend a bit less another day. Often I find myself wanting to food shop. Then I remember that there is plenty of food in my cupboards and freezer. So I start to ask myself again, *'What is it that I want and what do I actually need?'*

## 6. Repeat

Every month you're choosing and directing where every penny is going to go. You're following the plan. This is *Mindful Finance*. It isn't easy, but it gets easier with practice! So repeat!

If it feels a bit repetitive or boring, well it is! It's brick-laying! It's building a good financial habit, month by month, day by day, moment by moment. From the moment you wake up in the morning and set your mind on your goal, to when you go to sleep at night. And all those temptations and spending opportunities in between!

As I said before, you can adjust your categories to suit you. It's *your* spending plan after all! But the basic categories are here on my budget template. It can be a big step to write your first budget as it means you're taking responsibility for your finances. So don't be hard on yourself. You're making amazing progress!

It can also be a bit scary to see where all your money is going. For me, the first thing I noticed was how much I was spending on restaurant bills. I would often eat out rather than cook at home. What should have been a special treat had become a necessity. Once I realised that, it was relatively easy to get into a new habit of cooking at home, planning my meals, cooking food in batches and freezing it in advance. I started taking lunches to work rather than buying expensive canteen food. It was cheaper, healthier and I started to enjoy cooking more!

There are ways to make the process fun. You can turn it into a game. Some of my shopping apps have coupons and prizes. I get so excited when I win a free loaf of bread or a croissant! Try and out-budget your spouse and your friends! Don't forget to celebrate the little wins (in ways that don't cost a lot of money, as that sort of defeats the purpose, doesn't it!)

## How To Use Margin to Reach Your Goals

So, you've done your first budget! Congratulations! Now it's time to learn how to put margin to work and build your financial house. Remember, we've created a zero-based budget. That means that what goes in must be the same as what goes out. That way, every penny is accounted for.

When we created our budget you'll notice that we had categories for giving and saving. This was the margin in our budget (remember, **margin** = your **income** minus your **expenses**). Margin is the difference between what we earn and what we spend. If you're in a season of paying off debt, then you direct any margin you have towards paying it off instead. We'll talk about that more in *Chapter 4: Possessions and Debt.*

Of course, it's not quite as easy as earning more and spending less, in the same way that there's more to sustainable weight loss than eating less and moving more! Money management is behaviour, not maths. It's psychology and saving money is hard. As the saying goes, most people find they've got 'too much *month* at the end of the *money*!'

Most people do their spending first and then try to save what's left over (which usually isn't very much). There's a reason why this doesn't work. After some research, I've discovered it's because of **Parkinson's Law**. But we can turn that to our advantage!

Parkinson's Law was an observation made by a British Naval Historian called Cyril Northcote Parkinson. He wrote an essay published in *The Economist* in 1955.[28] He was originally talking about bureaucracies, and how officials have a natural tendency to make more work for each other, but his law seems to hold true for many other things too. In essence, Parkinson's Law implies that *'the demand upon a resource tends to expand to match the supply of the resource.'*[29]

Some people use this to explain how work expands to fill the time we have to complete it. It's why people get a pay increase but find that their lifestyle rises to meet it so they still struggle to save money. It's why a lot of people end up living paycheque to paycheque because it feels so natural to spend everything you make each month. And it explains my own observation that no matter how big your freezer is, you will always fill it ( *'Esther's theory of freezers'* ).[30]

How do we get around this law? Well, the answer is simple. We need to learn to pay ourselves first and live on the rest. It's a life hack that has the potential to accelerate your margin creation. Again, if you're already doing this, that's great! For everyone else, it's a great life skill to learn. It will help you go from having *never enough* to having *more than enough.*

I first heard about this principle from Pastor Luke Bryant in my late twenties. But it took me a few years to actually start doing it. I've since come across other people recommending it and I found that it works for me!

You'll also hear this idea called *enforced* or *artificial scarcity*. You have to trick yourself into believing that the money you've put aside for spending is all you have. It's all too tempting to think that the money you've allocated for giving, saving or paying off debt is money that can be spent on a fun night out or a new outfit.

If we **take our margin out of the equation first**, then we've got: Your **income** minus your **expenses**.

So if we remove our margin from the equation, then everything we have left is our (artificially lower) income. It feels natural to spend it all.

In fact, we now have permission to spend it all! It's that same feeling of freedom that the budget gives us by setting limits. It's permission to spend without feeling guilty!

I'm going to show you several different ways of taking margin out of the equation. Then we can put it to work and learn to live on the rest. It might sound a bit complicated, but this upside-down approach can be really effective.

Of course, you may be in a season where your income is low. You may be living at or below the poverty line. You may be out of work or facing a health issue. In that case, it can be very difficult for you to create margin without first finding a way to increase your income.

It may still be possible to save a little bit over a longer period or avoid getting into debt. In this season, that would be a win.

For many of us who are working and still find that money is tight, we may be experiencing *lifestyle creep*. This is where our lifestyle rises to meet our income. It's where we get confused between what we *want* and what we *need*. For the majority of people in this situation, it's possible to reframe our view and reset our spending.

For many people the idea of living on 90% of your income (or even less) might feel a bit scary right now. But your brain will get used to it and your lifestyle will adjust.

You can start with a smaller percentage if you want to and increase it gradually over time. Some people get a pay increase and make a conscious decision to keep their spending the same so that they can save more. Overcoming Parkinson's Law feels unnatural, but it can be done!

\* \* \*

## Get Your Priorities Right

Another way to look at this is to use the concept of *prioritisation*. You've probably heard of this when it comes to time management, but it's a key part of creating financial margin too.

Have you heard the story of someone who is given a container, a load of rocks of different sizes and some sand? Then they're told to fill the container. They try lots of different combinations. Sand first and then some rocks. A few rocks, then a layer of sand, then a few more rocks. But actually there's only one way to guarantee you'll fit everything into the container every time. You have to *prioritise*.

**You've got to put the big rocks in first.**

If you put the sand in first – the tiny distractions, the unimportant things that can waste our time, like hours of social media scrolling and binge-watching TV – then you'll have no room for the big rocks. These represent important things like quality time with family, achieving a goal, doing a project, or reading a book like this!

When it comes to our finances, the big rocks might be things like saving, giving or paying down debt. Other rocks could be paying our rent and bills as well as other essentials. It's the sand that can be the problem – the impulse buys, the expensive coffees, the takeaways and restaurants, the little bits here and there that really mount up.

If you put the sand in first, you'll never be able to create margin. If we don't make the time for important things, then it's used up before we blink and wasted. If we don't put money aside, we spend it all and it slips through our fingers.

It's easy to pour in sand. But we have to make a habit of prioritising the big rocks first. These will become the corner stones or foundation stones, the important things that get us where we want to be, the building blocks for success. You'll struggle to do the daily habits that lead to achieving your big goals if there's too much sand in the way.

"The foundation stones for a balanced success are honesty, character, integrity, faith, love and loyalty."
~ Zig Ziglar

Rocks first, then sand

"Success is neither magical nor mysterious. Success is the natural consequence of consistently applying the basic fundamentals."
~ Jim Rohn

Make sure you put in your big rocks first – the essential ones. Then put in the smaller rocks. Lastly, you can pour in the sand. There. Your life is full of the things that matter.

Whether it's managing tasks at work, managing your time, managing your relationships, your spiritual life, creating a morning routine or managing your finances, it's the same principle at work. You'll never get everything you want done. So you have to choose what's important and make it a priority to do those things first.

## Pay Yourself First

*'Do not save what is left after spending, but spend what is left after saving'*
~ WARREN BUFFETT

After I heard Pastor Luke Bryant from Liverpool One Church talking about *paying yourself first*, I started to find it in lots of other places. I came across Jim Rohn and he would tell people to read a book called *'The Richest Man in Babylon'* by George Clason.[31] It was published in 1926 and many authors have been inspired by its message, including Robert Kiyosaki, Dave Ramsey and David Bach.

The richest man in Babylon is a fictional character called Arkad. The book is a series of parables and conversations where Arkad tells his story. He started off as a poor scribe, learning about money through a series of common mishaps (traps that many of us fall into too), before being sold into slavery.

He has a mentor who teaches him about financial wisdom. He starts to apply it and shares the mistakes he made along the way to eventually become the richest man in Babylon. It's an old book but still very relevant a century later.

I encourage you to read it, watch a YouTube summary or listen to an audio version. I've listened to it several times. It's not very long but packed full of useful principles and memorable stories.

# Seven cures for a lean purse

**1. PAY YOURSELF FIRST** - Save 10% of your income. Keep one coin out of every 10. For every £100 you earn, save £10 and live on £90.

**2. CONTROL YOUR EXPENSES** — avoid getting luxuries mixed up with necessities. Don't confuse what you need with what you want. If you get used to having luxuries, you'll start to think you need them.

**3. MULTIPLY YOUR WEALTH** — put the 10% you've saved to work, so that it makes more money. Arkad says of compound interest: "Learn to make your treasure work for you. Make it your slave. Make its children and its children's children work for you."

**4. GUARD YOUR WEALTH** — avoid get-rich-quick schemes, don't invest in things you don't understand, or you'll risk losing the wealth you've worked hard to build. This is sometimes called getting rich slow.

**5. OWN YOUR OWN HOUSE** - Arkad advises buying versus renting your principal residence, and to use your residence to establish a business.

**6. ENSURE A FUTURE INCOME** - Arkad advises on having a future retirement income. We don't like to imagine a time when we're no longer young or may not be able to work. Do we still want to be doing active or heavy work as we get older or when our health isn't so good?

**7. INCREASE YOUR ABILITY TO EARN** — the greatest investment we can make is into ourselves. Arkad suggests that the more wisdom we know, the more we may earn. If we learn more of our craft we will be richly rewarded. Ask yourself if you're working a job or building a career. How easy are you to replace? Is there career progression?

One of Arkad's strategies is called *Seven Cures for a Lean Purse*. I've written these out on the page opposite. The first two principles are about living on less than you make and controlling your expenses. In the book, Arkad recommends saving 10% of everything you make and putting it into investments to grow more money.

This is a good place to start. But I like to take if further and think about intentional generosity too. While Arkad is generous with his money once he becomes wealthy, a lot of finance experts believe in being generous during the journey of wealth-building too. After all, it's easier to give when the numbers are small to make it a lifelong habit.

I'm going to dedicate a whole chapter to the principle of intentional giving. But since I learnt about it from my church first, this seems like a good time to introduce you to the concept of *'Tithing.'*

Tithing was originally an Old Testament Biblical principle at a time when people's wealth took the form of crops or cattle. They would honour God by giving the *'first fruits'* of their increase to the local storehouse to feed the priests.[32]

*Tithe* means 10 per cent. Some of today's Christians decide to tithe by giving 10% of their income to their local church. Not all Christian traditions teach about tithing, nor is there historical agreement on what it means exactly.

All I can say is, it's something that I've done personally and it has really blessed me. It made me get organised with my finances in a way I never dreamed possible. It reminds me to put God first in my finances and trust Him to meet my needs. It also means I'm helping my local church to help others, which is something I'm really passionate about.

If you've got questions on tithing before we get to *Chapter 6: Generosity* I've found some FAQs that the Ramsey Solutions team has put together that might help you understand more.[33]

As Dave Ramsey says, there are only three things we can do with money: *Give, Save and Spend.* When it comes to managing our money, it's important to do all three. If we focus on one area at the expense of another, our life can easily get out of balance. There's something exciting about doing your giving first. That way, you can say you've made it a priority. It increases your chances of actually doing it and making a difference in the world.

So for people who want to tithe, whether they're Christians or not, it looks like this:

- Pay God first (tithe – pay 10% to your local church)
- Pay yourself next (margin: extra giving, saving and investing)
- Live on the rest (spend)

## Models of Giving, Saving and Spending

Now I want to introduce you to a few different models of paying yourself first. When it comes to income, some of these models talk about *gross income* (before tax) or *net income* (after tax). I like to use gross income to divide up my giving, saving and spending. But other people just divide up their monthly pay, which is usually their net income. You'll have to work out how to apply these principles to your specific situation and find which model works for you.

## 1. Pastor Luke Bryant - The 10 / 10 / 80 Model

I first heard about this model from Pastor Luke Bryant at Liverpool One Church. LOC is founded on three main principles: *Humility, Unity* and *Generosity.* LOC is a church that teaches about and encourages people to tithe, which means giving 10% of their income to the local church. Pastors Luke and Emma have consistently taught this model and passed it on to their three sons as they were growing up. It inspired me to start my debt-free journey and was the first time I saw what it was to live a life with financial margin.

Luke recommends giving the first 10% of your income to the local church as a tithe (paying God first). The second 10% is yours to save (paying yourself second). The remaining 80% is yours to live on (spend the rest). Luke teaches that God can do more with our 90% than we could have done with our 100% on our own.

I've personally seen that to be true in my life. Before I started tithing I had no idea what my income was, let alone what 10% of it was! So, by learning to tithe, this was the first step to motivating me to get my finances in order. It became much easier then to free up money to pay off debt and that, in turn, gave me the skills to save and invest.

I'd like to thank Pastors Luke and Emma Bryant, Dave Alexander, Nathan and Megan Rutledge and many others for getting me started and encouraging me on this incredible journey of financial stewardship. I'm blessed to now be able to give, save and invest more than 10%. But this was where I started and I'll be forever grateful.

## 2. Robert Kiyosaki – Think Like A Business Owner

Robert Kiyosaki is a very popular author and speaker in the world of finance. We'll talk more about his teachings in *Chapter 4: Possessions and Debt*. When it comes to his views on debt, he takes the exact opposite of Dave Ramsey. His famous book *'Rich Dad Poor Dad'* was first published in 2017.[34]

Robert Kiyosaki's version of paying yourself first is to see yourself as a business owner. When you run a business, you have income coming in and expenses going out. A business only gets taxed on its profits (the difference between income and expenses). That profit can be used to pay yourself a salary, but it can also be used to buy assets that create more income. Kiyosaki doesn't believe in saving. Instead, he teaches that you should put your money to work and invest it (he made his fortune from investing in property and real estate).

There are all sorts of legal tax advantages available for people who run a business (or run their finances like a business). It's these tools that can help people become wealthy, such as claiming tax-relief on business expenses or getting tax-relief on pension contributions. So it's worth doing some more research to see how you can apply this to your personal situation.

His view is that to become rich (grow your wealth) you should buy assets that generate cash flow. Meanwhile, poor people only have expenses and liabilities, which is why they stay poor (they can't grow wealth). With this mindset, it's okay to take on debt to help you grow your assets, just like a business owner wanting to grow their business.

After doing some research I discovered that Kiyosaki also believes in tithing and generosity. He has been quoted as saying, *'Most people know they should save, tithe, and invest. The problem is, after paying their expenses, most people don't have any money left to do so. The reason is because they consider saving, tithing, and investing as a last priority.'*

There isn't a strict formula to his version of paying yourself first. But it would probably look like this: give at least 10% to charity, invest as much as you possibly can, then spend last.

## 3. Jim Rohn – The 70 / 30 Rule

Jim Rohn proposes living off just 70% of your after-tax income.[35] He allocates the remaining money in the following way: 10% is allocated for charitable giving. The next 10% is for what he calls *capital investment*, money used to create wealth. This could be to become an entrepreneur, create a part-time business, or be used to develop yourself. The last 10% he puts into savings, preparing for the winters of life. It's a way of making sure you are being generous and building wealth at the same time.

Jim started his career in network marketing and was a powerful motivational speaker, so it's no surprise that he suggests investing money into yourself and your business. I discovered Jim Rohn during my debt-free journey and his teachings are very memorable, which is why I quote him so often in this book.

# Pay Yourself First

There are 3 things you can do with money

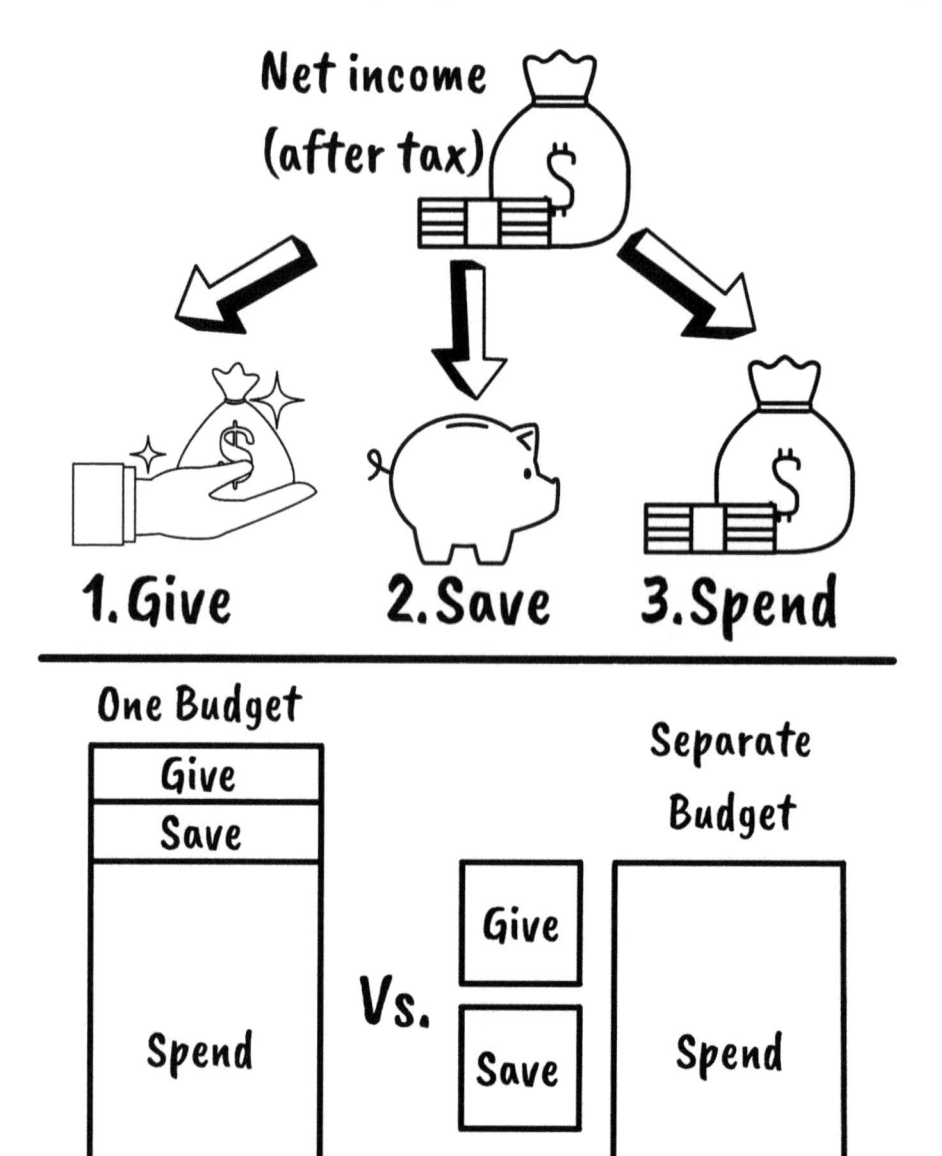

Net income (after tax)

1. Give  2. Save  3. Spend

**One Budget**
- Give
- Save
- Spend

Vs.

**Separate Budget**
- Give
- Save
- Spend

## 4. Dave Ramsey – Give 10%, invest 15% for retirement

Dave Ramsey is famous for helping millions of people get out of crushing debt through his radio show, books, courses and classes, with the help of his team at Ramsey Solutions. While some of his views may seem a bit extreme (he hates debt and recommends people live on beans and rice whilst paying it off) there's no doubt that his *7 Baby Steps*[36] have transformed the lives of many.

He comes from the *'buckle of the Bible belt,'* near Nashville, Tennessee, so it is not surprising that he is someone who teaches that you should tithe the first 10% of your income. Beyond that, he recommends putting your money towards the Baby Steps.

Ultimately once you've paid off your consumer debt, got your emergency fund and built a solid financial foundation, you'll be ready to start investing 15% of your household income into retirement. After this, he likes people to pay off their house. With no payments whatsoever, Dave encourages people to turn their full attention to building wealth and living lives of outrageous generosity.

## 5. The Money Guy Show – Give 10%, 25% for retirement

Brian Preston and Bo Hanson from T*he Money Guy Show* are Dave Ramsey's neighbours near Nashville, Tennessee, and teach the principle of tithing. They have a tolerance for debt that is somewhere between Dave Ramsey and Robert Kiyosaki. They don't mind people using credit cards as long as they don't keep a monthly balance. They don't mind people taking out a car loan as long as it fits certain criteria. Their guide to wealth building is called the *Financial Order of Operations* [37] and it takes Dave Ramsey's model to the next level of complexity.

They don't feel the need to pay off a mortgage early. But they also acknowledge that for some people saving 15% of their income towards retirement just isn't enough. Depending on your age, especially people starting later on in their 40s and 50s, the number to invest may need to be 25% of their income or even more. That's why they have 25% as an investment target but recommend that your savings rate should reflect your age and goals. They have created helpful resources to calculate how much you should be saving towards retirement.[38]

## Managing Your Margin – Using a 3-Account Strategy

So, what does paying yourself first look like in practice? Pastor Luke Bryant has often given examples of how he'd talk his youngest son through this process of dividing up his money into giving, saving and spending categories.[39]

Imagine £100 in £10 notes. If you were doing the 10/10/80 strategy, you'd put the first £10 in a giving pot, you'd put the second £10 into a savings pot, and the other £80 would be yours to spend. If you had more money, the numbers just get bigger, but the proportions would stay the same.

You can use *Give, Save and Spend jars* to teach kids how to manage their pocket money. Well, we can do something similar with our bank accounts too. It works especially well if you have online banking or banking apps to easily move your money around.

*Christians Against Poverty* have their own version of a 3-account strategy: one for bills, one for discretionary spending and one for savings.[40] But I'm going to talk you through what I do, using Robert Kiyosaki's idea of paying yourself like a business and *The Money Guy Show*'s idea of artificial scarcity. I've called these '*phases*', so we don't get mixed up with the 3-step margin plan from earlier on.

Check out my **3-account strategy flow chart** so you can follow what I'm talking about a bit more easily. It'll probably make more sense when you start putting it into practice.

MINDFUL FINANCE - 89

# Pay Yourself First

## Example of a Three Account Method

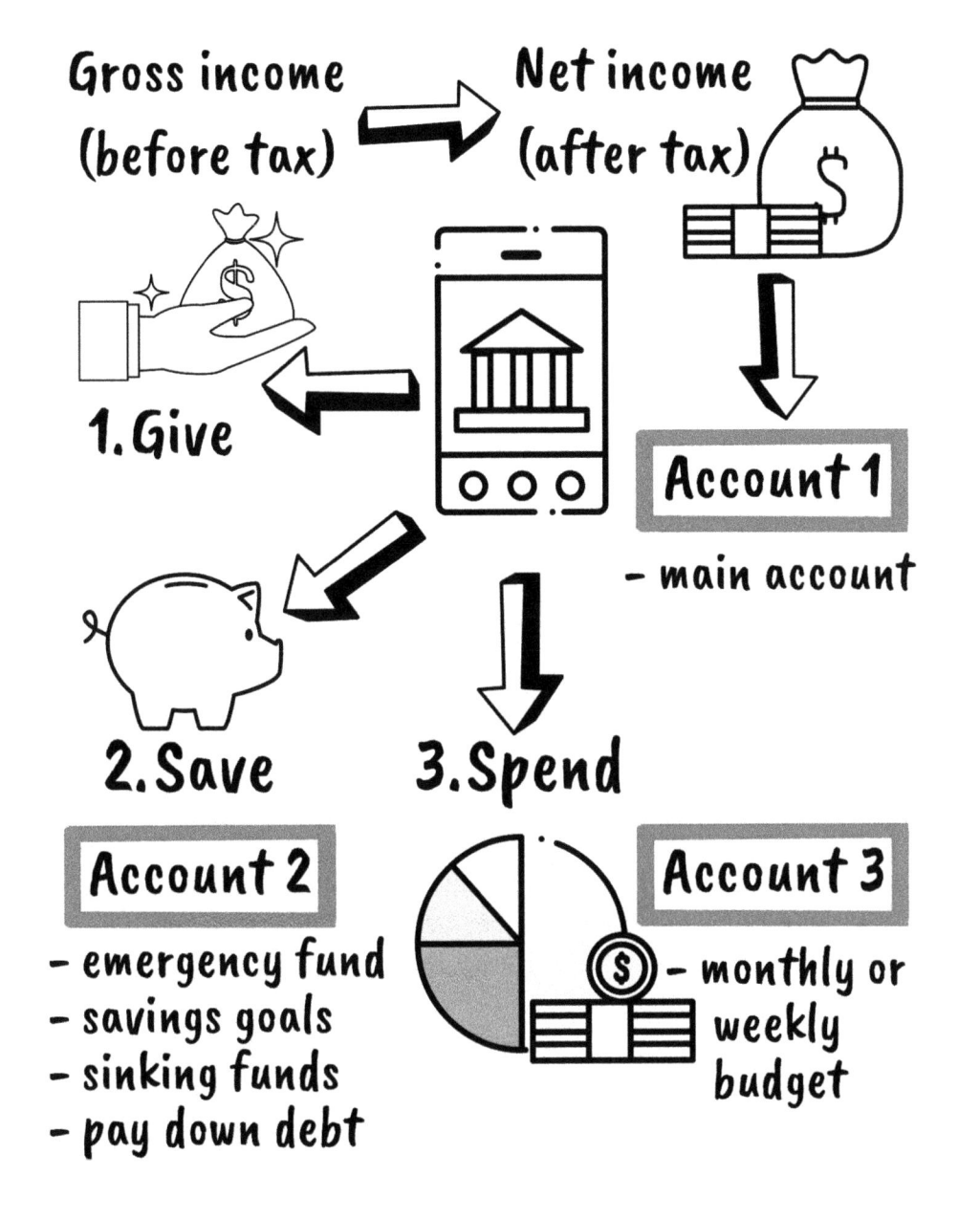

Gross income (before tax) → Net income (after tax)

**1. Give**

**Account 1**
- main account

**2. Save**

**Account 2**
- emergency fund
- savings goals
- sinking funds
- pay down debt

**3. Spend**

**Account 3**
- monthly or weekly budget

## Phase 1: The Main Account

I get paid a salary for the contract work I do. That **money all gets paid into my main bank account** each month. This is my net income as I've already paid income tax and national insurance contributions on it. Because of the way I work, the amount I earn can vary from month to month.

This is why I decided to live on the same amount each month and budget based on this. This makes it easier to plan my spending. If I don't have enough income, I borrow from my sinking fund. If I have more than enough income, then I have some margin left over. I can either give, save or spend that extra money each month.

I decided to run my finances like a business. A business owner receives an income and pays out expenses. The money left over is called profit and they pay tax on this. Then they get to decide how much they want to pay themselves as a salary. Any money left over is *'margin'*. You can decide how much to pay yourself and how much to have as margin.

I plan my giving, saving and spending at the beginning of each month. I do most of my giving out of the main account. I divide my saving and spending into different bank accounts. This stops me spending money by accident. I know it sounds complicated, but you'll soon get the idea. Make sure you're tracking me on the flow diagram.

## Phase 2: Giving

So each month after I get paid into my main account, the first thing I do is give a tithe of 10% of my gross (before tax) income to my local church. By giving first, it's like putting the big rock in the container. *I make giving my first priority.*

It's up to you how and who you give to. But percentage giving has all sorts of benefits which we'll explore in *Chapter 6: Generosity*. Some people make a giving envelope for spontaneous giving. Some people save up their giving and do it at Christmas as a family. Other people do payroll giving (so that it's automatic) or invest it in a donor-advised fund (so it can grow and they get tax benefits before they give it away).

You get to decide what giving looks like for you. The key is that we get into the habit of giving as it's good for us!

## Phase 3: Savings Account

I work out in advance what I'm going to pay myself to live on in a budget. Often I can live on less than I make. That means that I'm always going to have some margin which I can use to save and invest.

So next, I pay this **margin money into a savings account**. I can decide what I'm going to do with it later. This is *paying yourself first*.

For some people, they may be using their margin to pay down their debt. For others, it could look like putting 10% into a savings account. It depends on where you are on your financial plan, your savings goals, your income and how much you're willing to sacrifice to keep your expenses low.

In reality, I have multiple savings accounts, pensions and ISAs. But to keep our example simple, I'm putting it into a basic savings account. That's another rock in the container. That way I can't accidentally spend my savings.

## Phase 4: Spending Account

Finally, **I get to pay myself a salary**! This is the spending part of my **monthly budget** and it gets an account all on its own. It's a zero-based budget, so I've calculated the minimum amount I need to pay my bills and then added some extra for discretionary spending like food, entertainment and clothes.

You'll notice that by doing it this way, the giving and spending parts of the budget have already been paid. That means we can fully embrace Parkinson's Law and spend the rest! It's like finally pouring in the sand and my container is completely full.

## Phase 5: Adapt The Strategy

Of course, we've got to make sure we have a big enough budget to help us stick to it and not overspend on discretionary things like food and entertainment. Or else we'll still be struggling to pay our bills.

If you struggle to stick to the spending plan, then maybe having a strategy like *Christians Against Poverty*'s 3-Account Strategy might be for you. They recommend putting your *non-discretionary* money for bills in one account and putting your *discretionary* spending money in another. That way, you can see exactly what you have left to spend.

In practice, we're all different and we develop as people over time. There may be a season where you have to be stricter with the spending plan than others. Maybe you're going through a difficult struggle and can't afford to give or save as much as you'd like. Maybe you've got a particular savings goal coming up and want to cut your expenses right down so that you can save more.

Your life situation may change. You may be getting married. Perhaps you add a new baby, pet or family member to your household. Perhaps your home needs renovating or you have some other expense coming up. You may find that you need to increase your spending for a season, then cut back again later.

The budget is there as a tool for you to use and adapt to your individual circumstances. You can have one bank account or five bank accounts. You might have a joint account and separate accounts. You'll find a way that works for you and your situation.

The key is to make sure that you can do all three things - give, save *and* spend - with intentionality.

## Automatic Finance – The Pros and Cons

It's good to explore opinions we don't always agree with. That's the key to having a conversation about money. It's what stops us from feeling like we're in an echo chamber where everyone is saying the same thing. Hearing only what we want to hear can lead to *confirmation bias* where we seek out people and resources with a worldview that confirms what we already believe. Social media algorithms amplify this effect and you can get caught up in a story that may not be the only one.

Well, that's why I want to talk about *Automatic Finance*. This is the *Anti-Budget*! Even though it can be at odds with *Mindful Finance* at times, there are still things we can learn from it.

When something is automatic, it's done spontaneously or unconsciously. It's like a machine is doing it rather than a thinking being. It's involuntarily, self-acting or self-regulating. In other words, it's done *mindlessly*. The key thing is to be *mindful* of the fact that we're automating our finances.

*Automating* your finances doesn't have to be *mindless* finance. We still need a plan. If we *pre-decide* how we're going to behave to help us reach our goals, then it's okay to automate the process.

Automation makes payments easier and it can help us stay on track. If we set up a direct debit that automatically pays our bills, then it removes a barrier. We could avoid late payment fees. It saves time, energy and effort. That's *good* automatic finance.

But we can also have automated recurring payments for things like TV subscriptions, music and magazine subscriptions, store cards and credit cards, buy now and pay later services.

Some of these start as free trials, special offers and great deals, which suck us in. But these can also take our time (if they're distracting) and drain our money (especially if we don't even use the service or end up paying interest). That's *bad* automatic finance.

## The Automatic Millionaire

If the mindful finance approach – knowing where every penny is going – isn't for you, then maybe you'd like to try the Automatic Millionaire approach. Perhaps you've tried budgeting and it just isn't working out the way you'd hoped. You need to find a different way that works for you.

David Bach's book *'The Automatic Millionaire'* was published in 2004.[41] Just like me, David Bach is aiming his book at financial beginners or intermediates. There's nothing particularly new or revolutionary in his book. But common sense wisdom isn't that common. It may seem revolutionary to you right now, just like it was to me a few years ago.

David Bach controversially claims that you can become a millionaire automatically without using a budget, because, he claims *"budgets don't work."* (Of course, I don't share this opinion). He thinks we're just too good at misbehaving with money. Instead, he suggests automating our bills, our savings (by paying ourselves first, of course) and automating our giving. Then we live on what's left over. I think this approach is similar to Parkinson's Law we spoke about before.

I do agree with automating as much as possible. But I personally still need a spending plan to hold myself accountable. I still need to check in with myself at least once a week and course-correct if needed. Even once the important things are paid for, you can still run out of spending money before the month is finished. There still has to be a degree of mindfulness in the automatic millionaire plan. It's still easy to overspend and go into the red. We need the willpower and self-control to stop us from dropping into our overdraft or reaching for the credit card.

Another of the famous and controversial concepts in *'The Automatic Millionaire'* is what David Bach calls the *'Latte Factor.'* He claims that we all have one. There will be unconscious spending habits that could be robbing you of your future fortune. David Bach doesn't identify the *latte factor* as a mindfulness technique, but I think it is. He wants us to reflect on and become aware of our unconscious spending habits so we can make a change.

So, what area of your spending might you be taking for granted? Where could we be saving money? He gives the example of someone who buys their coffee and breakfast each morning at the café on the way to work, instead of having it at home. Or someone who goes to the shop to buy their lunch each day, rather than making a packed lunch. These savings add up each day, each week, each year. If invested over the course of a few decades, it could add up to hundreds of thousands of pounds over a lifetime.

Some people get annoyed at the idea of the *latte factor* because they'd prefer to go and enjoy a cup of coffee! After all, it takes more than saving a latte a day to become a millionaire, doesn't it? Making the little changes and adjustments, building up daily habits over time, can have a big impact. Maybe it's a start rather than the complete answer. So is having an automatic financial plan and no budget better than having a mindful finance spending plan? What about *automatic investing*? Would *mindful finance* or *intentional investing* be better?

I think there's a difference between trying to do something automatically (without intentionality) and automating the process (with intentionality). So I don't mind David Bach's Automatic Millionaire plan as long as it's done *mindfully*.

## Auto-Enrolment: Britons Aren't Saving Enough

We only need to look at the UK's automatic enrolment of employees into workplace pension schemes to realise why automation has limitations. The problem is that when finance is automatic it can go unnoticed. It's the opposite of *mindful finance*! Many people assume that the state or employer will just take care of them. They think they'll get by on their state pension, or that their workplace pension will be enough. They assume that because it's automatic, it's enough.

Unfortunately, for many people, their automatic investments are not enough. The saving rate is just too low. Auto-enrolment is nowhere near *Ramsey Solutions'* 15% target or *The Money Guy Show*'s 25% target. The harsh reality is that unless people wake up and take control of their finances, they may not have enough money to retire and may have to keep working longer than they wanted to.

When a pay increase comes, it's all too easy to increase your lifestyle rather than your savings. We have to be intentional with our retirement planning and investing, just like we have to mindfully build the rest of our financial house. The sooner you start, the easier it will be.

## Round Up Apps: Small Savings, Small Results

The same is true if you're relying on round-up apps to help you save for the future. These make small savings that you barely feel and automatically put them towards your future financial goals. But if you are only saving pennies, you'll probably only get pennies back. If you intentionally invest, you're more likely to grow some significant wealth over time. If you don't notice the friction of saving and investing, there's a strong chance that it won't become a habit.

There are different round-up apps available in the USA[42] and in the UK.[43] This is not a recommendation and I don't use them personally. But I want you to be aware of everything that's out there. If you want to try any apps, make sure you check out the fees and research the pros and cons yourself.

While the saying goes that *'from little acorns, mighty oak trees grow,'* you have to be careful or you might just end up with a pile of acorns. Seeds have to be planted, watered and have the right conditions to grow. The same is true with our investments. They need to be planted in the right place and tended to with intentionality, even if you're going to use a set-it-and-forget-it approach or automate the process.

Unfortunately, it's highly unlikely that you'll become a millionaire by saving a few pennies on your shopping, in the same way that you won't become a millionaire with air miles or loyalty points alone. In fact, round-up apps may actually be undermining your budget by taking extra money away without you knowing. It's hard to build a habit of living on a budget when you're giving up control to something else.

I believe it's far better, in the long run, to develop financial mindfulness and build consistent habits, helping you develop the self-discipline you need to reach your goals. If you can't do that, then by all means, try a round-up app. At least you'll manage to save something. But don't expect the same results as someone who is being intentional with their savings and investments.

## Mindful Spending

Some people make fun of Millennials for their love of avocado toast (which costs many times more to buy from a restaurant than to make at home). Gen Z are often characterised by their YOLO (*'You Only Live Once'*) mentality. Some people claim that David Bach is making you feel guilty for enjoying your overpriced coffee and expensive fancy toast in the here and now. This is something I've heard lots of finance podcasts talking about. How do we balance enjoying life now with ensuring we have enough for the future?

It's good to save money where we can. Martin Lewis's *Money Saving Expert* has built a whole brand focused on teaching people ways to save money.[44] It could be switching your energy providers, shopping around for insurance, or simply knowing when to turn your heating and appliances on and off. It's easy to go overboard and get obsessed with the little details. But arguably it's your *behaviour over time* that matters. If you save regularly, consistently and for the long term, then you can build wealth. That means it's okay to enjoy a cup of coffee here and there.

# What's your spending habit?

**western_spiral_art** I've been so blessed this weekend to be able to spend time with friends, catch up on what's been going on in our lives, over a cuppa or three. Thank you SciFi, Kallie and Laura ☺ xxx

*March 7 2020*

*One of my last café visits before the 2020 lockdown*

*Treats are okay! But remember to enjoy them! Make every latte count!*

### Reflective Questions: Automatic Finance — help or hindrance?

- What's your 'Latte factor'?
- What are the little habits that could cost you big in the long run?
- What's a necessity or a special treat? Do you take that thing for granted? Do you have an attitude of thankfulness and gratitude?
- Are you making saving (or investing) a regular habit?
- Are you only saving dimes when you could be investing dollars?
- If your budget is set to autopilot, are you paying the right amounts? Are you paying for subscriptions you don't use? Are you being overcharged in any areas? Could you get a better deal?
- What is your priority for your money right now?

This is where *mindful spending* comes in. Here's one of my social media posts from March 2020.[45] I'd been catching up with friends. Little did we know that several weeks later and the UK would be entering a series of lockdowns during the COVID-19 pandemic. Being able to go to a café and order a cup of coffee became impossible. We were no longer allowed to see friends and family. It makes you look at a cup of coffee differently, knowing about David Bach's *latte factor* and remembering the things we couldn't do during the lockdowns. It reminds me to *really* enjoy a cup of coffee.

If you experience a season where you decide to make some sacrifices and go without a favourite treat, whatever your *latte factor* might be, initially you'll be overjoyed to have that thing back in your life. But the novelty will eventually wear off. It'll feel normal again. The key is remembering to enjoy the moment.

*Mindful spending* acknowledges that there's more to spending money than just the thing you're buying. A shop-bought coffee can mean spending time with friends, family or having some *me time* in a café. It's a luxury. I need to remember not to take it for granted.

## Conclusion:

Thanks for sticking with me. This is probably the most in-depth and practical of all the chapters. That's the foundation of your financial house built! If you do nothing but go through this chapter a few times over it will set you up for a lifetime of wealth-building! If you'd like to learn more, remember to check out the Resources Chapter for some useful videos.

Hopefully, you've learnt the fundamentals and started to put your toolkit together. You've learnt about spending plans, budgeting tips and the importance of living on less than you make. You've learnt how to create margin. Now we're going to put that margin to work and look at ways to accelerate your progress, building your financial house and helping you reach your wealth-building goals.

# Build your four walls

1. Food
2. Clothes
3. Shelter & utilities
4. Transportation

# | 2 |

## Chapter 2: The Four Walls

*'No matter how blessed or distressed you are financially, your first priority every month is to cover what I call the Four Walls. Think of it as the four walls that hold your house together. They are food, shelter, clothing, and transportation. If you have food in your belly, a roof over your head, clothes on your back, and a way to get to work tomorrow, you'll live to fight another day.'*

~ DAVE RAMSEY

Now we've built a solid foundation of good financial habits, you can start get your financial house built. Perhaps your financial house is already under construction. Now is the time to sort out any cracks that might cause you problems in future. Again, this may seem like basic common sense, but we need to fix these issues early if we want our financial plan to be structurally sound for years to come.

I first heard about the four walls principle from Dave Ramsey. You might find some variation in what's included in the four walls. It's making sure that you have the basic necessities for life covered. Our income is our greatest wealth-building tool, so to protect it we've got to make sure our household is secure and we can get to work. As Dave Ramsey puts it, making sure *'you'll live to fight another day.'*

My version of *The Four Walls* principle includes:

1. **Food**
2. **Clothes**
3. **Shelter and utility bills**
4. **Transportation**

These are based on *'Maslow's Hierarchy of Needs.'*[46] In psychology, this is the concept that we need to have our basic physiological needs covered before we can satisfy our higher needs. We need food and shelter before anything else. At the very top of our needs hierarchy, after building strong relationships and self-esteem, is something called self-actualisation. This is where we fulfil our desire to become the best that we can be.

The four walls are the key things you need to protect yourself and your family from danger. We need them for our mental and physical wellbeing. That's why it's important to prioritise building the walls of your financial house next. These are essential and help you to keep earning an income, which in turn creates the margin you need to reach your financial goals.

It's hard to work effectively, think strategically or make wise decisions when you're cold, hungry and worried you might lose your house. So it's important to stabilise your situation first. Remember, if your debts are overwhelming and you think you're in a spiralling debt crisis, then you need to get professional help.

Of course, there are also people in the UK and globally that live below the poverty level. For them, keeping the four walls may be a daily struggle and priority. I've come across two key definitions of poverty. These are known as *'absolute'* and *'relative'* poverty.[47]

When we're talking about the four walls we're actually looking at an *'absolute'* view of poverty, condensed down to the physical essentials like food and shelter.

MINDFUL FINANCE - 103

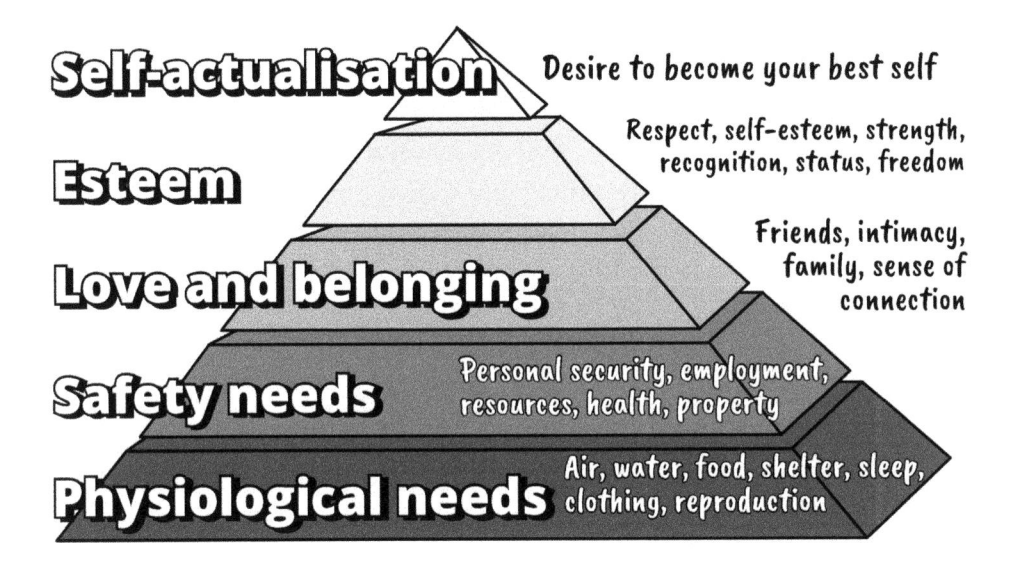

# Maslow's Hierarchy of Needs

**Self-actualisation** — Desire to become your best self

**Esteem** — Respect, self-esteem, strength, recognition, status, freedom

**Love and belonging** — Friends, intimacy, family, sense of connection

**Safety needs** — Personal security, employment, resources, health, property

**Physiological needs** — Air, water, food, shelter, sleep, clothing, reproduction

Maslow's hierarchy of needs is a motivational theory in psychology. There are 5 tiers of human needs, often depicted as hierarchical levels within a pyramid. When one need is fulfilled a person seeks to fulfil the next one, and so on. Every person is capable and has the desire to move up the hierarchy toward a level of self-actualization.

Unfortunately, progress is often disrupted when lower needs are unmet. Life experiences, including divorce and loss of a job, may cause an individual to fluctuate between levels of the hierarchy. Therefore, not everyone will move through the hierarchy in a uni-directional manner but may move back and forth between the different types of needs.

### Simplypsychology.org / Dr Saul McLeod / Feb 5 2007

For those of us with an modest or higher income, this hierarchy of needs can give us a new perspective. Being mindful of our basic needs increases our gratitude for the things we often take for granted. It can also help us to become more aware of the needs of others.

There is also a *'relativist'* view of poverty, which includes other aspects of life that go beyond the four walls. These include our standard of living and things that enable us to participate in society, like access to computers and the internet, washing machines and phones. In our modern Western world, these things are seen as essentials when in the not too distant past they would have been considered luxuries.

## Priority Debts

You might have heard of *Priority Debts*. Certain types of debt need to be paid as a priority as they may come with a penalty. It could be a fine, a criminal record, or even a prison sentence. You could end up losing something essential that you rely on like your internet, mobile phone, electricity, home or car.

What debts to prioritise will also depend on the country you live in. In the UK, your supplier isn't allowed to cut off your water. So that becomes a non-priority debt. The *Citizens Advice* website can talk you through which debts to focus on first and give you advice on what to do if you're behind with any of them.[48]

Priority debts include house payments, council tax, energy bills, phone and internet bills, TV licence payments, court fines, overpaid tax credits, hire purchase or conditional sales (like household appliances, or your car), unpaid taxes and unpaid child maintenance. These priority debts correspond closely with the four walls. You need to make sure you prioritise these over your other consumer debts. We'll focus on paying off the non-priority debts in *Chapter 4: Possession and Debt*.

But, for now, we just need to keep the wolf from the door. That means paying minimum payments on all the essential bills. It means deciding not to go deeper into debt. If you're familiar with Dave

Ramsey's Baby Steps, you'll sometimes hear this referred to informally as *'Baby Step Zero.'* I want you to ask yourself some questions:

- How much does it cost to cover my *essential* needs?
- What is a *want* rather than a *need*?
- What does *enough* mean for me?
- Is there anywhere I can save money?
- How can I make my money go further?

Every time we spend money on something there is an opportunity cost. It means we can't use it to buy something else. We can't save it, invest it or give it away. If we consume it, then it's gone forever. We can no longer use it to grow our wealth.

In this chapter, as a thought-experiment, we'll strip back our spending to the bare essentials as if we're in emergency mode, even if we're not. It will help us become mindful of what is a *need* and what is a *want*.

If you ever decide to aggressively pay down debt or find yourself in a season of hardship, then this chapter will cover some spending tips that you might find useful.

## A Message for Young Adults

I'm lucky to have friends of all ages. I love supporting the Young Adults (YA) ministry at my church and I'm writing this book with them in mind. You guys have time on your side! One day, I was speaking to a friend who was in her early twenties. I was trying to explain to her how powerful time can be when it comes to investing. I wish I'd been able to tell myself 10 or 15 years ago that our decisions in our early adult years matter more than we sometimes realise.

*The Money Guy Show* has calculated that every dollar invested at age twenty has the power to multiply 88 times over by the time you get to age 65. You can download their free deliverable showing you how compound interest can work for you depending on how old you are.[49] It's hard to emphasise enough just how powerful it could be to start investing early. There's an equally powerful negative effect of debt working against you.

The later you leave it, the more you need to invest to achieve the same results. That's because exponential growth is a curve. To give yourself a better chance of success, you should start as soon as you can.

Ironically, it's when we're young that we usually have the least money available to invest. It's tempting in your twenties and thirties to spend money on food, clothes and going out. It's easy to take on debt and keep accumulating. As we get older, our expenses increase along with our responsibilities.

We have an opportunity to choose what we do with our money and that includes planning for the future. Would you rather have one pair of shoes now or 88 pairs of shoes in 45 years' time? That might seem like a silly example. We'd need to adjust for inflation too. But that's the sort of trade-off we're making. Every £1 we spend now is £88 we can't spend 45 years from now.

I was explaining to another friend that it is possible to become a millionaire if you invest regularly for long enough. The earlier you start, the less you have to invest each month to reach your long-term goal. "But I don't want to be a millionaire," she said in reply. It may seem abstract and impossible, but financial independence is attainable for everyday people and you might become a millionaire in the process.

The unfortunate reality is that to retire with the lifestyle many of us desire, some of us will need to be millionaires to afford it. If we don't save enough or start early enough, then we may end up needing to work harder for longer or cut our lifestyle in retirement.

To become a millionaire you need a net worth of £1 million (net worth is the difference between what you own and what you owe). It doesn't mean you earn £1 million. The stock market goes up and down but generally goes up over the long term. Calculations suggest that you could invest as little as $200 a month to reach $1 million over 40 years. An article from *The Motley Fool* has the numbers to back this up.[50]

I'm not suggesting that everyone in their twenties needs to start investing. There is a time and place for investing. You need to have built your financial house first before you grow your financial garden.

But I want you to be mindful of where your money is going and why you're building wealth in the first place. £200 a month might seem like a lot of money to save right now, but I assure you, it's very easy to spend £200 without thinking.

For those of you later in life, it's not too late to start your mindful finance journey. But be prepared to increase your savings rate to play catch up. As our time horizon diminishes, money has less opportunity to grow. Compound interest can still be powerful; just, not as powerful.

## Financial Minimalism and The FIRE Movement

I've learnt a lot from my friends who live on a low fixed income, such as those living on benefits or student loans. I have retired friends and family who remember World War II and food rationing. Frugality for them is a way of life that they have continued.

I appreciate that for some of you reading this, living on a low income is a necessity. So I'll try to be sensitive to that. There's lots we can learn from each other.

For some people, extreme frugality is a choice. They deliberately live a lifestyle costing much less than they earn. This is called *Financial Minimalism*.[51] It's a stripped-back way of living where spending is kept to a minimum, usually to dramatically increase their savings rate. Or sometimes they just want a simpler way of life with less emphasis on material possessions.

Financial minimalism is often associated with the **FIRE (Financial Independence, Retire Early) movement.**[52] We'll spend some more time looking at the FIRE Movement in *Chapter 8: Roadmap to Your Financial Future* when we crunch your retirement numbers. You can watch some videos in the Resources Chapter if you'd like to find out more.

Some people in the *FIRE movement* have decided to make lifestyle sacrifices, usually in their twenties and thirties, so that they can save and invest enough to become financially independent.

*Financial independence* means that they have enough money (wealth generated from their businesses or passive income from investments) to allow them to stop working if they want to. Some people decide to work part-time or take a lower-paying job. Some people want time-freedom (to work when they want) or geographical-freedom (to work from anywhere they want).

You'll see lots of different types of *FIRE* described, depending on how much you want to live on and how aggressively you cut your expenses to get there.

**Coast FIRE** is one of my favourites because it's one of the easiest to achieve. This means having enough money invested earlier in life so you can *coast* your way to retirement, letting your investments grow while you continue working a job that pays your expenses.

There's a version called **Barista FIRE** which is similar, but people typically continue to work part-time, for example, in a coffee shop, while sometimes drawing from their investments.

**Lean FIRE** is where you live on less both whilst saving and during retirement, a true financial minimalist.

**Fat FIRE** is where you aim to live a luxury lifestyle in retirement, which usually means you need a higher-than-average income while you're working so that you're not cutting your lifestyle too much.

You may not want to retire early, but I think most of us would like to retire *someday*. So that's lots we can learn from the *FIRE movement*, including money-saving and investment tips. They are great at creating margin and build their financial house quickly. That way they can focus on becoming financial gardeners and grow their wealth as much as they can.

So let's take a look at our four walls in detail.

## 1. Food

Food is one of our most basic human needs and it's close to my heart. I love food! It's so easy to overspend in this area. I've already told you about my unconscious restaurant habit, my version of the *latte factor*, right? Restaurants were convenient and comforting.

Food is the ultimate form of consumption. Perhaps it's a weekend takeaway habit or a daily habit of buying lunch at work. It can quickly get expensive if you're not paying attention.

This was one of the main areas where I needed to become mindful and change my habits. So when I was getting debt-free, I cut back on eating out and did my cooking at home instead. I tried batch cooking and cut down on food waste. I ate a lot of budget ready-meals for lunch (not the healthiest choice perhaps, but certainly cheap and okay for a season). I didn't mind eating the same thing every day. For a time, I became a sort of food minimalist.

### *"Cost of Living Crisis"*

While I've been writing this book, 2023 has seen the UK enter the highest period of inflation for 30 years.[53] Food prices in the UK had stayed relatively low during the last few decades, probably because of competition between supermarkets. However, we experienced supply shortages and panic buying during the COVID-19 pandemic (including limited availability of toilet rolls, eggs and fresh salad).

Russia's invasion of Ukraine in February 2022, a leading exporter of grain, contributed to a significant increase in food prices around the world.[54] It made us realise just how vulnerable our supply chain is.

I don't want to undermine people's reliance on food banks and food pantries. These provide an important service and people shouldn't feel ashamed to access them if they need to. They are usually available through referrals by organisations like *Citizens Advice*.

There are lots of ways to make the most of your food budget. We can change how and where we shop. Cooking from scratch or in batches is generally cheaper. I choose relatively cheap fresh fruit and vegetables that don't go off quickly – apples, onions, carrots and cabbage. Frozen fruit and veg is a great option too. I try to minimise food waste, shop locally and buy food in season, when I can.

For people who don't have access to cookers and ovens, non-cook recipes are available. Food is a culturally sensitive issue. I've put some links in the Resources Chapter to websites with healthy recipes and cuisines from around the world.

There's a difference between the food we *need* and the food we *want*. There's also a balance between eating what is cheap (and convenient) and eating a healthy balanced diet. It's not easy to eat healthily on a budget, but it is possible. We need to be mindful about how food effects our wallet, waistline, gut-health and our planet.

### *"Rice and Beans"*

When times are uncertain, some people have the wisdom to plan ahead for difficult times, such as a job loss or food shortage. They stock up on extra food in advance. You can keep basic necessities in your cupboard that last a long time, like noodles and pasta. But we need vitamins too which is why you may have heard of the phrase *'living on rice and beans.'*

There's a group of people called *'preppers'* who dedicate themselves to being prepared for emergencies, like supply chain shocks, wars and zombie apocalypses – you know the kind of thing I'm talking about. Well, beans and rice are favourite staples for people preparing for the next crisis or disaster to hit.[55]

Rice and beans are cheap, nutritious and easy to store. They're a good source of carbohydrates, fibre and plant protein.[56] It's a food staple around the world, especially in poorer countries. For some people, beans and rice represent the essential food needed for survival.

If you listen to Dave Ramsey long enough, you'll probably hear his catchphrase, *"Beans and Rice, Rice and Beans."* This is a euphemism for cutting your expenses dramatically so you can pay off debt faster.

It's also a popular dish in Latin America and parts of the American South (remember, Dave Ramsey is based in Tennessee, USA). He uses this phrase to describe financial minimalism and food minimalism during difficult seasons of financial strain. If we make sure we have enough to eat, then it can free up extra money to help us stabilise our financial situation.

For most of us reading this book in the developed world, the concept of rice and beans should increase our gratitude that we are blessed to have so many food options available. It's easy to take a varied diet for granted. Food is imported to us from all over the world. Fresh food is available all year round. In the past, people used preservation methods such as canning, pickling, bottling, making jams etc. to preserve food for use out of season. In some countries, this is still the case.

If we've got a particular goal – such as paying off debt – taking our food category down to the basics for a season might be the sacrifice that helps us reach our goal quicker. It doesn't have to literally be rice and beans. But it could be something just as cheap and nutritious.

There are lots of ways to make meals more appetising - adding herbs, spices, sauces, seasonings. The key is that you can cut your lifestyle for a short time and still be okay.

While I didn't exactly live on rice and beans while I was paying off my debt, I did get through several large bags of rice. Buying in bulk can be more expensive in the short term. But home cooking can work out cheaper and healthier than buying fast food and ultra-processed convenience food over the long term.

When you cook dinner, you can save the left overs to eat the next day. Some people do this deliberately to meal-prep. You can multiply your recipe servings which usually doesn't take much extra cooking time. It's amazing to see how much you can fit into a well-organised fridge or freezer.

# Home Cooking

## Useful cupboard items

- Cooking oil
- Tinned tomatoes
- Onions / Garlic
- Soy sauce/sesame oil
- Dried chili flakes
- Tinned tuna/salmon
- Tinned Chickpeas
- Stock cubes
- Salt / pepper
- Cleaning products
- Bin liners

- Dried pasta/noodles
- Rice / grains
- Couscous / Lentils
- Oats / muesli
- Nuts and seeds
- Tinned sweetcorn
- Baked beans
- Honey
- Olive oil / seed oil
- Laundry detergent
- Freezer bags

- UHT milk / alternatives
- Coffee / teabags
- Hot chocolate
- Tinned Soups
- Cooking sauces
- Herbs and seasonings
- Replacement condiments
- Corn flour / Other flour
- Sugar / sweeteners
- Dried Fruit
- Kombucha (healthy drink)

## Useful fridge items

- Tomato Ketchup
- Mayonnaise
- Milk / alternatives
- Eggs
- Cheese / Butter
- Salad Dressings
- Kimchi / sauerkraut

- Fruit / Veg
- Tomato puree
- Yoghurts
- Puddings
- Lemon / lime juice
- Left over meals
- Salsa / dips

- Jam / preserves
- Chutneys
- Condiments e.g. mustard, sauces
- Miso paste
- Chocolate!
- Different sauces

*These are just some of my ideas. Did I miss any of your favourites? Know what you've got and the date you opened it!*

### *Mindful Food Storage*

I didn't realise that during my mindful finance journey, I would also be practising food minimalism. I needed some help though. My sister Liz has a gift for sorting cupboards. Whenever she visits me, she takes out all the out-of-date cooking sauces and helps me to make an inventory. She rotates my tins, jars and cans, moving the newer stuff towards the back and keeping what needs to be used sooner at the front.

When you know what's in your cupboards (or your pantry, cellar, fridge, freezer or wardrobe – wherever it is you store your food!) you'll be less likely to go out and buy stuff you already have. Mindful food shopping and keeping a kitchen inventory (even if it's just in your mind, rather than written down) means less food waste. There are even apps which help you with this. It's better for your bank balance and the environment. Hopefully, you'll enjoy the cooking experience more and be less likely to get fast food or a takeaway when there's a cheap and healthy alternative waiting for you at home.

It makes sense to keep some non-perishable foods in stock, things that last a while (like tins, grains and pasta). You can build this up over time, just like you would an emergency fund. Just remember to keep an eye on the dates and rotate your stock every so often.

It's tempting to hoard and overstock, so you need to find a balance. Just how much extra food you have in case of an emergency will change depending on your risk tolerance and where you are in your wealth-building journey. It may be cheaper to buy in bulk, but it may not make sense to do this if you're in a season of paying down debt.

I've made a list of some of my favourite kitchen essentials. I always have pasta, onions, garlic, tinned tomatoes and cheese in the house so that I can make an easy meal in just a few minutes. Some foods are safe to eat even beyond their best-by or sell-by date.[57] They will eventually lose their flavour and their texture may alter. Just make sure you're sensible. Some stuff is better thrown out. What are your food staples? Will you try something new?

One food minimalism technique is having different supplies in different places. I have my day-to-day essentials in the kitchen cupboard. But after learning about the preppers, I decided to keep some backup supplies (in the wardrobe). That way, I can keep my cupboards less cluttered.

I've only got a small freezer, so I need to know what's in it to make the most of the space available. You remember my theory about freezers, right? Parkinson's Law applies to food storage: *'No matter how big your freezer is, you will always fill it.'*

Having a small freezer means I have to be extra efficient and mindful of what I put in there. If it's not defrosted, I can fit in even less! So I have to remember to defrost my freezer if it starts to look like an ice cave. It's more energy efficient to have a full freezer, with not too much ice and room for air to circulate.

The fridge is where I find it's easiest to waste food. That's where I keep perishable things like fresh vegetables and milk. I like to meal plan but also stay flexible enough so that I can use up my fridge items.

Over time, I've changed my veg choices to things that stay fresh for longer. I've also put myself on a condiment ban. I used to go through phases of buying chutneys and jams, only to forget that they were there. Even though they last a long time, I don't allow myself to buy any more until I've used up what I already have.

We can learn a lot from food minimalists and preppers, as well as people from our grandparents' era, who know how to make a little go a long way. For those of us who are blessed with so much, we may take living surrounded by abundance for granted, with a tendency to over-indulge and waste food.

I found a blog by Jen Schmidt where she introduces the idea of a *'No Spend Pantry Challenge.'*[58] What creative meals can you think up using things you've already got in your cupboards and freezer? How would you do in a no-spend pantry challenge? What weird and wonderful ingredients have you got hidden away that are waiting to be used? Is it time to try a new recipe idea?

## *Budget Recipes*

It's amazing what sorts of things you can cook on a budget. I've included a list of some recipe ideas that you can make in bulk and freeze. When I was paying off my debt, I used to find ingredients nearing their sell-by date in local supermarkets and convenience stores to turn into soup or pop in a freezer bag.

One day I managed to find packs of 6 tomatoes marked down to 10p! Sometimes I freeze ripe bananas to make smoothies. These go really well with frozen blackberries foraged from my local park.

My friends and family are keen to swap recipe ideas. Sometimes I'll search for recipes online or watch cooking videos on YouTube. It's easy to double up or quadruple recipe portions. I will sometimes cook 6 to 8 portions and it only takes a little more time than if I were preparing a single meal (more chopping is needed!). I've linked to some useful videos on food minimalism, food prepping and budget recipes in the Resources Chapter.

One of my favourite YouTube channels is called *'Great Depression Cooking.'* Clara was a 98-year-old cook who vibrantly shares memories of her childhood growing up in the Great Depression era. She was filmed between 2007-2012 by her Grandson, Film Director Christopher Cannucciari. Clara sadly passed away in 2013 but has left a legacy of fascinating insights and memories through her recipe books and videos.

Clara shares the struggles and strategies American households adopted to cope during tough economic times in the 1930s. Things we take for granted now, like coffee and biscuits, were special treats back then. We should be grateful that we don't need to make dandelion leaves into salads, though it's useful to know that we can, should the need ever arise.

## Home Cooking

## Simple Soup recipe ideas

Tomato Soup - fresh tomato, tinned tomatoes, stock, onion, (optional carrots, celery, red pepper), herbs, salt, pepper

Winter Veg - parsnips, carrots, winter squash (e.g. butternut squash or pumpkin) or sweet potato, onions, stock, seasoned with paprika, chilli or a little curry powder, Crème Fraîche

Celery Soup - celery, onion, potatoes, vegetable stock, milk

## Batch cook ideas and things to freeze

| | | |
|---|---|---|
| Curries and somosas | Meatballs | Puddings and cakes |
| Bolognaise / pasta sauce | Burgers | Crumpets |
| Chilli con carne | Pizza | Chips / roast potatoes |
| Cottage pie (beef) | Soups | Blanched vegetables |
| Shepherd's pie (lamb) | Sausages | Fish portions |
| Lasagne / Pasta bake | Frozen bread | Meat portions |
| Stews / Casseroles | Frozen milk | Frozen fruit / smoothie |
| Vegetarian alternatives | Frozen butter | Yorkshire puddings |

Search online for recipe ideas for good home-cooking on a budget. These are some of my favourite freezer items!

Being aware of what we're eating is important too. It was only when I tried calorie counting for the first time using the *My Fitness Pal* app[59] that I realised what a single adult-sized portion of cereal is meant to look like. It's good for your budget and your waistline when you're mindful of your portion sizes.

I've also learned from *The ZOE Science & Nutrition Podcast* (www.Zoe.com) that most breakfast cereals are *ultra-processed*. While fortified with vitamins and minerals, they also have all sorts of additives you wouldn't find in a standard kitchen.

Many convenience foods with a long shelf-life are actually ultra-processed. Mass produced foods like fruit-flavoured yogurts, bread, crisps and biscuits may be high in sugar, salt, or saturated fat. It's not just the quantity of what we eat, but the quality that matters. *The Zoe Science & Nutrition podcast* also has episodes on how to eat healthily on a budget.

I also follow Graeme Tomlinson, *TheFitnessChef_* on Instagram.[60] He is a nutritionist who uses his deadpan, humorous videos to educate people to become mindful about what they're eating. He talks about the psychology of eating in the same way that we've been looking at the psychology of spending. He coaches people not to feel guilty about falling off a diet plan.

He also compares the different costs and nutritional values of food to make you aware of portion sizes and food quality. There may be a healthier, cheaper alternative. It might even taste better! He reminds me to not take any dietary advice too seriously.

You'll find many different definitions of h*ealthy eating*, diet plans and people claiming one is better than another. *The British Society of Lifestyle Medicine* is  agnostic on which type of diet is best, as long as it's sustainable and based on science. New science at the moment includes the impact of food on our gut microbiome and the health benefits of fermented food. That's why I've added kefir, kimchi, kombucha, nuts and seeds to my regular shopping list in 2024 just to see what happens.

### *Where You Shop Matters*

It may seem obvious, but where you shop makes a difference. In the UK, there are a wide variety of places where we can buy food, anywhere from a market stall to a high-end supermarket. But there's a big price difference between supermarkets like Aldi and Lidl compared to an organic farm shop.

We also pay a premium for convenience, so you may find the highest prices at your local corner shop. But you can also find some bargains in these places, like marked-down fruit and veg that are still good to eat, but nearing their sell-by date. Depending on your savings goals, you may need to adjust your lifestyle for a season and decide to shop differently. You can even turn frugality into a game.

Marketing also plays a big role in our food selection. Do we need the expensive branded product or can we swap to a cheaper unbranded alternative? Are we caught up by an advert or the smell of freshly baked bread? They say never shop when you're hungry, right? Supermarkets are clever. They'll put sweets within reach of small children and make you walk right through the store to buy your pint of milk, meaning you go in for one thing and come out with half a dozen items or more!

Let's start by doing some mindful shopping. Do you shop weekly or drop in daily? Little and often can cause your spending to mount up if you're not careful. But weekly shopping also means that food can go off before you get around to eating it all. So you need to make sure you're storing your food mindfully, as we've already discussed, or maybe do a main shop and top-up shops.

Do you shop in that particular store because you've always shopped there? Have you tried anywhere else even if it means taking you out of your comfort zone? Maybe there is a shopping app that gives you points, vouchers, discounts, coupons or special offers. But you need to make sure those bargains don't make you overspend - were you going to buy those things in the first place?

I've finally given in and signed up for a variety of supermarket apps. Some offer rewards for spending over a certain amount. Others turn shopping into a game by offering scratch cards, spin the wheels and arcade games. So I have to ask myself these questions often!

It's good to reflect on whether you're an impulse buyer or a strategic buyer. In this case, it might be sensible to make a shopping list. Some supermarket apps have the option to create one so you can tick items off as you shop. That way, you can avoid the centre aisles at Lidl and Aldi. You can avoid the situation where you go in for a loaf of bread and come out with power tools and garden furniture!

There are also apps to reduce food waste by allowing businesses to sell at a discount, so food doesn't have to be thrown away. Some apps allow food and other items to be shared between neighbours. There are even apps to help you keep track of what food is in your cupboards so you can meal plan accordingly.[61]

### *Online Food Shopping*

For some people, online shopping is a more convenient way to shop. Ordering online and having your shopping delivered can save you time and energy. Some people find that having a virtual shopping list helps them stick to their budget.

These websites can still bombard you with special offers and discounts, so you have to stay on your guard against overspending. Some people choose to pay a small monthly fee to get discounted deliveries as it can work out cheaper over the long run, especially if you're doing your shopping weekly. Just be aware that some online supermarkets have a minimum spend, meaning you may need to do a big shop fortnightly instead.

I have a friend who is now retired who grew up in Liverpool during World War II. She is disabled, which means that she can't get to the shops easily. She has adopted lots of strategies to make sure she has enough food and supplies in stock, just in case. She remembers food rationing and you can tell by the way she shops.

My friend enjoys good quality items but also practises frugality. She always has reserves of durable goods, such as long-life milk and tinned food. She buys a one-year supply of bin liners, teabags and coffee online. She likes wholesalers (like Costco and Amazon) for bulk-buying essential items. She was well-positioned for the toilet roll shortage of 2020. I've learnt a lot from her and have taken on some of her habits.

Proverbs 21:20 (New International Version (NIV)) says, *'In the house of the wise are stores of choice food and oil.'* I feel she definitely fits that picture of wisdom. However, there's a balance between storing wisely and hoarding unnecessarily (which can indicate harmful or dysfunctional behaviour). I've seen both sides of the spectrum.

You may find that by practising financial minimalism, especially when it comes to food, you're relearning the frugality that was necessary for our grandparent's generation during World War II and the great depression before that. These are life skills that we have mostly forgotten but we can rediscover them.

## Different Shops for Different Stuff

It's rare for me to do all my grocery shopping in one place. When I was on my debt-free journey, one of my friends introduced me to cheap ready meals and snacks from places like Home Bargains and B&M. This was revolutionary for me at the time.

I'd never thought of bargain stores to do my grocery shopping. I've since discovered some healthier alternatives, but it was okay for a season. It started me on a journey of exploring new shops.

If you've got nutritious delicious and convenient food at home, then restaurants and takeaway deliveries will be special treats, rather than the norm. I now do the majority of my shopping at Lidl and Sainsbury's. Both of these now do shopping apps with added discounts.

When I go to a high-end store, like Marks & Spencer, it's usually with a particular ingredient in mind or I'm just looking for a bargain. If you want to save money on your shopping, where you shop matters!

During the COVID-19 pandemic, I treated myself to the occasional recipe box (there was an NHS discount at the time). I also used the lockdowns as an opportunity to explore the international food shops on Liverpool's London Road (because food shopping was an adventure back then). We were only allowed to go out once a day and I would take my backpack. I felt like I was going on a hiking trip. I could always use food shopping as a reason if the police pulled me over to ask where I was headed.

I've always enjoyed wandering around Asian supermarkets (even though I recognise very few of the exotic ingredients) but I'm getting more familiar with some of the things I've previously been wary of, most recently, frozen dumplings!

You can play the price comparison game. In the UK, I'm sure you've heard of Lurpak butter. But did you know that Aldi has Nordpak? And Lidl has Danpak! You may find that these alternatives cost a fraction of the price, but the packaging and taste are similar!

Whether it's Kellogg's or a supermarket's own brand of cereal, Nutella or an unbranded chocolate hazelnut spread, Biscoff or biscuit spread, you can usually find cheaper alternatives that don't taste too different. Though some people can't give up the original.

There are always reasons for paying extra. Perhaps you would rather pay for quality or ethical reasons, like Fair Trade, free-range or organic. But there may be a season where cost saving becomes the priority for a time. We can shop with sustainability and the environment in mind once our financial situation is stabilised.

# Mindful Shopping

## Where do your groceries come from? (UK)

### 1. Low
- Lidl
- Aldi
- Home Bargains
- B&M
- Heron Foods
- Iceland

### 2. Middle
- Tesco
- Morrisons
- Sainsbury's
- ASDA

### 3. High
- M&S
- Waitrose
- Co-op
- Ocado
- Booths
- Farm Shops
- Holland & Barret

### 4. Buying in bulk
- CostCo
- Amazon
- Online
- Other wholesalers

### 5. Convenience
- One Stop
- Corner shops
- Spar
- Petrol Stations

### 6. Recipe Boxes
Examples:
- Mindful Chef
- Hello Fresh
- Gousto etc.

### 7. Alternatives
- Asian Supermarkets
- Independent shops
- International Grocers
- Market stalls

This is not a recommendation! Just some ideas to get you thinking! Where do you shop? Time for a change?

## 2. Clothes

Clothes are another essential human need. We need clothes to keep us warm and give us dignity. We need different clothes for different seasons and different occasions. Clean socks and underwear are everyday essentials. There may be a dress code for work or school. We need different clothes for exercise, going out, relaxing and sleeping in.

There's also a social aspect to clothes, expressing our fashion and style, our personality. Just like there's a difference between basic and luxury food, the same is also true for our clothes.

Clothes can easily become an entrapment, a source of comparison, a way to try and impress others or fit in with a group of people. Named brands and labels can become a way of showing off our status, seeking approval or trying to feel good about ourselves. When it comes to clothes, there really is no upper limit to how much we can spend. So we have to be mindful of the psychology behind clothes – why we wear what we wear, the pitfalls of shopping without a plan, or playing the comparison game.

How often do we go to a sale and buy clothes because they're on offer, whether we need them or not? I've done my fair share of impulse buying in the past. It's easy to buy clothes we liked at that moment but later didn't like. Sometimes we even buy clothes that don't even fit us, hoping that we'll fit into them one day. They end up in storage with the price tag still attached.

Clothes minimalists keep the number of clothes items they own down to a minimum. However, they sometimes decide to pay more for quality, wearability and durability. Again, think of our grandparents' generation. Back then, clothes were made to last – a good pair of shoes, a decent coat. These things were treasured possessions and kept you warm and dry, sometimes for decades.

My sister Liz has tried clothes minimalism whilst travelling and living out of a suitcase. She tells me she had two of each item of clothing and tried to give the rest away to charity. She describes herself as partially successful (some clothes have still ended up in family members' wardrobes!). Minimalism won't be for everyone, but it might be for a season.

Just like the food in our cupboards, it's good to do a clothes inventory and get to know what's already in our wardrobe. Then we can do something about it. Minimalists have a lot to teach us about clothing too.

### *Basic Clothes*

Most of you reading this, even if you're getting out of debt right now, will probably have some basic clothes already. When it comes to the four walls, we need to make sure we have the basic clothes covered, things like shoes and clothes for work. If you need a uniform or a suit to allow you to earn an income, then that should be a priority.

When you're getting current with your bills or in a season of paying off debt, you may decide to keep the clothing part of your budget deliberately low. Perhaps the sacrifice for creating margin in this season is wearing the clothes you have or finding inexpensive ways to renew your wardrobe.

I had a very strange relationship with clothes and spending before my mindful finance journey. I don't know if you can relate. I used to feel depressed and stressed, but I couldn't work out why exactly. The truth is that I was struggling because my finances were disorganised. But because I couldn't see it, I'd try some retail therapy instead. I was spending money on clothes to make myself feel better for not being able to afford clothes! Humans do crazy things, right?

Of course, the happy feeling was temporary and I'd feel stressed again soon. I think that's how I ended up with wardrobes full of random clothes, some of which I'd collected over the years and forgot I even had. Do you ever buy an outfit for an event and only wear it once? We all seem to do it.

So when I started my debt-free journey, I decided to look at my clothes differently. I realised that I actually had everything I needed for that season. I had work trousers, tops, and work shoes. I had the basics covered. If I hadn't, then that would have been my next focus.

### *Make Do and Mend*

I started looking through the bags, boxes and draws. It was like discovering a whole new wardrobe from things I already had. If you're working towards a particular money goal, I encourage you to have a good think about what clothes you already have, what you need and what you would like.

Buying clothes doesn't have to break the bank either. My friend, Cynthia Ajayi, is a self-acclaimed *'Queen of charity shops.'* She sometimes shares her passion for frugality and fashion on her Instagram and YouTube channel.[62,63] I have other friends who've traded second-hand clothes online or through vintage apps. I've been to clothes swap parties where we've tried out each others' old or unwanted clothes (some with the price label still attached, never worn).

While it is possible to buy cheap clothes, sometimes it's at the expense of quality or questionable manufacturing processes. The social responsibility and ethical aspects of clothes are something else to consider. Some clothes are now made from new natural fibres or recycled plastics. We need to make sure that there's no modern-day slavery or human trafficking in the supply chain. Thinking about where our clothes come from is also part of mindfulness and stewardship.

If you've got the time, you can also make or customise your own clothes. I've got friends who crochet, knit and sew. My mum is a whiz at sewing and altering dresses. I've got Steampunk friends who've made their own costumes and outfits, Victorian skirts from dress patterns and curtain material, just like Maria in *The Sound of Music.*

Programmes like *'The Great British Sewing Bee'* may have popularised a handmade approach to fashion. But the saying *'Make Do and Mend'* was popularised during World War II due to scarce resources. It was a government-backed scheme to encourage people to revive and repair worn-out clothes.[64] While food was rationed from 1940, clothes were also rationed from 1941 to free up fabric for uniforms and increase war production.

People were encouraged to sew, mending clothes with patches (these were the days before ripped jeans were fashionable). Women used non-rationed materials, such as blackout curtains and men's suits, to turn into dresses. There were even clothing exchanges (just like the clothes swap parties of today). We may not be facing a clothes shortage, but we can rediscover how to make the most of what we have.

## 3.1 Shelter

We all need somewhere to live. It's another basic human need. This looks different for us in different seasons. It could be renting or buying. It could be a house or apartment. It could be a hostel or temporary housing. It could be moving in with your parents, friends or family for a short time to save money to reach a financial goal. Some people do this when saving for a house deposit, getting through uni, or as a last resort.

I know people who do volunteering and get shelter provided for them for free or at a discount. For some people, accommodation is included as part of their work (such as house-sitting, pet-sitting and live-in care work).

My sister Liz has travelled around the world in this way, staying at Airbnb rentals and volunteering. She stayed with a host in exchange for providing a service (such as editing websites, videography and marketing). Later on, she volunteered at various yoga retreats and meditation centres in exchange for food and accommodation.

The *FIRE movement* has popularised minimalistic ways of living, such as living in a *tiny house* (which often costs less to build but can be harder to re-sell) or house-hacking (where you can take in a lodger to help pay for your housing). Of course, there are pros and cons to doing this, so do your research.

Saving for a house deposit is something we'll look at separately and equates to Dave Ramsey's Baby Step 3b (after you've paid off consumer debt and got an emergency fund in place). I want to focus on the importance of keeping a roof over your head.

### *How Much Should I Spend on Housing?*

For most people, your accommodation cost will take up a big part of your monthly budget.[65] Keeping up with your rent or mortgage payments is an essential part of building your four walls. But how much is too much to spend on housing?

Ramsey Solutions has a handy *Home Buying Calculator* for people in the USA.[66] Dave Ramsey suggests that you shouldn't spend any more than 25% of your net income (your after-tax take-home pay) on housing.

American lenders often use the 28/36 rule to calculate financing for a mortgage. This means spending no more than 28% of your gross income (before tax) on housing and no more than 36% of your income on total debt payments (including mortgage, student loan, credit cards, car loans etc.)

From what I can tell, we don't have the same lending rules in the UK. Mortgage lenders take into account how much you earn and what your expenses are, to calculate how much house you can afford, usually four-and-a-half times your annual income.[67]

So, if you're thinking of getting a house in future, having a handle on your finances is a good thing as it proves to the lender that you can afford the mortgage you're applying for.

# Rent Vs. Buy

## Remember, renting can be a good thing!

## You're only ready to buy a house if...

- You have a steady income
- You have a deposit (a bigger deposit may mean lower mortgage rates)
- You've found an area where you'd love to live
- You're going to be living there more than 5-7 years
- You have built a strong financial foundation
- You're on a budget
- You're able to demonstrate you're living within your means (not too much consumer debt, living on less than you make)
- You've got an emergency fund
- You've got extra house expenses covered such as fees, moving costs, furniture, maintenance costs
- If you've got a good credit score, then great, but it's not essential, as long as you can show that your finances are in control. You may need to consider manual underwriting.

## Your housing cost should be...

- Less than 25% of take home (net) pay or 28% of gross pay
- Not at the very limits of what you can afford – make sure you have some margin if mortgage rates go up or your circumstances change. Don't be house poor!

In 2022-23, we saw the Bank of England increase the base rate.[68] This means people with a variable interest mortgage saw costs rise significantly. Making sure you're not spending too much on housing means making sure that you're not pushed to the limits of what you can afford.

The principle of not paying too much for your housing is to ensure that you're not *house poor*. This is when so much of your budget is spent on housing that you don't have enough additional money for other important things, like food, fun, saving and paying off debt. You may *feel* rich because you have a big house that is going up in value. But you don't want the big house to have you.

So as a general rule, you want to make sure your accommodation is right for the season you're in.

## Debunking Some Housing Myths

In this section, I want to debunk some common housing myths. Society, our parents, families and friends will tell you all sorts of things about home ownership. I hope this section helps you find peace in your situation, even if you're renting. Renting is okay – it gives you options.

### *"I need a good credit score"*

You'll often hear people say you need *'a good credit score'*. A credit score is calculated by companies called Credit Reference Agencies and represents how good you are at borrowing money.[69] You'll hear some people taking on debt and credit cards to build their credit score so that they can get a mortgage at a better rate in future.

However, some people, like Dave Ramsey, teach you how to get a mortgage with a *'zero credit score'* (i.e. you're debt-free with no credit cards). To do this you need to prove you can afford the mortgage by showing that you're sticking to a budget, that you're living on less than you make. It means you might have to go to a mortgage lender and ask for *manual underwriting* (where a human does the work rather than a computer). It may be more difficult to get a mortgage this way, but may be better than falling into a debt trap in the pursuit of more debt.

### "I'm buying a forever home"

There's also no such thing as a *forever home*. People don't tend to stay in one house for longer than a few years or decades, because life changes: your family might grow, your job can change, your dreams can change too.

There's also a phenomenon in psychology called *hedonic adaptation*.[70] This is where something initially makes us happy, but then we quickly return to our baseline level of happiness. It happens when you get a new car, win the lottery, or buy something we've seen in an advert. The novelty will wear off. What once felt special soon feels ordinary again. Our dream house quickly becomes just a house. We move on from the now to the next.

### "Renting is throwing away money"

I hope this takes the burden off you if you feel pressurised to buy a house. It's okay to rent! There are lots of benefits to renting, as long as you've got a good landlord, property management company or housing association. Guess what, there can be some home ownership horror stories as well. *Money.co.uk* has a good article on the pros and cons of renting versus buying a house.[71]

Firstly, you probably shouldn't be buying a house unless you plan to live there for at least a few years. This is referred to as the *5-year rule*, but it's a general principle that suggests you live in your house long enough to build up equity, even if there's a housing market downturn. It also keeps buying and selling costs to a minimum.[72]

# Saving on Accommodation

## Living with family
- This can be a great option. But make sure you've got a clear time frame and boundaries. Will you pay rent or contribute towards food and bills? Maybe make a written contract

## House mates
- I did this as a student. It can work out cheaper to live in a house with others. Again, work out who pays what bills, share housework, set boundaries, be prepared to compromise

## House Hacking
- This is where you can rent out part of your house and take in lodgers. You will need to ask your landlord's permission. Or you can do this with a house you own. It started in the USA, but it's growing in popularity in the UK too.

## Alternative Housing (FIRE movement)
- Live on a canal boat
- Get a flatpack house or Tiny House
- Live in a converted van
- Live in a caravan
- Live in a converted shipping container
- Live in a tent / yurt
- Some jobs include accommodation!
- Pet sitting
- Luxury house sitting
- Volunteering (e.g. spiritual retreats)
- Join a commune (intentional community)

Still sceptical? I know, it's so ingrained in our society that home ownership is the best way. The COVID-19 pandemic of 2020 saw a rush of people moving into home ownership. It also saw a wave of regret afterwards as some people realised they'd taken on more house than they could afford.

I've put together some YouTube videos in the Resources Chapter for you if you want to learn more. I want your house to be a help and not a hindrance; a blessing, not a curse. After all, your house is probably the largest purchase you will ever make. So you want to make sure you can do it with no regrets.

## 3.2 Utilities

When I first moved into my rental property in 2014, I was still blissfully unaware of things like budgets and utility bills. Looking back at my records, it was at least a year later when I received an energy bill for £800. The water company was also asking for an amount that just didn't look right.

I didn't have a smart meter. My bills had been included with my rent prior to this. I had to rely on meter reading estimates by the utility companies. That's when I realised I had to do regular meter readings myself and become mindful of how much energy and water I was using.

After phone calls, letters, and complaints to the utility companies, we finally got it sorted. It may have been an estimated reading of the wrong meter – the serial numbers were wrong. They'd even spelt my name incorrectly. I eventually got a £400 refund. But, looking at my records, that was almost two years after I'd moved in.

This is why it's so important to become mindful of your water and energy usage and make sure it matches what the utility bills say. I learnt the hard way how important it is to be aware and keep good records.

More recently, 2022-23 saw a dramatic increase in our energy bills. It's become even more important to be doing regular meter readings, get a smart meter or be mindful with your energy usage.

MINDFUL FINANCE - 133

# Mindful Utilities

## How much are you spending on energy?

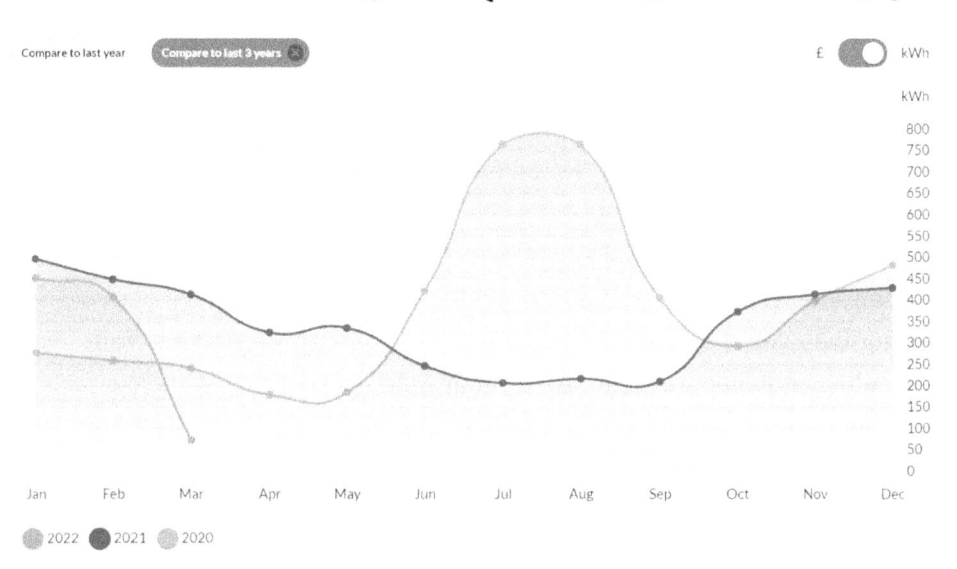

| Compare to last year | **Compare to last 3 years** | | £ ⬤ kWh |

```
kWh
800
750
700
650
600
550
500
450
400
350
300
250
200
150
100
 50
  0
Jan  Feb  Mar  Apr  May  Jun  Jul  Aug  Sep  Oct  Nov  Dec
```

● 2022  ● 2021  ● 2020

Utility companies often allow you to keep an eye on your energy usage and costs. This graph compares my energy usage over the past few years. I was writing this chapter in March of 2022. My energy usage spiked in summer of 2020, probably because I was at home more than usual due to my COVID-19 shift patterns at the hospital.

### *Keeping The Lights On*

Gas and electricity were on the list of *priority debts.* If you don't pay your bills, then eventually the utility companies could switch off your power. That would mean no lights or heating. It would make it hard to live, cook or function long-term. In the UK, your water bill is not classed as a priority debt as utility companies are not allowed to turn off your water. However, you should still try to keep up with all of your bills if you can.

Whether you're on a Pay As You Go meter, have a direct debit arrangement, or a smart meter, if you know how much energy you're using then you won't get any surprise bills. You may need to cut your spending elsewhere to make paying your bills a priority.

Paying your energy bill is another area of our budget where we can automate payments. But it's important to be aware of what energy you are using and whether you can afford to make the payments. If you're older, then there may be fuel payments that you're entitled to. In 2022-23 the UK government gave many of us fuel payments to help with the rising cost of energy. If you're in financial difficulty, then it's worthwhile talking to your energy company about it. Help may be available that you didn't know about yet.[73]

### *Have a Sinking Fund*

It may seem obvious, but we use more or less energy depending on the time of year. If we're home more, we use more energy. If it's cold, we can put on extra layers or put on the central heating. In some parts of the USA, it's impossible to get through a summer without an AC unit. In the UK, it may be possible to save during the warm summer months so that you have money in reserve for the cold winter months. If you have extra margin in your budget, you may want to put some in a sinking fund to prepare for the cost of future energy bills.

### *Energy and Cost-Saving Tips*

Energy supply is a complex global issue. The world is trying to transition away from fossil fuels to renewable sources of energy. In the investing world, there is a growing movement called *ESG* which stands for *'Environmental, Social and Governance.'* It is part of financial and environmental stewardship.

Some things seem so big and complicated, so we need to focus on what's in our power to change. On an individual level, some people are keen to do what they can to help reduce their carbon footprint and prevent the acceleration of global warming. Switching to renewable sources of energy is one of these ways.

Unfortunately, *green energy* tends to be more expensive. So there may be other things you can do, like supporting tree-planting initiatives and changing your behaviour in other ways.

When it comes to saving money and using less energy, a great place to start is Martin Lewis's *Money Saving Expert* website.[74] This has many articles and guides looking at energy-saving tips, news on energy prices, advice if you're struggling to pay your bills, and lots of related topics. You may be able to claim the winter fuel payment or access other financial support.[75]

It may be time to switch suppliers for a cheaper energy deal. It may be adjusting your thermostat. It can be adjusting your boiler or investing in better home insulation. There are lots of little changes you can make that add up over time to help you use less energy.

If you're not doing regular meter readings, I recommend that you start to become aware of how much energy you're using. It took me several years to get confident with this. Now I use my phone to take photos of my meters and I keep records in a folder on my computer. If you don't know how to read your meter, there are guides available online, such as the *Citizens Advice* website.[76]

## 4. Transportation

We've reached the last of our four walls - transportation. We all need to get from A to B – perhaps it's to get food from the shops, commute to work, get the kids to school and for trips further afield. It's so basic, it's easy to overlook in our spending plan.

I've got many friends who rely on walking, cycling or public transport to get about. If you don't need a car, then these might be more cost-effective ways to get by. Some families may need more than one car. Where I live in Liverpool, like many other cities, there are now E-scooters to provide an alternative mode of local transport.

There are alternative transport options that can be better for the environment, such as car-pooling or car sharing.[77] As individuals, there are ways to minimise or offset our carbon footprint. Unfortunately, we can't rely on the government to reach the goal of halving carbon emissions by 2030. So we need to consider making some changes ourselves.

Whatever our transport requirement, we need to make sure we've got it covered in the budget. I'm going to look specifically at cars as this is how many people get to work. But it's also where many people find themselves getting into financial difficulty. If you have overwhelming car debt, it may be one of the things you have to prioritise.

### *How Much Does It Cost To Run A Car?*

It can be more expensive to run a car than you realise. In July 2020, a survey was done of 2000 adults in the UK. It was found that 73% of people asked owned a car. Of those car owners, 65% had no idea how much they were paying to run their vehicle and 64% said this was their most expensive outgoing after their housing costs.[78]

It's not just the price of the car and any financing arrangement that you might have. There's also the cost of car insurance, maintenance, fuel, breakdown cover, MOT, and road tax. The *Nerdwallet* website has a handy calculator to help you work out what percentage of your income is being spent on transport. It helps you know if can afford the car you're driving.[32]

When it's comes to car insurance, it's good to shop around. I'm sure you already know about price comparison websites. You may not have thought about the amount of car tax you pay. In the UK, this is linked to how environmentally-friendly your car is.[79]

There are environmental considerations, with the UK planning to ban the sale of all new fossil fuel cars by the 2030 electrical vehicle *'switchover'* deadline. Many people are opting for electric or hybrid cars before that date, though the UK government needs to make sure the infrastructure is in place to make this a reality.[80]

There's also a difference in running costs between a basic car and a luxury car. In general, cheaper cars are also cheaper to maintain. It's easier to get parts for Fords and Vauxhalls which can usually be fixed at a local garage. More expensive cars, on the other hand, such as BMW, Mercedes or Bentley, will need specialist parts and are more expensive to repair and maintain.[81] So your choice of car can make a big difference.

How you buy a car also makes a difference. You can pay cash, take out a loan, hire purchase, personal contract purchase (PCP), or lease a car. *Moneyhelper* has a website which helps weigh up the pros and cons of these various payment methods.[82]

There's also a big difference between buying a car second-hand or new. Here's the thing to remember. New cars typically go down in price dramatically. As soon as you drive away from the car dealership, a new car starts to go down in value.

The main exception to this rule was during the 2020 COVID-19 pandemic where second-hand car values started going up. This was put down to supply chain disruptions and a shortage of microchips.

On average, a typical car loses 15-35% of its value in the first 12 months and loses around 80% of its value by 10 years.[83] So buying a second-hand car that is at least 3 to 5 years old is a great way of buying a car which has already taken the biggest depreciation hit.

Other things to consider include the age, mileage and condition of the car. As long as it's been well looked after and has a good service history, it doesn't necessarily matter that it's an older car with a higher mileage. It can still be a safe and reliable option.[84-86]

### How To Get out of Car Debt

You may have calculated that you've got more car than you can afford. You may have rolled over your finance and found out that you're now *underwater* or *upside-down* with a car loan that is more than your vehicle is worth. This is a common scenario from callers on Dave Ramsey's radio show. If you find yourself in this position, the team at *Ramsey Solutions* have put together some advice on how to get yourself out of an unwanted car loan.[87]

The worse thing you can do is let your car be repossessed as you often get back much less than the vehicle is worth and still have to pay off the debt. The key is taking back control of the situation and deciding whether it's worth it to keep the car or sell it.

Of course, you'll want to get your four walls stabilised first. You just need a cheap and reliable way to get to work. But you may find that paying down your car debt becomes one of your priorities when we get to *Chapter 4: Possessions and Debt*.

> *'Don't try to rationalize an expensive car purchase.*
> *A reliable used car is what most millionaires buy'*
> ~ DAVE RAMSEY

### Different Approaches to Buying a Car

Of course, one of the best ways to avoid the situation of having a huge amount of car debt is to avoid it in the first place. Dave Ramsey is famous for advocating buying a cheap car with cash, especially when you're in a season of paying off debt. If you want to buy a more expensive car, he sometimes recommends paying yourself the money you'd otherwise spend on a car loan and levelling up to a more expensive car when you've saved for it.

The *Ramsey Solutions* team have put together a comprehensive article arguing why a second-hand car is better than a new car. It also talks about the benefits of buying a car with cash rather than financing a car. They use evidence from the *Ramsey Solutions* study of 10,000 millionaires which found that *'the average millionaire is driving a four-year-old car with 41,000 miles on it.'* They also found that eight out of ten millionaire car drivers paid with cash.[88]

If you don't have a car payment, then that's extra margin each month that you could be putting to work on building your financial house. Imagine putting £500 a month into investments, rather than it disappearing on a car payment! Over time, that one car decision could actually cost you millions.

If you still want to buy a car using a financing arrangement, *The Money Guy Show* are proponents of the 20/3/8 rule. Brian Preston has a set of ground rules that help you determine whether you can afford your car.[89] He suggests that you should pay at least 20% of the car's value when purchasing your car. Next, you should aim to have the car paid off in 3 years. Then, your monthly payment for all vehicles in your household should not exceed 8% of your monthly (before tax) household gross income.

Lastly, and most importantly, to make sure you're going forward with your finances and not backwards, he also recommends making sure you're investing more into your retirement funds than you are spending on car payments. Again, it's that awareness that we shouldn't be letting a luxury item in the now rob us of our future wealth-building.

So, what vehicle are you driving? Will reading this chapter influence what you choose to drive next?

## Reflection questions:

- *What is the minimum amount of money I need each month to cover the basics? (The four walls of food, clothing, shelter and utilities, transportation)*
- *Am I up to date with my minimum payments?*
- *Am I behind with minimum payments on any of my priority debts?*
- *Am I in a debt spiral where I need to ask for help?*
- *Are there any ways I can save money?*
- *What luxuries can I give up for a time?*
- *Is there a difference between what I need and what I want?*
- *How can I make the most of what I already have?*
- *Are there things that I don't use any more that I can sell?*

I hope this chapter has given you some things to think about. It certainly helps me to think about the minimum amount I need to cover my basics. I have so many fixed expenses (like bills and insurance) that in reality, there are only a few things in my spending plan that I can control. So decisions like how much I spend on food and clothes, my choice of where I live and what I drive, do make a big difference.

With our four walls built, next we're going to take a look at protecting what we've built so far by building a roof of protection over our financial house.

## Build a roof of protection

# | 3 |

# Chapter 3: Roof of Protection

*'It's not how much money you make, but how much money you keep, how hard it works for you and how many generations you keep it for.'*
~ ROBERT KIYOSAKI

In this section, we're going to talk about wealth protection. I know this may all seem a bit dry or underwhelming, but this is an important step you don't want to miss. In the same way that building a wall, brick by brick, isn't necessarily very exciting (unless you're passionate about that sort of thing), laying roof tiles probably isn't going to be very exciting either. Neither is building a rainy day fund. These things take time and effort to put in place but they can make all the difference if something unexpected happens.

The truth is that if I'd had an emergency fund back in 2017, I probably wouldn't have run out of cash. I wouldn't have needed to borrow money from my parents to pay my rent. Nor would I have discovered all the wisdom in this book, at least, not as quickly.

Going broke kickstarted my mindful finance journey. It taught me the importance of having a spending plan, to make sure I had the basics covered and put some protections in place to stop me going backwards. Even though it was painful at the time, I'm grateful that it was a process I had to go through to get to where I am now.

Building a roof of protection means planning for emergencies before they happen. It includes building up your savings into an emergency fund so that you can self-insure when small emergencies happen. It's taking out insurance policies for the big emergencies that are too expensive for us to pay for by ourselves.

These wealth protection methods are there to put a cushion between you and life, in the hope that you'll never need to use them. But you'll be very glad you've got them if anything were to happen.

We'll whizz through the basics. You can go and read up on any areas where you want to know more. As always, I'm going to point you in the direction of my favourite content creators who can explain these things far better than me. You'll find these in the Resources Chapter.

In summary, in this chapter, we're going to look at what an emergency fund looks like and what different types of insurance you need. That way you can protect the wealth you're building for the long term.

## Emergency Fund ~ Short Term Protection

*'If you fail to plan, you are planning to fail'*
~ BENJAMIN FRANKLIN

Once upon a time, I *sort of* had an emergency fund. And then I didn't anymore. That's because I didn't call it an emergency fund. I didn't have a plan. I had some savings that were available. So I used them for all sorts of things that, in retrospect, were not true emergencies.

If you don't define what an *emergency* is, then it just becomes a pot of money that can disappear all too easily. You end up spending it on things that you think are important at the time, but when something unexpected happens the money may not be there when you need it. So we need to ask ourselves before we dip into our emergency savings account, *'Is this a true emergency?'*

# Emergency Fund

## Define what an emergency is in advance

Your starter emergency fund is £1000 and covers a basic emergency. So work out how much you need to live on each month, the bare minimum to cover your expenses. Your full emergency fund is generally enough to cover 3 to 6 months of expenses, depending on your circumstances.

### Emergency

- Car breakdown / repair
- Boiler breaks / burst pipes
- Home repairs
- Unexpected job loss
- Missed or delayed paycheque
- Injury or illness
- Relationship breakdown
- Natural disasters
- Global pandemics
- Unexpected bills
- Anything unexpected, necessary & urgent

### Not an emergency

- A luxury car
- New car tyres / maintenance
- Children's braces / planned health issues
- Holiday/ Christmas/ Vacation
- Kitchen renovations
- Birthday presents
- Romantic dinner for two
- Luxury goods / treats
- Expected bills
- Anything expected, unnecessary & not urgent

An *emergency* is something *unexpected, serious, sudden* and *urgent*. It could be *anything*, affecting any area of our lives. It could happen at any time and unfortunately they tend to come in clusters. Our emergency fund may not be enough to cover the whole emergency, but at least we've tried to protect ourselves and our wealth from something that might derail our wealth-building plans. We'll usually be better off than if we didn't have one at all.

On the previous page, I've made a list of some things that are true emergencies and a list of things that are not. There is a subtle difference between an unexpected emergency and an expected event with unpredictable timing. It's the difference between a sudden job loss and a job that sometimes has seasonal slowdowns. It's the difference between your car needing an unexpected major repair and the inevitable wear and tear where you need to replace your tyres every so often.

Some things are obvious. **Christmas is not an emergency**; it's predictable and always comes around at the same time each year, although many people treat it like an emergency. Having a **summer holiday is not an emergency**, although many people fail to save for one and think of it as an entitlement.

> *'Nothing helps you sleep better at night*
> *than knowing you have money tucked away for a rainy day.'*
> ~ GREG MCBRIDE, CFA

Some people call an emergency fund a *'Rainy Day Fund.'* That's because it's needed when the storms of life hit. There are many wise sayings about umbrellas and making sure you're adequately prepared. I like Dave Ramsey's anecdote where he talks about the storms of life and the need for a rainy day fund. When someone tells him to be positive. His reply is this: *'I am positive it is going to rain!'*

You've probably heard it said that if you're not in a storm or coming out of one, then you'll be heading into a storm soon. In life, there will always be downturns, dramas, and disasters. But, just like natural storms, they are often temporary and associated with our greatest personal growth. Rain may not be pleasant at the time, but we need it to turn our desert into a garden.

Many negative life events begin with the letter 'D' – divorce, demotion or dismissal, debt, depression, disease, displacement, disappointment and death. Of course, there's only so much we can do to prepare for these things in advance. But it certainly helps if we can give ourselves a financial buffer.

Dave Ramsey says, '*A crisis becomes an inconvenience when you have an emergency fund.*'[90] This has certainly been true in my experience.

It was Benjamin Franklin who famously wrote in a letter to his friend, '*But, in this world, nothing is certain except death and taxes.*' Both are inevitable, and yet many people decide not to prepare for them.

Why? I suppose some things are just too horrible to think about. Or they may seem abstract and far away; like they will never happen to us. There's always that little superstition at the back of our minds that preparing for something, writing a will or buying life insurance, will somehow tempt fate. It's ridiculous when you think about it. Or is it just human nature to put off thinking about these things?

### Where Should I Put My Emergency Fund?

It's usually recommended that you keep your emergency fund somewhere accessible and liquid (easy to convert into cash), not tied up in investments or fixed-term financial products (that may go down in value or be difficult to access). Typically that means keeping your emergency savings in an easy-access savings account in a bank, somewhere you can get to it quickly without paying a penalty for early withdrawals.

In the olden days, people used to stuff their emergency money under mattresses or bury it in the back garden – that's not generally recommended these days. Other people buy bars of gold and keep them in home safes or vaults – again, it's not for everyone. I've even heard of people putting dollar bills behind picture frames or freezing their bank cards in ice cubes so that there is some resistance which stops them from accidentally spending their emergency money.

At the time of writing in 2022-23, interest rates on savings accounts have gone up for the first time in years. So you may be able to make a little money on your emergency savings. Just remember, an emergency fund is not meant to make money. It's your self-insurance policy in case life takes an unexpected downturn. So it's okay to keep your rainy day fund in cash or cash equivalents like money market funds, or Premium Bonds (savings backed by the UK government).

## How Big Should My Emergency Fund Be?

*'Save 3 to 6 months of expenses in a Rainy Day Fund. Know Why? Cause it is going to rain, and you aren't the exception.'*
~ DAVE RAMSEY

Finance articles usually estimate that around 4 in 10 adults in the USA would struggle to get together $1000 for an unexpected emergency. *Bankrate.com* did a survey in 2021 that found that a quarter of people didn't have any emergency savings at all.[91] That means a good number of ordinary people even in the richest countries in the world could be living on a knife edge, just like I was.

Depending on which financial plan you follow, you'll see different recommendations for how big your emergency fund should be and when to build one. Some plans want you to build an emergency fund first and pay off high-interest consumer debt second. Some plans want you to attack the debt first without an emergency fund.

It all depends on what your priorities are, how uncomfortable you feel without an emergency fund and how likely you are to need to use one whilst building the rest of your financial house.

I've put the roof-building and wealth protection step before paying off debt in our chapter order. But in reality, you're likely to be turning your attention from one to the other and back again. It depends on the stage you're at and your individual circumstances.

*Ramsey Solutions* recommend building a £1000 or $1000 starter emergency fund before paying off debt. Not only does this get you into a savings habit early on. It gives you a boost of satisfaction, knowing that you've completed an important milestone. It's also a *misfortune deterrent.* There's something about having a small cushion between you and life that seems to prevent every small crisis from knocking you sideways.

Dave Ramsey says it keeps *'Murphy at bay.'* We call it *Sod's Law* in the UK, the idea that *'if something can go wrong, it will go wrong.'* Usually, it's everything, all at once. For me, it was a health situation, job insecurity, relationship strain and financial struggle, as well as a spiritual battle, identity crisis and search for purpose. Remember, money can affect every area of our lives.

Your starter emergency fund is a great motivator. It's not meant to cover all your emergencies. It just stops you from sliding backwards in those early crucial days of changing your financial habits. It may even motivate you to get out of debt quicker so that you can build up your full emergency fund once you're debt-free

Many finance experts suggest that your emergency fund should be around 3- to 6-months of expenses. That's your basic monthly costs, what you would need to survive in an emergency. It's just the bare essentials with no luxuries. It could be £12,000 or $36,000. Or maybe that $1000 starter emergency fund is alright for now - not ideal, but okay.

Imagine if your income were to stop and you needed to survive on your emergency fund alone. Look at your situation now and ask yourself how long would you be able to last? What happens if your next paycheque is delayed? Could you get by?

Again, don't worry if it feels overwhelming. The key is working out how much margin you can create in your spending plan each month and setting achievable goals. There are plenty of podcasts and online communities of people doing exactly the same thing as you to reach financial freedom. **So start with that £1000 emergency fund and celebrate!**

When I was at this stage of building my financial house, I was working a volatile job that could have ended at any time. So I decided to build an emergency fund (or a *sinking fund/hills and valley account*) alongside paying off debt. Remember, for me, I only had one big debt left – a £20,000 student loan. I knew it would take some time and I wanted to be covered in case my contract came to an end or I changed jobs (which has happened multiple times since then).

So, to decide how big an emergency fund you need and whether you do it before or after paying off your high-interest consumer debt, you need to ask yourself some questions:

> - How secure is my job?
> - Do I have people depending on my income?
> - Am I debt-free? Do I have any priority debts?
> - Do I have super high-interest debts that I need to prioritise paying off, like payday loans?
> - What other assets do I have (things you can sell, like gold, jewellery, collectables, antiques, second-hand clothes, books etc.)?
> - How long would it take to access these funds in an emergency?

Some finance experts recommend even larger emergency funds in certain situations, like retirement. Your emergency fund may need to be 1 or 2 years of expenses. This is called a *'bucket strategy'* and means you can draw money from different *buckets* in case there's a market crash or economic downturn. That way you can live on your cash and avoid using your investments at the worst possible time.

## Insurance Policies ~ Long Term Protection

*'When wealth is lost, nothing is lost; when health is lost, something is lost; when character is lost, all is lost'*
~ BILLY GRAHAM

There are lots of different types of insurance. Some of them are people wanting to make money off you, usually unnecessary extended warrantees. Other types of insurance are absolutely essential if you want to protect your wealth over the long term. The key is knowing how to tell the difference.

We've talked about self-insuring for a short-term crisis by building an emergency fund. For anything beyond that, we'll need to consider an insurance policy.

An insurance policy is where lots of people pay a premium which creates a pool of money (that gets invested on our behalf). We hope that we'll never need to make a claim. But if something happens to us or our belongings, we have peace of mind knowing that we will be covered financially.

We don't want to think about our car being damaged, our home destroyed, losing our job, getting ill or dying. But these things do happen and we can get financial cover just in case, to protect our wealth for the future and for those who depend on us.

As I said before, getting insurance doesn't mean something bad is going to happen soon. It means we've prepared in advance and decided to build a roof of protection over our financial house, so the storms of life can't destroy the wealth we've built.

## Types of Insurance

Some types of insurance are to cover your belongings if you can't afford to replace them. Other types of insurance protect your greatest wealth-building tool – your income.

Types of insurance that you should strongly consider include:

- Car insurance
- Contents insurance and home owner's insurance
- Travel or holiday insurance
- Pet insurance
- Income protection insurance
- Critical illness cover
- Life insurance

We're lucky in the UK not to have to worry about paying *Health Insurance.* The NHS is funded from the taxes we pay so that we can get free healthcare, but sometimes with a long waiting list and less choice. Some people decide to take out private healthcare plans so that they can access medical treatment quicker. In the USA, health insurance is sometimes provided with a job or there are different savings accounts that can be used, like Health Savings Accounts (HSAs).

In the USA, there is also a way of ensuring you'll get the care you need in old age. It's called *Long Term Care Insurance.* We don't have this yet in the UK. It means that we're relying on our own wealth to fund the care packages or care homes we need in future.

Health and Social Care in the UK has been under great strain for decades. The state will pay for it if you haven't got the wealth built up, but you get less choice over what that care will look like. Once again, having enough wealth one day gives you the option to self-insure.

You can check out my Resources Chapter to find more about insurance. My favourite podcast on this topic is Pete Matthew's *Meaningful Money Podcast* episode called *'The Ultimate Guide to Wealth Protection.'* [92] It's 36 minutes long and will set you up to build a strong roof of protection over your finances. The first types of insurance are pretty self-explanatory. So let's take a look at the last 3 types of insurance on the list which you may not have come across before.

## 1. Income Protection Insurance

As I said earlier, your income is your greatest wealth-building tool. If you have an illness or develop a disability, then you might not be able to do your job anymore. If you have a family or someone depending on you to pay the bills, losing your income can feel even more stressful.

If you are single and don't have another source of income, this makes you particularly vulnerable. It's easy to take your health for granted and assume you will always be able to work. But I have personal experience and friends who found themselves in the position of becoming unable to work for health reasons.

If you have a health crisis and can't work, then sick pay (if you're entitled to it) will only last a certain number of weeks.[93] If you don't qualify for sick pay or it runs out, your emergency fund will likely only last for a few months. After that, you would be reliant on government benefits, such as *Universal Credit*.[94] So we need to prepare for this situation ourselves with income protection insurance.

The *Citizen's Advice* website has a great explanation of what income protection insurance is and whether you need it, based on your circumstances.[95] Income protection insurance pays you a regular income if you can't work because of illness or disability. It continues until you return to paid work or until you retire.

The period before your income protection insurance kicks in is called the *waiting period*. The shorter your waiting period, typically the higher the premium you pay because you'll be more likely to make a claim. So having an emergency fund to self-insure for a few months is a good way to reduce the cost of your insurance.

The premium may seem quite expensive. But remember, if you develop a serious illness that means you can't work, then the policy is going to cover you for your whole working life until you retire. It's a potential pay out of hundreds of thousands in income over the decades. Some people may have to claim during their twenties or thirties, while others may never have to claim. That's how insurance works – it's for your peace of mind. You buy it and hope you never need it.

The only other way to generate an income for the rest of your working life would be to build up enough wealth to live off your investment income and become financially independent. Until then, we can't assume that our health will always be good. There may be a diagnosis just around the corner that turns our world upside down.

I experienced this myself in 2015 when a health condition came out of the blue and I needed several months off work for an operation. Thankfully I made a good recovery and I was covered by sick pay. Had it happened a year or two later when I was self-employed, I wouldn't have qualified for sick pay and the situation could have been very different. So it made me aware of just how important income protection insurance can be.

You need to do your research. Some types of income protection are career-specific, while others aren't. Some income protection won't pay out if you can do a different job, so you need to read the fine print. The premiums will also differ greatly so you need to make sure you can afford it. You may not qualify if you have pre-existing medical problems, or your insurer may write an exemption into the policy. You may need to increase your coverage as your income increases and make sure it adjusts for inflation.

It's something to be mindful of and reassess regularly. It may seem expensive, but the true cost is *not* having insurance. If you couldn't work for health reasons, you could find your quality of life drastically altered.

## 2. Critical Illness Cover

The *Citizens Advice* website also has a helpful overview of critical illness insurance and explains how it works.[96] Critical illness insurance pays you a lump sum of money when you're diagnosed with a particular illness or disability. These are usually long-term or very serious conditions such as heart attacks, strokes, loss of limbs, diseases such as cancer, multiple sclerosis or Parkinson's disease.

They usually only pay out if you are extremely unwell or very disabled. There's no fixed way to spend this money, but some people use it to pay off their mortgage early or supplement their income. It may just be some extra money to boost your emergency fund in case of unforeseen events. The alternative is building wealth with the money that would otherwise have been spent on premiums.

It's different from income protection insurance as it's usually a lump sum, not a regular monthly payment. Again, you need to do your research and find out if this is something you need. I don't currently have this myself as I prefer income protection insurance. You need to find out what's right for you.

## 3. Life Insurance

Life insurance isn't needed by everyone. If you're single or unmarried, without kids, with nobody else depending on you for your income, then you probably don't need life insurance right now. But it's good to know about it, because you may need it someday.

As soon as your circumstances change – you get married, have a baby, or have someone else relying on your income – then life insurance is a great way to protect them in case you're not around anymore.

It's not something we like to think about, a world without us in it anymore. But if you listen to Dave Ramsey or any of the financial experts, they can tell you some of the most heartbreaking stories of people who didn't take out a life insurance policy, who left behind a grieving spouse with several children and no income. Not only have they lost the person they love, but they could be facing incredible financial stress as well.

On the other hand, there are inspiring stories of people who did take out a life insurance policy the right way. These families were comforted in their grief knowing their loved one had taken care of them in advance before they died. Often they receive enough money to pay off their house and replace the missing income so that their loved one's legacy could continue long after they've gone.

There are two main types of life insurance: *Term Life Insurance* and *Whole Life Insurance*. You need to make sure you research them well and pick the right one for you. They sound similar, but don't get them mixed up! They are very different!

Just like with other types of insurance, you can use comparison sites or life insurance brokers to help you get a good deal.

Sometimes life insurance is included as a benefit from your employer. But you could lose your insurance along with your job, so you need to be particularly mindful if facing a job loss or career change.

Similarly, if you're situation changes, for example having another child or dependent, you may need to take out an extra insurance policy to cover you. Yes, you can have more than one life insurance policy at the same time (though this could of course change if the UK government decided to change the law).

## i). Term Life Insurance

You can find out more about term life insurance on the *Which?* website.[97] This sort of insurance covers you for a particular term, usually 15 to 20 years. This should provide financial cover while your children are growing up and allow you time to build wealth to become financially independent and self-insure. At this point you will no longer need life insurance, though some people choose to keep it anyway for peace of mind.

You can choose a shorter or longer term. Most finance experts recommend level term insurance, rather than increasing or decreasing term insurance. That's where the pay out is fixed rather than going up or down over time.

You can also take out additional policies to increase your cover if your circumstances change, such as having additional children, buying a house, or if your income increases. Ultimately, your family will get used to a certain lifestyle based on your household income, so that's what you need to aim to replace should you not be around any more.

Similarly, it's important not to forget the economic value of a stay at home parent. It would cost a lot of money to replace what they do by employing someone else to do it, such as childcare and cleaning services. You may want to get a term life insurance policy on both you and your spouse, even if one of you is *'working inside the home.'*

In general, the younger and healthier you are when you take out life insurance, the cheaper the monthly premium will be over the duration of the term. But if you stop paying the premium, your protection goes away in 30 days or so. It can be expensive to start a new policy once you're older or have pre-existing health conditions.

You'll find financial advisors recommending a term life insurance policy which is 10 to 15 times your annual income.[98] Once paid out, some people use this money to pay off their mortgage. Other people decide to invest the money and live off the interest. There's no exact way to do it, but ultimately you leave your family in a much better financial position if you have a term life insurance policy in place.

## ii). Whole Life Insurance

The other type of life insurance is called *Whole Life*, or *Whole of Life Insurance*. Other names for this include *Cash Value Life Insurance* or *Permanent Life Insurance.'*[99] This covers the whole of the policy-holder's life. It's like an insurance and cash savings product rolled in to one.

Sounds too good to be true? Well, the financial experts can be very scathing about this product which is heavily marketed by salesmen as a way of saving for retirement, when there are usually much better ways available.

Whole life insurance is usually more expensive than term life insurance. Unlike term life insurance, the value of the insurance policy doesn't come with a deadline, which is why it's called *Whole Life*. But they still need to make money and they do this, at least in part, from their more expensive premiums.

Make sure you do your research and don't believe everything the insurance salesmen tell you. These policies are very heavily marketed, especially in the USA, as they pay salesmen a commission. They may even try to sell whole life insurance products to cover your children. It can be a money trap. Remember, your child probably doesn't need life insurance unless you're relying on them to add to your household income.[100]

There are only a few reasons why someone should get whole life insurance, for example, if you have pre-existing medical conditions which make term life insurance too expensive. You may have started a whole life insurance policy early enough and build up a considerable cash value which can be used for a house deposit or retirement savings. But, on the whole, there are better ways to do this.[101]

## Conclusion: The 4 Walls

So there you have it – that's an introduction to how to build a roof of protection over your financial house: an emergency fund to protect your wealth in the short term, and insurance policies to protect your wealth in the long term. You'll have to do your research to see which of these you need to consider for your specific circumstances.

There are times in your financial plan where you need to be focusing on building emergency cash reserves – which could be before, during or after paying off debt – depending on your risk tolerance, family and work situation.

It is always a good time to be thinking about insurance. But you need to make sure you can afford to keep paying the premiums over the long term. On the whole, the sooner you start, the cheaper it will be. But nobody can predict the future and how their life will change.

Don't forget to check out Pete Matthew's *'Ultimate Guide to Wealth Protection'* in the Resources Chapter if you want to learn more.

## Reflection Questions:

- *Could I come up with £1000 in an emergency?*
- *What's the minimum amount I need each month to run my household?*
- *How long could I get by if my income stopped after my next paycheque?*
- *How big do I want my emergency fund to be?*
- *Where will I put my emergency fund so I can get to it easily?*
- *Do I need income protection insurance or critical illness cover?*
- *Are there people dependant on me for my income?*
- *In that case do I need to consider life insurance?*
- *Do I have insurance policies that I don't need, such as life insurance policies on my children or extended warranties – money that could be better used elsewhere?*
- *Have I discussed life insurance with my spouse or life partner?*
- *Have my friends and family heard about wealth protection?*
- *Who else can I talk to about wealth protection?*

Possessions &

# | 4 |

# Chapter 4: Possessions and Debt

*'In the house of the wise are stores of choice food and oil, but a foolish man devours all he has.'*
~ PROVERBS 21: 20, New International Version (NIV)

This is probably the chapter that I'm the most excited and nervous to write about because it's going to touch a nerve for all of us. We're going to tackle two controversial topics – *material possessions* and *debt*.

You'll come across lots of people with different attitudes to spending money: on house décor and home improvements, gadgets, gizmos, collectables, stuff in general. Some people will choose to borrow money to do it.

Whatever you decide to spend money on says a lot about your priorities. You'll hear it said that if someone wants to know what's important to you, they only need to look at where your money goes.

It's okay to have a strong opinion about this and it's okay to change your mind. I've changed my views about possessions and debt many times over the past few years as I've done more research and took the decision to become debt-free.

Ultimately, we're the product of our upbringing and what the people around us think about. This includes how we choose to spend money. Our society and culture shouts to us loudly about what we should and shouldn't have to make us happy, content, normal or accepted.

We already touched on this in the introduction when we talked about what *success* means, how it's defined by our culture and how we can redefine success for ourselves. Well, this chapter might just turn what you thought you knew about spending money on its head.

We're going to wrestle with some challenging questions: is all debt inherently bad? Is having nice stuff evil? Am I trying to look *rich* or am I building *true wealth*?

When it comes to spending and debt, some people frame it as a simple maths problem: you spent more than you made and therefore you got into debt. But, as we'll see going forward, it's actually a behaviour problem that comes from our unconscious thoughts, beliefs, emotions and desires. And if it's a behaviour problem, then it needs a behaviour solution. That's where many people come unstuck.

> 'As I stare at it, I can feel little invisible strings, silently tugging me toward it. I have to touch it. I have to wear it. It's the most beautiful thing I've ever seen'
> ~ SOPHIE KINSELLA, *'Confessions of a Shopaholic'*

This chapter is divided into two halves. Firstly, we'll look at your **POSESSIONS** - your assets, things we own, items of value. This will include looking at materialism and our love of stuff, the comparison trap, as well as answering the question, *'Is it okay to have material things?'*

In the second half, we'll look at **DEBT** - your liabilities, things we owe and sometimes pay interest on. We'll look at types of debt, whether there's such a thing as good or bad debt, look at whether we should pay our debt off, and if the answer is "yes" we'll look at some ways to do it.

## Help with your debts

Again, I want to remind you that if you do find yourself struggling with debt, don't feel ashamed or embarrassed. It's important to accept that there is a problem and reach out for help.

As I've mentioned before, one of the best UK resources is the *Money Saving Expert* website.[102] This will walk you through the steps you need to take and questions you need to ask yourself to identify whether you are in a debt spiral. This includes whether you're struggling to pay all your basic outgoings (the 4 walls we talked about in Chapter 2) or whether your debts are bigger than a year's income. If either applies to you, then you will probably need more help than this book can provide.

If you *are* in a debt crisis, then the *Money Saving Expert* website can signpost you to resources and debt charities that can help you. But remember to ask yourself the question, *"how did I get into debt in the first place?"* This will help you turn your attention to the underlying patterns in your spending. Perhaps the next section on possessions will help shed some light on the psychology of money and why many people find themselves taking on more debt than they can afford.

## Ideologies: Performance, Possessions and Popularity

> *'A lot of people live in a proving mode. They can't feel good about themselves unless they prove to people they're important. They're always having to outdo, outperform, outdrive, outdress. It's very freeing when you realise you don't have to impress people. It takes a lot of energy to compete, to impress. Get off that treadmill. You're working hard, but you're not going anywhere. You don't have to prove anything.'*
>
> ~ JOEL OLSTEEN

We're going to start by having a look at why we do what we do with money. I've heard motivational speakers, like Steve Harvey and Joel Olsteen, talk about people falling into the comparison trap. They try to gain value or a sense of self-worth through their *performance, possessions* or *popularity*.

Often, we can fall into a behaviour pattern of wanting to show off or impress people by what we do, what we have or who we know. Sometimes it comes from a deep-seated longing to be accepted. We can look to these things to satisfy us. But as we've explored in the introduction, none of these things can fully satisfy us.

Once we obtain our goal, we can be left feeling empty and go looking for the next challenge. The novelty quickly wears off the shiny new toy. The new car smell fades. We find the big new forever house looks a lot smaller once we've settled in. It's *hedonic adaptation*.

It's human nature to be hungry and dissatisfied. We all have a longing for more. Often Christians refer to this a *God-shaped hole* as they believe that only the Holy Spirit can truly fill the gap and satisfy us, bringing peace and an end to striving. Seeking comfort and completeness, finding ways of self-soothing, to heal our inner traumas with or without the help of a higher power, is thought to be behind many addictions and behaviour patterns. Toxic spending is no different.

Do you remember from the introduction how one definition of *success* is not in achieving a distant goal, but the process of becoming the best version of ourselves as we try to live our best life? It's not necessarily about what we own, how we dress or what we do in order to fit someone else's ideal of what a successful person looks like. Success is the journey itself and who we become along the way.

We also talked in the introduction about the difference between looking *rich* and building *true wealth*. We also looked at the difference between *material wealth* and *spiritual wealth*. You can go back and remind yourself of these topics if you like.

# STEVE HARVEY

"PERFORMANCE BASED IDEOLOGIES SAYS I AM WHAT I DO. I AM WHAT I HAVE. I MUST BE GREAT; I MAKE MONEY. I MUST BE GREAT; I HAVE A BIG HOUSE. I MUST BE GREAT; I'M PRETTY.

IF YOU'RE ALWAYS SEEKING A CERTAIN STATUS TO VALIDATE WHO YOU ARE, YOU'RE NEVER GOING TO HAVE PEACE.

YOU CAN'T CLIMB UP TO FIND YOURSELF. YOU HAVE TO FIND YOURSELF SO YOU CAN CLIMB UP. SO THAT MEANS YOU COULD BE RICH WHILE YOU'RE BROKE. YOU COULD BE HEALED WHILE YOU'RE SICK. YOU COULD BE LOOSE WHILE YOU'RE BOUND. IT DOES NOT YET APPEAR WHAT YOU SHALL BE. BUT YOU GOT TO **BE IT** BEFORE YOU CAN **GET IT**"

> '*Advertising* – *The gentle art of persuading the public to believe that they want something they don't need.*'
> ~ AD SENSE, 1905

In this chapter I want you to ask yourself some questions: w*hat does wealth mean to you and why is it important? If it isn't important to you, then what are the things that are?*

The truth is, we live in a society of consumerism that wants us to spend money. If you're living in the Western world, then there are capitalist forces at play. Companies spend vast sums of money on advertising. Big businesses want us to buy the latest model. They're trying to sell us a dream. Our economy is fuelled by debt and borrowing and it would collapse if we all stopped spending at the same time. If we're not aware of these things, then it's easy to get sucked in by all the adverts promising us happiness and fulfilment from buying stuff.

Ads play on our sense of purpose and meaning. But if we remind ourselves that we are already valuable without having to buy a load of valuables, then we don't need the big house, the fancy car and the social media following to prove our worth.

However, everything around us - popular culture, social media, magazines, TV shows, movies and adverts – is trying to convince us that we *do* need these things.

There are lots of mindfulness techniques that can help us reflect on our innate value, heal our inner wounds and nurture a sense of self-love. This can help to make us immune to the ideology that performance, possessions and popularity are what matter when, really, **we already matter.**

Buying things can become an addiction. You've probably heard of *Shopaholism, impulse buying* and *retail therapy*. But there's also a recognised psychiatric diagnosis, similar to OCD, called *compulsive buying disorder* (CBD) or o*niomania*. Our relationship with shopping is a spectrum from healthy to dysfunctional.

*'**Americanism**: Using money you haven't earned
to buy things you don't need to impress people you don't like.'*
~ ROBERT QUILLEN, 1928

It's similar to comfort eating or gambling, binge-watching a TV series, overindulging in chocolate, alcohol, smoking, sex and drugs. These things can all give you a powerful dopamine hit (the brain's '*feel good*' hormone). But the effect is always temporary and leaves you wanting more. It always takes more stimulus to get the same response next time. Some of these things can seem quite innocent at first until they become all-consuming.

We use lots of different ways to self-soothe, satisfy our spiritual hunger, to heal ourselves from inner pain and longing. These are often unhealthy habits that can have negative consequences on our health and wellbeing long-term. They can lead to feelings of guilt, shame and low self-esteem which can make the cycle worse. A habit can easily become a stronghold, which then becomes an addiction. It can take years to break free from a habit or addiction that took decades to establish, but many people can and do succeed.

When it comes to 12-step recovery programmes, like *Alcoholics Anonymous*[103] or *Celebrate Recovery*,[104] the first step is admitting that there is a problem in the first place. If you're in debt, there may well have been some sort of life event that contributed to you getting ensnared by debt. But it may also be time to admit that you have a problem with your spending.

Maybe you feel powerless, like you've lost control, that your life has become unmanageable because you haven't been managing money properly. It may be time to pause and ask if there are any behaviour patterns that aren't serving you well. As Tony Robbins says, "*Change happens when the pain of staying the same is greater than the pain of change.*"

Does this apply to you? Do you ever describe yourself as a shopaholic or impulse buyer? Do you speak negative affirmations over yourself and tell people, *"I'll never be good with money"*? Perhaps you haven't been paying attention to where your money is going lately. Do you fall for ads promising you success, health, wealth and happiness through material possessions?

Don't worry, we've all been there! I can't tell you the number of times I've fallen for fast-food ads and felt guilty afterwards when the reality didn't meet my expectations (now I acknowledge that it's a special treat and try to enjoy the moment. I'll eat healthy later). I added chocolate to my list of addictions (though now I try to enjoy a piece of dark chocolate rather than eating a whole bar of the sugary stuff). That's part of mindful eating.

This is just an opportunity for some self-reflection. You can only turn things around when you realise that you're not going in the right direction. It starts with a shift in your mindset. It's becoming mindful of your finances and asking why we do what we do with money.

## The Comparison Trap

*'Those who want to get rich fall into temptation and a trap and into many foolish and harmful desires that plunge people into ruin and destruction. For the love of money is a root of all kinds of evil. Some people, eager for money, have wandered from the faith and pierced themselves with many griefs.'*
~ 1 TIMOTHY 6: 9-10, New International Version (NIV)

Knowing that we are innately valuable without the need to prove it takes away a lot of the exhausting striving. Playing the comparison game can have all sorts of negative consequences. It can lead to mental health issues, anxiety, depression, a critical spirit, jealousy, anger and low self-worth. It seems to be a universal human condition to never feel good enough. Comparing ourselves to others just serves to re-inforce that belief.

There will always be someone with more stuff, a bigger house or shinier car, a more prestigious job, more friends, more money, more of whatever it is that we think we need to be happy.

We have to remind ourselves that we often don't see the journey they've been on to get there. We don't get to see the struggles and sacrifices they have made, the work they've put in behind the scenes. We just wish we had it too. We want to be where they are, but are we ready to put in the work? Is that sacrifice a price we're willing to pay?

Or it could be far worse: perhaps they've taken out debt to build the life they think a rich person should have because they're playing the comparison game too. Comparison can be contagious.

Social media and technology have taken the comparison game to another level. Now we don't just see what other people have in real life - our neighbour down the street. It's presented to us like a Hollywood movie, fictional but based on a true story. Whether it's a showreel or a snapshot of our lives, what we put out for others to see is a carefully curated version, airbrushed and filtered, at times barely resembling reality at all. This can cause all sorts of problems when we forget that the identity we create for ourselves is manufactured and so is everyone else's.

The danger comes when we're tempted to spend excessive money, time and energy on *looking rich*. We may take on debt to try to live the lifestyle we think we should be living because it's what we've seen other people doing or we think it's what they expect of us. It's a comparison *trap* because the illusion is hard to break free from, like the illusion of being inside *The Matrix*. Many people end up broke and broken because of it.

Developing a sense of gratitude for what we already have is a great way of countering the insatiable desire for more. It may seem counterintuitive, but giving and generosity are great ways to stay grounded. It makes us aware of how wealthy we truly are, not just materially but spiritually as well.

## Is It Okay To Have Material Things?

*'I'm not so in love with material things that I'll do anything for money. That allows me the luxury of doing things of value.'*
~ ESTHER ROLLE

As long as we are aware of the ideology of performance, possessions and popularity, it's still okay to want to achieve our goals, have nice things and build great relationships. As Dave Ramsey says in his book *The Legacy Journey*, 'I want you to have some nice stuff; I just don't want your nice stuff to have you.'[105]

It's a paradox, but we shouldn't be striving and climbing the mountain to become successful at all. We're climbing the mountain because we are *already* successful. We're doing it because we can, so we must. We're becoming the person we were created to be, ignoring what the critics think of us, working out our unique purpose, whatever passion or dream has been put in our hearts. That's when we'll find ourselves doing things beyond our wildest dreams, helping the people we want to help the most, and having the things we want to have – because our heart will be right.

If our attitude towards material things is healthy – if we're not idolising money, if we're not a slave to it, if we can let go of it if we need to – then having material things will be a blessing, not a curse.

## What's Your Relationship With Stuff?

*'It is human nature to want it and want it now; it is a sign of immaturity. Being willing to delay pleasure for a greater result is a sign of maturity.'*
~ DAVE RAMSEY

In our *Buy Now, Pay Later* culture, it's tempting to take shortcuts. It takes discipline and maturity to save for the things we want and wait until we have the money to pay for them, rather than putting it on a credit card. It makes us ask ourselves questions: *Is it worth sacrificing for? Why do we want it? Will it truly make us happy? Did you see an advert, promising that it will change your life? On reflection, did those things we wanted so badly in the past deliver satisfaction and how long did it last?*

We are a product of our upbringing and experiences. I grew up in a house with lots of material possessions. Some of it was clutter. Some of it was sentimental. Some of it was valuable and could have been sold at auction. Sometimes it was hard to tell the difference.

There were collectables, nostalgic things, cultural things, things that might be useful one day. Because it's what I saw every day, it became normal to me. Eventually, I decided to join in the collecting. As a child, I joined a book club and started my own book collection. There were piles of old Radio Times magazines, VHS videos, DVDs, art and all sorts of other stuff. As I was growing up, I found having stuff around comfortable and normal.

When I moved out and got a place of my own, some of these habits followed me into my adult life. I moved house a lot as a student, which made it hard to accumulate material possessions. My life at that time had to fit in a car or two. But whenever I stayed put for long enough, the stuff quickly started to pile up.

After a lot of self-reflection and conversations with others, I've come to realise that people have different experiences and expectations of what their home environment should look like. For example, my grandma can't abide mess. Her house is always neat, clean and tidy. Her possessions, ornaments, photos, and trinkets are neatly displayed or tidied away. Everything has its place.

I have another friend from that generation who talks about her tidying habit. She would sometimes be told off by her late husband for throwing the newspaper away before he'd even had a chance to read it.

I know people with Instagram picture-perfect houses; they may be beautiful and tidy in that moment, but there may be a load of clutter out of camera shot. Who knows how long they stay that way! I also know people with young kids where nothing stays put very long. Are they real (or reel) life?

It's a cultural stereotype that Americans, in particular, own a lot of stuff. They even have extra storage for stuff that won't fit into their houses, as explored in a humorous video by Laurence Brown.[106] His YouTube Channel called *Lost in the Pond* points out the differences and similarities between Great Britain and the USA. Unfortunately, both countries seem to have an obsession with stuff.

There are lots of reasons why people hold onto a lot of stuff. Perhaps it's an unconscious habit that brings comfort or a feeling of security. Some items have sentimental value, happy memories or are gifts from people we care about.

Some things we think will be useful in future, like tools, knick-knacks, string or whatever else fills up our sheds and garages. Unfortunately these can turn out to be useless, old fashioned or become obsolete. It could be collectables or investments, like trading cards or antiques. Whatever the reason, I think it's useful to reflect on why we have so much stuff and ask ourselves whether we need to hold on to it.

## We Can Change Our Relationship With Stuff

We've talked in the introduction and Chapter 2 about *financial minimalism,* how some people choose to declutter their house and their life so that they have only the minimum they need to get by. For some people, financial minimalism is a way to fight against materialism and consumerism. It makes them mindful of what they own. It increases gratitude for what they already have. They would rather have a few useful things than piles of clutter.

Sometimes financial minimalism is used as a way to accelerate people towards financial independence. It's means cutting costs and saving more money. Think of all the money people pay for junk or storage units! Or perhaps there's something you could sell and help you pay off your debt. The question you have to ask yourself is what matters to you more: paying off debt or having more stuff? (You can always buy stuff later when you're debt free).

I've been practising more financial minimalism in recent years without really knowing it. I decided to reduce the amount of new stuff I acquired. I make use of what I have already rather than buying more, or invest in useful things. I'm trying to reduce waste and buy things that are better for the environment. It's not always easy but I think I'm getting better at it. I've found contentment and don't feel a pressure to buy the latest gadgets.

I know I prefer quality time more than receiving gifts, so I try to communicate that to my friends and loved ones. I'm slowly decluttering my life - throwing away, recycling, reusing, upcycling, giving away, selling stuff and tidying things in storage containers. After all, do I still need my university notes from 18 years ago? My 3 art boxes has expanded to several art cabinets, but at least they're tidy and I know what's in them. Sometimes stuff builds up again or I start a new project that takes up more space. I just have to be mindful and try again.

Over the years, I've also taken the time to get my financial documents in order. I try to keep them sorted into folders in a box or filed electronically on my computer. Between tidy-ups, they tend to pile up in a heap. So I have to take some time to sort the letters. I sort them into separate categories (bank accounts, insurance, car, health etc.) and divide them into cardboard folders.

Having access to the past few years of utility bills, bank statements, council tax bills, or payslips can be useful for ID checks, job applications or tax returns. In the UK, the DBS service often ask for these sorts of documents. It's much easier if you've got your paperwork to hand.

Having a decluttered environment can help you have a less cluttered mind. It can be easier to find things, rather than wading through piles of stuff you forgot you had. Our home environment has all sorts of effects on us. The atmosphere we set affects our mood and ability to study, for example. We may not even realise the effect our environment has on our sleep patterns or general wellbeing. It also changes how we feel about opening our home up to invite others in.

## A Note on Collectables As Physical Assets

*'Money is not good or evil. It has no morals or intentions of its own. Money reflects the character of the user.'*
~ DAVE RAMSEY

I've got lots of friends who collect things. Often you can become a specialist or collect things in a niche area. People collect all sorts of interesting things: first-edition books, wargaming models, autographs, stamps and postcards, LEGO, musical instruments, trading cards, watches, and jewellery. I'm sure you can think of lots of other things people collect and TV shows that turn bargain hunting for antiques into a game.

However, it's important to think about why we're collecting these things. Are they just nice to have or are we buying them as an investment? If we own a toy or model, do we choose to play with it or keep it in the box, thinking it might be worth something one day?

When it comes to collectables, often their value in the marketplace is based on what people are prepared to pay for them. Value tends to increase with scarcity, but the things that are popular now can go out of fashion later. Just because something is old doesn't mean it's valuable. This is why becoming an expert collector matters.

If you've built up a lovely collection for yourself, it's important to know what your exit strategy is. Is this something you're going to hold on to forever and pass on to your heirs? What are they going to do with it? Would you give them to another collector or could they be part of an exhibition? Sometimes families don't know what to do with things they inherit. They may not know the value of a collectables, other than sentimental value.

Or would you sell your collection one day? If you're relying on collectables to be part of your retirement plan, do you know how you're going to turn them into cash so you can pay the bills and eat?

If you're a specialist collector and your family isn't, then it might make sense to sell some of your collectables on their behalf and invest it in something else. If you've got expert knowledge, you can use that to your advantage. You'll know who to sell to and what a fair price is. *Antiques Roadshow* is a TV programme that shows how difficult it can be for families to know what things they inherit are actually worth.

Selling or giving away some of your collection may be a test to see how attached to material possessions you are. That way you'll know the position of your head and heart, what's emotion and what's maths.

Also make sure you know the tax rules for selling your collectables. In the UK, you may need to pay capital gains tax if you make more than £6000 from sales in a financial year. This includes jewellery, paintings, antiques, coins and stamps, as well as possessions that are part of a set. But you don't have to pay capital gains tax on items with a limited lifespan of less than 50 years, including machinery like antique clocks and watches. So be careful the next time you have a yard sale or sell a few things on eBay. Make sure you've looked up the latest regulations.[107]

## The Real Cost of Material Things

Every time we spend money, there is an *opportunity cost*. It's money we could have spent on something else. When we spend on *consumption* (e.g. goods that get used up, services that we use only once) or if we buy things that lose their value over time (*depreciating assets*), our net worth tends to go backwards.

Instead, we could be paying off debt or investing it in things that go up in value, like collectables and antiques, gold, stocks and shares, bonds, houses or land.

Everything we spend and consume means we can't put that money to work in other ways.

As we'll explore later, there are other ways to invest, like investing in ourselves and careers through qualifications and education, which can increase our future earning potential.

Some material things aren't valuable to collectors, but they're valuable to us. We can't put a price on family heirlooms with sentimental value, letters from loved ones, photographs, home videos or children's artwork. They're irreplaceable. But in a way, they're also just stuff. There may come a time when the loft, full of childhood things, gets cleared out and we need to make space for the new.

Similarly, in the introduction we talked about spiritual wealth. These are often immaterial things, like building relationships with friends and family, being part of a community, having fun experiences and making memories. Sometimes these things can fulfil us more than material things. But money may still be needed to help us pay for the time off, meals, holidays and fun. How we spend and invest our time, talent and treasures is a key part of financial stewardship.

## Conclusion: Possessions

Many people teach that it's okay to have nice things as long as they don't have an unhealthy hold over us. We need to make sure we understand the heart behind why we buy and hold onto material things. The ultimate test would be if we were to lose everything. We can learn from people who have experienced conflict and natural disasters, like war, housefires, floods and earthquakes. How would we feel or respond if we lost everything and had to rebuild our lives?

If you live with other people, you need to recognise if you're a hoarder or a person who throws things away. It can be a cause of conflict and the source of many arguments. It's important to be self-aware and be willing to make a compromise with those you live with. The environment you create and the behaviour you demonstrate will also affect your children and other family members.

There are also environment, social and governance (ESG) considerations when it comes to how we consume and collect material possessions. Pretty much everything we use, eat and wear involves fossil fuels – plastics, man-made fibres, fertilisers, manufacturing and transport.

Are we buying quality items that will last for decades or buying single use plastics, clothes we'll only wear once, or things wrapped in non-biodegradable packaging?

We also need to be mindful of supply chains and make sure we're not promoting unethical practices like child labour, modern day slavery and human trafficking.

We may choose to pay more for better quality, ensuring that farmers are paid fairly through fair trade initiatives and sustainability programmes. This is called ethical consumption. What we consume affects what the big corporations will supply.

Monocropping and loss of biodiversity in some of the poorest countries in the world are the result of our first-world greed and consumption. We need to ask ourselves questions: Are our air miles contributing to our carbon footprint? What can be recycled and reused?

It can feel overwhelming, but if we all do something and make a little change to how we spend money, together we can make a difference. We can lobby governments, support charities and NGOs, educate ourselves and raise awareness by telling our friends and family.

We look back at history, the evils of the Transatlantic Slave Trade or the cruel working conditions of the Industrial Revolution. Back then, there were abolitionists and reformers who spoke out and changed society. How will we be remembered 200 years from now? Will people look back and wonder why we didn't do anything to end our own social injustices?

When it comes to spirituality, there's a saying that money is a mirror or an amplifier – it reveals more of what we already are. You'll hear the Bible misquoted and people saying money is evil. That isn't the case. It's just a bit of metal, a piece of paper or a number on a screen.

The Bible says *'for the love of money is a root of all kinds of evil.'*[108] It's our mindset and attitude toward money that makes the difference. The pursuit of money, like the pursuit of power, can corrupt and lead people to do evil things.

If you feel material possessions or wealth are starting to turn you into someone you don't want to be, amplifying our unhealthy personality traits (these exist on a scale from helpful to toxic; you can look up *The Enneagram Test* to learn more), then there are things that we can do.

We might need to continue the journey of self-discovery and self-compassion, to identify and heal the route cause of our anger, envy or dissatisfaction, to understand that we are truly valuable as we are. You might need to sell some stuff or give it away. Perhaps doing gratitude exercises might help. *Chapter 6: Generosity* may well be the antidote for you.

I've put together a few videos in the Resources Chapter on mindful consumption, ethical supply chains, financial minimalism and fighting modern day slavery.

BEN BÜYÜYÜNCE
Gülten Dayıoğlu
Apartman Çocukları
etkili iletişim
GERÇEK
OLSUN
KİŞİSEL GEL
EYECEK

## Ways To Think About Debt and How To Manage It

*'He who is quick to borrow is slow to pay'*
~ GERMAN PROVERB

Now we've thought about our relationships with material possessions and stuff, in the second half of this chapter I want to talk about our relationship with debt. People often use debt to acquire stuff and live the lifestyle they've grown accustomed too. This can be destructive if it gets out of control. But debt can be useful too, helping people to acquire things that they wouldn't ordinarily be able to afford, like houses and education, as well as leveraging the power of debt to grow a business or side hustle.

So what is debt and is it all bad? In its simplest terms, debt is where we borrow something (e.g. money) from someone else or an institution, usually to buy something we couldn't afford under normal circumstances.[109]

Just like we saw with money and possessions, debt isn't inherently good or bad. It's how we use it that matters, our mindset and attitude surrounding it, that determines whether it becomes a blessing or a curse.

In this section, we'll explore some mindful finance techniques to help us avoid debt traps and learn how to use debt responsibly. We'll also look at some terms you might have heard of, like *good debt* and *bad debt*, as well as how to pay debt off should you decide to.

Debt is sometimes divided into four main types:[110]

1. Secured debt
2. Unsecured debt
3. Revolving debt
4. Mortgages

You don't need to know these in great detail. But it can be useful to think about how debt works.

Secured debts are backed by some sort of asset, known as *collateral*. This could be a car loan where the car could be repossessed if you don't make payments. Perhaps you've bought your furniture through a hire purchase agreement.[111] Having secured debt gives the lender more confidence that you will keep paying down your debt as they can take something valuable off you if you don't pay.

Unsecured debt, on the other hand, is based purely on the borrower's creditworthiness. This means the interest rate will be higher as the lender has to take more risk. Examples include personal loans, bank overdrafts, gym memberships and student loans.

One type of unsecured loan, in particular, you should avoid at all costs – the *payday loan*. These are now regulated in the UK, but costs can still spiral out of control. The *Money Helper* website and *Citizens Advice* give a good overview of payday loans and some alternative ways to borrow money to help you avoid becoming the prey of loan sharks.[112,113]

Revolving debts are where you can repeatedly borrow and pay them back again. The most common examples are credit cards and store cards. These are also unsecured debt which is why the interest rates on credit cards can be over 20%, though you'll often find deals – like 0% balance transfers – to lure you in.

The last type of debt is a mortgage which is used to buy a property. These get classed separately as they're unique. This debt is secured against your house. In the USA, you can find fixed interest rate mortgages of 15 or 30 years, though some people opt for a variable rate.

In the UK, things are a little different. Mortgage terms usually last between 25 and 40 years, but they're only fixed for the first few years. After that, they go to a variable interest rate which can fluctuate greatly. You can move to another fixed-rate deal when your fix comes to an end.

There can be penalties if you want to pay off your mortgage early, so doing some research into the different types is essential. There are also *offset mortgages* where you can use your savings to bring your interest rate down. The *Nerdwallet* website and *Which?* have a good overview of UK mortgages if you want to know more.[114,115]

## Debt Mindset

*'Procrastination is like a credit card: it's a lot of fun until you get the bill'*
~ CHRISTOPHER PARKER

People's attitude to debt depends on their different beliefs and experiences. Some people who have had their lives turned upside down by debt, for example, spending on a credit card that got out of control or a gambling addiction, often find that the safest way to go is to declare abstinence from debt. They cut up their credit cards, go to war on debt and decide never to use it ever again.

Deciding to live debt-free is certainly a valid choice for some people who've seen just how destructive uncontrolled debt can be. Only a handful of people choose to live that way – anecdotally, it's mostly our elderly relatives' generation or followers of Dave Ramsey.

It's possible to live and grow wealth without debt. It just takes a bit longer and you may have to work harder to do it. But there are certainly some advantages, such as less downside risk if economic conditions flip on you. Someone who is debt-free and loses their job will usually fare better than someone facing the same situation who is up to their eyeballs in debt repayments.

You'll also hear people dividing debt into arbitrary good and bad categories. But it doesn't mean that debt is evil. You can think of *good debt* as useful debt. It can provide opportunities and help us achieve our goals, like student loans and mortgages. On the other hand, *bad debt* can be a hindrance, keeping us stuck and taking us backwards on our wealth-building journey, like consumer debt and credit cards.

Whatever your relationship to debt, if you find yourself in financial difficulty then I want you to go and ask for help. If you're facing a debt crisis, then the *Money Saving Expert* website has a checklist of things you need to do and can signpost you towards the help you need.[116]

## We Live In A Debt-Based Society

*'Debt is like any other trap, easy enough to get into,
but hard enough to get out of.'*
~ HENRY WHEELER SHAW

As we've already explored, people take on debt for many reasons. Sometimes it's intentional and sometimes it's unintentional. Perhaps we take out debt because everyone else seems to be doing it.

Debt companies make it so easy. We might have underestimated just how dangerous taking on debt can become. We should always be asking ourselves whether we can afford the debt, especially if we have a drop in our income or some other event that rocks our world.

A credit card may come with all sorts of perks and features: bonus points, air miles and other freebies, or even exclusivity and prestige. *Buy Now, Pay Later* schemes seem to have popped up everywhere in recent years.

People can be lured into the belief that because they can afford the monthly payments, then they can afford the item. But in reality, it could be costing us more than we realise, both in excessive fees and complacency. If we make instant gratification our expectation, then it turns us into impatient risk-takers which could set us up for problems later on.

Just as compound interest can work miraculously to grow our wealth over time, so too will the interest penalty of debt be compounded against us to drain our future wealth. At the time of editing in August 2023, credit card rates in the UK have reached their highest rate for 30 years.[117]

Imagine what 20% annualised growth on your investments would feel like instead of having a credit card charging you 20%! Again, credit cards aren't inherently evil. It's how we use them that matters. Most finance experts are clear that holding a credit card balance (where you don't completely pay it off each month) is a big no-no.

Dave Ramsey certainly takes one of the most extreme anti-debt views and has claimed that, *'Credit cards are the most aggressively-marketed product in the history of humankind.'* Why? Because it's an offer that's too good to be true. You're rewarded for spending money. Of course, it's going to incentivise people to spend more!

Credit card companies understand the psychology of spending better than most people. It's human nature to spend more on plastic because we lose the sense of friction and money no longer feels real. It's easy to drift into debt. We succumb to an enticing welcome offer and then stop paying attention. The credit card balance can grow exponentially and interest repayments squeeze us like a boa constrictor. We can become entrapped, ensnared and powerless to dig our way out because of the hefty fees.

So what's the antidote? Yep, you guessed it. It's *Mindful Finance*: being aware of our relationship with debt and how we're using it. It's making sure we're in control of it and it's not controlling us. That way we can use debt (if we choose to) to accelerate us forward, rather than keeping us stuck.

## Debt As A Trap, Tool or Lever

I want to introduce you to three different content creators and show you how they think about debt. This will help you decide where you may be on the debt risk spectrum. They are:

1. **Dave Ramsey** from *The Ramsey Show*
2. **Brian Preston and Bo Hanson** from *The Money Guy Show*
3. **Robert Kiyosaki** from *Rich Dad, Poor Dad*

MINDFUL FINANCE - 185

# Attitudes to Debt

## Where are you on the debt risk spectrum?

### Dave Ramsey
"Debt is a snare"

⬇

### The Money Guy Show
"Debt is a chainsaw"

⬇

### Robert Kiyosaki
"Debt is a lever"

As you read about different attitudes to debt, ask yourself where you fall on the debt risk spectrum. Is your relationship with debt healthy or toxic? Are you in control or does it control you? Are you burdened by debt or is it a tool you can safely use to build wealth? The answer will be different for each of us. So give it some thought.

## 1. Dave Ramsey – Debt as a Snare

*'I always laugh and say I met God on the way up, and I got to know him on the way down. And so, as I'm crashing and losing everything, a lot of people run to God when they are struggling. And I was no exception'* ~ DAVE RAMSEY

Dave Ramsey is a familiar voice in personal finance in America. His views of money and debt are perceived to be quite extreme by some. But his tried and tested principles have helped millions of people get out of debt. His commitment to living a debt-free life comes from the terrifying experience of borrowing too much early in his real estate career and going bankrupt a few years later. He wants to make sure nobody has to go through the same pain.

His view of money is shaped by his Christian faith as his experiences led him on a journey to discover what the Bible has to say about financial wisdom. These are timeless principles that seem to follow what my grandma's generation said about money. Live on less than you make. Don't buy what you can't afford.

*'Free yourself, like a gazelle from the hand of the hunter,
like a bird from the snare of the fowler.'*
~ PROVERBS 6:5, New International Version (NIV)

Famously, Dave builds his teachings around the concept of *'Gazelle Intensity'* as an approach to paying off debt. This comes from *Proverbs 6*, where debt is described as a trap or a snare.[118] Just like a deer escaping a hunter, you have to run from debt as if your life depends on it. It will take all of your strength, perseverance and focus.

Only by attacking debt aggressively, typically over an 18- to 24-month period, by throwing everything you have at it, can you break free from the shackles of debt and never go back. Short-term sacrifice results in a lifetime of gain. It could change your family tree forever.

I've put some links in the Resources Chapter for you to discover more about Dave Ramsey's *7 Baby Steps* and how these can be adapted for a UK audience. In particular, his advice on USA student loans needs to be reinterpreted for UK students.

> *'Debt is not a tool; it is a method to make the banks wealthy, not you. The borrower truly is slave to the lender.'*
> ~ DAVE RAMSEY

In Dave Ramsey's view, debt is framed as something dangerous and best avoided. It steals from your future prosperity by bringing forward the things that we should have saved up to buy tomorrow. To Dave Ramsey, there is no such thing as *good debt*. He views it all as *bad* with the potential to entrap or ensnare you.

As a small concession, he will allow people to take out a mortgage. But cars are best paid for with cash. Holidays and other expenses need to be saved up for. He teaches Americans how to go to college without student loans. It may be harder work and take longer, but he teaches that living debt-free is possible.

> *'Neither a borrower nor a lender be; For loan oft loses both itself and friend.'*
> ~ WILLIAM SHAKESPEARE, 'HAMLET, ACT 1, SCENE III'

Dave Ramsey warns strongly about borrowing money from friends and family. This includes co-signing on loans (where someone promises to pay on someone else's behalf). This can create relationship strain and be like putting a price on a friendship. He would rather people give money as a gift without any strings attached than enslave someone into debt which creates an unhealthy power dynamic.

## 2. The Money Guy Show – Debt as a Tool

*'Debt is a chainsaw. It's a very powerful tool,*
*but if not used responsibly, there can be horrible consequences.'*
~ BRIAN PRESTON, *'The Money Guy Show'*

There's a sort of middle ground that sees debt being used responsibly and the possible dangers respected. I've heard Brian Preston and Bo Hanson discussing many times on *The Money Guy Show* how debt can be thought of like a chainsaw. It's a powerful tool – extremely useful but potentially dangerous – to be handled with caution and used in the right way.

This view acknowledges that our modern-day society is built on debt. We shouldn't feel guilty for using it, as long as we have a plan and are in control of our finances. It's a view that gives more freedom and choice. There's no such thing as purely good or bad debt. It depends on our circumstances. It challenges us to think about which debts are helping and which ones are a hindrance.

In reality, we will all probably take out some debts to get by – to buy a home, to get a car, to have an education. But it makes us ask ourselves questions like are we taking out too much debt? Are we paying off our credit card each month so it doesn't carry a balance? How much student loan are we taking out and is our aim to pay it off one day or not?

From this viewpoint, if you're in control of your finances, then it's okay to use debt for some things. *The Money Guy Show* team admit that this method only works for people who have self-control. If someone can't handle debt safely, then they signpost people to Dave Ramsey, advising them to cut up their credit cards and avoid debt altogether. They've even appeared on each other's shows!

You can check out *The Money Guy Show Resources* website for guides and checklists on how to buy a car or house correctly, as well as their financial roadmap, *'The Financial Order of Operations.'*[119]

## 3. Robert Kiyosaki - Debt as a Lever

*'Bad debt is debt that makes you poorer. I count the mortgage on my home as bad debt, because I'm the one paying on it. Other forms of bad debt are car payments, credit card balances, or other consumer loans.'*

~ ROBERT KIYOSAKI

As we've already said, there's nothing inherently good or bad about debt. It's what we do with it and our tolerance to risk that matters. I first introduced you to Robert Kiyosaki when we looked at building a foundation and the concept of paying yourself first.

Instead of thinking all debt is bad, as Kiyosaki's *'poor dad'* believed, his *'rich dad'* taught him that some debt can be used for good. He teaches that it's okay to use debt to buy assets that are going up in value (like real estate investments). But he doesn't see the mortgage on his own personal residence as an investment.

Just like Dave Ramsey, Kiyosaki thinks depreciating assets (like cars, TVs and luxury items) should be paid for with cash. Getting into debt to buy these things keeps you poor.[120]

I like to think of Robert Kiyosaki as the anti-Dave Ramsey. They both made their initial fortune from real estate. But Dave Ramsey got burned and Robert Kiyosaki didn't. It's left them with very different views about debt.

Kiyosaki teaches people how to build businesses and become property investors using debt as a way to build wealth faster, like a lever. In fact, debt is sometimes called *'leverage'* for this reason. This is a way of borrowing money to make money. He sees his own home as a liability – it's just somewhere you live that costs you money. The real power is building up a real estate portfolio, where renters are paying the mortgage for you.

It's certainly a high-risk approach, especially when you do it with lots of debt. It only takes an economic recession or a house price crash for things to come tumbling down, which is what happened when the stock market crashed during 2008 and 2009.[121] Taking out debt to build wealth only works if everything is going to plan.

So, where are you on the debt risk spectrum? Perhaps you'll find out as you read on.

## Maths Versus Behaviour, Head or Heart?

*'But the way you start saving is to get rid of the debt.*
*Once you don't have to make payments, you can start to save.*
*And you have to make saving an emotional priority.'*
~ DAVE RAMSEY

Both Brian Preston from *The Money Guy Show* and Martin Lewis from *Money Saving Expert* are maths people. Their good debt/bad debt advice is often based on calculations of how the numbers would look over a 30- or 40-year period, all things being equal.

But things are not always equal because humans are emotional as well as thinking beings, which leads us to do irrational things. We fall off the wagon and need to force ourselves to get back on again. Sometimes we pay off debt faster if we feel we're making progress, even if it doesn't make mathematical sense based on interest rates alone.

What I like about Dave Ramsey's approach is that it sees debt as a behaviour problem based on emotion. It's 80% behaviour, 20% head knowledge. You don't reason your way into debt: you feel it – debt is pleasure in the short term and regret in the long term. You can't reason your way out of debt: you have to feel it too – often you need to have that *"I've had it!"* moment. You need hope and a sense of traction.

# Good Debt vs. Bad Debt

## Which of these debts is helpful or harmful?

Whether debt is 'good' or 'bad' depends on the situation. Is it adding value by giving you opportunities sooner, or stealing from your future prosperity? Often, it depends on your individual circumstances. Here are some general rules:

## Bad Debt

- Credit Card with a balance
- Car loans you can't afford
- Student loans (USA system)
- Mortgage on your own house
- Mortgage on investment property when there's an economic crash
- Debt on depreciating assets
- Payday Loans (high interest)
- Some personal loans
- Money owed to friends/family

## Good Debt

- Credit Card paid off monthly
- Car loans (using 20/3/8 rule)
- Student loans (UK System)
- Mortgage on your own house
- Mortgage on investment property when the economy is working great
- Investing in yourself e.g. for education, courses and certificates
- Mobile phone contracts

## Should I Pay Off My Student Loan early?

I've put together a page for you with examples of so-called good and bad debts. As you can tell from the views of the three different content creators, opinions vary greatly as to whether debt should be divided up in this way. Some debts fall into both categories, depending on your circumstances. The issue of student loan debt is one of those.

Just because I had the opportunity to pay off my student loan early doesn't mean that it makes sense for everyone to do it. My situation will not be the same as yours.

For me, I calculated that my student loan would have paid off within 4 years if I stayed on my current trajectory. In the end, I was sick and tired of having a £20,000 bill hanging over me and charging me interest. So I decided to attack it, the way Dave Ramsey teaches, mainly to prove to myself that I could do it.

It marked a turning point in my life that got me interested in personal finance, a passion that goes beyond just becoming debt free.

\* \* \*

I've put some links in the Resources Chapter for you to explore the topic of student loan debt further. One of the most prominent British personal finance educators is **Martin Lewis**, founder of the *Money Saving Expert* website. He also has a successful TV show and often gives interviews discussing money matters in the UK.

Martin Lewis is also a big advocate for UK students and talks with the UK government on their behalf to make sure they're getting a good deal with their student finance. He wishes that student loan debt would be reclassed as a *'graduate contribution system'* or *'tax'* as he acknowledges that the majority of UK students will never pay their loans off and therefore shouldn't worry about it.

For most people in the UK, their student loan debt will hopefully be forgiven one day. The information on this topic is constantly changing and being updated, but there are helpful articles on the *Money Saving Expert* website which is a good place to start.[122,123]

However, Martin Lewis also recognises that there is a difference between what the maths says and how debt makes you feel:
'*Those with no self-control – be careful... This guide is written from a financial, not an emotional, perspective [...] For those who've been badly burned by debt, or have no self-control, sometimes it's best to ignore the sums and do what you feel comfortable with. If you'll just end up spending or wasting the cash, then at least overpaying the student loan is playing it safe. It's far better than ignoring the fact you've no self-control or frivolously building up more borrowing.*'[15]

\* \* \*

On the other hand, Dave Ramsey's view of the impending USA student loan crisis is outlined dramatically in the podcast *Borrowed Future*.[124] In the USA, there is no guarantee that student loans will be forgiven. Some people are promised student loan forgiveness only to find that they don't qualify.

The anxiety, depression and psychological burden of what feels like impossibly high student loan debt in America shouldn't be underestimated. It changes people's patterns of behaviour. They may decide to work in a different career field, feel relationship strain and worry about their children's financial future. They may even put off marriage, kids and house purchases because of their overwhelming debt burden.

They may feel like it's a hopeless situation. But the *Borrowed Future* podcast does give hope. There are real-life interviews with people who have managed to pay off their student loan debt, or who have gone through college with scholarships or part-time jobs. There is also a call for change, highlighting the need for the government to fix a broken system.

# UK Student Loans

## Are UK student loans a good or bad debt?

Student loans are the way most people pay for higher education in the UK. The UK student loan system is very different to elsewhere in the world as there is a debt forgiveness programme built into it (at the moment). Here are some pros and cons of UK student loans.

### Pros

- Anyone can afford to go to University by taking out loans to cover the cost of tuition and living expenses
- It's an investment in yourself
- Some people may never pay anything (or very little) back
- Eventually the debt is wiped
- The more you borrow, the more you'll have forgiven
- It helps improve your future

### Cons

- Middle to high earners may need to pay more back over the course of their career than low earners
- University isn't for everyone
- People may earn less due to fears of loan repayments
- The total bill gets bigger
- The government can change the rules at any time
- You can't predict the future

## How Do I Pay Off Debt?

*'Borrowing today to pay tomorrow is harrowing;*
*loan sharks will arrow your marrow till sorrow wash over you.'*
~ VINCENT OKAY NWACHUKWU
*'Weighty 'n' Worthy African Proverbs – Volume 1'*

If you decide that you want to pay off some debt, then there are a few different approaches you can use. Some are more analytical, based on maths and head knowledge, whilst others are behaviour hacks that rely on your emotions for motivation.

I'm going to talk about 3 different approaches to paying off consumer debt. Each has different pros or cons and will suit different people depending on your personality type. These are:

1. **The Debt Snowball Method**
2. **The Debt Avalanche Method**
3. **The Debt Snowflake Method**

*'No matter how smart you are, nothing much happens in terms of results until you put it into action. Yes, we need to be dreamers. Yes, we need to be architects for the future. For the architect can draw all day long. But unless somebody is willing to lay bricks...? So get going'*
~ JIM ROHN

So far we've been talking about theory. Now it's time to take action. I heard someone once say, *"the only way to pay off debt is to pay off debt."* It seems obvious, but it means pretending to be your own debt management service and paying your debts off, not just moving the debt around. Before you start paying off your consumer debts, there are a few things you need to do.

# How to pay off debt

## Get your priorities right

**01** — **BUILD A FINANCIAL FOUNDATION**
-> get a spending plan (budget), increase income, cut spending, create margin to throw at your debt.

**02** — **BUILD YOUR 4 WALLS**
-> make sure you've got the basics: food, shelter, utilities and transport. Pay minimum debt payments.

**03** — **GET A £1000 EMERGENCY FUND**
-> build a starter emergency fund to stop you going back into debt when an emergency comes up.

**04** — **FIND AND LIST YOUR DEBTS**
-> make a list of your debts, know what you owe, pull your credit report if you need to. Face reality.

**05** — **PAY PRIORITY DEBTS FIRST**
-> research which debts are a priority e.g. council tax, income tax, child maintenance, car loan, rent arrears, court fines. Make sure you pay these first!

**06** — **PICK A DEBT PAYMENT METHOD**
-> for non-priority debts, choose to Debt Snowball, Avalanche or Snowflake your way to debt freedom! How will you stay motivated? Good luck!

First, you need to get good at laying bricks. Whether it's building an emergency fund, paying off debt or saving money, to build wealth it's exactly the same process! We need our foundational financial habits in place (*Chapter 1: Foundations*).

It's making a regular spending plan (such as a monthly budget), creating margin (money left over to save or pay off debt) and putting it to use. Remember, the more you can cut your lifestyle, increase your income, work overtime, sell things, do whatever it takes, the sooner you will be able to pay off your debt.

The next thing you need to do is stabilise your finances (*Chapter 2: The 4 Walls*). It's important to make sure you've got your shelter, utilities, clothes, food and transport covered, whilst making minimum payments on your debt. This stops you from going further into debt.

Then you need to build up a £1000 (or dollars, or equivalent in your currency) emergency fund (*Chapter 3: Roof of Protection*). This stops you from going backwards with your financial plan once you're ready to throw everything you have at the debt. This puts a cushion between you and life and means you're more likely to be successful.

The next step is to make a list of all your debts. You need to work out which ones are your priority debts and which ones are non-priority debts.[125,126] We talked about these back in *Chapter 2: The 4 Walls*. It's important to pay off your priority debts first or you could face a penalty, e.g. a prison sentence or your items may be repossessed. Paying minimum payments on your 4 Walls – house and car payments, keeping the power on and food on the table - should also be a priority.

Only then should you be focusing on paying off your non-priority debts. This is everything else, not including your mortgage (though some people do choose to pay off their mortgage early, but in a later step).

To pay off your non-priority debt you need to know what debts you actually have. For some of the methods, you need to know how big each debt is and what the interest rates are. You may need to pull your credit report and talk to your debt collectors to make sure the amounts are correct.[127]

Some debts may have gone into default (or *'gone into collections'* as they say in America), while others are still active. It makes sense to focus on the active ones first. The debts in default can usually wait and be dealt with eventually.[128]

The process can feel daunting. There may be threatening letters, people wanting to take you to court or send in the bailiffs. It may feel overwhelming. But there's lots of advice available on how to negotiate with debt collectors. There are resources to help you understand your rights, for example, when bailiffs are or aren't allowed to enter your property. This will help you to stand your ground especially when you feel intimidated or threatened.[129-131]

Finally, it's time to choose a debt repayment method for your non-priority debt. I'm going to talk through the three most popular methods, all of which are related to snow in some way. Then you can go and research the method you like the best and get after it. For additional support, you can phone a debt helpline, join an online community, find more content from the creators I've mentioned and come up with ways to spur yourself on.

We all need cheerleaders and accountability. Some ideas to encourage yourself to pay off debt are to help visualise the process and make it a game. You can make a paperchain representing your debt or financial goal, then break off a link of the chain with each £1000 that you pay off. It could be creating a good old-fashioned *Totalising Thermometer* (*'Totaliser'* or *'Total-ometer,'* like the ones on the TV show *Blue Peter*) to colour in as you achieve each milestone.

You can celebrate the wins and milestones along the way and find ways to stay motivated and encouraged. It gives you a psychological boost every time you pay off a debt. It helps to reinforce your belief that you're making progress and help you stay the course and maybe even get debt free more quickly.

MINDFUL FINANCE - 199

# How to pay off debt

## Emotions, mathematics or automatically?

### Debt Snowball

- Pay off your debt by arranging them from smallest to largest, irrespective of the interest rate.
- Pay minimum payments on all debt and attack the little one first. Any extra money goes to the next debt.
- The sense of traction with each win will motivate you to go faster.

### Debt Avalanche

- Pay off your debts efficiently by paying off the debts with the highest interest rates first.
- Mathematically it could save you money as you'll pay less interest.
- But you won't get the emotional hit of the debt snowball method.

### Debt Snowflake

- This is where you automate all debt repayments. Pay at least the minimum on all your debts.
- There's no emotion and no maths, it's just spare money paying debt off, like snowflakes building up.
- So you'll get there eventually, but it could take you a long time!

While there are some debt solutions in the UK, like IVAs, debt management plans and bankruptcy, if your debt burden isn't too heavy and you've got a big enough shovel (debt to income ratio) then there's a lot you can do on your own without needing to access those services. But if you've tried to pay off the debt yourself and can't, then it's okay to get help and these options might be for you.[132]

*The Debt Snowball* and *The Debt Avalanche* methods of paying off debt in particular work best when you've got multiple debts of different sizes or interest rates. That's why many finance experts recommend avoiding consolidation loans, unless you don't have the discipline to pay down debt yourself.

Some people are also tempted to refinance and add their debt onto their mortgage. Again, you'd only be moving the debt around without actually doing anything about it. You'd feel like you'd achieved something even though the debt is still there.

If you don't change your ways and build healthy money habits, then you may find yourself spending more and going deeper into debt. You've got to address the underlying issues that got you into debt in the first place, like overspending or not paying attention to your finances.[133]

Let's look at each method of paying off non-priority debt in turn.

## 1. The Debt Snowball Method

The Debt Snowball method was popularised by Dave Ramsey in the USA.[134] He's helped people pay off millions of dollars using this approach. Pete Matthew in the UK is also a big fan of the Debt Snowball Method and calls it *"the most effective way to clear debt I've ever come across."*[135]

Think of when you were a kid in the snow. Your snowball starts off small, maybe a handful of melting ice. But you pack a bit more snow against it and get rolling. As you roll, more snow sticks and you start to build up some momentum. As you keep rolling, layers of snow build on each other and before you know it you've got a giant ball or roll of white icy frosting. It's even more satisfying if you're pushing it down a hill.

The Debt Snowball method uses behavioural psychology to motivate you to build good money habits and pay off debt as fast as you can. When you've had a wake-up call, a moment where you become *'sick and tired of being sick and tired'*, you've reached the point where you've had it with debt and want it gone forever, then it's very satisfying to pay off your smallest debts first and celebrate these early wins.

When there are lots of little debts, it may feel like you're swiping at gnats. But as you start to knock out some bigger ones, you can really feel like you're building momentum which can motivate you to keep going.

To do your debt snowball, you need to take all your debts and lay them out in order, smallest to largest, irrespective of their interest rate. You pay minimum payments on all your debts, then attack the smallest one first. Once you've paid that off, then you'll have the extra margin to throw at the next debt, and so on, and so on. It builds momentum and you'll feel a sense of traction, that you're making progress and paying your debts down.[136]

Often, people get so motivated to do this that they often cut their spending even harder and maybe take on extra work to increase their income. Psychology is very powerful and unlike the other debt payment methods which mostly rely on maths, this method is the one that engages with our emotions the most.

Some people, maybe those of you who are more maths-minded, may be wondering why you would want to pay off smaller debts first, even though there could be bigger debts with a high-interest rate slowly accruing more debt. Wouldn't it make sense to pay off the debts that are hurting you the most?

The main argument against this is that the debt snowball is so effective in achieving motivation and momentum that the average household will be paying off their debts within a year or two, so the interest rate won't make too much difference. It may add a month or two to your debt repayment plan. Or it might even spur you on to pay off the debts faster.

Ultimately, for many people, even though the Debt Snowball Method may be more expensive than the avalanche method, you're more likely to stick to the plan and pay off debt this way.[137]

## 2. Debt Avalanche Method

For those of you who are more into maths, then the Debt Avalanche Method may be the one for you. This is the preferred method of *The Money Guy Show* team. They compare this with the debt snowball method in one of their podcast episodes and explain why they prefer it.[138]

This time you can think of an avalanche of snow crashing down a mountain, with sudden, sometimes deadly momentum. This momentum comes from the fact that you are attacking the debt with the highest interest rates first, so you're slowing down the accumulation of new debt. Mathematically, this means that paying off your debt should work out to be cheaper overall.

To do your avalanche, you lay out your debts in order of interest rate, irrespective of their size, and focus on paying off the highest interest rate debts first. Keep paying minimum payments on all your other debts. Again, focused intensity, attacking one debt at a time, helps build momentum. Each debt paid off frees up more margin to attack the next debt.

The main downside is that people don't usually feel maths. They feel the wins! If your first high-interest debt is huge compared to your other debts, then you may not realise you're making progress. It can feel like you're climbing a mountain, rather than coming down one like an avalanche. Some people get disheartened and give up early because they don't feel like they're winning when they probably are.[139]

## 3. Debt Snowflake Method

Just like we discussed in Chapter 1 when we looked at *'automatic finance'* and the *'Latte Factor,'* there are ways to automate your debt repayments as well as your savings. You may come across round-up apps that take small amounts of money when you spend to put towards your goals. In The Debt Snowflake method, it means that small, almost unnoticeable amounts of money are leaving your budget and forming a snowdrift on your debt goal without you realising it.

I'm not a fan of this method as I think it lacks intentionality. If you're paying down all your debts gradually, then you don't feel any traction or emotion (unlike the Debt Snowball Method) and you're not addressing the highest interest rate debts (unlike the Debt Avalanche Method). This is one of the reasons why it took me over 6 years to pay off the first half of my debt and less than 2 years to intentionally knock out the rest.

When you're using automated payments to clear your debt, it's still important to be mindful. You need to set a clear goal and make sure you're going in the right direction. If you don't pay attention, paying only minimum payments on your debt could take years to pay off. You may never pay it off at all, especially if you're being charged a high-interest rate.

Just like we talked about David Bach's *'Automatic Millionaire'* concept, there's nothing wrong with automating your debt repayments. Jennifer Thomson used a modified Debt Snowflake Method, called the 10% rule, to automate her budget and debt repayments. She decided to make 10% overpayments on all her household debts, irrespective of size or interest rates. That means making at least one extra payment a year on the debt.[140] In this way, she was able to pay off £22,000 ($28,000) of debt in 3 years.[141]

It isn't the intensive, aggressive, momentum-building, *throw-everything-at-your-debt* approach of the Snowball and Avalanche Methods. It could take longer to achieve debt freedom this way. But if it means you'll stick with it because it's less painful, if automating the process stops you from missing a payment, then this might be the method for you.

Your lifestyle will often adjust to your new reduced budget because of Parkinson's Law. The Snowflake approach focuses on longevity and sustainability; good money habits for the long term. Perhaps you can think of it as a healthy eating plan, rather than a crash diet. You can use it alongside the Snowball and Avalanche methods, adding additional Snowflakes using round-up apps.[142]

## Debunking The Debt Myths – It's Okay To Be Weird

*'Today must not borrow from tomorrow'*
~ GERMAN PROVERB

In this final section, we're going to look at some commonly held beliefs about debt. You may find your worldview turns upside down for a moment as the debt myths get exploded out of the water. But what culture says isn't always right and what most people say isn't always true. Common sense just isn't that common.

### *Myth 1: Debt is Necessary*

As we get older life tends to get more complicated. As well as having more stuff and responsibility, many people find that they accumulate debt as well. *'Normal'* for many people is acquiring a heavy debt burden because society tells us debt is necessary.

Perhaps we start adult life by taking out a student loan, or three. When we start work we might finance a new car with our first pay cheque. Then we get a credit card to build a credit score (because that's what everyone says we should do) as it helps us to take out a mortgage (debt on a house). When we move into the new house, maybe we decide to take out a home improvement loan to do some refurbishments.

Perhaps we get engaged and borrow money for a marriage ceremony and reception, with a wedding ring paid for with credit, before going on a once-in-a-lifetime honeymoon. Eventually, when kids come along, people usually find that there's just not enough space. Debt can help to buy a bigger car and house to contain everything.

But all this *normal* debt accumulation comes at a cost and it usually looks like living paycheque to paycheque. Is there a way to do things differently? As Dave Ramsey says, '*Normal is broke. Normal is a victim mentality. Normal sucks. BE WEIRD.*'

Our ancestors' post-war era frugality or behaviours that came out of the Great Depression in the USA proved that excessive debt is not necessary to become successful with money. People like Dave Ramsey and Jim Rohn who went broke earlier in life, managed to rebuild wealth without debt and have taught many others how to do so.[143] It's possible to build a life that keeps debt to a minimum. It's just unusual to do so.

## *Myth 2: Everyone Needs To Build Their Credit Score*

Everyone seems to believe that building your credit score is a good thing. According to *Nerdwallet*, a credit score '*shows how reliable you are at borrowing money.*'[144] Several credit reference agencies calculate how likely you are to repay your debts. In the UK, the three main ones are *Experian*, *Equifax* and *TransUnion*. These agencies also operate in the USA and you'll hear it referred to as a *FICO score*.[145]

These companies use a secret formula, taking into account your payment history, how much you owe, new credit applications, types of debt and how long you've had them. But your credit score can be affected by all sorts of things. There are big things like bankruptcies, but you might not have realised that something as simple as an unpaid parking ticket can have negative consequences for your credit score.[146,147]

A *good credit score* usually means you're more likely to be approved for a loan and get a better interest rate. But credit scores only show that you've paid debt off regularly in the past. They don't really represent your financial health overall, though many people hold them in high esteem. In real-life situations, you're far better off showing that you have your financial house in order.

To be truly weird, you don't need to worry about growing your credit score at all. After all, it's only for people who want to borrow money, which people committed to a debt-free life don't need. For some people who haven't borrowed debt for years, they may have a *zero credit score* (or a credit score that can't be calculated at all).

The *Ramsey Solutions* team have put together an article which tells you ways to navigate the challenges created by living without a credit score.[148] It can be really confusing for the person trying to sell you a house or a car! Without a credit score to guide their computer algorithms, sometimes their systems malfunction. But it's a nice problem to have to be so weird that you don't need to borrow money anymore.

Some people fall into the debt trap in the first place because they take out credit cards to build their credit scores. They can get obsessed with this arbitrary number. It's important to be mindful of why you might need a credit score in the first place. If you want to get a mortgage without a credit score, then you'll need something called *'manual underwriting'* where a human looks at your financial fitness.

If you still want to improve your credit score, then there are tools available to help you. For example, in the UK, *Experian Boost* is a service where you can improve your credit score by showing that you are saving and paying your bills regularly (as I'm committed to living debt-free, this is not a recommendation!). There is a guide on the Experian website which has some handy tips on how to build your credit history and improve your score. It helps you know how a credit reference agency thinks so you can play the game.[149]

## Mindful Finance Challenge 3 – *Financial Fitness Score*

So, weird people who want to live debt-free don't need to worry about credit scores. Instead, they can work on their *financial fitness*. That means having an emergency fund, living on less than you make, having a budget, not having debt you can't afford and working towards investing for your future. HSBC have come up with a handy calculator so you can calculate your *financial fitness score,* rather than your credit score.

As part of the next *Mindful Finance Challenge*, why not have a go at working out your financial fitness score? Have you got your financial house in order?

www.hsbc.co.uk/financial-fitness/fitness-score/ [150]

For more about busting debt myths, I've put some links to articles on the topic in the Resources Chapter.

## Conclusion: Debt

Whatever your beliefs and views on debt, I hope this chapter has helped you become more mindful of debt – what it is and how it affects us – both good and bad.

I hope this chapter starts some useful conversations to help you get on the same page with your finance. Perhaps it's a partner or spouse that you need to talk to and address the elephant in the room. Is an increasing debt burden starting to get out of control? Perhaps you're a parent and want to talk to your teenage children about the pros and cons of student loans. Perhaps you want to set up younger children strong with frugal habits.

It's up to you if you want to pay off your debt and how you want to go about it. It's also important to take your spouse and children along for the ride, if you have them. Remember how money fights and money problems can pull relationships apart? This could be the opportunity to get closer as a family.

For my single readers (unmarried, not doing finances jointly with someone else), then don't forget to get an accountability partner or method that works for you. Perhaps it's a mentor or a way of celebrating little wins.

Ultimately, for your long-term wealth building, it's recommended that you enter retirement (or financial independence) debt-free. This will lower your risk and accelerate your wealth-building because there won't be interest payments holding you back. By then, you may have also paid off your house which will mean a big chunk of your budget is free to be used as margin elsewhere.

Remember, just like possessions and money, debt isn't inherently good or bad. It's how it affects us that matters. We need to make wise choices. That means doing things that are a bit unusual and counter-cultural. It's okay to be *weird*. Because *normal* is broke.

## Reflection Questions:

- *Have you sat down and taken a look at how much debt you have?*
- *How does having debt make you feel?*
- *Do you define these as 'good debts' or 'bad debts?'*
- *Could you be in a debt crisis? Do you need outside help?*
- *Do you have a goal to pay off your debt and how long will it take?*
- *Have you calculated how much margin (extra money beyond your basic living expenses) you can create in your monthly budget to put towards giving, saving, spending and paying off debt?*
- *What would being debt-free allow you to do?*
- *Have you found out what your credit score is?*
- *Does your credit score worry you?*
- *Have you taken the financial fitness quiz?*
- *What are the areas where you would like to improve?*

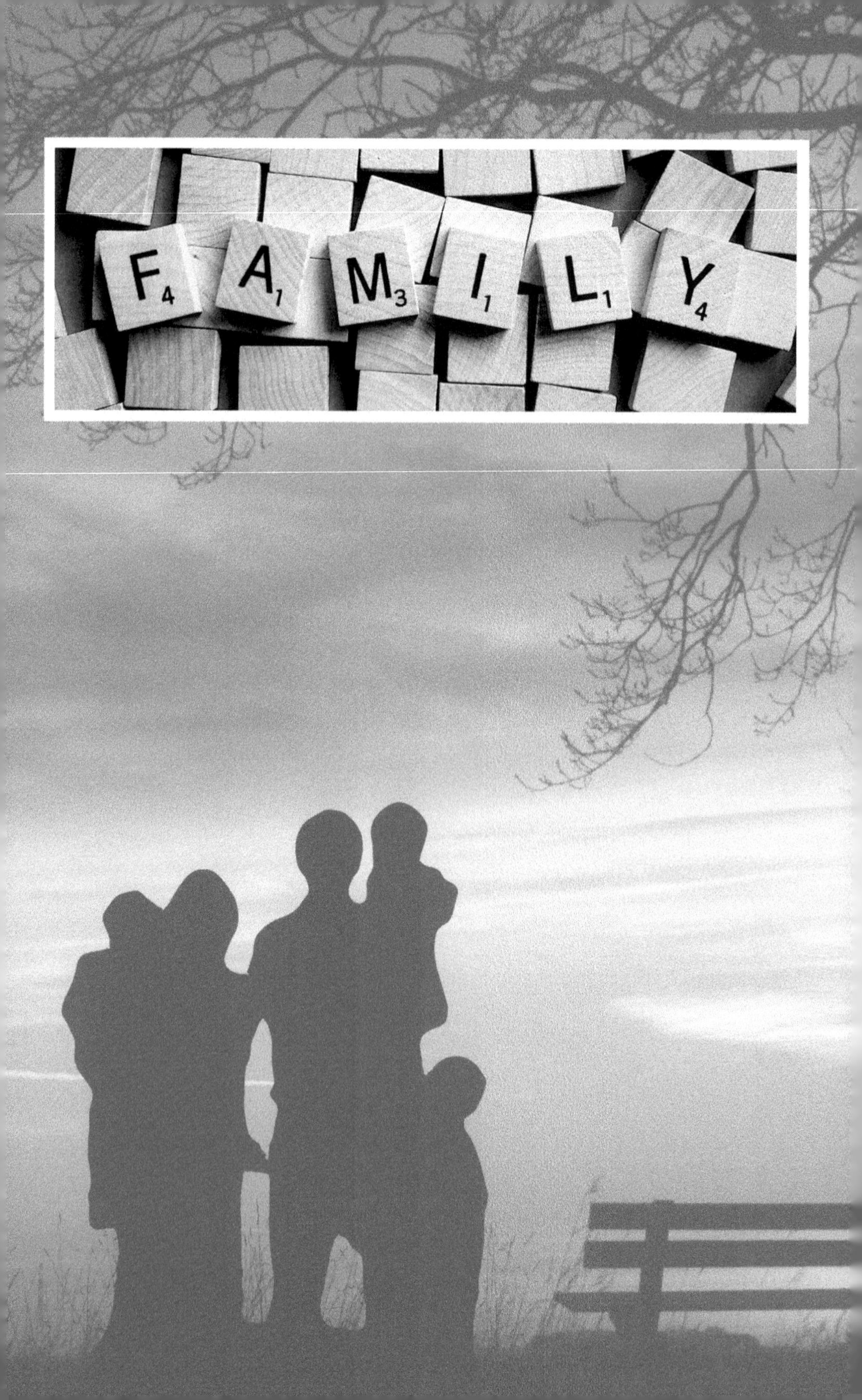
FAMILY

| 5 |

# Chapter 5: Family

*'If you want your children to turn out well,
spend twice as much time with them, and half as much money.'*
~ ABIGAIL VAN BUREN

### Turning Our Financial House Into A Home

You're making great progress! Our financial house is finally taking shape. It has a solid foundation, walls, roof and home décor. We've furnished it and filled it with our favourite things. Now it's time to start living in it. The next two chapters on family and generosity will overlap quite a lot. This is the final important section before we start focusing on growing wealth for the long term by cultivating our financial garden.

Just to recap, let's ask ourselves *'What's the purpose of a house?'* To my mind, it's fundamentally somewhere that provides shelter, protection and privacy. It's somewhere to spend our time, sleep, eat and live. It's also a store of wealth.

Our money can be used for all these purposes too. Money is important in the same way that a house is important. It keeps us safe and secure, and wealth gives us options that we wouldn't otherwise have.

But money isn't everything. It can only get us so far. The Bible reminds us that *'Wisdom is a shelter as money is a shelter, but the advantage of knowledge is this: Wisdom preserves those who have it.'*[151] The Bible also says that wisdom is worth more than silver, gold and precious jewels (*Proverbs 3: 14-15*). Wisdom is a form of *spiritual wealth* that may help us obtain *material wealth* along the way, as it did for King Solomon.

While money isn't the purpose of life, it's hard to do life without it. It affects almost every area of our life, whether we want it to or not. The person who says *"money isn't important"* is usually someone who hasn't known life without it.

So a house is ultimately just another material possession. I've heard finance experts say, *"There's a house on every corner."* We can sell up and buy a new house almost as easily as a hermit crab upgrading its shell (but it takes more paperwork and more effort to move our stuff).

A *home* on the other hand, is more than just bricks and mortar. *Home is where the heart is.* Home *'is the place where you have a foundation of love, warmth, and happy memories.'*[152] We can have many places to call *home*, both emotionally and spiritually. It may not even be a physical place. It may just mean being with our family and loved ones. In the words of Dorothy in *The Wizard of Oz,* "There's no place like home."

## So What Does 'Family' Mean To You?

Usually in financial planning, *'family'* typically refers to the traditional idea of a household made up of parents and children. But family in modern times often looks very different to this. Family means different things to different people. It could be a nuclear family, blended family, extended family, or even a community of people with similar interests and values.

The idea of family may bring to mind happy relationships and nostalgic memories. But perhaps it also causes pain, feelings of loss and separation, dysfunction and chaos. Families are often complicated.

There's always more that goes on behind closed doors than we realise. We often just assume that we're the odd ones and everyone else has got it all together.

In this chapter, I want to use the broadest definition of *family* possible. This is because estimates show that approximately 40% of adults in the UK are single (unmarried, not cohabiting) and 1 in 6 people live on their own.[153]

The phrase "*2.4 children*" to refer to a traditional nuclear family in the UK no longer applies. Birth rates have fluctuated greatly over the decades and generally seem to be on the decline. There are also other types of family units, such as childfree, single-parent and grandparent families that this stereotype seems to overlook.[154]

In this chapter, I want to go beyond the traditional basic unit of society to include all relationships that give us a sense of identity and belonging: friends like family, neighbours, work colleagues, social and religious groups, communities, choirs, clubs and classes, both in-person and online.

Whether you have children, parents and grandparents, first cousins once removed, animals, or none of the above, I believe we can all find meaningful relationships, mother and father figures, mentors and counsellors, as well as becoming family to others, especially if they don't have any of their own nearby.

## Don't Do Life Alone

Whether you have only a few key people to do life with or an extended network, we all need meaningful relationships to live a fulfilled and healthy life. It's not good to be alone all the time. Isolation can be a contributor to burnout, anxiety and depression. Sometimes we end up hearing only the echo chamber of our own thoughts which can lead us into a destructive spiral.

Isolation can lead us to make poor choices and decisions, the consequences of which can take us to places we don't want to be. Sometimes we need someone to encourage us and walk alongside us, especially in times of financial need, or to call us out if we're heading in the wrong direction.

The COVID-19 pandemic further exacerbated what has been called a *'loneliness pandemic'* in the UK. This is especially true among young people, not just the elderly.[155] It's easy to lose our sense of community and relationships.

Making relationships is an investment. It takes time, energy and intentionality. Sometimes it's a financial investment – through gifts and showing love through generosity, travelling the distance to visit face to face, sharing meals, special occasions, socialising and other things that cost money.

It's still possible to do things that are free or low cost, but having some money gives us options. It allows us to help others and bless others in ways we couldn't without it.

There's something very special about connecting with people face to face, not just over digital technology. But online communities can be a great support, especially when you're paying off debt and trying to reach your financial goals when nobody around you seems to be talking about it.

There's a saying, "*If you want to go fast, go alone. If you want to go far, go together.*" There's also a saying that "*success can feel lonely at the top.*" This definition of success feels wrong as the *'successful'* person hasn't been able to take people with them on the journey, which means they've perhaps been less successful than they first thought.

If you're on your mindful finance journey, I believe it's important to make sure you take as many people along with you as possible. The experts recommend that you include your spouse and close family in financial conversations.

As a family, you can come up with shared financial goals and make shared decisions which will inevitably take negotiation and compromise, so the burden doesn't fall on one person alone.

This may include talking to children about money in an age-appropriate way, which we'll explore later. That way you can sacrifice, strive and celebrate together, setting an example for the next generation. It can help strengthen relationships in a stressful time when you need each other and encouragement the most.

We all have influence, no matter how small. We can be leaders and set a good example for the people we come into contact with. It's brave to talk to your family, friends and work colleagues about *Mindful Finance*. We can change the culture and help people enter the conversation. We can pass on our wisdom to people a little way behind us on the journey.

Sharing your story or testimony can be extremely powerful and inspire others to change their lives for the better, hopefully without appearing boastful or self-righteous. That's why it's important to have humility and share your struggles as well. Don't be afraid or ashamed to tell people how you fell short and overcame your challenges. That's what makes your story powerful.

## Having Family Conversations About Money

In this section, I want to explore some topics related to family and money. These all involve having conversations with your family and loved ones about *Mindful Finance*, including:

1. **The myth of work-life balance**
2. **Breaking generational chains**
3. **Changing your family tree**
4. **Legacy and generational wealth**
5. **Wills and estate planning**

## 1. The Myth Of Work-Life Balance

I've heard lots of speakers and entrepreneurs talk about the difficulty of balancing work and relationships. Jim Rohn talks about how he would take his briefcase with him to the beach while on a family vacation, and yet at work would find his mind drifting back to wanting to be at the beach with his family.

It's good to work hard and maximise our income, especially during a season when we're trying to achieve a financial milestone. That's how we can set ourselves up financially to afford the holidays, special occasions and gifts. Often we want to give our families the good things we wish we'd had growing up. But there's an idea of balance. There's always an opportunity cost for our time.

Life should be work, rest *and* play. There are busy seasons, but we also need an opportunity to rest and recharge. For the sake of our health and wellbeing, this should ideally become a regular pattern and habit. In the same way that we've talked about financial goals, money habits and good routines, we need to invest in our relationships too.

We need to be intentional about scheduling phone calls, family time and remember to tell people how much they mean to us. We need to explore how we give and receive love. We need to find out how we, in turn, can communicate our love to our families and friends. This is something that I've tried to do more of in recent years.

Part of mindfulness is being aware of where we are in the present moment. So when we're at work, we can ask ourselves *'Am I actually working and giving it my all, or is my mind drifting elsewhere?'* We shouldn't sit meditating for too long though. There's work to be done!

When we're with family, we can ask ourselves *'Am I engaging and being involved? Am I having intimate conversations about things that matter? Or is the TV on in the background, drowning everything out? Am I more connected to social media than with the person sitting next to me?'*

We can be in proximity without being relationally close. This can happen in all sorts of situations. Perhaps we're on holiday together, doing our daily routine with others, or even hanging out with friends. We can be sat next to each other, but relationally a million miles away.

We often live in a dual reality with the artificial construction of our virtual identity sometimes becoming more important than our actual identity. It's important to build genuine relationships in the here and now. Being relationally present is something that we all need to be intentional about and with technological advances, it seems to be becoming harder to do.

I've come to realise that work-life balance is a myth. There is always tension and compromise, never an equilibrium as such. Sometimes I will take admin work with me when I visit family, but I try to make sure that we also have some dedicated family time too. I try to capture moments in photographs on my phone, but I also want to make real memories too.

Why do I mention the concept of work-life balance in a book about *Mindful Finance*? Well, it's because money affects everything, including our relationships. If you're going through a difficult season financially, then it affects your family and loved ones too.

Perhaps you're trying to work overtime to increase your income and pay off debt. Maybe you're working towards a certain savings goal. Or perhaps you're in a season of transition with your career where you have to dedicate time to learning and courses. In these seasons, you're just not as relationally available as you used to be. But it's usually only going to be temporary. Open and honest communication with your family about finance is key. Make sure you put boundaries and a timeline in place. Maybe schedule some quality time together. Again, it's all about negotiation and compromise.

I've heard of people working so hard that they pass like ships in the night when their shifts overlap, barely seeing each other. That might be okay for a year or two if it's for an important goal like paying off debt. Pretty much anything is possible if it's just for a little while. But if it's going to take more than 5 years then you'll probably find it's too hard a struggle to keep going. Is a better way possible?

*Ramsey Solutions* has put together a very useful article about how to get on the same page with your spouse and family and how to avoid money fights.[156] Money fights and money problems are a leading cause of divorce. So being able to talk about money with a spouse or as a family is going to help keep your relationships strong.

There is also a right time and place to talk about money. Try not to do it when you're tired, hungry or emotional. If the TV is blaring, kids are running around or tensions running high, it can probably wait until the environment is right. If you've built a regular habit of talking about money over the dinner table as part of asking your family how their day has been, that's great. If you know talking about money or politics over dinner leads to a food fight, maybe avoid it!

Sometimes, I find myself living in tension between all my different goals and commitments. But like many others, I'm learning that it's wise to be present wherever I find myself. I'm trying to set boundaries and divide up my time – an hour of project work here, an hour of family time there. It's impossible to make everyone happy all the time but you can do your best to try to navigate this tension.

I found myself replaying a video by Craig Groeschel on the topic of work-life balance.[157] It pops up on my YouTube feed at opportune moments, so I listen to it again. He talks about how we can get overwhelmed slowly, then all at once. Over time, life – with its increasing stresses and responsibilities – can all build up. We can be busy but find we're not going anywhere. He teaches what we can do to prioritise, manage our time, remove the hurry and create the space to breathe again. These are the same ideas explored by John Mark Comer in *The Ruthless Elimination of Hurry.*[158]

We need to take time to look after ourselves and make sure we get the rest we need. I've also learned that it's okay to neglect my housework for a few days if I'm working towards a particular goal that needs my time and attention. Very rarely I've spent some days focusing on cleaning (usually when I have a house inspection due, but I've done it and it's very therapeutic!). It's impossible to do it all. So you just do the best you can, where you are, with what you've got.

Remember, work-life balance is a myth. It's also good to remember that to be truly successful you need to make sure all areas of your life are flourishing, not to excel in one area at the expense of another. You may have heard of the person at the top of their career whose marriage is breaking down; the workaholic whose health suffers as a consequence of long hours and lack of sleep; the person with great wealth, but lacking in spiritual purpose.

When it comes to work-life balance, we may feel we're working hard to get money to support our family, but sometimes what they often want is just *us* – our time, attention and presence.

## 2. Breaking Generational Chains

> 'Then Jesus told them, "A prophet is honoured everywhere except in his own hometown and among his relatives and his own family."
> ~ MARK 6:4, New International Version (NIV)

You may have heard of '*The Law of Attraction*.' This is a sort of New Thought spiritual belief and philosophy, where practitioners believe that what happens to us in life is attracted or manifested because of what goes on in our subconscious mind.[159] There's an idea that what we think about, we see more of. What we focus on, we seem to attract – both positively and negatively.

Earl Nightingale, one of my favourite motivational speakers, famously said, '*We become what we think about most of the time*.' He also taught, '*Whatever we plant in our subconscious mind and nourish with repetition and emotion will one day become a reality*.' [160] He was inspired by a book called '*As A Man Thinketh*' by James Allen, published in 1903,[161] which in turn takes its title from *Proverbs 23:7*.[162]

I encourage you to seek out these books to read if you're interested in learning more about how to renew your mind. *The Law of Attraction* may seem a little far-fetched and resembles a pseudo-science at times. I'm sceptical too, but I've found that key principles, such as the laws of sowing and reaping, have really helped me on my journey.

Some effects of *The Law of Attraction* may have an alternative scientific explanation called the *'frequency illusion'* or *'Baader–Meinhof phenomenon.'*[463] Ever planned on buying a car and suddenly you see a particular colour or make of car everywhere? Or maybe you see an advert for something and now it's popping up everywhere.

Certainly, whilst writing this book over the last few years, resources and ideas have seemed to find me and flow in my direction. It could just be that we're just more aware of something that was always there. But it does at times feel like there's an inexplicable power at work when your brain is focused on a problem, even if you're not conscious of it, to make connections and gain insights.

Whatever you believe, most of us would probably admit that there's a lot about our minds that we can't fully explain. You'll sometimes hear people referring to our unconscious wiring or mental programming based on our childhood experiences. There are often hidden thought patterns, learned from observing our families' way of doing things, that shape our current beliefs. This includes watching how our families coped with crises, managed money and dealt with pain or stress. Whatever we experience as children just becomes normal for us – this is how we do things – and we tend to carry this into our adult life.

But we often have trauma and psychological wounds inflicted on us, intentionally or unintentionally, even without us being consciously aware of it. There can be pain caused by our parents, families, friends, teachers, caregivers, or strangers. Often it's the people who were meant to protect us but who let us down in some way.

It may not have been outright abuse. Perhaps they were just doing the best they could, based on the resources and knowledge they had at the time. We live in an imperfect, fallen world which is full of broken people. People are hurting and broken, so they can inadvertently pass on their trauma and inherited dysfunction to those around them.

We often carry thoughts, habits, attitudes, stories, excuses, narratives, explanations and behaviours with us into adulthood. Some patterns serve us well, whilst others can prove to be destructive. We can pick up the limitations and prejudices spoken over us and others by our families and communities. This is one explanation for why patterns of addiction, poverty or learnt hopelessness seem to be passed down from generation to generation, along with theories of *'Epigenetics.'*

If we come from a family that has struggled with debt or financial stress, it's possible to pass on that worry to a child. They may not know exactly what's going on, but they may sense the tension. They can develop feelings of guilt and shame surrounding money and may end up avoiding anything to do with budgets or spending plans because of the anxiety it triggers.

People respond to negative thoughts about money in several ways. Someone who has experienced lack may have a tendency to hoard and find security in material possessions. People who've lived through the Great Depression or World War II often find it hard to give up their frugal habits even in times of plenty. Some people find money conversations trigger deep-seated memories or associations of past hurt recalled from early life.

But good things can be passed down too, like healthy habits, resilience, coping strategies and helpful ways of self-soothing, a good work ethic, narratives of success, overcomers and achievers, financial wisdom and hope. You can be the first person in your family to break free from the negative patterns and change the direction of your family for the better. You can become debt-free and teach the next generation how to do the same.

I believe that it's possible to become mindful of our unconscious wiring, transform our thinking and renew our minds.[164] Scientists call this *'Neuroplasticity'* – *'the ability of the brain to grow, change and adapt throughout life.'*[165] Often, the battle is lost and won in the mind.

Negative memories, experiences and criticism have been scientifically shown to stick more easily than positive ones. We call this *'Negativity Bias.'*[466] When it comes to personal finance, our brains are more likely to remember the hardships and hurt, the times we've failed or fallen short. Often we're shaped by the money habits and attitudes of our parents and people around us which are often negative too.

If we recognise that negative thoughts and memories have more sticking power than all the positive, good, hopeful and uplifting ones, then we can reframe how we see them. Just because our negative thoughts are loud doesn't mean that they are true. We can try to identify where our thoughts and behaviours originated from. Then we can do some inner work to change them, especially if they're based on lies and flawed thinking.

But it's not going to be easy. We remember the bad stuff more easily than the good, so it's going to take a lot more positive affirming thoughts and voices to blot out the negative ones. It's the same as a negative throwaway comment overshadowing the dozens of positive compliments people give us, or that one negative review that casts doubt on hundreds of 5-star ratings.

There is a theory that everything we experience is thought. It underpins our habits, behaviour and emotions. While it isn't possible to stop thinking negative thoughts (trying not to think of something makes you think about it more, right?), we get to choose which thoughts we hold on to. We can learn to meditate on positive thoughts instead, which over time will create new thought patterns and make it easier to sustain healthy habits.

We know that the small choices we make daily, given enough time, can lead to incredible life changes. But to keep going, it takes more than willpower, optimism or positive thinking. It's almost like becoming a new person. When we face an inevitable setback we have to get up and go again.

Sometimes it can take years of counselling, self-reflection and self-discovery. Meanwhile, other people get inspired and feel different almost instantly. It's okay to get professional help or join a 12-step recovery programme. Sometimes there's a spiritual element too, like finding a higher power, a relationship with God to help us.

When we change our thoughts and the direction of our own life, this can help us create lasting change that influences our family tree forever. Perhaps your family tree has already been changed by someone who inspired you and taught you financial wisdom. Maybe it was a frugal grandparent or an entrepreneurial uncle. Perhaps you watched your parents become debt free and show you what to do. Or it could have been a mentor or friend who walked alongside you and told you their own story of how they overcame their personal challenges.

If not, then don't worry. You have the opportunity to break the cycle and become a person who has healthy thoughts about money, who is good at finance, and who can become a positive influence to those around you. You can change your family tree and set up future generations to win.

## Who We Hang Around With Matters

*'You cannot hang out with negative people and expect to live a positive life.'*
~ DARREN HARDY (Author of *'The Compound Effect'*)

You'll hear it said that we are the average of the five people we spend the most time with. Our income, political views, thinking and decisions will often be similar.[167] This doesn't mean we should ditch our family and friends as soon as we decide to go after a big goal. But it does mean that sometimes we need to put some distance and boundaries in place.

Perhaps we decide not to share our dreams and goals with negative people which opens us up to criticism and ridicule. Instead, we should be looking out for positive voices, new relationships, inspiring role models, mentors and people who we aspire to be like. They can help us by drowning out the negative voices that hold us back.

Our families can be our biggest cheerleaders. But they can also be the biggest dream killers. Even Jesus in the Bible faced this challenge when he was trying to do miracles in his home town of Nazareth.[168]

His community could only see the carpenter he used to be, not the man he had become, the teacher who was now doing miracles and inspiring huge crowds of people in the towns and cities. Because of their unbelief, Jesus was unable to have much of an impact there.[169]

Nazareth was a small town. It's estimated that around 200-400 people lived there in Jesus' day.[170] It would likely have been made up of extended families where everyone knew everyone. They didn't even refer to him as Jesus, but instead called him *Joseph's son*.[171] So when Jesus started trying to preach to them, they became angry. They questioned his credentials. They even turned violent.

Does it remind you of some towns, villages and city districts today?

Transformation can be messy. There's that chrysalis part where the caterpillar has to turn into a pupa and break down before being reformed into a butterfly. We need to be careful who we listen to during that vulnerable stage in the process of becoming the person we were created to be. They can make us feel unqualified, uninspired and make us doubt ourselves and our ability.

There's a saying that "*You can take the person out of the place, but you can't take the place out of the person.*" It reminds me of the Israelites fleeing from Egypt in the Old Testament of the Bible. They were held captive as slaves for over 400 years.

Eventually, they escaped. But even though they were physically free, they were still slaves in their minds. As a result, a whole generation died in the wilderness. It was their children who finally broke free from the generational chains that held them back and they eventually made it to the Promised Land.[172]

When someone knows where you came from, sometimes they can't see where you're going. They don't want you to leave and change into someone they don't recognise, a new version of us. There are lots of reasons why the personal development we undergo and developing a growth mindset can upset the people who love us.

Their reasons may not be altogether vindictive. Perhaps they believe that they are protecting us by not wanting us to go through pain. Perhaps they are projecting their limitations and fear onto us, not wanting to see us fail. They may still be trapped by generational chains themselves. But as we've said before, sometimes pain and sacrifice are necessary to push forward to a higher level. The risks can be worth the reward.

Just like a toddler learning to walk, our parents pick us up and encourage us to take another step, even if we fall down. Strangely, this is harder for people to accept when we're adults. This is probably one of the reasons why Dave Ramsey calls his financial plan the *'Baby Steps.'*

If we learned to walk as babies by trying and failing, then I'm sure we can achieve our financial goals in the same way. If we fall, then we can get up and go again. As John C. Maxwell put it, we can *'fail forward'* and learn from our mistakes. If we can grow and develop as children, then we can continue to grow and develop as adults.

## Overcoming Victim Mentality With Compassion

*'God, grant me the serenity to accept the things I cannot change,*
*the courage to change the things I can,*
*and the wisdom to know the difference.'*
~ *'Prayer For Serenity,'* attributed to REINHOLD NIEBUHR

There are lots of external factors that we can't change: we can't control other people or tell them how to think; we don't get to choose our biological family and who we're related to; we can't choose the circumstances we were born into or what events happen to us in life. There's no guarantee of a knight in shining armour coming to rescue us. We didn't ask for the patterns of negative thinking that subconsciously hold us back.

***The only thing we can control is ourselves.***

Dave Ramsey deliberately brings to mind the people who say *"the little man can't get ahead"* or *"rich people are crooks and did something immoral to get their money."* Some of this negative thinking or poverty mindset may well come from our society or the community we grew up in, especially if people have been stuck for a long time and have never seen anyone do anything differently.

When we blame others or our circumstances for what happens to us, this is sometimes referred to as a *'Victim Mentality.'* One of the criticisms of *The Law of Attraction* and New Age Teaching is that it focuses too much on self-responsibility and puts the sole onus of overcoming trauma onto us.

Sandra Lee Dennis wrote a blog post that addresses this issue, entitled *'Betrayal: Did You Choose Your Reality?*'[173] She describes people who try to give helpful advice and tell us to stop playing the victim. However, by doing this they insinuate that we are responsible for our negative circumstances because we didn't have the right attitude etc. If we feel pain, they presume it's self-inflicted and somehow we are responsible for our misfortune, which makes the trauma worse. She writes:

> 'When you most need validation and support to get through the worst pain of your life, to be confronted with the well-meaning, but quasi-religious fervor of these insidious half-truths can be deeply demoralizing. This kind of advice feeds guilt and shame, inhibits grieving, encourages grandiosity and can drive you to be alone to shield your vulnerability.'

I believe that the pain and trauma are real, even if they are based on faulty thinking. Healing starts with acceptance and acknowledgement of the reality of psychological discomfort. But that's only the beginning.

It's not healthy to stay in our pain for too long or we can find ourselves getting stuck there which can lead to all sorts of different health and wellbeing problems. We do need to move forward but we need to do it with compassion.

A friend of mine recently introduced me to the concepts of *'ACT: Acceptance and Commitment Therapy'*[174] and *'CFT: Compassion Focussed Therapy.'*[175] These are forms of psychological therapy that help to create self-compassion and compassion towards others.

This includes things we've been talking about in previous chapters, like gratitude and mindfulness practices, visualisations, and finding healthy ways to self-soothe and regulate our emotions. Of course, these approaches have their limitations too, but a compassionate approach to behaviour change will certainly suit some people.[176]

I think it's important to be mindful of these different approaches. Not everyone needs videos yelling at them to hustle, grind and outwork everyone else – though I do listen to these videos each morning as soon as I get up. I find them ironic because they're clearly not marketed at me and it makes me smile.

These short daily motivational videos certainly inspired me as I worked on my side-businesses or on this book. Some of them use more expletives than others, or try to bleep them out. Some are from a Christian perspective or have speeches from celebrities and motivational speakers with dramatic music that make you feel like you're in a Hollywood Movie.

I don't take them too seriously as most of the videos have macho bearded men as thumbnails. We don't need to be elite athletes or business executives to listen to them. They can still be useful to reset your thinking. So why not listen and see what happens.

Remember to take them with a pinch of salt. There are ways to do personal development that don't involve getting up at 4 a.m., doing a workout and taking a cold shower, though some people swear by it.

Instead, my morning routine involves some worship, prayer and spending time in God's Word, usually a devotional from the *YouVersion Bible App*.

I'll sing worship songs in the car and use my commute time to listen to positive messages from church leaders around the world. Many of them talk about positive life change and personal development. Many of them have found their way into this book. There are ways to hear healing positive voices, especially first thing in the morning before we start our day.

I also use meditation videos on YouTube and apps, like *Headspace*,[177] that promote mindfulness and self-compassion, self-love, gratitude and help us discover ways to manage anxiety. I tend to listen to these as I wind down for bed or first thing in the morning.

Often, it's the past failures and hurts of those around us that hold us back, their disappointments and struggles projected onto us. So fostering compassion towards our families, friends and communities is important too. Forgiveness for those who hurt us is a form of compassion that can release us from bitterness and help us heal.

It's possible to overcome these barriers. We can rebuild our self-esteem and increase our sense of self-worth. We can heal our inner wounds and childhood traumas. We can change our thinking, transform and renew our minds. You can even be the first person in your family to get on a budget, become debt-free, start a business or become a millionaire. You can become an inspiring example to others.

## Find Inspiring Examples and Encourage Yourself

Just like Roger Bannister breaking the four-minute mile in 1954, or Sir Edmund Hillary and Tenzing Norgay becoming the first people to climb to the summit of Mount Everest in 1953, it only takes one person to prove that it can be done to inspire others to follow their example.

The reason why I like listening to motivational speeches and podcasts is that you'll come across all sorts of people born into modest circumstances who went on to pursue success:

- **Steve Harvey**'s first marriage fell apart when he wanted to pursue a comedy career, but he did it anyway. He was homeless for 3 years, living in his car. His faith and mindset kept him going.
- **Les Brown** was bullied at school and labelled as stupid, *'the dumb twin.'* He was even ridiculed by one of his teachers for wanting a career in TV. However, another teacher inspired him to go after his dreams and not be held back by the opinions of others. He became a successful motivational speaker but acknowledges that he wished he'd done it sooner.
- **Tony Robbins** experienced childhood poverty, then ran away from home and started working for **Jim Rohn.** He went on to become a motivational speaker himself and built successful companies that now allow him to feed millions of people.
- **Oprah Winfrey**, one of the most famous TV personalities in America, came from a childhood of poverty and abuse. She was even told by a Baltimore TV producer that she was "unfit for television news." She believed in herself and proved him spectacularly wrong.

There are many other inspiring stories of people who were told they were useless or were fired from their jobs, only to go on to achieve great things. I've found an article outlining the surprising ways that celebrities failed before hitting the big time.[178]

Of course, these are just a few interesting examples from popular culture. I'm sure we all have inspiring people in our worlds who have overcome a challenge or obstacles in life.

These are the sorts of people we should be listening to and surrounding ourselves with to help us believe that if they've done it, then we can do it too.

## 3. Changing Your Family Tree

*'Your decisions from today forward will affect not only your life, but also your entire legacy.'*
~ DAVE RAMSEY

As we've said before, many families aren't able to have positive conversations about money and it can become a taboo subject. But you can take steps to change that for your family. Some people may remember seeing their parents arguing about money or a sense of lack. But you can change that for your children.

Your parents may not have taught you how to handle money and finances very well. But it's more than likely that nobody taught them either! They were just doing their best. But thankfully there's plenty of information available now on how to teach children about money.

In childhood, more is caught than taught. We pick up habits and norms from the few people we're close to. The good news is that if we learn to take control of our own finances, then we have an opportunity to pass on these habits to our children. That's why it's possible to change your family tree, not just for one generation, but for multiple generations to come.

### How To Talk To Your Family and Friends About Money

It can be very difficult to talk to your family and friends about money. Once you learn about personal finance for yourself, it's only natural to want to tell the rest of your loved ones about it. But you need to prepare to come against resistance. It's painful to watch other people misbehaving or mismanaging money. But we can't control what others do. We can only change ourselves and hope they ask us how we did it.

In the section on work-life balance, we talked about the challenges of talking to a spouse about money and avoiding money fights in your marriage. Well, talking to older family members about money often proves another challenge. Our parents, grandparents or parent figures have been doing life longer than we have. They often have an established role as leaders of the family. But we can still be leaders and cheerleaders without a title. We all have a platform and opportunity to influence others in positive ways.

The challenge comes from trying to pass on financial wisdom (or any other wisdom for that matter) to people who have known us for a long time, who knew us as babies or children, who knew us before we started our mindful finance journey. Dave Ramsey calls this *'Powdered Butt Syndrome.'* It's hard to take advice from someone you knew in nappies (or diapers). He has had to navigate this personally as he works with his daughter, Rachel Cruze, at *Ramsey Solutions*. They've put together an article with advice on how to talk to your parents about money.[179]

The key is having humility and compassion, maybe even acknowledging how awkward it's going to be to talk about money and estate planning. Sometimes our parents may not want to hear our advice or they may mistrust financial advisers. They've been doing it their way for so long. Why would they want to change now?

In these situations, the main thing you can do is lead by example. You can make the changes in your life and others will see that there is something different about you. This may ignite a spark of curiosity. Your friends and family will start to ask you how you've done it. This may provide the opening and opportunity you've been looking for to start to tell them about the financial foundations and money habits you've been applying. They may then want to have a go too.

### *Money Resources For Children*

While I don't currently have children of my own, I have many friends who do. I also do art workshops for kids and am part of the children's ministry at my local church. So for this section on teaching children about money, I'm mainly pointing you in the direction of resources that other people have written.

From what I've learnt and observed, children grow and develop at an astonishing rate. They are like little sponges, keen to learn everything they can and follow our lead. We may not realise that they are following what we do and say so closely, but they're taking it all in. You'll hear it said that more is caught than taught. This applies to how we manage money. This is why it's important to have early age-appropriate conversations about money, helping them appreciate where money comes from, the value of work and leading by example.

You don't need to tell children how much debt you have or what your net worth is unless they are old enough to understand it. But it's okay to involve them in family decision-making and share your debt-free journey with them. Kids will remember and respect you for being someone who had a goal and made sacrifices to work towards it. They can be part of that journey and celebrate with you along the way.

'Smart Money Smart Kids' is a book about money and parenting, written by Dave Ramsey and his daughter Rachel Cruze, is a good place to start if you want to find ways to teach children good money habits.[180] This book highlights the importance of teaching children where money comes from by rewarding them financially for doing chores or jobs around the house. You can teach the principles of paying yourself first, creating habits like generosity and saving, using *'Give, Save and Spend Jars.'*

Will Rainey, a UK author and speaker, wrote a book about money for his own children called *'Grandpa's Fortune Fables.*[481] This is aimed at children with an entrepreneurial spirit who want bedtime stories that teach them personal finance principles in a fun way. It's also getting incorporated into some UK school curriculums.

These books and other resources can help you to start having positive money conversations with children in an age-appropriate way that sets them up to win. This helps prevent them from turning into the spoilt trust fund babies we're going to look at in the next section.

As you turn your finances around, you can include your children in your family's journey. Remember those visuals, like cutting paper chains or colouring a box that represents another debt paid off? The ways we motivate ourselves will get kids excited too. They can choose what the next milestone celebration will be. Involving them and being open about the process, but protecting them from all the details and stress, will help demonstrate how making sacrifices today will help your family win in the future.

Later on, as they get older, you can guide your children to make wise decisions about their first car (e.g. encouraging them to save by doing a matching scheme, if you can afford it), their choice of university or college (being clear about what financial support you are willing or not willing to give), a part-time job or setting up a business as a teenager (with profits divided into giving, saving and spending categories).

If you've got their interest, you can talk to children about investing and the power of compound interest. You can even set up tax-efficient savings and investment accounts and give them regular updates to show how their money is growing. There are all sorts of practical ways that kids can learn personal finance habits from an early age that will take away some of the fear and dread as adults.

I'm sure you've heard inspiring stories of people describing how their single parent worked multiple jobs and sacrificed to raise them, how their parents emigrated to a new country and set up a business, or kicked an addiction to turn their life around, how previous generations overcame the odds to build a better life for their kids. Well, no pressure. But one day your kids could be saying things like that about you.

So why not be intentional about how you talk to your kids about money? You can turn personal finance into a game. It'll give board games like Monopoly a new meaning! There are all sorts of positive things that they will remember, planting seeds of hope that will set them up to win in later life.

\* \* \*

## 4. Legacy and Generational Wealth

*'I didn't drop the mic. And don't you drop it either. And something of what I said will make it into your book. And something of what you said will make it into the book of the person who read it. And that's how we have progressed for centuries, and eons, and millenniums. Because we passed the mic. We didn't drop it.'*
~ BISHOP T.D. JAKES

### *What is a Legacy?*

There are many ways to leave a legacy. Some people think of *'legacy'* as our impact on the world after we've gone. As I said before, we are all leaders because we all influence people. It may not be easy to think about a time when we're not around anymore and it wouldn't be healthy to focus on this all of the time. But it is important to think about how we live today based on how we want to be remembered, to live with purpose and make decisions with the end in mind.

Legacy can be thought of as a financial gift to people and causes we care about – *material wealth*. But the greatest legacy we leave will be similar to how we defined *spiritual wealth* – memories, stories, wisdom, relationships, purpose – all those intangible things that you can't put a price on.

Many of you reading this will have lost loved ones. It's a sad part of life that we will all face someday. Ultimately the legacy we leave behind is the essence of who we are as a person, how we make people feel, gifts of love, generosity, support, leadership and our presence.

While it may be painful to think of a time when we're not around anymore, I think it's important to reflect on these things now and again to keep us grounded and to give us perspective. While we can leave money and material possessions behind (we certainly can't take them with us), these aren't usually the things we think about when we look back at a life well-lived. What most people want is people and intimacy with others. The money side of our legacy usually comes second.

In summary, leaving a meaningful legacy has to be more than just money. Instead, we can:

- Pass on wisdom and knowledge
- Create memories together
- Share experiences
- Set healthy boundaries
- Pass on stories and family values
- Inspire others through leadership (our influence, character, authenticity, integrity and reputation)
- Share and show generosity to others
- Leave a financial legacy to people or causes we care about

## *What is Generational Wealth?*

This is the idea that material wealth can be passed on to the next generation and future generations.

But there has to be more to this than just money. We need to teach future generations how to manage money well and how to pass that wisdom on. If we don't, having lots of money can become a burden rather than a blessing, just like having a powerful car but not knowing how to drive it properly.

You may not be aware of this statistic: did you know that 70% of families lose their wealth by the second generation and 90% of families lose their wealth by the third generation? There are lots of reasons why this occurs which are explored in an article by David Kleinhandler.[182]

If we get wealth without working hard for it, then it's difficult to keep it. Building wealth from nothing takes resilience. Unfortunately, this resilience often isn't inherited by those who go on to inherit wealth. As David Kleinhandler says, *'Becoming wealthy requires a lot more* than knowledge. It requires hard work, discipline, sacrifice and many other traits that are very hard to teach and pass on.'

This is why so much of this book is focused on the basic building blocks of wealth. Building wealth and keeping wealth involves a similar mindset. The key principles of living with margin and not blowing your wealth on trying to live a rich lifestyle apply to everyone. This is why lottery winners and NBA players often end up in financial difficulty, so-called *'Sudden Wealth Syndrome.'*[183]

I was first writing about generational wealth back in May 2022, just as *The Money Guy Show* team were discussing it in an episode entitled *'The Dark Side of Being a Millionaire.*[184] They look at the statistics from Thomas Stanley and William Danko's book *'The Millionaire Next Door'* which revealed that 80% of the wealthy people studied are first-generation millionaires.[185] They outline 7 secrets of wealthy people, including how to ensure wealth is passed on to future generations.

I've listed these points in a summary on the opposite page. The research behind *'The Millionaire Next Door'* discovered that millionaires were more likely to teach their children how to be self-sufficient rather than giving them parental bailouts.

It may seem cruel, but these sorts of boundaries may be the thing that help our children thrive and succeed, letting them go out on their own and seeing if they sink or swim. It's okay to be there as a safety net if they fail, but it's not healthy to have them living in your basement for years playing computer games.

Proverbs 22:6 in the Bible says, *'Train up a child in the way he should go; even when he is old he will not depart from it.'*[186] While not a guarantee, it's a wise principle that often holds true. Unless parents and grandparents take time to teach future generations about where money comes from and how to manage it, then the family fortune may be all but spent within a few decades.

Future generations who have grown up knowing only a life of luxury can become entitled and idle trust fund babies. They may never get a job or career.

# The Millionaire Next Door

## By Thomas Stanley and William Danko

Here are the 7 common denominators among those who successfully build wealth in 'The Millionaire Next Door':

1. They live well below their means.

2. They allocate their time, energy, and money efficiently, in ways conducive to building wealth. e.g. they live on a budget, they're intentional with their money.

3. They believe that financial independence is more important than displaying high social status. Often, millionaires don't have fancy cars and they keep them for years.

4. Their parents did not provide economic outpatient care. Most millionaires were not financially supported by their parents.

5. Their adult children are economically self-sufficient.

6. They are proficient in targeting market opportunities.

7. They chose the right occupation, the right career for them. Small business owners were 4x more likely to become millionaires. But you could just have a regular job too.

Adapted from wikisummaries.org/the-millionaire-next-door/

When a rich kid is '*spoilt*' they may take money for granted and blow it all on material possessions or living on paradise islands. They don't learn how to delay gratification or the true value of wealth. The same thing can happen to children whose parents have been on benefits for generations and never worked. There can be a sense of entitlement there too.

Many wealthy people choose to keep their net worth a secret from their children until they're old enough to understand what it means. It's important to talk about money in an age-appropriate way with children, making it a normal part of everyday life. That way, they don't reach adulthood with unrealistic expectations and grow to resent you if you decide to give your wealth to charity rather than to them as an inheritance. It encourages them to go and find their own path in life. Then, if you want to, you can bless them with a house or pay off their student loan one day. But those things are not an automatic entitlement.

## 5. Wills and Estate Planning

*'Blessed is he who plants trees under whose shade he will never sit'*
~ INDIAN PROVERB

To be honest with you, I admit to being a procrastinator when it comes to estate planning. My main reasons for not thinking about it in the past were that I was young, I had no direct dependants and I was in debt, so I had no wealth to leave to anyone. To be honest, these are quite good reasons for not needing a will. But it was only a few years later that I was debt-free and starting to build wealth.

Then COVID-19 happened and I found myself working on the front line, dealing with life and death issues daily. Nobody knew what would happen. I looked after many elderly patients who sadly passed away, some of whom I had been looking after only a few days or weeks before and thought I had discharged to safety.

It's hard to describe that time. I heard of staff members getting ill and looked after some of my colleagues. I heard stories of people who knew people, even young and middle-aged people, taken before their time, leaving loved ones and young children behind.

I'm sure history will look back at that surreal time and not quite understand what it was like. We had no vaccines, no treatment options and no real knowledge of how COVID-19 would affect the world. While I already had an interest in end of life care, I didn't know that this would be my reality for a few years.

One of the first things I did was research and buy term life insurance. It felt a bit extreme, to hear about a new disease and then get life insurance straight away, but I wanted to make sure my family had something if I were to die before I'd built up any significant wealth to leave them. It took me a little longer to make a will because I had to do it over the telephone and via email as there were rules about social distancing. Eventually, I got that sorted too.

Throughout paying off debt, I'd listened to *The Ramsey Show* and other podcasts, hearing cases of people who had died young, leaving behind a spouse and children. There was a big difference between the ones who had done their estate planning and the ones who had not.

If someone died with enough life insurance in place, their family was now able to pay off the mortgage, with money left over to invest and produce an income, so they could stay at home with the kids, missing their spouse but feeling cared for in advance and very grateful. If someone died without life insurance, their spouse was now a single parent having to go to work full-time whilst still grieving, feeling the burden of regret.

We never think that it will happen to us.

I already mentioned in our deep dive into life insurance in *Chapter 2: The 4 Walls* that some people are superstitious when it comes to estate planning. But we shouldn't be. If we love our family, then estate planning is a no-brainer. It saves time, effort, heartache and maybe future legal fees. We assume that our family will know our mind but there's no guarantee.

So that's why we need to get it all written down and watertight so nobody is coming out of the woodwork to start a family feud when we're not around to stop it. Similarly, we can't just assume that our wealth or a particular heirloom will go to a spouse or family member unless we write it down. If we have children, we also need to prepare for the situation where either or both parents are no longer around. We may not want to think about these things, but they are all as much part of financial stewardship as building wealth in the first place.

## *How To Talk About Estate Planning While You're Alive*

Dave Ramsey often talks on his radio show about the importance of letting people know your intentions for your children, money or possessions while you're alive. That way, people are under no illusion of what may or may not be coming to them as an inheritance. It may feel a bit morbid, but there are ways to make this just a normal conversation about money. Or if there's going to be an argument about it, it's best to do it when you're around to speak your mind rather than risk a court battle when you're not around.[187]

If there is any doubt over a will it's easy to imagine the consequences. A quick Google search for *'celebrity will dispute'* generates a surprising list of famous people who didn't have a will and who left behind decades of court battles for their surviving relatives. Names include Martin Luther King, Pablo Picasso, Aretha Franklin, Prince, Robin Williams and others.

These stories are often quoted by estate planning websites, hoping to get you to use their services and avoid a similar legacy for your loved ones. For those of you in the UK, some of the reasons why you need a will are outlined in a useful PDF document from Age UK, entitled *'Wills and Estate Planning.*[188]

## Other Things You Can Do

I'm writing this chapter as a reminder for myself because there's something new we have to think about called our *digital legacy*. In the modern world, we leave behind a digital footprint – social media accounts, photographs, intellectual property, computer passwords, online banks and investments, digital creations, not to mention cryptocurrency keys and NFTs (if you have them) – all sorts of digital things that have the potential to outlive us, but which may be difficult for our families to deal with.

We need a plan for our digital assets too. Some social media providers have legacy pages after someone has died that can be maintained by our loved ones. There are services now available to help us plan our digital legacy. You can find out more on the *Digital Legacy Association* website.[189]

Some finance experts encourage people to create a legacy box. This is a way of making sure that your family is cared for if one of you were to die. It's a place to put information about your bank accounts and investments, a copy of your wills or life insurance documents. You can even put written instructions on who to go to in case of an emergency, such as a financial adviser. This could be where you store instructions for your digital legacy too. It could be as simple as a storage box under a coffee table or a particular cupboard.

The last thing to think about is setting up power of attorney for yourself or ageing loved ones. This is so that there is someone appointed to make decisions on your behalf should you lose the legal capacity to do this for yourself.

There are several types of power of attorney. You need different ones for property and finance, health and welfare.[190] There are also documents like *Advance Care Plans* (ACPs) or living wills, as well as *Do Not Attempt Resuscitation* (DNAR) orders and *Emergency Health Care Plans* (EHCPs).

These are all ways that you can plan for your future, anticipating a time when you may no longer be able to communicate your wishes. Like an insurance policy, these things are put in place hoping that they will never be needed. It's all about planning for a future scenario that saves your family from stress and strain later on, especially if they are worried about you, grieving or having to deal with uncertainty and loss.

It's not just about us – we may have ageing parents or grandparents who haven't thought of these issues before. We need to talk about these things as a family and find out, if possible, in advance what our loved ones would like.

If documents, like power of attorney, are not in place, it can be difficult for the next of kin (close family) to access finances. They may have to apply to the *Court of Protection* to be appointed as a deputy.

Doctors have ways of involving a patient's next of kin (close family) in best interest decision-making, but the family have limited legal rights. Without those legal documents, they can only inform the doctor what the patient would have wanted, rather than to make decisions about health directly on their behalf.

If you're interested in learning more about this heavy topic, I highly recommend listening to Pete Matthew's *'Ultimate Guide to Estate Planning.'* When not podcasting or making YouTube videos, Pete works as a financial planner who specialises in trusts and estate planning, so he's dealing with this stuff on a daily basis.[191]

## Reflection Questions:

- *What does 'family' mean to me?*
- *Am I spending enough time investing in my relationships?*
- *What are the main things I spend my time and money on?*
- *What distractions and traps are stealing my time and attention?*
- *What negative habits and narratives have I picked up that I would like to change? Has an unhelpful habit turned into a stronghold or an addiction?*

- *Who can I be a positive influence and mentor to?*
- *Are there children in my world who I can teach about money?*
- *Who might be a mentor to me? How do I make that connection?*
- *What would happen to my family if I wasn't around anymore?*
- *What do I have in place if I can't make decisions for myself?*
- *Have I got my affairs in order? What small thing can I do today?*
- *Have I got older family members who need help?*
- *Do I know where my bank account details are?*
- *Do I need to start a legacy box?*
- *Have I made a will and do I know where it is kept?*
- *Do my family know where my will is kept?*
- *What would I like my legacy to look like?*
- *How do I want to be remembered?*

# Chapter 6: Generosity

| 6 |

## Chapter 6: Generosity

*'You give but little when you give of your possessions.
It is when you give of yourself that you truly give.'*
~ KAHLIL GIBRAN, *'The Prophet'*

There's a reason why this chapter on generosity marks the mid-point of *Mindful Finance.* That's because I believe generosity and giving should be at *the heart* of what we do in life. Generosity can become the *'why'* behind what we do with our finances. It informs how we use our time and energy. It can become our purpose – to help others and be a channel to pass on the blessings that come into our hands, rather than storing them up for ourselves.

You may not feel very generous right now. You may not think you are positioned to be able to help others. Money may feel tight. You may not feel like you have any spare time or resources. You may think, *'I can't be generous because I don't have anything to give. I'll give when I've got more money. I'll volunteer when I have more time.'*

Did you know that it's still possible to become a *generous person?* Even without much money, there are still things we can do. It could be a smile or a hug, a note or a kind word. These are all ways of showing others that we love them, see them and honour them. They don't cost the earth. We can brighten someone else's day.

We can lead by example. Others may take notice and find more ways to be generous too. I can think of many examples of generous people who inspire me. While there are small ways we can be generous, it's also fun to shock people with outrageous, irrational generosity!

In order to become more generous, we can reframe our situation and change the way we see what we already have. Having an abundance or growth mindset helps us see the blessings we may have taken for granted, that we've forgotten to say thank you for. Our *never enough* can become *more than enough.*

Global poverty is a significant issue. Did you know that global wealth inequality is so extreme that if you have approximately $4000 in the bank, then you will be wealthier than half of the world's population?[192] According to *Oxfam*'s annual wealth inequality report, *'The richest 1% own almost half of the world's wealth, while the poorest half of the world own just 0.75%.*[193]

When we look for ways to create more margin in our lives, we can learn to think differently about generosity. More opportunities to be generous will find us.

When it comes to our money, we can change our priorities and choose to put giving right up there at the top. You may not know how it's going to work out yet. It can be a leap of faith. You may not feel like you've got anything to offer. But if you take one small step in the direction of generosity it can change the direction of your whole life. Some of the most powerful stories of giving are from people who didn't think they had much. For them the sacrifice means so much more.

*\*\*\**

Generosity certainly became one of my biggest motivations for paying off debt and getting my finances in order. I'll never forget the feeling of wanting to help the charities I now support so that I could do my bit to help fight global poverty and social injustice. But I had to put those payments on hold.

For a year and a half, I had to say no to helping others financially while I focussed on fixing my own money situation and paying off my own debt. It was a challenge for me as I'd just discovered how much joy I got from giving! It made me want to get out of debt faster. I didn't realise back then that I had a seed of potential within me, a heart for generosity, waiting to grow and bear fruit.

You know the analogy of being on a plane and putting oxygen on yourself before you can help anyone else? Well, the same is true when it comes to helping others, both financially and practically. We need to have a handle on our finances. We need to live a life with margin.

We can't give what we don't have ourselves. Sometimes giving too much leads to burnout and we find ourselves getting into difficulty. Yes, it's okay to step out in faith. But I've experienced times when I've overstretched myself with generosity, trying to run before I could walk. I was trying to invite people into my financial house. But it had no roof, or walls and a crumbling foundation. That's when I realised I needed to get myself sorted first.

*\*\**

We need healing, strength and stability in our own lives before trying to minister to others who are hurting and broken. It's hard to pull someone up when we're stuck in the mire with them. We may be able to help in small ways, but to make a real impact we need to be doing so from a position of strength. This can be the motivation we need to get our financial house in order.

When it comes to showing hospitality to others there are preparations to be made. When we intentionally invite someone over, the least we can do is chuck the laundry into the spare room and pretend we have it all together! (Although my closest friends and family don't seem to mind my mess). Then we can open the doors of hospitality to others, invite them into a welcoming environment and stick the kettle on.

Hospitality and generosity show people that we care about them. But it needs to overflow from the abundance of what we already have. Otherwise, we can feel depleted and exhausted. There's a toxic side of generosity, when we give way beyond our means and end up feeling resentful and used.

Or we can feel pressurised or coerced by an sad story, a sort of emotional blackmail. Sometimes we think we're going to be rewarded for our giving and we're disappointed when the admiration doesn't come. That isn't true generosity. It's neither sustainable nor healthy. We have to give with the right heart and motives.

So we need to make sure that there are *'stores of choice food and oil'*[194] – teabags, milk and sugar, maybe a spare packet of biscuits – so that we can pour a healing cuppa and be a shoulder to cry on. We need to make sure we've got financial margin, time in our diary, energy in our tank and emotional reserves. Trying to be outrageously generous in our own strength can lead us to financial and emotional bankruptcy. We need to be *spirit-filled* so that we can pour ourselves out for others, then be filled back up again, ready to give again.

We all have different ways to replenish our energy, recharge our batteries, to come back to a central place of peace. The tension is released, like the recoil of a stretched elastic band. Then there will be abundance and the oil will keep on flowing.

I hope that your mindful finance journey brings you to a place where you find that you have *more than enough*. In this way, you can find contentment and help someone else as well, even if you don't feel you have much right now.

What nobody seems to tell you is that you can get better with practice! Just like when I was a kid in PE and thought I was terrible at running, I would never have believed I would run a 10K one day, but I did – *back in 2010!* It took training and practice.

It turns out generosity works in the same way.

It may feel overwhelming to imagine giving away your hard-earned cash. But when you start small, when you give just a little, then you may well find it easier to give again next time. We can all practice generosity and get better at giving. You may find that over time generosity can even change you from the inside out. You may look back and find you barely recognise yourself.

In this chapter, we're going to look at a few key topics, including:

> 1. What are generosity and philanthropy?
> 2. How to live open-handedly
> 3. What is percentage giving and tithing?
> 4. How to grow a heart of generosity
> 5. What are the barriers to generosity?
> 6. Developing wisdom and discernment
> 7. Giving and abundance mindset
> 8. Leaving a legacy

Remember, there are only three things you can do with money – *give, save* and *spend* – preferably in that order. I hope this chapter helps you to understand why so many people choose to make generosity a priority and how this can change your life for the better.

## 1. What are Generosity and Philanthropy?

*'Help others without any reason
and give without the expectation of receiving anything in return.'*
~ ROY T. BENNETT

***Generosity*** can be thought of as giving to help people in need. This can go beyond financial and physical needs to include things like gifts of time and attention, hospitality, words of affirmation, our presence and company, and acts of service or kindness. It's a way of showing people that we love and care for them, even if they are strangers to us. It shows that we're willing to put their needs before our own.

**Philanthropy** is a word that means *'love of humanity'* in Greek. Some people use separate definitions for **philanthropy, volunteering** and **charity work**. But ultimately, these are all ways of promoting the welfare of others and supporting good causes. They are ways to have a positive impact on the world and they are all forms of generosity.

Generosity is a way that we can make a lasting impact on the world and leave behind a *legacy*. This could be through our daily interactions, acts of kindness, passing on wealth and wisdom, the things we looked at in the last chapter on generational wealth.

It could be servant-hearted leadership, influencing and inspiring others. It could be leaving money for a charity in your will. Creating a legacy is something we can work on every day, not just when we're gone.

There are things we can do on an individual level or by joining others. In the UK, we're lucky to live in a democracy with freedom of speech and the right to peaceful protest. We can fight for social justice and environmental issues through petitions to the government, raising awareness of important causes, sharing posts on social media, fundraising and writing letters to our MPs.

We can also open our homes and show hospitality to others. We can meet up with a friend or small group to catch up and encourage each other. There are all sorts of things we can do to help our neighbours, local community and further afield to make the world a better place.

As Kalil Gibran reminds us, generosity isn't just about money or possessions. When we give of our time, talents and resources we're actually giving of *ourselves*. It may be volunteering for an organisation or befriending someone lonely, fundraising for charity, campaigning for a good cause, cleaning someone's house, babysitting, childminding, pet-sitting, helping someone move or decorate a new home.

I'm sure you can think of all sorts of ways to be generous. Even if you're at the early stages of your mindful finance journey and just starting to get your financial house in order, there are still ways you can make generosity a habit without needing to spend lots of money.

## 2. How To Live Open-Handedly

*'Good will come to those who are generous and lend freely,*
*who conduct their affairs with justice.'*
~ PSALMS 112: 5, New International Version (NIV)

I like Pastor Craig Groeschel's definition of generosity outlined in a talk called *'When You Stop Holding Back.'*[195] It's not just about *giving*. It's about becoming a **generous person.** He talks about making irrational generosity an **intentional** act. It's about **pre-deciding** to be generous and **planning** to give in advance.

Instead of a spontaneous act where we feel emotionally prompted to give which can leave us scrambling for spare change, it's creating the margin in our budget to help others. If we want to do spontaneous giving, it's planning ahead of time by making sure we have funds available.

It's hard to be generous without margin. When we made our spending plan back in *Chapter 1: Foundations,* we made a separate 'giving' category. When we make generosity a priority, we'll find ourselves becoming a *generous person* – someone who plans their giving in advance.

You can even become a generously family and involve those around you in the giving process, for example, choosing a charity to donate to each Christmas. Soon you'll start looking for new ways to help people and strategies to make an even bigger impact.

Being a generous person means **learning to live with** *open hands*. I like the image of someone kneeling down, holding seeds in both hands. There are only two ways to hold them – with closed hands or open hands. Someone with closed hands won't drop a single seed, nor will they be able to receive more.

But someone who lives open-handedly opens themselves up to the risk that some of their seeds will fall onto the ground or become food for birds. But having open hands also opens you up to the possibility of receiving more yourself.

This is a beautiful example of how generosity works. By giving to someone in need we take a risk and make ourselves vulnerable as we have no control over how our generosity seeds will be used once they leave our hands. Generosity blesses both the gift-giver and the gift-receiver. The Bible says, *'It is more blessed to give than to receive.'*[196]

Some people may take advantage of our giving, but it also opens up to the possibility of more blessings ourselves. You'll know from the introduction that I don't believe in a prosperity mindset, where we give to receive.

But if we develop an **abundance mindset**, we have the opportunity to plant a seed of generosity and watch what we sow bear fruit in due season.

We are blessed in order to be a blessing to others. This blesses both us and others, creating a ripple effect, an abundance cycle, as generosity inspires generosity. True generosity is good for your heart and has an impact beyond what you can initially see.

Generosity shouldn't feel like an obligation. It's different to paying your taxes which is our duty as citizens of a country. It's a choice and we can choose to **give with gladness**. It's something we *get* to do. It's a *privilege* to be able to help others.

Generosity is the antidote against becoming ensnared by material wealth. There's something very powerful about giving and the effect it has on us. It increases the gratitude and contentment we feel towards what we already have. It makes us realise that there are often people worse off than us who we can help. Giving becomes a habit and a natural rhythm of life. It helps us hold onto money and possessions less tightly.

Sometimes we can feel too overwhelmed to be generous. When we're in the middle of a storm or emergency, when time and money are in short supply, when our margin feels squeezed, when the cost of living is going up and the economy is struggling, giving can feel like less of a priority.

But that's when generosity can also be the most impactful. When we give just a little when we don't have much it means so much more than giving when we have a lot. It reveals a heart of generosity and love for others, giving especially when it hurts, an act of faith and trust.[197]

Giving just a little when you don't have much is extremely powerful. Even a small act of generosity can go a long way to getting you started on your path to living an open-handed life. A seed can be tiny but can grow into an impressive tree one day.

Through **micro-philanthropy** or **micro-donations**, cumulatively we can have a massive impact. Together our little droplets can form an ocean of generosity and change the world. So don't ever think that your little act of generosity is unimportant.

Just like when we established our 4 walls, in order to get started with margin creation you may want to look at your budget again. You can ask yourself if the things you buy are really necessary.

Are there things you can change or sacrifice for a season? Are there TV subscription services that you rarely use, are you shopping for luxury brands or supermarket own brands? What is a *want* and what is a *need*?

Do you need the expensive coffee every morning or a store-bought lunch? Can you drink coffee at home for a fraction of the price or make a packed lunch to take to work? Are there swaps or substitute items that you can still enjoy that don't cost as much? Just something to think about.

Giving is going to look very different to each of us at different ages, life stages and wages. I still think that generosity is something that everyone should try. As long as the heart behind it is right. If you can't give right now, that's okay too. Just as I did, you can allow the desire to be generous *one day* motivate you in the present to change the direction of your life.

## 3. What Is Percentage Giving and Tithing?

*"'Bring the whole tithe into the storehouse, that there may be food in my house. Test me in this," says the Lord Almighty, "and see if I will not throw open the floodgates of heaven and pour out so much blessing that there will not be room enough to store it."*

*~ MALACHI 3:10, The Bible: New International Version (NIV)*

### *My Tithing Journey*

You may remember that I first talked about *'tithing'* and *'percentage giving'* in *Chapter 1: Foundations* when we looked at *models of giving, saving and spending*. In this chapter, I want to focus in on the *'giving'* element of these models. There's a reason why people recommend to give before they do anything else.

Because this is my personal story and faith is a the heart of it, I hope you won't mind us discussing the concept of *'tithing'* in more detail. I know you probably still have questions about it. It took me a while to get my head around it too. It may seem old fashioned or weird at first, but I think we've already established that sometimes weird is better.

Percentage giving and tithing is a principle that helped me to prioritise giving whilst also getting debt-free. Generosity became one of my main motivations for taking control of my finances, along with wanting to avoid the stress that comes from not knowing where my next paycheque is coming from.

The dream of being able to live a generous life helped me to look beyond the everyday disciplines, habits and sacrifices that I was making in the here and now towards a better future ahead.

Essentially, tithing means *'one-tenth'* of something (in Hebrew). Deciding to tithe sets a pattern and a rhythm for your life. Pre-deciding to be generous with a percentage of what we make may feel overwhelming, but we quickly adapt to our new lifestyle. It may take a few months and you don't need to start at 10%. Many people choose to start gradually and work their way up.

There's also nothing set in stone about whether to tithe whilst paying off debt, but you can if you want to. After all, it's meant to be *10% of your increase* and if you're in debt, your net worth is going backwards.

I wanted to try tithing since I'd heard so much about it. I wanted to prove to myself that I could do it. I knew that giving whilst getting debt-free would slow the process down a little, but I also knew it would help me manage the other 90% better for the long-term, knowing I'd got my priorities in the right order.

I usually do my monthly budget on payday, which for me is around the 28th day of the month. To calculate 10% of my income, I need to know what my income is. This is a game-changer in itself! I still don't know how I coped with no budget and no idea of what my monthly income was. As I said, we just adapt our lifestyle to whatever our bank balance says.

Once you get into the generosity habit, it's possible to give above and beyond the tithe to causes you care about. While 10% is a great generosity target to aim for, it's certainly not the limit. Some people decide to increase their generosity by 1% per year as their career develops. Others set up a giving budget each month or save up to do their giving at Christmas. It really is up to you.

Some people have a spiritual gift of generosity that they choose to nurture. I've heard several entrepreneurs and motivational speakers say that they recommend tithing and generosity because it has been life-changing for them and how they conduct their business. Generosity can be a way to build wealth, which seems counter-intuitive, but studies have shown that wealthy people often have a generous spirit.[198]

Percentage giving could mean giving to a charity, an organisation, or a cause you care about. For me, *tithing* means giving 10% to my local church and *offerings* are anything above that. I also give to charities I care about, as well as gifts to friends and family. Spontaneous giving is something I'd like to do more of in future, but I admit it makes me a little uncomfortable too (we'll explore this tension later on).

When I started my first budget in January 2018, I decided to practice *artificial scarcity* and set a budget well below my means. I made *the tithe* the very first line item of that budget. I was practising how to give 10% and live off the other 90%.

The extra money I had coming in each month varied. That was my *margin*. I deliberately didn't include it in my budget and instead threw it at my debt. So when I started out it wasn't a *whole tithe*, in the traditional sense. But it was 10% of my (artificial) regular income, building my giving habit and getting me ready for when I would be debt free with an income increase.

Now I'm debt-free, I pay the tithe of 10% off my gross income as soon as the month begins. Then I still pay myself an artificially low income. I now have regular charitable giving built into my monthly budget and I'll occasionally do lump sum donations on top of that if my financial situation allows.

Any additional money each month not included in the tithe or my budget becomes my *margin*. I'll put this towards my different financial goals, such as saving for a house deposit, replenishing my emergency fund or investing for retirement.

I'm so glad I decided to make giving a priority. It made me get organised. It made me pay attention. I found that this giving habit also helped me develop the discipline to save regularly. Giving increased my gratitude for the 90% that I was choosing to live off. I was able to find money to throw at my debt. And yes, it was a leap of faith and quite scary at the time, but very exciting and empowering too.

Your generosity journey may look different to mine. That's absolutely okay. I hope that one day you experience the same joy and freedom that I found through making generosity a natural part of my financial routine. Remember, it's okay to start small and build up. It doesn't matter what other people are doing. This is *your* mindful finance journey.

## *What Do Religious People Say About Tithing?*

Tithing isn't a universally accepted Christian principle. Nor is it something practised by many modern-day Jewish people. I've been to churches that never spoke about it and I've met people who feel it is something resigned to history. That's probably why I never paid much attention to it until later in life.

I can only tell you how much it has helped me on my mindful finance journey and I recommend everyone to at least try it. It feels so good to be able to sow into a cause you care about and build something bigger than yourself. Percentage giving helped me develop self-discipline, gratitude and awareness. It's changed the way I think and act. It's why I'm writing this book right now.

You'll see tithing mentioned in the Old Testament of the Bible. It was an instruction Moses gave to the Israelites for when they settled in the Promised Land, an act of worship to help support the priesthood and the temple.[199]

In fact, the Old Testament process was quite complicated with multiple tithes depending on the yearly farming cycles, so it wasn't exactly 10% at all. Pastor Peter Haas has written a blog about this if you're interested in learning more.[200] The Jewish tithing tradition seems to have ended with the destruction of the Temple in Jerusalem around 70 AD/CE.[201]

Some people argue that the concept of a 10% tithe of financial increase isn't mentioned in the New Testament of the Bible. However, there is a reference to the tithe of the religious leaders on their mint and herbs.

Jesus makes an example of the Pharisees for being so careful with their finances, but accuses them of neglecting other aspects of religious law – such as justice, mercy and faith.[202] We've got to be careful not to get swept up by ritualistic giving. It's more important to develop a generous heart.

The Bible goes on to give examples where the early churches were exceptionally generous. Generosity wasn't limited to a particular percentage and people would sometime sell all their possessions to share with those in need.[203]

So when you feel challenged to give 10% of your income, think about the early Christians who sometimes sold everything they had to give to the poor. We're not being asked to do that, but I wonder if it's something we would even be able to comprehend in this day and age.

While editing my book, I came across an interesting podcast by *The Bible Project* which helps put the Bible into historical context.[204] Tim Mackie and Jon Collins help explain how to make sense of these principles for us in the modern era. It's definitely worth a listen if you have any questions on what the Bible has to say about money and generosity.

They explore this topic from the point of view of two Harvard Business School graduates who are trying to answer the question, *'Should we tithe?'* Their conclusions are surprising. Many Christians they surveyed give substantially more than 10%. Ultimately, they discover that it's good to lead a generous life. But that will mean different things to each of us.

## 4. How To Grow A Heart Of Generosity

> *'Remember this: Whoever sows sparingly will also reap sparingly, and whoever sows generously will also reap generously. Each of you should give what you have decided in your heart to give, not reluctantly or under compulsion, for God loves a cheerful giver.'*
> ~ 2 CORINTHIANS 9:6-7, New International Version

Our **money** and our **heart** are closely connected. Acts of generosity change us from the inside out. Giving is good for you! When we give, it stretches us and exercises our ***giving muscle***, making it easier to give next time. It always feels like a lot when we're giving for the first time. It can feel tense and scary. We wonder how we'll ever do it. But often we find ourselves looking back at the progress we've made, wondering how we got there.

I remember when £10 felt like a lot. Then £100 felt like a lot. One day I was challenged to step up and give £3000. It felt like a lot too! Then I got the chance to do it again and I got excited. Each step of faith stretches you. As the amounts get bigger, they don't feel quite so scary. I look back now and it blows my mind how generosity has changed my heart. This can happen on your generosity journey too.

Giving helps us gain perspective by revealing people who are in need. We get the opportunity to make a difference. It's the antidote to selfishness. Generosity helps you develop a sense of gratitude for what you've already got. It helps your heart stay soft and open, not hard and cynical. When you get a taste for giving, you may find you *want to do it more* because of the joy it brings to you and others!

We need to make sure we're giving with the right heart and attitude. You may feel a million miles away from generosity at the moment. That's okay. It's another milestone on the journey that you're moving towards. I hope that there will be a time and place for generosity somewhere in your future.

The Bible is very clear that we should not be under any compulsion or coercion to give. We shouldn't feel emotionally manipulated. It's okay to ignore those emotive adverts designed to pull at the heartstrings. Giving should be a joyful act of free will. It should be a choice, not an obligation. If you're in a place of financial strain and giving feels like torture, then it's not the right time to give yet.

But you shouldn't let fear of giving rob you of the opportunity to step out in faith either. You'll have to search your own heart. In fact, it's healthy to be aware of the motive for your actions and put appropriate boundaries in place. You need to decide what the right amount is for you, the right time, and the right cause. There shouldn't be any pressure. But there may just be a blessing for you and someone else on the other side of your decision to say, *"Yes!"*

Keep building your strong foundation. Give a little along the way when you can. You can start small, go slow and make it a habit. When your financial house is built there will be opportunities to open the doors of hospitality and share with others. When you keep a look out for opportunities to bless someone, you may well find that you become the delivery guy. You may be the answer to someone else's problem or prayer. When we give, we're not necessarily losing something. We're letting go to make room for something far greater.

### Your Spending Reveals Your Heart

*'Wherever your treasure is, there the desires of your heart will also be'*
~ MATTHEW 6:21, New Living Translation

It's often said that you only need to look at your bank account or spending habits to see what your priorities are. We spend our money on things that we think are important. We give to causes that we care about. We give to the people we love. We explored in *Chapter 4: Possessions and Debt* how our spending is driven by psychology. Well, our giving is also an outworking of our heart, an indication of our thoughts, priorities and values.

But did you know that this principle works in reverse too? Where we put our money often pulls our attention in that direction. When we buy a lottery ticket, we suddenly become very interested in what the lottery numbers will be that week. If you make a bet on a sports event, suddenly you're interested in knowing who the winner is.

I experienced this refocusing of my attention when I started to invest. Before I opened up a self-invested pension I was learning the basics of investing but I'd never cared for investment news. As soon as I started to invest real money, I found myself learning about the stock market, watching the ups and downs of stock charts, finding the podcasts, signing up for newsletters and watching YouTube videos about economics and world events. It's just human nature.

*Where our heart goes, our money flows. And where our money flows our heart goes.* Does that make sense? That's why sometimes we just have to get started and the rest will follow.

In the same way, when we give money to something, we often start to care about it more. We want to know what's being done with our money. We may want to learn more about a charity and what projects they're working on. We buy the merchandise and carry the tote bag, join the community, fundraise, raise awareness and become a champion for that cause.

I found this when I started giving to my church. At first I was just a congregation member. But when I started to tithe, suddenly I was all in. I wanted to know where my money was going and who I was helping. I got to know more people, signed up to do more volunteering and I even occasionally wear the merchandise! I wanted to share my testimony and mindful finance journey. You're reading it now! Where our money goes shows where our priorities are and it also becomes our priority.

## 5. Barriers To Generosity

*'Generosity is giving more than you can,*
*and pride is taking less than you need'*
*~ KAHLIL GIBRAN*

Being a *'good steward'* means managing our finances responsibly, being intentional with our giving, saving and spending. It's using our money in a way that has a positive impact on the world. When money leaves our hands we don't get to control what happens to it. But if we're being wise, we have a responsibility to research and do our due diligence on the people and organisations we're choosing to give our money to.

I don't think it's just me who feels a tension when it comes to giving and generosity: *'Do I give now or invest it so that I can give more later?* Who should I give to and what will they do with my money? Why is one cause more worthy than another? Can I even afford to help right now? Will my little bit of giving make a difference anyway? Should I wait until I can give more?'

Sometimes we want to give freely and spontaneously, but we come across real-world barriers. We want to ensure our giving helps people, rather than hurting or enabling them. We want to know our money won't be wasted. We want our giving to have an impact. So what happens when we're walking down the street and someone starts asking us for money? What do we do then?

These are questions I battle with often. There may not be just one correct answer. But I can tell you what I learned when I grappled with this question a few years ago. I still live in the tension and I change my mind often. These days, I take it case by case.

If a stranger in the street asks me for money, my thoughts often do a sort of tug-of-war with my heart: 'Am I safe? What am I able to give? What coins or notes do I have on me? If I give money to this stranger what will they do with the money? Will I be aiding them in making poor life choices, such as buying drugs or alcohol? Or will my money make the difference between them finding a safe place to sleep or spending the night in a doorway with an empty stomach? Are they being exploited? Could they be a victim of human trafficking and modern day slavery? Are they exploiting me? Will they be back on the street tomorrow? How can I solve the problem of homelessness when it's so much bigger than this one decision?'

The reality is I have to make a judgment call. Some days if I have time I'll stop and chat with them. But sometimes I'm on my way somewhere in a rush so I just have to say, "Sorry, I don't have any change."

Ultimately, when someone is asking for money on the street, their situation could just as easily have happened to any one of us. We don't get to choose the circumstances we're born into and the things that happen to us. We're here but for the grace of God.

When I can, I try to listen to their story and remind myself that this is a person whose experiences may be very different to mine but they are still seen. I try to at least make eye contact.

They may be homeless. They may be a professional beggar or perhaps they're being controlled by someone. A lifestyle of dependency may be all they've known. We never know for sure if the story someone tells us is real. But if we're making judgments, we need to check ourselves and not jump to conclusions or see only stereotypes.

I'm sure you've asked yourself similar questions. Back in 2017, I was walking past homeless people most days in Liverpool and Manchester. I felt compelled to find out what I could do as I didn't feel comfortable giving them money. Though sometimes I did.

That's why I decided to support a charity called *Shelter*. *Shelter* advocates for people in uncertain housing situations and lobbies for change to the housing laws to prevent people from becoming homeless in the first place.[205]

Anyone can become homeless, for example, through an unexpected life event, health problem, addiction or exploitation, relationship breakdown or job loss, not being able to afford their rent or through discrimination.[206] *Shelter* helps remove the stigma and gives practical help. Giving a regular donation to *Shelter* wasn't the whole answer, but it made me feel like I was doing something.

I'm still looking for ways to do more, including what local projects are happening near me that I can support. Some charities and organisations give practical help like food, clothing or provide places to sleep. There are food banks, pantries and soup kitchens. There isn't an easy answer to solving the problem of homelessness and poverty. So I'm going to try and do what I can.

So when a stranger in the street asks me for money I still often have to say, *"Sorry, no."* There have been times when I've given financially to strangers if the opportunity arose. Some of those times I was left with feelings of regret, wondering if I'd done the right thing or been taken advantage of. I guess I'll never know for sure if my giving helped or harmed them. That's what led me to do more research.

I recently met a young man near where I live who had fallen on hard times. He told me he was transitioning between homeless shelters. He'd been sent to the wrong place and his belongings were somewhere else, including his medication. I could tell he was stressed and frustrated. I was able to lend him my phone to make the calls he needed to make. After hearing his story, I paid for a taxi to get him to where he needed to be.

It was something small, but I knew where the money was going and that it would directly help him. I could tell he appreciated it. He didn't want my money, which is exactly why it made sense to give him this gift. His hug of gratitude meant a lot. Sometimes small acts of kindness help people feel seen and known. Even when the problem is huge at society level, there may be something we can do to help just one person.

## *How Can We Tackle Poverty?*

There are lots of ways to tackle poverty. There are charities and non-profit organisations set up to help people living in poverty across the world. Some of them are in desperate need of funding.

Beyond this, there are ways we can help including volunteering, education, donations, activism and petitions, and spreading the word through social media.[207] Sometimes poverty feels so big that we'll never be able to tackle it alone. But there are lots of things we can do collectively to make a difference.

Poverty is one of the main reasons why people around the world are vulnerable and in need of help. As we talked about in the introduction, poverty can lead to worse health outcomes, crime, human trafficking, exploitation and discrimination, as well as a loss of representation. Climate issues often disproportionately affect the poorest in society. Yet it isn't until the impact is felt by the wealthy that governments are moved to act.

Some of the most beautiful and biologically diverse areas in the world - our rainforests, coral reefs and other threatened ecosystems - are located in some of the poorest countries in the world. The voice of the poor often goes unheard, leaving them feeling disenfranchised and marginalised.

I wonder how history will judge us. Will people look back at us, the way we do at the Victorians and ask *'why didn't they do more to help people and end suffering?'* What is the modern equivalent of Ebenezer Scrooge in Dickens' *A Christmas Carol* asking, "Are their no prisons [...] and the Union workhouses?"

A motivation for writing this book was to help people find ways to become good financial stewards. This may include lifting themselves out of poverty and avoiding debt traps. I hope this book inspires you to do something to help fight poverty as well. You can inspire others. Together we can make a difference.

It's up to each of us individually to decide how to help vulnerable people in need. My thoughts on this change frequently and I'm not convinced I've got the right answer yet. I'm on a journey to learn more about social justice and discover what part I can play.

We all have local services, networks, charities, church groups and not-for-profit organisations that we can go looking for. Some of them will need our help in these tough economic times. I recently discovered '*Together Liverpool: Network of Kindness*,' a Christian organisation connecting individuals and organisations across Liverpool that helps provide local food banks and pantries, debt advice, companionship and modern day slavery initiatives.[208]

I'm part of the *Hope For Justice Liverpool & Wirral Abolition Group* which raises awareness of modern day slavery and human trafficking, an issue that disproportionately affects people in poverty.[209] We take part in the Annual *A21 Walk For Freedom* each October, do *Spot The Signs* training and organise regular fundraising events. We're looking to support other anti-slavery organisations and connect with like-minded people.

I find myself drawn to charities that focus on issues, such as tackling global poverty, with on the ground practical help and support at a community level. I've also become very interested in nature conservation, both in the UK and around the world. There will be something that resonates with you too.

I'm sure there will be charities that are close to your heart for different reasons. Perhaps it's scientific research into a particular health condition, providing funding for hospices, tackling mental health issues, helping vulnerable or disenfranchised people such as refugees and asylum seekers, training guide dogs or funding animal rescue centres. The list of people and causes in need of help is endless. Some people end up starting an organisation of their own.

There will be lots of ways we can use our time, skills and money to help poor and marginalised people. It could be as simple as befriending someone who is isolated and help build community. I see it as paying it forward as one day it could be us.

This internal struggle we feel as potential donors, of wanting to know how our money will be used before we give it away, is just one of many barriers that explain why people don't give.

I found an article from *Barclays Bank* from 2019 looking at why **high-net-worth individuals** *(HNWI)* don't give to charity.[210] The main findings from their survey are summarised here:

- **75%** believe philanthropy is the responsibility of people wealthier than themselves
- **54%** believe that it's the responsibility of the government to support charities
- **42%** believe that making extra donations wouldn't be enough to have a significant impact
- **23%** cite a lack of knowledge, experience and contact with the charity sector as a hurdle to overcome when considering large donations.

If these barriers are present for high-net-worth individuals, then surely we must feel them too! In reality, it is the combined efforts of many people working together that can make a big impact. It's the £1, $5 and $10 donations that can build up like drops of water to create an ocean.

If high-net-worth individuals are waiting for someone more wealthy to do something, then what about the rest of us? Do you believe that many small efforts can join together to make an impact? There are always things we can do to help and we don't need a high net worth to do it.

If we're waiting for the government, then we may be waiting a long time. There also seems to be a mistrust of the charity sector in general. However, charities are under a lot of pressure as they have to do their advertising and marketing, cover their staff overheads and yet be seen to be giving as much money as possible to the cause they are set up to serve. It's hard for them to grow and invest in themselves the way most businesses can, yet we still expect charities to grow and flourish.

Have you thought about what your barriers to generosity are?

I found an article that outlines some of the reasons why people don't give to charity.[211] The main reasons are summarised below:

1. **43%** don't feel they have the financial resources
2. **20%** volunteer instead of making donations
3. **17%** donate goods and/or services instead of making a donation
4. **12%** don't trust organizations to spend their money well
5. **6%** prefer to spend their money on their family and friends
6. **2%** don't believe that organizations make a positive difference

Do you share any of these opinions? Do you feel like you don't have enough to give? Do you trust individuals, charities or organisations to put your money to good use?

## How To Help Without Causing Harm

Of course, poverty and it's impact is multi-factorial and complex, especially on a global scale. *The People's Charter For Health* states: *'Inequality, poverty, exploitation, violence and injustice are at the root of ill-health and the deaths of poor and marginalised people.*[212]

There is certainly tension, wanting to help others without enabling them to misbehave or make unwise choices. We want to encourage people without making them dependent on us for ongoing help and support.

Sometimes we need to ask *'is the person we're trying to help willing to help themselves?'* If we want people to help themselves out of poverty, sometimes there are things people need to do, painful decisions to make and lessons to learn. We can equip them with the resources and knowledge to do so.

I'm not just talking about global poverty. This also applies to our broke friends or family members, people who may come to us asking for money, but we can see them making unwise decisions!

There is a theory that people living in poverty have certain habits that keep them stuck and wealthy people have habits that help them become wealthy. This could be the way they spend money or their mindset. It explains why the US government stimulus cheques were quickly spent during the COVID-19 pandemic. Poor people spend money; wealthy people invest it.

Jim Rohn tells a story that if all the money in the world was redistributed evenly, over time money would flow from the poor into the hands of the wealthy because of their habits. If everyone were to be given money indiscriminately without any personal financial education, the money would most likely trickle back to the people with wealthy people habits.

On the opposite page, I've summarised what finance experts call **Poor People Habits** and **Wealthy People Habits.** This doesn't mean we should blame people for being poor. But it can be a reminder to us that we need to become good stewards to avoid the poverty trap ourselves.

# Habits of wealthy people

## Poor People Habits:

- Spend more than they make (live without margin), are consumers
- Take out debt to buy depreciating assets e.g. car loans (bad debt)
- Use their time on things that make themselves feel better but don't grow themselves (e.g. trashy TV, entertainment)
- Are in debt or living paycheque to paycheque
- Care what other people think e.g. about how they look, status
- Victim or poverty mindset (never having enough)
- May not have the margin to give or mindset of generosity
- Go to bed late/get up late, poor morning routine, go to work late
- Drifting rather than moving towards a goal
- Want to feel good now rather than sacrificing for future gain

## Wealthy People Habits:

- Live on less than they make (create margin) and create things
- Take out (good) debt to buy appreciating assets e.g. business loans
- Use their time on things that make themselves feel better and grow themselves (e.g. taking care of their bodies, personal development, classes and tutorials, growing skills, investing in themselves)
- Are investors (compound interest works to grow their wealth)
- Often look surprisingly ordinary, living within their means
- Growth and abundance mindset
- Get up early and have good morning routine, get to work on time
- Set goals and work towards a plan
- Have discipline to delay gratification

When we put good habits in place and do what wealthy people do, then we're more likely to become wealthy too. On the whole, wealthy people create and add value, while poor people consume and use up all they have. Wealthy people have a life with margin; poor people don't.

When it comes to generosity, we have a responsibility to give wisely and control what's in our power to control. If we give without due diligence and proper boundaries, this may open us up to being scammed, used or taken advantage of.

Where do we draw the line between helping and enabling? When we give, are we still expecting to get something in return? Whether it's a family member facing financial hardship or a stranger we've never met before whose motives we can't be sure of, should we keep giving and pouring ourselves out? Should we give even when we can't guarantee the outcome?

Here's a different scenario. What if a family member or friend asks to borrow money from us? Should we give them money?

Here's what *Ramsey Solutions* recommends: **Never lend to a family member and never co-sign on a loan**. It fundamentally changes your relationship dynamic and can cause all sorts of emotional strain. It's better to give a gift, without expecting the money to be returned, than to lend and entrap that person with a debt they can't repay.[213]

Ask yourself what price are you willing to put on your relationship? That's why it's better to give and never lend expecting a return.

If we're worried that our money may enable someone to continue to make poor choices, to perpetuate the bad habits that got them into trouble in the first place, then perhaps we can give in different ways, including non-monetary gifts, such as our time and attention, advice, love, encouragement and practical help. We can give food, clothing and support.

It was in August 2021 when I had a day off work and decided to do some research. I wanted to try to answer some of these questions that were making me feel so uncomfortable. I looked up resources on the topic of *Christian Stewardship* to see what advice there is on helping the poor. I wanted to know if my generosity was helping or enabling harmful behaviour. The answer is probably somewhere in between and I had to make peace with that. **I concluded that it's still better to give anyway.**

My biggest generosity barrier was addressed by Pastor John Lindell in a YouTube message called *'A Heart For The Poor.'* It was like he was calling me out. He said:

*"Ours is not to sit and render a judgement on how they got there, why they're there and how they can get out of there. Ours is to look through eyes of compassion because that's the heart of God. And to recognise that when we honour the poor, this is the Christian ethic, when we do it for them it's like we're doing it for Him. It's like we're honouring God. God has a heart for the poor."*[214]

I encourage you to listen to this message in full and allow yourself to be challenged by it, just as I was. In particular, he quotes from a sermon given by Robert Murray McCheyne in 1830s Scotland, preaching on the text *'It is more blessed to give than to receive.'*[215]

It's a powerful passage that explains the Christian message of generosity, challenging us to follow Jesus' example. It highlights how Jesus had not only a heart for the poor, but for all of us. Ultimately we are all undeserving of such love and grace, but it was given to us anyway. So it's up to us to show that love to others as well.

Sometimes we just have to live in the tension, like the pendulum swing between grace and truth. It's okay to give and plant a generosity seed, even though it's not in our power to control the outcome and consequences of that generosity. Some of our giving will be fruitful, but there's no guarantee how it will be received.

## 6. Developing Wisdom and Discernment

*'The most truly generous persons are those who give silently without hope of praise or reward.'*
~ CAROL RYRIE BRINK

The funny thing about common sense is that it isn't very common. Your mindful finance journey won't be all straight paths and sunshine. There may sometimes be treacherous terrain to navigate. Remember what I said in the introduction about becoming prey for sleazy salesmen and highway robbers? Well, there's a target on your back now.

It seems like a good moment to pause and mention some common scams you may come across. It's important to educate yourself on how to avoid getting scammed. As you start to watch the YouTube videos, the algorithms are going to direct the clickbait ads towards you. As you interact with the finance YouTube comments and conversations, the bots are going to interact with you in disguise. It's time to protect yourself.

The scammers are often sophisticated, ruthless and determined to take your money. They have no morals. They show no mercy, especially for the elderly, vulnerable or technologically illiterate.

So you need to train yourself in how to recognise these scams and avoid the pitfalls and dangers. You may want to tell your friends and relatives about them too. The louder we shout, the harder it will be for these scammers to win.

There is also a group of dedicated YouTubers who are fighting back against the scammers. These are the scam-baiting community, a group of like-minded people, using technology, intelligence and humour (occasionally foul language) to fight back. Sometimes their techniques are very creative e.g. glitter bombs, cockroaches, rodents and even hacking their telephone lines and CCTV.[216]

A lot of the telephone scammers are based South Asia, in call centres, masquerading as genuine businesses, though they also operate in countries around the world.

The scammers, while they may have ulterior motives, can also be victims of the system, working for dangerous bosses and fearing what will happen to themselves or their families should they try to escape to a more legitimate line of work.

There's growing evidence, highlighted by charities such as *International Justice Mission* (IJM) that some scammers are victims of a new form of human trafficking - *enforced scamming*. Tricked into applying for jobs that don't exist, they find themselves trapped in compounds and forced to scam under threat of violence.

It's hard to end both scamming and enforced scamming for the same reasons. It's an organised crime network, stemming from poor countries while their victims are usually in the affluent West.

Police departments and governments have difficulties tackling this international problem as it involves collaborative work across the globe, with limited resources.

Some law-enforcement agencies are also subject to corruption, put under pressure by powerful businessmen trying to cover up the scams.

One of the most common types of scams is the tech support scam. This is where the scammer will get you to download some software to hack your device. They can then take you to a fake version of your bank account, deliberately fake an overpayment, and coerce people to pay them back with cash or gift cards.

There are also relationship scams where someone fakes an entire long-distance relationship to take someone's money over the years. They can be expert manipulators.

Scams can also be done in several different ways, including in person, via mail, telephone, text and email.[217] They may pretend to be a genuine company or charity. The key is to be suspicious if anyone is asking you for personal information, if it seems too good to be true, if someone is asking you to transfer money quickly or is putting extreme pressure on you.[218]

It's recommended to educate yourself, recognise scams and avoid them. Ideally, you shouldn't be trying to become a scam-baiter yourself. Leave it to the police, professionals and scam-baiting community.

I've included some links to my favourite YouTube scam-baiters in the Resources Chapter. One of my favourite scam-baiters is called *'Scammer Payback,'* also known as *Pierogi*. He brings together scam-baiters from across the world each year to create *The People's Call Centre*.[219] It's an emotional rollercoaster to watch as some of the best scam-baiters in the world intercept the scammers' phone calls and try to save victims.

There are plenty of scams targeting you on social media. When you're on YouTube and you think a content creator is saying hello to you and asking you to contact them on WhatsApp, don't fall for it. These are bots that have cloned their YouTube account. A content creator will never ask you for money or contact you in this way.

Again, you'll probably become a target for adverts trying to sell you get-rich-quick-schemes, courses and winning trading strategies. If it feels like a sales pitch, then it probably is. Ignore them, skip them, block them. They are usually just wanting to make money from you.

You will, however, notice that there are legitimate ways that financial YouTubers use affiliate marketing to fund their channels. These are things like product placement and sponsorships. These may be a bit annoying, but it's just part of how YouTube works. It's how content creators are incentivised to get paid and make great content. So I've come to accept this as normal, just like the adverts on commercial radio.

So keep your wits about you as you navigate the world of online personal finance education and, as Pierogi says, *"Don't get scammed!"*

## 7. Giving and Abundance Mindset

*'Giving is not a debt you owe. It's a seed you sow'*
~ PASTOR RICK WARREN

Throughout this book, you'll notice that I talk about seeds and growth. That's part of the abundance mindset. You can't get something from nothing. But one small seed can result in a tree that produces much fruit, which has the potential to grow more seeds and fruit.

Generosity is sometimes described as a seed. A seed can't unlock its potential unless it's planted. When we give something away or invest our money, then we're planting the seed. We're giving it up so that it will have the opportunity to grow. It has to die to itself in order to be transformed into something else.

We have no control over what happens to the seeds we plant. We can prepare the soil, dig the weeds and water the seeds, but ultimately it's not up to us to provide the sun and the rain. We plant a seed of generosity, then we have to wait.

We may never see the fruit of our generosity and impact of our giving in our own lifetime. The miracle of multiplication isn't up to us. It's an act of faith.

I learned a lot of my giving philosophy from Dave Ramsey and Jim Rohn during a season of growth and personal development. These were the two main voices speaking to me at that time as I sorted my job situation and decided to become debt free. They introduced me to many ideas in this book and have inspired countless other people.

While I was getting my finances in order I filled my mind with positive voices and encouragement. I listened to success stories and reminded myself that if they could do it, I could too. I had to change my mindset, transform my thoughts and put good habits in place that would hopefully last a lifetime.

Dave Ramsey talks about the Jewish *Havdalah Ceremony* in his book *'The Legacy Journey'*.[220] During the ceremony, a cup is filled to the brim with wine and then spills over into a tray. It's a symbol of overflow and abundance, of having enough for ourselves and even more to bless others. Abundance mindset is the idea of us being so full of blessings, spiritually and financially, that we have enough to meet our needs and it can overflow to help those around us.[221]

Jim Rohn took inspiration from the Biblical laws of sowing and reaping. I also discovered a wonderful series by Pastor Rick Warren called *'Financial Fitness'* which uses the same imagery (I was listening to it whilst picking blackberries in Everton Park in July 2022). All this inspired me to write this chapter and the gardening chapter coming up.

You'll find this, along with other content in the Resources Chapter, with videos and talks relating to generosity, the laws of multiplication and growth. Feel free to explore these at your leisure. I've included them because they helped me. I know there's a lot!

Back in August 2022, I re-listened to Dave Ramsey's annual giving show. This is something he tries to do in the run-up to Christmas each year, showcasing stories of generous people or recipients of outrageous generosity. So it was a bit odd to be listening to it during the height of summer, but inspiring never the less.

In particular, his introduction stood out to me:

*"The highest and best use of money, the reason to become a Babysteps Millionaire, an everyday Millionaire, the reason to save and invest is something more than just the piling up of stuff. We all know that it is better to give than to receive. Some know that more than others. But changing your family tree and outrageous generosity are the highest and best callings of wealth. By the way, those are the most fun things you'll ever do with wealth."*[222]

Just as Dave Ramsey says, giving is the most fun that we can have with money. Generosity can be the reason why we build wealth and the way to build wealth. Ultimately, it teaches us to hold on to material possessions less tightly and to become an expert gardener.

We can become spiritually fruitful and give that fruit away. After all, what else is fruit good for when we have more than we need? Let me give you a suggestion: for making jam and preserves, and they makes excellent gifts too.

## 8. Leaving a Legacy

In *Chapter 5: Family*, we did a deep dive into generational wealth and the different ways we can leave a legacy, not just financial. But have you given much thought to how you could practically leave a financial legacy to the people and causes you care about?

As I mentioned before, there's a question we have to ask ourselves about whether we give to charity in the here and now or whether we invest this money to grow it and give later. Maybe we just write it into our will or give part of our estate when we die.

It's not an easy question to answer. If we give while we're alive, we're more likely to see our giving having an impact. It can be addictive. It gets easier to give big when we practice giving small amounts and build a generosity habit over our lifetime. We get to enjoy being generous too. You may find you give more than you ever dreamed possible. Generosity can bless you on your wealth building journey in so many ways.

But if we leave all our giving until later (when we're wealthier, when our situation changes etc.) will we actually be able to give? Will it feel too overwhelming? Will we hold on to our money and possessions too tightly if we haven't practiced generosity and living open-handed?

If you rely on *the future version of you* to be generous while you're still living it up in the present, spending all you have (*YOLO: 'You Only Live Once'* mentality), even if you're not aware that's what you're doing, the insidious lifestyle creep, then we can fall into a trap of inertia and procrastination.

You may be worried about giving when you're younger. You might think there won't be enough for your future financial goals or your retirement. So you say, "*I'll give when I retire*" or "*I'll leave a legacy in my will when I'm gone.*" But what if you get to retirement and find that you need all that money to live on? You may end up spending everything you have and never give anything at all.

For some people, of course, this is their goal or version of success. But *Proverbs 13:22 (NIV)* says, '*A good person leaves an inheritance for their children's children, but a sinner's wealth is stored up for the righteous.*' So perhaps there is a way that is better.

There isn't a universal answer when it comes to leaving a financial legacy. I think it comes down to what our values are and how we want to be remembered. I personally would like to be known as generous in life and generous after I die as well. I've discovered that giving is too much fun not to do while you're alive to enjoy it!

You'll also hear about people who lived a frugal life and amassed a secret fortune which was only discovered after they'd died. I can imagine the satisfaction they must have felt knowing that they were going to shock the people who'd known them their whole lives, who saw how they lived and thought they were nothing special. There's something very heartwarming about that.

One such person was janitor, Ronald Read, who died in 2014 at age 92. He turned out to be worth $8 million which he donated to his local hospital and library.[223] I first heard about his story in Morgan Housel's book *'The Psychology of Money.*[224] I encourage you to look up this story and read it for yourself.

The Resources Chapter includes Pete Matthew's *'Ultimate Guide to Estate Planning'* and a podcast called *'Strategies for Impactful Giving.'* These are practical guides for any of you who are in the UK. Pete talks about things that you might not have looked into, like tax-advantaged giving and how things like inheritance tax and capital gains tax work.

Again, this is just the starting place for you to do your own research. You may need to get financial advice tailored to your situation. There are all sorts of things you might want to look into, including weighing up the pros and cons of trusts or donor-advised funds, payroll giving and how to claim gift aid. You can also give to charity through your business (different tax rules apply depending on business structure).

## Reflection Questions:

- *Is there any margin in your budget for giving?*
- *Do you currently make giving a priority?*
- *Have you ever tried percentage giving or tithing?*
- *What are your experiences of generosity? Positive or negative?*
- *Are there times where you've been generous in the past?*
- *Have you experienced someone else's generosity towards you?*
- *How does talking about giving and generosity make you feel?*
- *What are your barriers to generosity?*
- *Have you found that giving gets easier with practice?*
- *Do you have any generosity goals?*
- *What small step could you take today to become more generous?*
- *Is there a time you wish you'd been more discerning?*
- *Have you ever been scammed or know someone else who has?*
- *What habits can you start today to grow your giving muscle?*

# PART 2

## JOURNEY TO FINANCIAL SUCCESS

# PART 2: JOURNEY TO FINANCIAL SUCCESS

*'Success is not a destination, it's a journey.'*
~ ZIG ZIGLAR

Congratulations! You've reached a major milestone in the book – the halfway point. Think of this as a place to stop and rest before we journey onwards.

You've come a long way, dear traveller. I hope you've enjoyed designing your financial house, learning to lay bricks and building a foundation of good money habits. You might have found the stuff about mindset and psychology a bit abstract and waffly. But I hope this has set you up for a lifetime of wealth-building ahead. Now it's time to go to the next level.

Did you know, I debated whether I should write two separate books – one on the basics of personal finance and a second one on investing? But I couldn't do it. I just knew that if Part 2 was a separate book then nobody would read Part 1! I'm right, aren't I?

Everyone wants the glamour of the stock market and nobody wants the bricks and mortar basics of the budget. But it's the small, seemingly insignificant steps – each day, month and year – that will change the direction of your life.

Yet, it only takes one emotional decision for investing to go very very wrong. One error of judgement and people can give up on investing forever, thinking it's too risky. There's no one right way to go about building wealth. I'm going to share with you what I've learnt.

I'm glad you've stuck with me this far. All the experts will tell you that if you don't get your financial house in order then there is zero chance of building wealth. That's why even high-income earners can go broke. Nobody is successful by chance. It's like swimming against the current.

If you did nothing but read *Chapter 1: Foundations* over and over, then learn to apply those foundational principles, then you'd be well on your way to success, whatever that looks like for you.

So now you can sit back and enjoy part 2 of the book... the movie sequel... the bonus tracks... however you want to think of it.

In this section, I'll talk you through how to design your garden (a portfolio of investments). We'll talk about goal-setting and dreaming about the future. I'll show you how to make it a reality.

There'll be practical stuff about different types of investments and where to put them. Along the way, you'll discover your investment style, your attitude to risk and find out if investing is for you.

**SPOILER ALERT:**

*You may get to the end of this entire book and find out that investing in the stock market is not for you. That's absolutely okay. Don't be disappointed. You'll discover that there are many other ways to invest and grow wealth.*

There will also be a lot about psychology and mindset. So prepare yourself for some more extended metaphors!

I hope you've brought your gardening gloves, trowel and secateurs. It's time to get our hands dirty. Let's create your dream garden!

"**Handle** the upcoming winters. **Don't wish away** the upcoming winters. That's called naïve. Wish for the **strength**. Wish for the **wisdom**"

~ Jim Rohn

# Make Your Garden Grow

# | 7 |

# Chapter 7: Make Your Garden Grow

*'Even if I knew that tomorrow the world would go to pieces, I would still plant my apple tree.'*
~ Attributed to MARTIN LUTHER

Some people have a fascination with gardens. I was at a party where a friend was telling us about her new-found gardening obsession. It was a smallish patio space transformed with containers, fairy lights and shrubs. It was proving to be an expensive and time-consuming hobby, she confided, but she was already dreaming of her ideal garden and couldn't wait to get ready to plant again next spring.

I introduced her to another friend at the party, someone older who I knew had been gardening for decades. Her garden was massive – a double plot – beautifully managed with stunning flowers.

I told them how I was writing this book and how everything they were talking about was a great metaphor for life: *don't compare gardens*. You'll never know the hard work and effort that went on behind the scenes for someone to get to where they are today. It's best not to compare your humble beginnings with someone else's destination.

Turns out I was right. My second friend had originally had a boggy garden that needed to be drained and redesigned by a professional landscape gardener. It was now transformed into a tranquil paradise with both a greenhouse and a summerhouse where she could spend her retirement with her granddaughter.

It had taken a massive effort to turn a muddy mess into the garden of her dreams. The grass always looks greener when you compare your garden with someone else's, *especially someone who has invested in an artificial lawn!* Because that's exactly what she'd done! You just have to water your own garden instead.

I only have a communal garden, so I don't get to do much gardening yet. You may not have a garden in real life but I'm sure you can appreciate the love of gardening in others.

My mum, Brenda, has an allotment. So a lot of this chapter has been inspired by her. I've also been doing a few jobs in another friend's garden. Her tomato harvest last year was a triumph. She also taught me how to prune and plant bulbs.

I recently become interested in a local Liverpool legend, William Roscoe.[225] There is a garden on Mount Pleasant named after him where he is buried. He was a botanist, philanthropist, member of parliament and one of the country's earliest abolitionists of the transatlantic slave trade.

Roscoe was a self-made man who left school at age 12, so it appears personal development was alive and well back in the 18th century. He was one of the founders of a botanical garden in Liverpool, the remnants of which still exist but are in dire need of conservation. Unfortunately, he was better at gardening than finance. He was a partner in a bank which failed and he was forced to sell off many of his assets.

Just like Voltaire's *Candide*, who ends up back on his farm after a sequence of unfortunate events, there are numerous examples of people trying to get back to the innocence and simplicity of the *Garden of Eden* (*Candide:* "*We must cultivate our garden*").

Here's me (in the middle) with mum Brenda and sister Liz. Summer is a great time to visit mum's allotment and help with the harvest.

# Mum's Allotment

There's something very special about green spaces and getting back to nature. In mindfulness terms, there are recognised health benefits of *'nature connectedness.'* Being connected to nature is good for our health and wellbeing. We often feel less isolated, less stressed and more secure.

What's more, there is an association between lack of green spaces and worsened health inequalities. Remember poverty and those *social determinants of health* we talked about? Having a park or garden nearby may be a luxury or privilege many of us take for granted.

Of course, individuals respond very differently to green spaces. It very much depends on our experiences, the memories and associations we form with nature.

Certainly, I've spent the past few summers getting inspiration for the book by connecting to nature, mostly foraging for blackberries in Everton Park. Whenever I talk about harvests and fruitfulness imagine my fingers stained purple! Gardens are a great metaphor for both life and our finances.

There's another purpose for talking about gardens since the cost of living crisis and supply chain issues associated with the COVID-19 pandemic. You might remember the *'preppers'* we learnt about in *Chapter 2: The 4 Walls*. Back then we looked at food minimalism, preparedness and self-sufficiency. Gardening takes on a new meaning when we're talking about people who live a minimalist lifestyle and rely on their gardens to survive if the worst were to happen.

Some people choose to live off-grid, keep chickens, stockpile food in case of an emergency, grow their own vegetables, harvest rainwater and solar energy. While it's an extreme lifestyle, they can teach us a lot about preparedness, especially if something catastrophic were to happen. It won't matter how much gold or money we have if civilisation collapses. We'd be back to the 4 walls, the necessities of life – food, water, shelter, power, clothes and transportation.[226]

I've also been inspired by a book about creating vegetable gardens in small spaces, Marta Teegen's *Homegrown*.[227] In the book, Marta systematically shows a beginner how to set up a kitchen garden, one step at a time, with handy pictures and personal experience. I learnt a lot about soil from her.

So hopefully by now you've realised I'm not a financial expert or a gardening expert! You definitely need to go do your own research. I just want to give you a useful framework for thinking about money when the time comes for you to grow your wealth. We're going to look at the following topics:

> 1. Mindful investing is like cultivating a garden
> 2. Designing your dream garden
> 3. How to live off the land
> 4. The importance of diversification
> 5. Preparing the soil
> 6. Knowing where to plant
> 7. The Laws of Sowing and Reaping

## 1. Mindful Investing Is Like Cultivating A Garden

*'A garden returns 50x the investment you put into it.*
*Not just food, but joy, peace and a real connection with creation.*
*A spiritual retreat from a noisy world and hurried people.*
*Grow a garden!'*
~ JOHN AND JONI SCHMIEDT
*Sprossen Farms, Deer Park, Washington, USA*

As I've been preparing and writing this book for a few years, you can imagine how my visits to gardens have been transformed by what I've been learning about personal finance. There are plenty of parallels to draw between growing plants and growing wealth.

Gardens don't just grow themselves into neat lawns and flower beds. Weeds are the natural consequence of doing nothing. It's easy for weeds to grow in all areas of our lives: we can neglect our important relationships or show up late for appointments; we can drift off course if we don't look where we're going; we can miss the target if we don't set any goals; we can fall into debt if we're not paying attention to our money.

Mindful investing is like cultivating a garden. If we want the garden of our dreams, then we have to roll up our sleeves and get our hands dirty. Growing wealth and growing a garden takes planning, preparation, intentionality, hard work and discipline. It takes time and there are different seasons to navigate. It's not a *set-it-and-forget-it approach*, at least, not in the early stages. We might be able to automate the process, but it takes effort to set things up initially.

Gardeners have to make a plan and follow it through. They prepare the ground, removing any large rocks and debris. They need to make sure that the soil is right. Even when the plants are fully grown, there's work to be done: a harvest to reap; seeds to collect for replanting; fruit and vegetables to process, preserve and store; there's pruning and preparing for next year. Only then can we sit back and finally enjoy the fruits of our labour.

Similarly, if we don't pay attention or do the work to cultivate our financial garden, then we could end up with a tangle of briars and weeds rather than the investment portfolio of our dreams. We may not get a lovely garden where we can relax and spend time in our retirement. We could find ourselves with no savings at all, or scattered pension pots from previous jobs that are gathering dust, underperforming or lost investments – in essence, *a financial mess*.

Most of us will want to retire one day. But some people just assume that everything will work out without putting in any effort. They think the government will take care of them when they reach state retirement age. The sad reality is that some people will suddenly realise they don't have enough to retire or perhaps they have to give up the lifestyle they've grown accustomed to. Nobody is accidentally successful.

For those of you who are relying on the state for your retirement, did you know that the State Pension in the UK and Social Security in the USA were never meant to be sufficient to fund the lifestyles we have grown accustomed to? There are also plenty of experts who think that these funds may be reduced or run out in a few decades, making it more important than ever to focus on your journey to financial independence.[228]

Maybe you're in your twenties or thirties. You might feel like retirement planning is something you'll do when you're older. After all, *you're only young once* and *retirement is ages away*, right?

Perhaps you're already older and you're worried you've left it too late. You've probably heard the saying *'The best time to plant a tree was 20 years ago. The second best time is now.'* Trust me, *Future You* will be grateful that you're sorting your finances and planting seeds today!

I believe our future rests in our own hands. It's not entirely up to us, but we're the only factor we really have any control over. I spent too many years procrastinating, thinking I'd meet someone who would do this stuff for me. We all have different starting places, skill sets, social backgrounds, life experiences, hurts and traumas that shape us.

But if Ronald Read – the janitor from Vermont – can do it, then so can we! We can build wealth, define success in our own terms, become who we were created to be and leave a legacy of outrageous generosity if we so choose.

Listening to Jim Rohn and Earl Nightingale in particular has taught me that ultimately it's up to us to get to where we want to go. We can't blame the weather, the seasons or the economic climate. We can't rely on a lottery jackpot or a sudden financial windfall. We create our own luck. We need to take personal responsibility to control what is in our power to control, to make the changes in ourselves and do the work.

The decisions we make today – to plant the seeds, cultivate them and allow them to multiply – will make a huge difference to our financial future, not only for ourselves but for generations to come.

\*\*\*

## 2. Designing Your Dream Garden

*'Anyone who thinks that gardening begins in the spring and ends in the fall is missing the best part of the whole year; for gardening begins in January with the dream.'*
~ JOSEPHINE NEUSE

So, before we get practical, I want to get theoretical again. Let's dream about your future financial garden. I want you to imagine what your investment portfolio could look like.

Will it be big or small? Will it be a flourishing wildflower meadow or a neatly manicured lawn with flower beds surrounding it? Will there be a leafy fruit tree orchard or a carefully tended vegetable plot, laid out in rows? Don't worry, these things are all a financial metaphor for different investment styles, as you'll soon see.

When it comes to designing your dream financial portfolio there's not just one way to do it. Some people take a passive management approach, buying the whole stock market, scattering seeds across a wide area. Meanwhile, other people prefer active management, paying someone to pick stocks for them and plant their investment seeds deliberately into the ground at what they think is the right time.

Some people have a DIY approach and do all the investing themselves, while other people involve a professional, a landscape gardener or financial expert, to help them design their investment portfolio. There are pros and cons to each approach.

You may already have some investing experience. Perhaps you've been paying into a workplace pension for a few years but aren't sure what it's invested in – you're still an investor!

To make the topic of investing less scary I'm going to explain how growing your financial garden works in simple terms, using vegetables to tell a story. If it worked for *VeggieTales*, it can work for us!

If this all seems really obvious or basic, feel free to skip ahead to the next part of the journey (I'll see you in the next chapter).

## 3. How To Live Off The Land

*'A farmer depends on himself, and the land and the weather. If you're a farmer, you raise what you eat, you raise what you wear, and you keep warm with wood out of your own timber. You work hard, but you work as you please, and no man can tell you to go or come. You'll be free and independent, son, on a farm.'*
~ LAURA INGALLS WILDER, *'Farmer Boy'*

I remember having an epiphany moment in my early twenties when I asked myself what I'd do if I won big on the lottery (just a hypothetical situation, as I don't buy lottery tickets, as a rule). I remember thinking, *'What if I could put those millions into some kind of account that would generate enough interest to live on?'*

I also remember thinking, *'I wish I had money invested when I was a baby. What would it be worth now, twenty-plus years later?'* I was asking the right questions. But it took me years to find the answers.

Well, essentially this is how investing for retirement works. It's about building wealth gradually over time, letting compound interest work its miracle over decades. You could even end up an everyday millionaire.

Eventually, you would have enough money invested to draw from in retirement. Your savings and investments may generate interest or pay you an income in the form of a dividend. Ultimately your money would keep growing.

Perhaps you could pay yourself an income to replace your job or work part-time. Or you may even decide to keep working. Some people even start a business or second career during retirement!

Remember the *FI* or *FIRE movement* from *Chapter 2: The 4 walls?* This is what many people are trying to do, to gain *Financial Independence* and sometimes *Retire Early*.[229,230] While some people may find it a bit extreme or unacceptable to sacrifice that amount of time, energy and lifestyle earlier in life to retire *early*, I believe it's still important to get into an investing habit and make some sacrifices to get to retire *one day*. That's why I like to learn about the *FIRE movement* as it motivates me to start thinking about retirement in general and to keep going. I just want to make doubly sure I get there!

If I were to put this into plant-based gardening terms, financial independence would mean having enough plants to feed you, all year round, for the rest of your life.

In the same way that your investments grow over time, you can eat the growth of some plants – their roots, leaves and stems. Other investments produce interest or pay a dividend, in the same way that some plants produce fruit, nuts or seeds at certain times of the year. There are also ways to store value, to harvest and preserve what you grow to replant or eat later.

Some plants grow quickly and some grow slowly. This is true of different types of investments too. We need a wide variety of plants in the same way we need a varied diet to make sure we have an income all year round once we retire.

## 4. The Importance Of Diversification

*'Riches are like muck which stink in a heap, but,*
*when spread abroad, make the earth fruitful.'*
~ *'A COMPLEAT COLLECTION OF ENGLISH PROVERBS' (1737)*

### Single Stocks Are The Riskiest Way To Invest

You can't just rely on one type of plant to feed you forever, nor can you rely on a single stock investment to fund you forever. That would be like buying only Apple stock and hoping for the best. You can't just rely on the apple orchard to survive! You can't just live on apples, no matter how much you love your iPhone!

If you don't spread out your investments you will be at the mercy of the seasons: a scorching summer, a bitter winter; a poor harvest or a blight that wipes out your crop. Just like we need to diversify the plants in our garden, the same is true of our investments. *Don't put all your eggs in one basket.*

When you buy **single stocks** in a company based on what the guy down the pub said, or what the YouTube video said, or what the internet forum said, then you're making yourself vulnerable.

It doesn't even have to be an economic downturn. It might be something random like a news article that makes people fearful about the business. The share price drop may drop suddenly only to bounce back the next day.

Single-stock investing is risky. You'll feel every bump of emotion when riding the ups and downs of the stock market rollercoaster. It means you're more likely to jump off at the wrong moment and sell when the market is down, missing the next leg up.

## What Is Diversification?

*'Diversification'* means spreading money around. You can invest in different stocks or asset classes.[231] It's adding variety, reducing the risk of all our investments doing badly at the same time. If any one of our investments has a down year, then there should be other investments that do better. We'll be more likely to keep going over the long term.

Of course, there are some expert stock pickers out there who call it *'de-worsification'* - they believe that spreading investments out waters down their performance. But they're experts. They have the time, energy and know-how to analyse stocks and work out which ones are more likely to perform better. They're not *you and me*. They're not always right. Nobody can accurately time the market or predict the future.

There are many asset classes to invest in.[232] To help you remember, I'm going to describe some of them in terms of garden plants!

### Trading The Stock Market (Microgreens & Beetroots)

Another risky way to make money on the stock market is called *'day trading'*. These are the people you may immediately think of when someone says *'investing'*, the drama, suits and ties, yelling *"buy, buy, buy!"* and *"sell, sell, sell!"*

Traders buy and hold an investment for just a few hours or even minutes before selling it again, trying to make a quick profit.

The nearest thing I can think of to this in gardening terms are things like microgreens for salad that sprout and are harvested in just a couple of weeks. Some vegetables, like beetroots, grow quickly and are ready to harvest in 7 to 12 weeks.[233]

While the potential reward for day trading is high, for most people the risk of failure is far higher. Many inexperienced retail traders lose money, especially if they don't know what they're doing.[234]

You may have heard of the *'meme stock'* craze from 2020 onwards. Lots of people started trading for the first time during the COVID-19 pandemic, hoping to make a quick profit. People had extra time and money, so they took big risks. Some made a fortune while others lost huge sums of money very quickly.[235]

### Fixed Income Assets (Lettuces)

Some investments are a bit boring, like salad leaves, lettuces and chard. They have a fixed predictable growing season and you can take a few leaves at a time as you need them. The same is true of fixed-income investments, like bonds.

Government bonds in the UK are called *gilts*, while in the USA they are called *Treasury bills* (or T bills). Some private companies issue corporate bonds but these tend to be riskier. A company can go bust, but hopefully a government never will.

Bonds are IOUs where the issuer borrows money from you for a fixed time period. It could be for a few months or even decades. In return, they pay a regular coupon payment each month. They also pay you back your money at the end of the term.

Historically, bonds have been considered boring, safe, low-risk assets. They typically go up when the stock market panics to keep a portfolio balanced. However, this didn't happen in January 2022 when US bonds had a meltdown, their worst performance in 250 years.[236] Confusingly, bond prices go down when yields (coupon payments) go up.

Coincidentally, 2022 also saw a shortage of lettuce due to an insect-borne virus.[237] Some California growers lost 50-80% of their harvest, proving once again that you shouldn't rely on just one plant to survive. It's important to spread your risk over different asset classes.

### *Stocks and Shares / Index Funds (Fruit Trees)*

Other plants mature and develop over several years. These can provide a regular harvest for a long time, just like apple trees, cherry trees or fruit bushes. In investing terms, these resemble stocks and shares, also known as equities.

Owning a stock or share is like owning a little bit of a company. Some companies focus on growth, like the tech companies Google (Alphabet), Tesla and Amazon.[238]

Some businesses are well-established, like solid sturdy trees. They focus less on growth and instead pay out a regular dividend as a reward to investors (like a fruit harvest). These are known as income stocks, companies such as Walmart, Coca-Cola, big banks and energy companies.[239]

You can buy a basket of stocks and shares in a fund. You may hear these referred to as ETFs (Exchange Traded Funds), Mutual Funds and other names. They are sometimes active funds where a manager selects the stocks and shares they think will perform the best. Or you can invest passively into an index fund.

Index funds automatically track an index, the top companies selected by specific criteria. These include the S&P 500, Nasdaq or Dow Jones in the USA and FTSE indices in the UK. Index funds may track a particular market, country or the whole world. Funds are a way of owning hundreds, if not thousands, of individual companies at the same time.

### *Gold and Precious Metals (Canned Food and Preserves)*

Gold is often thought of as a store of value and has been tried and tested for thousands of years. Not everyone decides to invest in gold. But many experts suggest owning a small amount of gold in case of an emergency.

You can invest in physical gold (coins, bars, jewellery etc.), paper gold or digital gold (funds that invest in gold for you), gold miners and gold royalties. There are also gold leasing schemes that pay interest.

Silver has uses in industry as well as in jewellery production. It's price tends to go up and down more dramatically than gold. Other precious metals include platinum and palladium.

The garden analogy would be like home canning, preserving and storing your harvest in a pantry for emergencies. Storing food doesn't grow or produce any more fruit, but it's there when you need it.

Of course, in a real-life apocalyptic-type emergency, if the power grid went down or war broke out, you wouldn't be able to eat your gold. Ironically, you would have been better off with the cans of food. But you could trade your gold to get them. That's why gold is typically kept as a small part of an investment strategy, just in case the world as we know it falls apart.[240]

You may want to think like a *'prepper'* and keep a little gold or ammo around in case of a *Shaun of the Dead* type of scenario.

### *Cash (Seeds and Grains)*

Don't forget that cash is also an important asset class. While cash isn't an investment as such, it's more like an insurance policy. Many experts suggest holding some cash reserves in your investment portfolio, in the same way that it's wise to have some seeds or grain in reserve. After all, you don't know what difficulties or opportunities may arise. You might need to eat up your cash if times are tough or have cash to re-invest in future if there's a good buying opportunity.

In the same way that seeds sitting on the shelf don't grow unless they're planted, cash doesn't grow unless it's put to work. Typically cash loses value over time due to inflation. While editing this chapter in the Summer and Autumn of 2023, bank accounts were actually paying some interest on savings again as the USA and UK central banks raised interest rates to the highest levels since 2008 to combat inflation.

If you have a short-term savings goal (less than 3-5 years) it's recommended that you keep money in cash. It needs to be easy to access. You don't want it to go down in value just when you need it most. Beyond that, it's wise to invest your cash. That way your investments have the potential to grow and produce an income in the long-term.

As I've said before, our income is our greatest wealth-building tool. So you need to make sure that you've got spare cash to invest. Everything you learned in Part 1 of the book has set you up for Part 2. Eventually, your portfolio will grow and start paying cash back to you.

### Alternative Assets (Tulip Bulbs)

You'll come across several other asset classes, such as commodities (the raw materials used to create the products consumers buy), property (either becoming a landlord or buying a REIT – real estate investment trust) or farmland.

Commodities include base metals, like copper, zinc and iron. There are rare earth minerals like cobalt and lithium (used in some electric car batteries). There are also elements used in the nuclear industry, like uranium.

Other examples of commodities include oil and natural gas. You can also invest in soybeans, wheat, lumbar, coffee and sugar. Many of these things are specialist investments, so you need to know what you're doing and be prepared for unpredictable swings in prices.

There are also alternative investments, like art and collectables, antiques, wine and whiskey, cryptocurrencies and blockchain technology (like Bitcoin, Ethereum, Altcoins and NFTs (digital art and collectables)). In the past, people even invested in tulip bulbs – but that's a story we'll explore in *Chapter 9*.

Some alternative asset classes tend to be more risky and unpredictable, as proven by the investment bubbles throughout history. They're called bubbles because they inflate slowly and pop suddenly. Again, it's all about psychology. We'll talk about that later too.

### *Investing Into Yourself and Others*

Dave Ramsey paraphrases the old 18th-century English Proverb like this: *'Investments are like manure. Left in one pile, it starts to stink. But when you spread it around, it grows things.'*

There are many other ways to invest that go beyond the obvious financial investments we've already mentioned. You can also invest in yourself, spending money on courses, qualifications and professional development that can enrich your career and your life. This may potentially increase your future income and ultimately benefit others.

We already talked about sowing generosity seeds. You can think of giving as investing in charities and causes you care about. There are even donor-advised funds and investment accounts you can set up that give to charity. It's also possible to donate your investment assets directly to charity.

You can also invest in your relationships, your spiritual, physical and mental health. This may require some money, but it could also be the way you spend your time and energy.

I want you to think as broadly as possible about what investing means to you. What ways can you think of to spread your money around so that you can help people and allow blessings to grow in your life? Are you heaping up your money in a pile or spreading it around to help the roses grow?

### Investors on YouTube Who Are Also Gardeners

I'm not the only person who has drawn parallels between gardening and investing. I've borrowed quite a few ideas in this Chapter from some investors I found on YouTube with a keen interest in gardening. They share their personal experiences, financial wisdom, gardening tips and philosophy on life. You can watch these videos in the Resources Chapter if you're interested in learning more.

## 5. Preparing The Soil

> *'Still other seed fell on good soil, where it produced a crop—*
> *a hundred, sixty or thirty times what was sown.'*
> ~ MATTHEW 13:8, New International Version (NIV)

You'll see lots of *soil metaphors* in the personal development and finance space. Soil can represent anything from our spiritual walk, to our daily habits, our mindset (a fertile space for thoughts to grow) and the struggles we face (dirt and resistance). I'll try not to get too bogged down here (pun intended). Before we look at some soil analogies, I want to briefly talk about what soil is in scientific terms.

### What is Good Soil?

Just like our financial house needs a secure foundation, the soil is the foundation of our financial garden. Different plants need different soil types to grow and flourish. But what is soil *really*?

Soil isn't just dirt or mud. It's an ecosystem. According to *Wikipedia*, it's a mixture of organic matter, water, nutrients, minerals, gas, bacteria, insects and other living organisms. It's a matrix of solids, liquids and gases that interact with the chemicals and things that live in it. Soil is alive and always changing.[241]

One of the first chapters of Marta Teegen's *Homegrown* is called *'Creating Amazing Soil.'* She talks about different types of manure and compost, the importance of pH (*'soil testing'*) and worms, to make sure your soil is fluffy and nutrient-rich. **Good soil** is essential to support life.

So what's the opposite of good soil? Well, that would be **bad soil**: contamination with poisonous chemicals or heavy metals; the wrong mix or pH; too much or too little water. You can have stony ground where there's hardly any soil at all, rocks everywhere that need to be cleared so that roots can grow properly. Don't forget about the weeds that can ensnare and entangle new seedlings.

One of the best descriptions of different types of soil comes from *The Parable of the Sower* in the New Testament of the Bible.[242] This describes four different environments:

- **The path** where there is no soil
- **Rocky places** where the soil is shallow
- Soil with **thorns and weeds**
- **Good soil**

You can read the rest of the passage yourself to see how Jesus goes on to interpret the parable in terms of faith and spiritual growth, explaining why some people decide to follow him and why others decide to walk away. But I think it applies to our money mindset too.

### Mindset: The Psychology of Investing

*Be fearful when others are greedy, and greedy when others are fearful'*
~ WARREN BUFFETT *(a.k.a. The Oracle of Omaha)*

When it comes to our finances we also come across different types of psychological soil: our **money mindset**. Sometimes, seed falls on the path where there is no soil: people hear but they don't take action.

They may not understand or choose not to listen. They may hear the advice, but don't apply it.

There may rocky ground where the soil is shallow: people get excited and start quickly but they don't put down deep enough roots so they fall away when the first financial crisis hits.

There may be thorns and weeds: some people never invest, overwhelmed by fear, choked by weeds of distraction or procrastination. The entrapments of maintaining a luxury lifestyle means they have no money to spare.

It's only the people who learn to create *margin* in their lives, who build *good financial habits* and plant their investment seeds in *good soil* that go on to see *financial fruitfulness*. They'll be able to carry the weight of responsibility of financial stewardship and not let the love of wealth corrupt them.

It's a challenge. But Part 1 of this book was really a giant compost machine for your mind. Hopefully, you've been working on your mindset and now you've got some good soil.

When it comes to investing, we can be our own worst enemy. We often do the worst thing possible at the worst possible time. It's human nature to be emotional or irrational when it comes to investing. So we need to overcome our emotional impulses and cognitive biases (the tricks our brains play on us). There are whole areas of research dedicated to the topics of *behavioural finance* and *behavioural economics*.

You can think of *'good soil'* as *preparing the ground* to invest. I've put a link in the Resources Chapter to a brilliant podcast series by Pete Matthew from *Meaningful Money* called 'New Accumalators.'[243] He tells you all about the practical steps and mental preparations you can put in place to make sure you're building wealth on a firm foundation. He includes resources on behaviour finance and understanding your risk tolerance.

Warren Buffet, one of the world's top investors, is famous for saying, *"Be fearful when others are greedy, and greedy when others are fearful."* This is because stock market movements are often driven by *herd mentality*. When we do the opposite of everyone else, this is called being a *contrarian*. Sometimes it's good to be different and go against the herd. When it comes to investing, sometimes we need to acknowledge how we feel and then do the exact opposite.

When the stock market is crashing and we feel like we want the pain to stop, that's exactly when we need to hold on and invest more! And it's at the height of the stock market when everyone thinks the good times will last forever and throws in every last penny that a financial crash is usually around the corner.

Let me give you a personal example that shows you just how important it is to prepare your mind before you start to invest. There are things you can do, like getting your finances in order and getting some knowledge. But ultimately you need to get to know yourself.

## My Investing Journey

Here's what happened to me when I started to invest. Hopefully, this will give you some insight into why it's important to make sure you're investing in good soil. That means having the right financial preparations in place - like good money habits, an emergency fund, mindset, knowledge and self-awareness - before you start.

So far, I've told you how I started my first budget in January 2018 and how it took me 17 months to pay off all my debt and put my emergency fund in place. I had a regular income and margin each month in my budget. Well, by the time I got to early 2020, I was ready to start investing for the first time!

I'd been listening to some podcasts in preparation. I didn't know many people who invested and I certainly didn't feel confident asking them about it. So I decided to go and learn about it for myself.

To invest in something you need to make sure you fully understand it for yourself. That's why I've included many of my favourite investing educational content creators in *Chapter 10*.

I opened up a couple of self-invested personal pensions (SIPPs) and started to drip-feed money into a globally diversified stock market index fund. Remember, this isn't a financial recommendation. This is just what I did when I started investing.

I also knew that I wanted to do something called *'pound-cost averaging'* (or *dollar-cost averaging* if you're in the USA) where you invest a regular amount of money over the long term, no matter whether the stock market is going up or down. This takes away a lot of the emotional turmoil that comes with investing so you can stay in the market over the long haul.

Well, in January 2020, every motivational message I listened to was talking about having 20/20 vision. And yet nobody saw a global pandemic coming. When COVID-19 showed up in March 2020, everything went crazy. Fear rocked the stock market. Countries went into lockdown. Supply chains were messed up. People started panic buying toilet rolls and milk. Governments started giving out free money, stimulus cheques and paying people not to work. Nobody expected that the stock market would crash over 30% until it happened.[244]

This is why preparation matters. I knew that the stock market tends to go up over the long-term.[245] I knew that sometimes the greatest gains in the stock market come after the biggest losses, so you have to stay invested to take advantage of them.

I remembered Warren Buffet's sage advice (to use other people's fear as a buying opportunity). So instead of panicking, selling and never investing again (which can happen if people give in to their emotions), I decided to invest more. Stocks were on sale! 30% off! A bargain! Time to plant more investment seeds.

The 2020 stock market crash proved to be short-lived and bounced back with a vengeance. Of course, every time is different. We have no idea what is around the corner or what will happen the next time. Nobody can perfectly time the stock market.

You'll hear it said that **'*time in* the market, is more important than *timing* the market.'** If you're investing with a 20- or 30-year time horizon, that crash will probably just look like a tiny blip when you take a step backwards from the chart. So one way to invest is to develop a long-term view and keep investing consistently.

Experts always say to make an investment plan and stick to it. So you need to prepare yourself before the crises come and encourage yourself when times get tough. If you need someone to help you and keep you calm when a storm hits, then it's okay to work with a finance professional.

The key is to invest for the long term. You don't want to make an emotional decision at the wrong time that puts you off investing forever. The most costly decision you may ever make is not to invest at all. So whatever you do, you need to be able to stick to the plan. Don't jump off the rollercoaster!

## 6. Knowing Where To Plant

Different plants thrive in different places. They prefer different growing conditions: specific types of soil, levels of sunshine and water. It can be difficult to move a plant once it's significantly grown. A fully grown tree is hard to dig up when it's put roots down.

In a similar way, some investments do better in certain economic conditions. Investment seeds can be sown into various tax-advantaged accounts but once they're established, they can be difficult to move around. That's why where your investment grows matters.

Just like a gardener who has to decide between a greenhouse, planting directly into the ground, a hanging basket, a container garden or a raised bed, an investor has to choose where to invest. So what are the options for where can you put your savings and investments?

In the UK, it could be an ISA, pension, savings account, premium bonds or a general investment account.[246] In the USA, it could be a money market fund, 401k or 403b, a Roth IRA, a HSA (Health Savings Account) or an education account.[247]

Each type of account has its own rules, tax advantages and age restrictions. Once your investments are growing inside a particular financial vehicle, you can buy and sell within them, but it's hard to pull your assets out of them. There can be all sorts of penalties and fees. That's why it's important to understand what types of investment accounts are available in your country and which ones are right for you.

Ultimately, there isn't just one answer to where you should invest your money. It depends on your specific circumstances and priorities, such as your age and when you need to access your money. In reality, your portfolio will probably be made up of several different sorts of accounts. You may need to access these at different stages of your financial independence journey.

If you're in the UK and want to know more about *'tax wrappers'* and *'investment platforms,'* then I want to point you in the direction of Pete Matthew from *Meaningful Money*.[248] He has lots of explainer videos on types of investment accounts in the UK, including whether you should invest in a pension, an ISA or both.

I've put some links in the Resources Chapter which can be your next step to finding out how to get started with investing for the first time. Just be aware that the rules for pensions and ISAs keep on changing. So you can keep an eye out for the latest updates by subscribing to your favourite financial YouTube channels.

*Don't tell me where your priorities are. Show me where you spend your money, and I'll tell you what they are*

~ James W. Frick

*Your life does not get better by chance, it gets better by change*

~ Jim Rohn

## 7. The Laws of Sowing and Reaping

*'Money grows on the tree of persistence'*
~ JAPANESE PROVERB

As I said before, I only have a communal garden. Today I'm sitting in it while I edit this chapter, enjoying the sunshine. I was harvesting blackberries back in the summer of 2022 and discovered Pastor Rick Warren's series, entitled *'Financial Fitness.*[249] Pastor Rick talks about the laws of sowing and reaping and how these apply to our finances.

These principles were extremely important to people in Biblical times who relied on farming and agriculture as the main source of their livelihood. That's why principles from nature – like seeds, growth and crops – were often used in the Bible to explain how to live life well and how to grow spiritually.

The laws of sowing and reaping can be applied to many areas of life. While I want to focus mainly on applying these principles to investing, you can also apply these principles to personal development, setting goals, developing daily habits, generosity, relationships, health and fitness, or any area of your life where the small things you do each day have far-reaching consequences over the months, years and decades.

So let's take a look at how the laws of sowing and reaping can be applied to your personal finances.

i. In order to reap, first you must sow
ii. You reap only what you sow
iii. You will reap more than what you sow
iv. The more you sow, the more you will reap
v. You are subject to the seasons
vi. There is always a wait from planting to harvest
vii. You need faith in a future you can't yet see

## i. In Order to Reap, First You Must Sow

To be fruitful, first you've got to do some planting. To get wealth, first you've got to sow a financial seed. It's impossible to get a harvest when we don't plant anything in the first place. It's difficult to flourish in life if you're just waiting around for stuff to happen without putting in any initial effort. Planting seeds changes us from the inside out and makes life change possible.

Remember when we looked at how the seeds of potential pass through our hands? When we earn money, it's up to us not to consume it all. It's those basic foundations again: be aware of your income, get on a budget, make saving a monthly habit, then intentionally put those savings into investment pots. You've got to plant them in order to see them multiply.

So far, we've talked about seeds of generosity and investing. But did you know that you can also sow into your vision for the future? We'll talk about this in depth in *Chapter 8: Roadmap to your Financial Future* when we look at setting goals and how to achieve your dreams. In essence, if you aren't where you want to be, then you can still choose to sow into someone else, especially if they have already attained the dream that's in your heart.

Maybe you're single but want to be married one day: you can bless a couple with a meal voucher. Perhaps you want children, but you're in a waiting season: then you can love on parents and give their children gifts at Christmas. There's something very powerful about these small intentional acts of sowing.

I first heard about planting generosity seeds when Pastor Emma Bryant introduced me to books and videos by Terri Savelle Foy.[250] Terri uses *vision boards* and *dream books* to help set goals. They are tools to help you imagine what a successful future might look like.

We already talked about how your heart goes where your money goes. Well, what we focus our attention on is where our energy flows. Sowing into a cause related to your goal, or blessing someone else, creates a powerful focus for our attention. It'll help you picture the dream house, car, life partner, career, retirement, purpose or whatever it is that you desire for your life.

When our heart is set on seeing our goal become a reality, somehow we find opportunities and ways to make it happen. Sometimes we even get unexpected blessings. The *Money Guy Show* team call it '*The Invisible Hand*'. Some people call it the '*Law of Attraction*'. It could just be a mindset shift where we see things differently. However it works, sowing a generosity seed can move you in the direction of your desired future.

This is a great example of the *abundance cycle* in action. This is a concept that Brian Preston and Bo Hanson talk about on *The Money Guy Show*. They sow into their audience with free resources so that one day they will build wealth and perhaps even come back to them as clients.[251] I see generosity as being a form of abundance cycle, blessing someone else, yet in return we are blessed in ways we don't expect.

When you feel like you're losing hope, that you're never going to make progress on your financial finance journey, or you're dreaming of something big that feels impossible, then it's okay to start sowing just a little anyway. Whether it's an investment seed or a generosity seed, you never know what impact it will have.

This is why I like to sow into charities like *Ripple Effect*, a charity that supplies people in Africa with livestock, farming and business knowledge that helps to lift communities out of poverty. It encourages people to pass on the first-born female of their livestock, their knowledge and learning to help friends and neighbours, creating a ripple effect where many more people are helped over time.[252]

I'm hoping that this book may be a seed, part of the abundance cycle. I hope it creates a ripple effect of positive money conversations and generosity. I already feel so blessed to be able to write and share my story, to pass on what I've learned. I am where I am now because people have sown into me and I get to pass that on. Imagine what could happen if this seed were to grow and produce fruit in your life too and the people you go on to inspire.

Planting a seed may come to nothing. But to grow something you have to plant something. You've got to at least give it a try. Earl Nightingale says, "*We become what we think about most of the time.*" So all we can do is plant the seeds, then sit back and wait. We are what we think.

## ii. You Reap Only What You Sow

> '*Let us not become weary in doing good,*
> *for at the proper time we will reap a harvest if we do not give up.*'
> ~ GALATIONS 6:9, New International Version (NIV)

You'll hear it said that you always reap what you sow. This is a law of nature: if you plant apple seeds, you will only get apple trees growing, not oranges. Typically, whatever you sow you'll see more of show up in your life (it could be generosity, good or bad habits, time, energy, money etc.) That's why it's good to speak encouraging words and positive affirmations over yourself and others.

Sometimes the phrase '*you'll reap what you sow*' has negative connotations. A judgemental person may look at someone's life and assume that if it's a mess, it must have been because of the seeds they planted years before that got them there. That's the *prosperity mindset* again - that blessings come from good behaviour and punishments come from bad behaviour. It's a way of thinking that's all too easy to fall into.

The reality is more complicated than that. We've all made mistakes, battled with bad habits or chosen things that may not be good for us in the long term. Our decisions can have negative long-term consequences. On the other hand, we can all experience bad luck or events beyond our control, uncertainty and confusion. Struggles, storms and strife can come to anyone at any time. The rain can destroy a farmer's crop just before harvest. There was no reason for it. Nobody deserved it. It just happens.

Still, there are things we can do to prepare for life's trials, in the same way we can make sure we've got an umbrella in case it rains.

As I've said before, a rainy day fund and good money habits can turn an emergency into an inconvenience. It's only our thoughts, feelings, behaviours and habits that are within our power to control (though sometimes we need some help, of course!).

This can make all the difference if something unexpected happens, sheltering us from the storm we don't see coming, which might be just around the corner.

Some people say that wealthy people got lucky. But that's not the whole story either. As we said before, wealthy people often create their own luck. Someone who is labelled an *'overnight success'* has often spent years working hard in the background, making the boring, necessary changes – day in, day out – just for their talent to be discovered at the right time.

Studies have shown that most wealthy people didn't win the lottery or rely on an inheritance to create their wealth. Often, they've worked hard, developed discipline and had good money habits over a long period of time.[253] They've planted seeds, watered them and waited for them to grow. Good fruit eventually comes from good seeds.

So we can't give in to fate and think that luck is the only thing that can get us unstuck. Nor can we rely on creating the future we desire through hard work and effort alone. The reality is somewhere in between. I like to think of it from an *abundance* perspective. We plant good seeds of potential and if they are destroyed, we go again! We keep planting good seeds. Good seeds may one day bear good fruit.

> 'You should have a strategic asset allocation mix
> that assumes that you don't know what the future is going to hold.'
> ~ RAY DALIO

When it comes to investing, the kinds of seed we sow matters. Different asset classes tend to perform a certain way, based on history. Of course, there's no way to predict the future growth of our investments.

But there's still a principle at work that what you get out depends on what you put in.

You might hear the term *'asset allocation'*. You can think of your investment portfolio as a pie, divided up into different proportions of investments. You may decide to have a slice of relatively *'safe'* assets, which are low risk, low return. These are things like cash, low-yielding bonds and money market accounts. If you invest there, you won't get the big stock market swings, but you won't see any big returns either.

If you're looking to grow your investment portfolio, especially if you are young with a long time horizon, then you may choose to put more of your investment pie into riskier assets. Things will be more volatile, with big swings up and down. But over the long term, your investments have more potential to grow. These are things like equities, stock and shares.

Some people decide to divide their investment portfolio into two pies – a core portfolio where the majority of their investments go and a smaller satellite portfolio of fun investments where they get to play a bit more. This satisfies the urge to buy and sell, while leaving the majority of the portfolio to grow untouched.

Typically, people have a mixture of assets in their portfolio. You'll come across something called the *'60/40 portfolio.'* These were also called *'balanced portfolios'* and were popular in the 1980s and 1990s when it was standard practice to have 60% of your portfolio in equities and 40% in fixed-income assets, like bonds.

But since 2000 onwards, with lower interest rates, these have not performed well due to poor bond yields, meaning people had to take on more risk to get the same sorts of returns. They've had to put more of their money into equities and alternative assets.[254] Portfolios these days can look more like a pizza, sliced into many different-sized portions.

> *'An asset allocation plan is based on your personal circumstances, goals, time-horizon, and need and willingness to take risk.'*
> ~ MICHAEL LEBOEUF

It's up to you to work out what sort of investment seeds you want to plant and to pick an asset allocation that's right for you. Your risk profile will be individual to you and can change at different times in your life.

Traditionally, younger people with a longer investment horizon can afford to take on more risk in the early years because there's more time for downturns in the stock market to recover. For someone nearing retirement, the focus may be on wealth preservation. You haven't got as much time or opportunity to rebuild your wealth.

That's why *Target Date Funds* exist. They move from equities in the early years (when you can focus more on growth) to having more bonds at the end (to focus on wealth preservation). However, many people choose to keep a higher proportion of equities into their retirement as people are living longer and retirement could last for 30 years or more. Your money needs to keep growing.

### iii. You Will Reap More Than What You Sow

> *'Compound interest is the eighth wonder of the world.*
> *He who understands it earns it. He who doesn't, pays it.'*
> ~ Attributed to ALBERT EINSTEIN

It sounds obvious to say, but when you plant a seed you often get out much more than what you put in. The seed has the potential to produce a plant that will bear lots of fruit, and each fruit can contain many more seeds of potential. If you were to plant all those seeds back into the ground, could you imagine just how many plants you would have? One seed could turn into thousands of plants given enough time! This is sometimes referred to as **The Principle of Multiplication'**.

In finance terms, we call this *'compound interest.*[255] Not only do you get paid interest on your initial savings (*'simple interest'*), but you also get paid interest on any future growth or re-invested dividends. You can think of it as replanting the seeds your initial plant produces and all the future seeds as well. It's generating interest on your interest.

*'Every gold piece you save is a slave to work for you. Every copper it earns is its child that also can earn for you. If you would become wealthy, then what you save must earn, and its children must earn, that all may help to give you the abundance you crave.'*

~ GEORGE CLASON, from *'The Richest Man in Babylon'*

In *'The Richest Man in Babylon'* George Clason says compound interest is putting your money to work and having it produce children, who also work for you. The slavery terminology may seem dated (it was written in 1926 and set in Ancient Babylonia, after all). But I think the main idea Clason was trying to get across is that we need to take control of our finances and have authority over it, allowing it to multiply for us.

Perhaps you prefer the idea of being a military general over your investments, which is why *The Money Guy Show* uses an image of taking charge of your *'army of dollar bills.'*

I personally prefer the image of a gardener or farmer growing crops to describe the abundance that can result from compound interest and the exponential growth that it can achieve. It's a lot less violent.

If you've not heard of it before, *'exponential growth'* is where the amount you have doubles, then doubles again, then doubles again, and so on. You'll see pictures of the exponential growth curve, where the numbers start small, but as more time goes on there's a sudden skyrocketing upwards as the doubling takes effect.

It may not feel like you're investing much at first, but given enough time and the compounding effect, growth can be significant and can help you reach seemingly impossible goals. You don't need to earn a million to be a millionaire. You just have to wait long enough for your investments to grow.

## *The Principle of Multiplication:*

Let's look at the principle of multiplication in a bit more detail. There are different versions, but ultimately this rule states:

**Wealth = Margin (put to use)** multiplied by **Time**

In case you've forgotten it, the margin equation from *Chapter 1* was:

**Margin** = your **income** minus your **expenses**

So, if you can create spare money in your monthly budget, put it to work in a focused way (through generosity, paying down debt, saving or investing etc.) and give it enough time, eventually you'll become wealthy. It's a simple principle that explains how the majority of ordinary people build wealth over time.

Wealth building starts small. It starts with saving, planting and waiting. If you create margin, put it to use and give it enough time, you can reach a seemingly impossible goal.

Do you believe it could be possible for you? Could you create just a little more margin in your budget? What could you do now with some spare cash to build a better future? How long are you willing to give the process without giving up, even when you don't see any results?

If you plant a financial seed, let it grow and multiply, one day you could have an abundant harvest.

## iv. The More You Sow, The More You Will Reap

Again, it sounds obvious, but the more financial seeds you sow, the more potential there is for a bumper harvest later. As there's only so much that each individual plant can grow and limits on how much fruit it can produce, to build wealth you need to plant more seeds so that you can have more crops.

I've heard some experts say that it's not about your rate of return (how much your investment grows each year). It doesn't matter if you get 6%, 8%, 10%. The key factor that sets you up to win is regular consistent investing over time. How much you can invest as a proportion of your income each year is called your '*savings rate.*'

Investing is a marathon, not a sprint. You don't want to burn out by trying to invest too much too quickly. This won't be sustainable and you will probably give up early. You also don't want to take on so much risk that you have a bad experience, get frightened and stop investing. You want to invest for the long-term, with a savings rate that you can afford, with the right risk profile for you.

The key to mindful investing, like the rest of mindful finance, is that you are aware of where you are in the present moment, pay attention to your thoughts and emotions, then make intentional choices that move you in the direction of your goals.

## *How much should I invest?*

Some experts, like the *Ramsey Solutions* team, recommend putting 15% of your income towards you're retirement nest egg. Of course, that's after you've paid off your consumer debt and built an emergency fund.[256] Meanwhile, *The Money Guy Show* team suggests investing 25% of your income towards retirement.[257]

So which one is it? How much is too little or too much to invest? Well, it's just a guideline. The actual savings rate target for you will depend on your age and income projection, as well as the sort of lifestyle you want in retirement and how much you can afford.

It's technically possible to invest too much. Just like you can be *house-poor* when too much of your monthly income is going on your mortgage or you can get overwhelmed by too many debt payments, investing for the future can be at the expense of living today. So you need to find the right balance for you and your family.

It's okay to invest more if you can, for example, if you get a boost to your income or a financial windfall, like a bonus or inheritance.

Perhaps your life situation means you can continue to live well below your means for a season.

It's okay to aim to have more than enough invested for the future, but maybe think about putting money in investment pots that are accessible before retirement age. If you're in the UK, maybe think about making the most of your ISA allowance and Personal Savings Allowance (unless you're a higher rate tax payer; in which case, the tax relief on a pension looks very appealing).

Whatever saving rate you choose or work your way towards, you need to make sure that you're being intentional about it. The key is making saving and investing a habit, something you feel comfortable doing, almost without thinking. You can automate the process. Perhaps you can start with 5 or 10% of your income and slowly increase the amount you invest each year, giving yourself time to adjust your budget and lifestyle accordingly.

In the UK, people can now be put into workplace pension schemes by *'automatic enrolment.*[258] But because it's automatic, people may assume that it's enough. Unfortunately, for most people, auto-enrolment is a good start but there's more we need to do.

Remember, each investment seed (pound or dollar) will only be able to grow a limited amount. So the more investment seeds you sow, the more wealth you can build over time.

## v. You Are Subject To The Seasons:

You'll find lots of models of how to plan for retirement. We'll crunch the numbers in the next chapter. Just like in nature, retirement planning has seasons and different times for sowing and reaping.

- The first part is called the *'accumulation phase.'* This is where you build your wealth – working, planting seeds and allowing your investments to grow.
- There may be a *'transition phase'* or *'wealth preservation phase'* where you may decide to work less, do a part-time job, and put preparations in place to retire fully.
- Then there is a *'deaccumulation phase'* where you live on what you've saved away, harvesting your wealth and eventually stopping work.

Did you know that the economy and the stock market have seasons and cycles too? There are changes in the economic weather. This why economists often resemble weather forecasters, trying to predict when the next financial storm is coming. They're not usually as successful as meteorologists.

The emotions of the stock market go up and down with the economic weather conditions, but not always in a predictable way. Just like in real life, sometimes bad news is interpreted as good news, and vice versa. It doesn't always make sense because it's just too complicated. There are too many variables; it's like *The Butterfly Effect* (in *Chaos Theory)*. Some economists think the stock market is irrational and unpredictable, though many still try to predict what price it will go to.

So just like you can prepare for different sorts of weather, you can position your investment portfolio accordingly. Just like some people love it when it rains because they know it's watering their garden and they can collect water in barrels, investors can see dips in the stock market as opportunities to buy more stocks at a discount. It's a matter of perspective and preparation.

When there's lots of economic bad news, this is called an **Economic Winter**. Sometimes it fits the criteria for a recession, depression or a market downturn. These are times when banks are reluctant to lend money, companies lay people off and jobs are hard to come by.

In these dark gloomy days, people get fearful and stop spending as much money, preparing for tough times ahead. They don't want to take on as much investment risk and often have less money to invest in the first place. They often move to safer assets, storing up cash, causing the stock market to crash.

When people get very depressed and scared that their investments are crashing, they may panic and sell their investments. Often this is at the worst time, just as other people are doing the same. This is known as *'Market Capitulation'*. This is where many people get burned and some decide never to invest again. It's part of the emotional cycle that retail investors, like you and I, are especially vulnerable to.[259]

Sometimes this represents a stock market bottom, the darkest midwinter night, when everything looks bleak and we wonder if we'll ever see the sun again. But as we know, it often looks darkest before the dawn and economic spring is often just around the corner.

Just like in nature, an **Economic Spring** or **Summer** is usually when the mood of the stock market improves. You'll hear it said that the greatest gains in the stock market often happen after the biggest drops. So you don't want to miss them by jumping off the stock market rollercoaster at the wrong time.

There can be booms and euphoria. These are plentiful times when the sun is shining, people feel wealthy, jobs are easy to acquire, banks lend lots of money for people to spend and the economy is soaring. This sort of exuberance was present in the *'Roaring Twenties'* just before the stock market crash of 1929 and the Great Depression of the 1930s.[260]

During different economic seasons, different asset classes tend to do better than others. There's no exact pattern to it, but when people feel positive about the economy, they often take more risks and speculate on investments that they think might have incredible growth which sometimes makes that growth a reality (of course, this can also fail spectacularly, especially when the bubble bursts).

On the other hand, when they feel worried about the economy, they tend to invest in assets that are felt to be safer and more reliable, such as cash or bonds (though these may not turn out to be very safe at all due to inflation). This draws money out of stocks and so the stock market crashes.

There are also things that governments and central banks do to try to manipulate markets and interfere with economic cycles, like adjusting interest rates and printing more money. You can read about this in *Chapter 9* if you want to know more.

What we ought to focus on (especially as new retail investors) is how to ride the choppy seas and get to our destination without capsizing the boat. Let's look at some tips from gardeners which can help us navigate towards a safe retirement harbour (sorry, I'm mixing metaphors!)

### *Crop Rotation and Pruning*

It's possible to rotate investment assets in the same way gardeners do *'crop rotation'*.[261] In gardening terms, crop rotation is a way of keeping your soil healthy and plants pest-free by rotating the family of plants growing in an area of your garden. For example, you may grow green leafy vegetables one year, and root vegetables, such as potatoes, the next.

In investing terms, it would be like changing your asset allocation with the changing seasons, picking ones that do well for a particular economic climate. Different assets - like stocks, bonds, gold, cryptocurrency and commodities - tend to behave differently depending depending on economic conditions.

But just like we can't time the market, it's difficult to predict how assets will respond to the changing economic seasons. Some investors, such as Ray Dalio, have designed *'all-weather portfolios'* aimed at consistent performance despite what the economy is doing.[262]

Meanwhile, some portfolio managers and traders have strategies that actively change the asset allocation depending on the season, moving into cash when they think winter is approaching, investing more in the spring. Sometimes they rotate from popular stocks that have done well to unloved assets when they're undervalued.[263]

An alternative strategy is a passive index approach, where you don't worry about timing the market or about the seasons at all. This is sometimes called *'buy-and-hold investing*' because you buy a basket of stocks in an index fund and don't sell it until retirement.[264] You just keep planting seeds, whatever the weather, no matter what happens. This is known as *pound cost averaging* (of *dollar cost averaging* in the USA, or whatever currency you're using to invest).[265]

Instead of swapping assets in one go, we can prune investments by *'rebalancing'* our portfolio.[266] In gardening terms, pruning is where gardeners improve the appearance and productivity of their garden by cutting back on overgrown plants. It usually makes them more fruitful.

In investing terms, *'rebalancing'* your portfolio has a similar effect.[267, 268] This is where you sell assets that are outperforming (like an overgrown plant) and sow investment seeds back into those that are underperforming (which may be undervalued and more likely to grow in future). It can be done once a year or more frequently. You need to be careful not to do it too often as it costs money to buy and sell assets.

We talked before about the traditional *60/40 portfolio*, made up of 60% equities to 40% bonds. An example of rebalancing would be if the equity portion of the portfolio grew so that the balance shifted to 70/30. In this case, you would sell a percentage of your equities and buy more bonds to get the balance back to your target.

This is a way of *'selling high and buying low'* which can be good for growth in the long term. It also makes sure you aren't taking on more risk than you initially planned. Some multi-asset funds in the UK do this for you, such as Vanguard's *LifeStrategy* range (passively managed) and BlackRock's *MyMap* range (actively managed) - this isn't a recommendation; it's just somewhere to go do some research of your own. Ramin Nakisa from *PensionCraft* compares the two different fund providers and the pros and cons of each of these strategies.[269]

So remember, investing – just like gardening – has seasons. A stock market downturn or economic winter is not forever and the spring will eventually come. Winter is often a time to prepare, build cash reserves and get ready to plant more investment seeds. Spring and summer are a time to sow seeds, build wealth and cultivate growth. For people entering retirement, the *autumn years*, now is the time to harvest and enjoy the fruits of your investments.

## vi. There Is Always A Wait From Planting To Harvest

> *'Time is your friend, impulse is your enemy.*
> *Take advantage of compound interest and*
> *don't be captivated by the siren song of the market.'*
> ~ WARREN BUFFET *(inspired by Jack C. Bogle)*

We've already looked at the importance of giving your investments time to grow. It's one of the key components in *'The Principle of Multiplication'*. The longer your time horizon, the longer you have for compound interest to work.

**Keep reminding yourself:** *timing the stock market is impossible*. If you wait for precisely the right moment to plant your investment seeds, you're likely to keep your seeds on the shelf and never plant them at all. All your money would stay in cash and never be invested.

Even if you did time the market and sell right at the top before it crashed, there's no guarantee you'd be lucky a second time and get back in at the bottom. People who wait to invest can get stuck on the sidelines. They end up watching the stock market go back up without them. They can get an overwhelming feeling of regret. It can mean that they invest too late and miss the best days of the stock market. Sometimes they never invest again – it's either too painful or they're still waiting for the perfect entry point that never comes.

If you're prone to feeling the emotions of the stock market, then a long-term strategy where you invest consistently over decades may be more appropriate for you. Having a long time horizon takes away the significance of the day-to-day fluctuations of the market and the emotions that can come with it. It turns a stock market drop from a disaster into an opportunity to buy at a discount.

For people with a shorter time horizon, as long as you're investing for more than 5 years, there's still an opportunity to build wealth through investing. If you're nearing retirement and want to know if investing could still be for you, you may want to get some professional advice to see whether you're on track to hit your goals and help you decide how much risk to take.

There is always a wait involved in both gardening and investing. It can take years for your investments to start bearing fruit. So don't expect your bare plot of land to suddenly become the garden of your dreams overnight.

Stay the course, keep investing and wait patiently. You don't go to the gym or eat an apple and expect to see your health improve on day one. Investing also takes time. You can course correct and adjust your investments if you need to, but don't keep checking your investments moment by moment. As Warren Buffett says, *"don't watch the market too closely."* The daily up and down fluctuations of the stock market waves will drive you crazy.

It could take 10 or 20 years (or more) to get to your destination. Get to know yourself and you can decide how often to check your portfolio – for some people, once or twice a year is enough. Jack C. Bogle suggested never looking at all! The waiting can be the hardest part.

On the opposite page are some quotes from the experts on how to manage your emotions and investing behaviour while waiting for your portfolio to grow over the long term.[270]

'Investing should be more like watching paint dry or watching grass grow. If you want excitement, take $800 and go to Las Vegas'
~ PAUL SAMUELSON (American Economist)

'Invest for the long haul.
Don't get too greedy and don't get too scared'
~ SHELBY M.C. DAVIS (Philanthropist, retired investor)

'A market downturn doesn't bother us. It is an opportunity to increase our ownership of great companies with great management at good prices'
~ WARREN BUFFETT
(Chairman and CEO of Berkshire Hathaway)

'Far more money has been lost by investors trying to anticipate corrections, than lost in the corrections themselves'
~ PETER LYNCH (American Investor and philanthropist)

'Though tempting, trying to time the market is a loser's game. $10,000 continuously invested in the market over the past 20 years grew to more than $48,000. If you missed just the best 30 days, your investment was reduced to $9,900'
~ CHRISTOPHER DAVIS (Investment Manager)

'The idea that a bell rings to signal when to get into or out of the stock market is simply not credible. After nearly fifty years in this business, I don't know anybody who has done it successfully and consistently. I don't even know anybody who knows anybody who has'
~ JACK C. BOGLE (Founder of Vanguard)

'A 10% decline in the market is fairly common—it happens about once a year. Investors who realize this are less likely to sell in a panic, and more likely to remain invested, benefitting from the wealth building power of stocks'
~ CHRISTOPHER DAVIS

'Your success in investing will depend in part on your character and guts and in part on your ability to realize, at the height of ebullience and the depth of despair alike, that this too, shall pass'
~ JACK C. BOGLE

'The lesson for investors: The weeds wither away in significance as the flowers bloom. Over time, it takes just a few winners to work wonders. And, yes, it helps to start early and live into your 90s as well'
~ WARREN BUFFETT, 'Annual letter to shareholders' Berkshire Hathoway, released 25 February 2023

## vii. You Need Faith In A Future You Can't Yet See

*'The future cannot be predicted, but futures can be invented. It was man's ability to invent which has made human society what it is. The mental processes of inventions are still mysterious.'*
~ DENNIS GABOR, *'Inventing the Future,'* 1963

While it's impossible to predict the future (just like it's impossible to completely accurately predict the weather), a few things are relatively certain: uncertainty is a given, so we've got to accept it and plan accordingly; if we don't plant seeds, we can't expect any plants to grow; our perfect garden won't appear overnight – it takes time, energy and discipline.

What is true of gardening is also true of your investment portfolio. No future is guaranteed, but there are steps we can take today to create a better future. As Dennis Gabor and others have suggested, while we can't predict the future, we can invent one for ourselves by putting our ingenuity and creativity to work in the here and now.

I'll say it again: where our money flows, that's where our heart goes. So why would we invest our hard-earned money into something we don't believe in? There's a degree of faith required to believe in a future not yet seen, a dream not yet realised, that could be many years or even decades away. Why else would we give up on the pleasure and immediate gratification of spending money now and instead make the sacrifice to save and invest for a better future?

Having a clear vision for what the future could be like is the key not only to getting started, but also to staying the course. That's why we took a bit of time at the beginning of this chapter to visualise our dream garden and what our future finances could look like.

Coming up next is *Chapter 8: 'Roadmap to your Financial Future.'* That's where we'll be putting numbers and timelines to your dreams and goals.

When it comes to having faith in a future we can't yet see, there are a few things we can do to keep ourselves motivated and focused on our goals. Firstly, we can learn from history. Although history doesn't repeat itself in exactly the same way, it often rhymes.

As I mentioned in the introduction, you'll often hear the warning that '*past performance is no guarantee of future results.*'[271] But unfortunately it's all we have to go on.

We can look at what previous economic cycles and stock market crashes looked like. We can look at data of how things have performed in the past in different economic conditions. We can look at previous speculative bubbles, investing fads and failures.[272] We'll see what we can learn from history in Chapter 9: 'A Brief History of Money'.

The other thing we can do is borrow wisdom from people who have already achieved success in the area we want. This could be in the form of quotes, books, podcasts, interviews, courses and tutorials by famous investors, such as those quoted above.

It could also mean working with a professional finance advisor or portfolio manager.[273] It could be joining a personal finance community and sharing ideas and tips. We'll look at different investment styles and communities you can join in Chapter 10: 'Ways to Invest.'

So, let's leave our garden for now and go back inside the house to grab a cuppa, a calculator and start crunching some numbers.

# ROADMAP

## TO YOUR FINANCIAL FUTURE

| 8 |

# Chapter 8: Roadmap To Your Financial Future

*'All you need is the plan, the road map,
and the courage to press on to your destination.'*
~ EARL NIGHTINGALE

So far we've been travelling on this mindful finance journey without a roadmap. Now it's time to start putting some numbers and a timeline to your dreams. That's how you go from a wish to a goal.

We've already talked in the introduction about how some people define success as working towards worthy goals. Well, now it's time for you to start to make some targets of your own.

You may remember the Zig Ziglar quote, *'If you aim at nothing, you'll hit it every time.'* Well, there's another quote I like from Les Brown who says, *'Most people fail in life not because they aim too high and miss, but because they aim too low and hit.'*

This chapter will point you in the direction of the resources you need to help you set realistic and achievable goals. It will show you how to get after them and encourage you to keep going!

We're going to look at several topics including:

- Why we need a roadmap
- Common ways to get lost
- How to navigate your way to financial success
- How to create a net worth statement
- How to set goals and work towards them

What you learn in this chapter can apply to goals in any area of your life, but I'm going to focus on retirement planning for now. That's because I believe it's one of the main financial goals that we all aspire to, in some shape or form. But it's also the one that people seem to want to talk about the least.

## Rethinking Retirement:

As I've been writing and editing this book, I've become more interested in the concept of *healthy aging*. We have a growing aging population. I often look after elderly patients when I'm working as a hospital doctor. It's amazing that health and scientific advances mean people are living longer and of course that should be celebrated! But we want to live well for longer too.

I also see the challenges that living longer can bring - complex health issues and frailty, the need for more social support, the loss of community and increased isolation and loneliness, financial strains and the need for future planning. Again, there are things we can do as individuals. But some of these things are systemic issues which we need governments, public health measures and society as a whole to change.

This is where *Lifestyle Medicine* comes in. It's about preventing illness in the first place, to help people live healthier and disease-free for longer. We can sometimes get away with a certain lifestyle for decades before the consequences eventually catch up with us. *Lifestyle Medicine* is about encouraging people to make healthy choices and build daily habits that take them in the direction of better health and wellbeing.

But what about our finances? Living longer puts more strain on our money as we need it to last for longer. If we want to retire one day and have the life we dream of, it won't happen by accident. That's why financial fitness is so important, along with our physical fitness.

What *mindful finance* choices can we make today and what healthy money habits can we start to make sure that our financial wellbeing is also taken care of as we get older?

It's never too early to start thinking about retirement. Though maybe we need to reframe the way we think about it. A quick search of the internet reveals multiple surveys in the UK that show one in three people think they won't be able to afford to retire when they reach State Pension Age. I don't want this chapter to be depressing or cause anxiety. I want it to motivate and empower you! No matter how old or young you are, there are things you can do to help you reach your retirement goals.

We've already talked at length about the *FIRE movement*, people who save and invest to work towards financial freedom and sometimes decide to retire early. I'm sure we all expect to retire *someday*, so there's still a lot we can learn from them.

But did you know that '*retirement*,' as we understand it, is a relatively new concept? In a blog post in 2017, a precursor to his book '*The Psychology of Money*,' Morgan Housel talks about retirement this way: *'Fifty years ago, the entire concept of retirement was reserved for the wealthy. The majority of men over age 65 were still in the labor force as recently as the 1950s. Most people worked until they died.'*[274]

We appear to have forgotten that retirement is a luxury.

Ultimately, in recent times, people in the UK and USA talk about retirement as if it's something they are automatically entitled to. But we shouldn't take the ability to retire with a decent standard of living for granted. We can't assume that we'll all be able to retire one day with the lifestyle we desire, not unless we make that our goal and work towards it. Luck has nothing to do with it.

We've already talked a little bit about how people aren't saving enough for the future. There is a potential retirement funding crisis facing us in the future as governments struggle to balance the books when it comes to the State Pension (UK) and Social Security (USA).

If we want to retire, we need to be intentional and make it happen. That means preparing for maybe 15, 20, or even 30 years. After that, we then need to make our retirement fund last for potentially another 20 years or more. The skills you've been learning in this book will set you up for a lifetime!

If you're in your teens, 20s, 30s or 40s - the sooner you start your *mindful finance* journey the better. If you're reading this in your 50s, 60s or later, if you're nearing retirement age and aren't sure what to do, then try not to panic. The worst thing you can do is remain on auto-pilot. It's okay to pull over and ask for directions if you're feeling lost.

In the UK, you'll hear all sorts of advice, people telling you to stop working at State Pension Age, to take the tax free cash out of your pension etc. But that's not right for everyone.

Your retirement savings are called a '*Nest Egg*' for a reason. Once you scramble them, that's it: there's no going back!

Like everything else in *Mindful Finance* so far, it's okay to stop and pause, to ask yourself why you'd want to do this and whether there's a better way for you. It's time to work out where you are and where to go from here.

It was a huge wake-up call for me when I changed jobs and could no longer pay into the NHS pension scheme. Suddenly, I couldn't do life on autopilot anymore. I found myself asking, '*How do other people save and invest for retirement? What do I do now? Is there another way?*'

That's what started me on a journey to find out what other ways there are to plan for retirement. Sometimes we have to think differently. And it's okay to ask for help if you don't know the answers.

MINDFUL FINANCE - 337

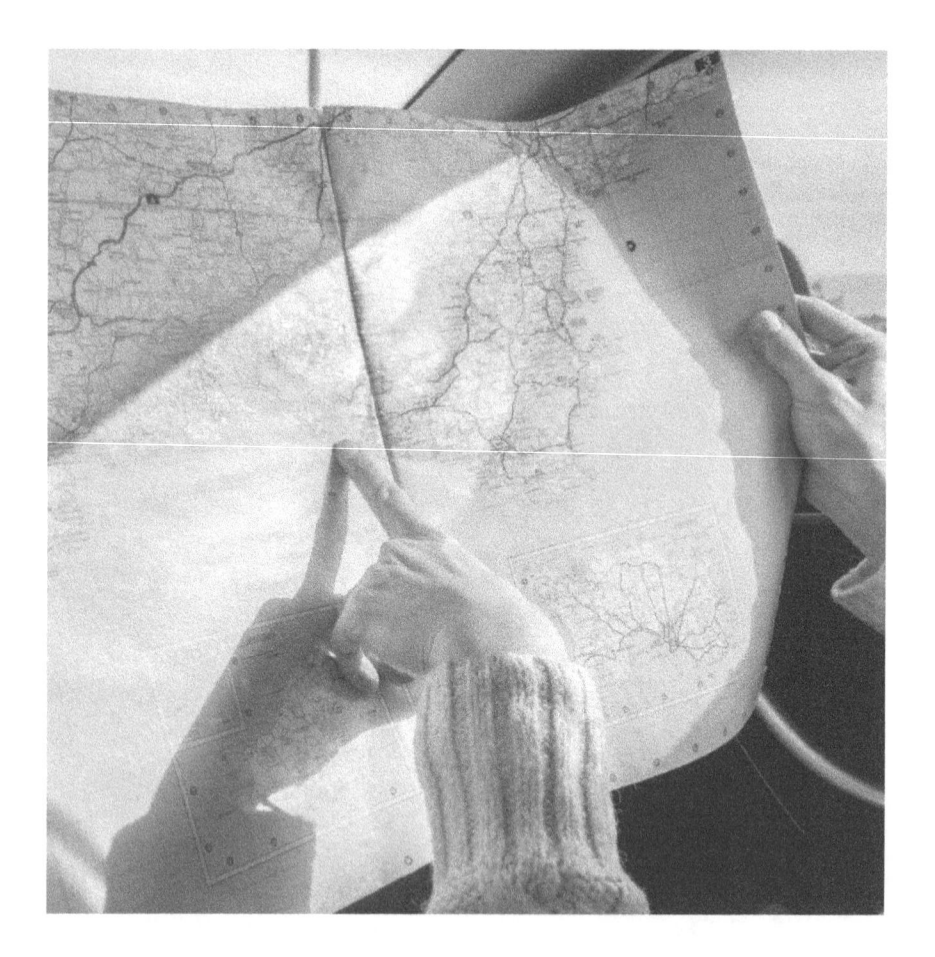

## Why do I need a Roadmap?

In this day and age, we've pretty much all experienced travel to unfamiliar places. It could be a road trip across the country or going on holiday abroad. It could even be checking out a new place in town or trying to get to a friend's house for the first time. We may only have a postcode or a street address to go on or a vague set of directions, but a map makes getting there a lot easier.

I remember when I was a child, we always kept a bright yellow and black roadmap in the back pocket of one of the seats of the car. I now realise that it was the *AA Great Britain and Ireland Road Atlas.* It was rarely ever used, but it was always there if we needed it.

In fact, a road atlas helped me a few years ago when I was stuck in a motorway diversion. The road ahead was blocked. But my Sat Nav kept taking me back to the motorway, no matter how hard I tried to find another way. I was going around in circles until I came across a service station where the shop assistant very kindly let me photograph the pages from a road atlas. At last I could follow the B-roads and take a different route.

Roadmaps are essential tools to help us get to where we want to go, especially if an obstacle gets in the way. The technology we have today is impressive. We essentially have a roadmap in our pockets in the form of our phones. We may have a Sat Nav built into our car. We can plan our journey on route planning websites. We can navigate to our holiday destination through a booking website.

When we get lost, we don't have to stop off and find a phone box like in the old days. We rarely need to ask someone in the street for directions anymore because we have a phone in our pocket and a satellite navigation system close at hand.

When it comes to our finances we can have a roadmap too. This is usually in the form of a **financial plan**. I've already mentioned a couple of these: Dave Ramsey's *7 Baby Steps* and *The Money Guy Show*'s *Financial Order of Operations*. These are just two examples of financial roadmaps that you can use to get you to the goal of financial independence or retirement. They tell you what to do in what order, just like when we built our financial house based on the architect's blueprint.

Unfortunately, we don't have a satellite navigation system, as such, to tell us where we are on our mindful finance journey. While there are apps and calculators available, I'm going to take you through some exercises to help you work out where you are and where you need to go. All you'll need for that is a pen and paper.

Keep that idea of a paper roadmap or road atlas in mind. If you aren't great at directions, don't worry. We'll work it out together and you can always get a co-pilot (financial professional) to help you navigate if you still feel lost.

## Common Ways To Get Lost

I'm sure you'll have a personal story of getting lost. You might know someone who has got lost on a rural walk or out with their dog. Maybe their phone battery went flat or they couldn't get a signal. Perhaps their map or map-reading skills weren't up to scratch. It's easy to get lost without the right roadmap or if you don't know how to use one properly.

In the USA's national parks, between 1992 and 2007 there were 65,439 search and rescue incidents, especially in mountainous regions or canyons. Unfortunately, not every story had a happy ending: most people (93%) were found within 24 hours, but sadly 3% of the search missions ended with the missing person never found, such is the vastness of America's terrain.[275]

This research outlined some of the key reasons why people get lost. This illustration can teach us a lot about why some people never reach their goals or miss their target destination in life. Examples included:

- Misjudging distances
- Not paying attention to their surroundings
- Over-confidence and refusing to ask for directions
- Difficult terrain
- Map failures
- Taking a wrong turn, a shortcut or a false trail
- Getting caught in the dark without a light
- A change in weather conditions
- Getting separated from the group

These are all things that can derail our financial and personal development journey too. Perhaps we're missing a rainy day fund and there's nowhere to shelter from the storm. We can get distracted and miss a turning when a key part of our financial plan is missing. Maybe it gets dark - we lose vision of where we're meant to be going and drift off course. What's more, our pride can get in the way and we don't ask for help until it's too late.

It can seem like a great idea to take a financial short cut, but a *too-good-to-be-true* offer or *get-rich-quick scheme* can tempt us to wander off-track. Similarly, it's easy to go into a daydream and drift off-course - that's what happened to me when I did life without a budget. It's so easy to overspend when we're not paying attention.

Do we even know where we are on our financial journey? It's easy to get lost when you're not aware of what's going on around you. When we panic, our situational awareness can evaporate.

When it comes to difficulty reading maps, the worst Sat Nav fail is probably the infamous story of the Syrian lorry driver who got very lost indeed. In fact, he ended up 1600 miles off course. He had a consignment of luxury cars from Turkey and was bound for Gibraltar on the Spanish coast.

All was going well, until he discovered that he was in Skegness, at *Gibraltar Point* (part of the Lincolnshire Wildlife Reserve overlooking the North Sea). He only realised his mistake when he reached the UK coastline and asked for directions from a group of confused-looking birdwatchers.[276]

If we don't follow the financial roadmap correctly we can end up way off course as well. So often we wish for a particular outcome but it's not clearly defined. We get disappointed when reality doesn't meet our expectations. If we don't have a clear goal, a plan or a roadmap to follow, this explains why sometimes in life we can feel completely lost or stuck with no idea where we are, how we got there or how to get back on the right path.

## How To Navigate Your Way To Financial Success

When it comes to going after our financial goals, such as financial independence or retirement, there are some things we need to know in advance:

1. **Work out where you are now** - create a *net worth statement*
2. **Decide where you are going** - *financial independence "FI" number*
3. **Plan how to get there** - *SMART goals*, daily habits
4. **Course correct** - adjust your plan, do a U-turn if necessary
5. **Don't travel alone** – join a community, work with a professional

So what lessons can we learn here to apply to our financial journey? Ultimately, *mindful finance* is key to navigating the long road to financial freedom. So many of these behavioural traps are within our power to control. Instead of drifting, we can start to gain awareness of where we are in the present moment and direct our steps more purposefully.

We need a roadmap from someone experienced who has gone ahead of us on the journey. That way, we can be sure it works. Just like a successful explorer, they have come back from climbing the mountain to share the story of how they did it. They map out a path that we can follow, a tried and tested method. So, start to do what wealthy people do and you can become wealthy too.

Sometimes many different routes lead to the same destination. So we don't have to travel exactly the same way as everyone else. If something unexpected turns up on our journey, like a financial road block, job loss or health issue, then we may need to take a diversion or detour. The roadmap will still help you find a way around it to correct your course. It might take a bit longer, but you can still get to where you're going safely!

Remember, you don't have to travel alone. If you're married, you should take your spouse along with you. You can do the exercises with a friend. You can find people going in the same direction as you who can share their experiences, fellow travellers along the road. You can invest in a co-pilot or navigator who can guide you. It's ok to get expert financial help and advice if you need it.

## 1. Work Out Where You Are Now

*'The real value in setting goals is not in their achievement [...]*
*The major reason for setting goals is to compel you*
*to become the person it takes to achieve them.'*
~ JIM ROHN

I was taught the basics of map reading at school. Did you ever do orienteering? In PE class, we were given a map and had to navigate to different check points where we could punch a card to prove we'd been there. It was like a treasure hunt with running involved.

I wasn't very fit as a kid (mainly because I hadn't learnt that I could get better with practice). So I'd be left reading the map and I would direct my friend to run and stamp the card for us! We were a good team – and yes, technically we cheated.

Anyway, to use a map properly, firstly you need to know where you are. That's why tourist maps mounted on big boards usually have a nice friendly arrow to announce, *"You Are Here!"* It's why when you use a Sat Nav the first thing it does is find your location.

Whether you're deep in debt or a millionaire, a key part of *mindful finance* is knowing where you are right now, in the valley or up the mountain.

You may already know that you've got unwanted debt. But it can be easier to bury your head in the sand and pretend it's not happening. We all know that ignoring a stressful problem doesn't make it go away, but it's still tempting to try. The debt will still pile up, even if you don't know how big it is.

Ultimately, when you're in a hole, the first step is to admit that you're stuck. Stop digging further (try not to get into more debt) and start to look for a way out (don't forget to ask for help if you need to).

On the other hand, perhaps you've been investing regularly or paying into a workplace pension for a few decades. Maybe you've never really looked at how much is in your different bank accounts and savings pots. If you stop and look at where you are, you may realise that you've got enough to retire sooner than you thought. Maybe you can afford to work part-time and enjoy some more hobbies or spend more time with your family.

We can work out where we on on our mindful finance journey by creating a **Net Worth Statement.** This is a great tool that can help you track your progress. It sounds technical and it can take a bit of effort to find your financial paperwork. But it'll be worth it. Remember, where you are now doesn't necessarily reflect where you're going to end up. You can adjust your course and keep moving forward. But you do need to know where you are.

## What Is A Net Worth Statement?

A net worth statement is a snapshot of your wealth at a particular moment. It'll help you work out whether you're in debt or on your way to building wealth. You can calculate your net worth by working out what you own and taking away what you owe, like this:

**Net worth = what you own – what you owe**

In other words, your net worth is the difference between your assets and your liabilities. The number can be positive or negative depending on whether you have more debts versus things of value. Once again I want to remind you: *Your true value is not measured by your valuables* and *you are worth more than your net worth.*

A net worth calculation is just a tool in your toolkit. It's a pinpoint on the financial roadmap and you don't have to stay there. You can do something about it.

Some content creators (like *The Money Guy Show* team) recommend doing a net worth statement once a year, like a financial MOT. I didn't find out about net worth statements until after I became debt free, so I decided to calculate them retrospectively. It amazes me to look back at where I started from to see where I travelled to next.

You'll remember from my story that I still can't say for sure how much debt I started with. Each year, as I paid off debt and grew my savings, I got a little further out of the hole. At some point, I reached a zero net worth where my savings matched my outstanding debt. Then finally, I made the phone call and the student loan was paid off.

After that, I started to focus on my emergency fund and investing. I could chart my net worth and see my savings grow year-on-year. It's just like putting pins in an Atlas of the world to remind yourself of where you've travelled to.

It's motivating to see how you can move from a negative net worth to a positive net worth. It's those simple habits we've talked about previously that can help us get there – by living on less than you make and putting that extra margin towards your financial goals. If you're feeling really geeky, you can even make it into a graph!

*The Money Guy Show* resources website has many handy tools including the *Net Worth Template*.[277] They also do an annual YouTube show comparing the net worth of people from different age groups.[278]

Of course, we've already talked about the dangers of toxic comparison. But comparing your net worth with your peers isn't meant to be something that makes you feel inadequate or competitive.

Rather, it's meant to inspire you. It shows you what's possible and where you could be aiming for. It's really useful to know if you're on track and whether you need to course correct so you end up where you want to be eventually.

If you have more debts than things of value, then you have a **negative net worth**. As we looked at in *Chapter 4: Possessions and Debt*, this might be a helpful debt, like a UK student loan, that helps you get on the career ladder. On the other hand, it could be the pit of consumer debt where it's hard to dig ourselves out.

Facing the debt black hole starts with opening the overdue bills and bank statements, locating your credit reports and finding out just how in the red you are. Most people would rather hide the letters somewhere. It's a brave thing to open them up and write all those numbers down.

It's painful to admit you're underwater. But this is a useful milestone on your financial freedom journey. It's putting a stake in the ground and saying, *"Right, I'm here! This is where I'm at."* Hopefully you'll be able to look back at that moment and see just how far you've come.

### Mindful finance Challenge 4 – Net Worth Statement

We're going to pause here for another mindful finance challenge. It's time to put together your own net worth statement, if you want to. I encourage you to have a go. For some people, this may be one of the hardest things they've ever done. It's really challenging to admit that you don't know where you are financially. So well done for giving this a go! You're taking the first steps towards changing your life and building a better future.

If you want to create a net worth statement, it really is as simple as writing down what you own and what you owe and working out the difference between the two.

You can download *The Money Guy Show*'s free *Net Worth Template*.[5] Otherwise, you can search online for a calculator or template. If you want to, you can get an old-fashioned pen and paper and write down your numbers, then add up the totals with a calculator.

On the next page, you'll find some examples of assets (things you own) and liabilities (things you owe). This isn't a complete list, but it gives you an idea of where your money or debts might be hiding.

It takes time and effort to find out what you've got and where it is. Don't feel you need to do this all at once. It's a process. So I encourage you to make a start and get to know where you are financially.

Think of it as a treasure hunt. Your assets and liabilities are out there somewhere, waiting to be found!

## *Where Do I Find My Liabilities?*

If you want some more information on locating your debts, I suggest you go back to *Chapter 4: Possessions and Debt*. There are resources in the debt section on how to find out how much debt you have and how you can pay it off.

## *Where Can I Find My Assets?*

When it comes to working out your assets – what you own – some people may decide that certain items, like your house or car, are optional. You might want to take an inventory of things like collectables, valuables and jewellery as this will help if you when getting things like contents insurance.

# Net Worth Statement

## Do you know where you are financially?

Assets are positive items on the balance sheet. They can go up (appreciating) or down (depreciating). Liabilities are negative items on the balance sheet. They tend to cost you money to own, like the bad debt we looked at in Chapter 4.

### Assets

- Cash / savings accounts / current account
- ISA / pension / general investment account
- Home equity / whole life insurance (cash value)
- Bonds / stocks and shares / gold / annuities / pensions
- Car / collectables / jewellery / furniture / cryptocurrency

### Liabilities

- Credit card / personal loans / store cards
- Owed taxes / legal fees / council tax
- Mortgage / loan on life insurance
- Money owed to family / others / IOU's
- Car loan / student loan (this may be optional to include)

There are plenty of websites where you can find out roughly how much similar houses in your local area recently sold for. Some people decide to create two net worth statements, one including your house and one without.

The housing market can fluctuate and contribute to the '*wealth effect.*' This is where people feel wealthy in good economic times when house prices are usually higher, so they tend to spend more. So skipping your house in your net worth statement can help you keep on track. Remember, your estimated house value doesn't mean very much until you sell it.

According to *Investopedia.com*, '*There is a bit of controversy surrounding the usefulness and appropriateness of including your home in your net worth calculation. Proponents believe that your home is your most valuable asset and should definitely be included in your net worth calculation. Opponents argue that you should not count it because if you sold it (for example, during retirement) where would you live?*'[279]

To get the value of your personal accounts and investments, you will need to access things like your bank statements and pension records. Do you have an old building society account that you've lost track of? Maybe you've got premium bonds left to you by a grandparent? It's worth thinking about any assets that you might have forgotten about. Savings and investments that have sat gathering dust can be put to better use.

While doing some research for this book I discovered that in the UK your accounts can become dormant if you don't access them for a period of time. Typically this is between 3 and 15 years. The money may even be reclaimed and given to good causes. This blog from *MoneySuperMarket.com* tells you what to do if you live in the UK and this applies to you.[280]

You may have changed jobs in the past and lost track of what retirement schemes you've paid into. The *Money Helper* website has advice on how to track down your old pension pots if you live in the UK.[281] Some companies in the UK will encourage you to consolidate all your pensions into one place using their service. This is optional. As long as you stay intentional, it's up to you.

It's also important to be aware that there are limits on how much of your money is insured by each bank or investment platform. At the time of writing, the Financial Services Compensation Scheme (FSCS) in the UK will insure you up to £85,000 if your bank or investment platform fails for whatever reason.[282]

In the USA, the FDIC will insure up to $250,000.[283] Some banks are actually covered by the same insurance policy, so it makes sense to do your research and make sure you're spreading your risk across different banks or organisations, just in case. This is important because there were several notable bank failures in 2022. So it is possible it could happen again.[284]

## Declutter Your Finance Statements

You may be a naturally organised person. Or like me when I first started, you may find you've got piles of bank statements and utility bills mixed together in a box somewhere.

In the process of getting debt-free, I also organised my records by category – bank accounts, insurance documents, car documents and financing, health records, student loans etc.

You could make folders on your computer to download your digital bank statements into. Or you could go stationery shopping and get some paper folders or a storage system for your documents.

If you do this once and put a system in place for your financial records, I assure you it'll be much easier to maintain going forward. It will also help you and your family in future, especially if you need help with your finances one day.

Decluttering your financial documents also helps you when meeting with a finance professional, doing your tax return or creating a legacy box for your family. You might want to revisit *Chapter 5: Family* to remind yourself about legacy boxes.

## 2. Decide Where You Are Going

*'If you don't know where you are going, you'll end up someplace else.'*
~ YOGI BERRA

The next thing you need to do when reading a map is to work out where you want to end up. This is true for any goal. But what does it mean for your retirement goal? To keep things simple, we're going to call this by its other name - *financial independence.*

The vast majority of the *FIRE community* is working towards the goal of financial independence. This is the point at which you have enough wealth invested to generate an income that replaces your job and allows you to stop working. It means we can work because we want to, not because we have to. Some people see this as the ultimate *financial freedom.* It may also allow them *time freedom* (to work when they want) and *geographical freedom* (to work where they want).

So to know how much you need invested to retire, you can start by calculating your **Financial Independence (FI) Number**. It's not the whole story, but it gives you a rough ballpark figure.

Here are some of the other factors we need to consider:

- What age do I want to retire? How many years away is that?
- Will I qualify for the State Pension (or Social Security in USA)?
- Will I have any other income streams? (e.g. property, a business)
- Is there anyone else dependent on my income?
- What is my health like? How long do I expect to live for?
- Do I have any debt or a mortgage? Do I have other expenses?
- Do I plan to pay for my children's university education?
- What would my minimum retirement income need to be?
- What sort of lifestyle would I like to have in retirement?
- How generous do I want to be in retirement?
- Do I want to leave a legacy or use up all my wealth?

We need to dream about retirement the same way that we designed our dream garden. Our portfolio of investments needs to be cultivated to make sure that it bears fruit at the right time to sustain us when we need it to. There are so many things to think about! The key is to **dream in high definition**.

In reality, retirement will look very different for each of us. It could involve part-time work or *mini-retirements,* while other people start a new career or keep working.

Some people plan to retire earlier or later than the State Retirement Age. If you're married, you may want to coordinate your retirement date with your spouse.

If you're married, you need to make sure your spouse is on board so you don't end up in two remote destinations. How would retirement work for each of you? What's your age difference? Will one of you still be working while the other is off playing golf? How is your health? Will one of you become a carer for the other at some point?

The usual trajectory of retirement is that people tend to spend more at the beginning when they are more active and their health is better. They buy the camper van, go on cruises, go out to eat and travel. But as you get older, you probably won't have those expenses. Instead, you may end up with health and social care costs to consider.

The other thing working against us is inflation. Do you remember how things tend to get more expensive over time? So things like food, housing, goods and services cost more years from now. Some people choose to take this into account when calculating how much they need to retire, especially since retirement can last 30 years or more. We need to make sure we're beating inflation or planning for it.

Try to imagine what your ideal retirement might look like. It's okay to dream, but then we need to look at what's possible in reality and get practical. We can't just cross our fingers and hope for the best!

After you've crunched the numbers, you may realise that you need to manage your expectations or up your savings rate. Or maybe you're well on track and can afford to spend a bit more in the hear and now.

Before calculating your *Financial Independence (FI) Number*, if you're a maths person, you might want to know some of the background to how the calculation works. If maths isn't your thing, don't worry; you'll just have to trust that the calculation comes from economic data. You can skip this next bit.

### The '80% Rule'

This rule suggests that you'll only need about 80% of your pre-retirement income during retirement. This assumes that you won't have a few key expenses in retirement, such as commuting, a mortgage or saving for retirement. Some expenses, such as healthcare and travel abroad may go up. It's not exact, but it's a good starting place to estimate how much you'll need each year to live on in retirement.[285]

### The '25x Rule' or '4% Rule'

You'll often come across this rule used by the *FIRE community*. It's sometimes called the *'safe withdrawal rate.'* It's based on research that suggests that you can safely withdraw around 4% of your investment pot each year (based on average growth and inflation) without your money running out.

It's also called the 25x Rule as you'll need 25 times your annual spending to be invested to achieve the same results.[286] For example, if you want to live on £25,000 a year in retirement, you would need to have £625,000 invested. If you want to live on £50,000 a year in retirement, you'd need to have £1.25 million invested. Get the idea?

The 4% rule has come under criticism for being an oversimplification. It doesn't work well if you retire early, which means your retirement is going to be longer than usual, more than the 30-year traditional retirement people imagine. Nor does it work well if inflation is running higher or if stock market growth is less than the historical average.

For this reason, it may be safer to withdraw 3% of your investment pot as this gives you a greater likelihood of your retirement funds not running out. This is sometimes referred to as the '33x Rule.' So to safely withdraw £25,000 a year you would need £825,000 invested. For £50,000 a year you'd need a whopping £1.65 million invested.

But don't be disheartened if the numbers look impossible. Most of this money comes from the growth of your investments due to compound interest, not what you save upfront.

If you're nearing retirement and don't have anywhere near enough to retire the way you had hoped, there are still things you can do. It might involve working for longer or working part time. It could be reducing your living standards in retirement.

The key thing is not to panic and do anything impulsive. There are lots of websites with free information on your retirement options. It may be worthwhile getting advice from a financial professional as well.

You can start by looking at this UK government website to see what to do next :

**www.gov.uk/plan-retirement-income/get-financial-advice**

Remember, we're gardeners now: we grow our investments over time. The more time we have, the easier it will be to reach our target. If time isn't on your side, there is still hope.

## *Today's Numbers or Adjust For Inflation?*

Nobody knows what the future holds, but as I said before, you can be pretty sure that your money will probably be worth less in future due to inflation. Central banks have a habit of printing more money and devaluing their currencies over time.

History is the only guide we have to go on and it shows we've had more periods of inflation (where money loses buying power) than deflation (where money gains buying power).

When calculating your retirement number you may want to take into account the effect of inflation on your investments.

One million pounds or dollars in today's money won't have the same buying power 30 or 40 years from now. Just look at average UK house prices in the 1960s; the average home cost around £2500 compared to over £280,000 according to 2022 data.[287]

If you want to play around with some numbers, you can check out the inflation calculator on the Bank of England website which shows how prices have changed from 1209 until now.[288] According to the calculator, £10 in 1209 would be worth over £16,000 by 2023!

Obviously, this is an extreme example, but inflation can apply to anything from average incomes and house prices, to the price of a loaf of bread.

Some retirement calculators will allow you to adjust for future inflation, so be aware of this when calculating your FI number. Ultimately, the purpose of investing for the future is to make sure your money is keeping up with or growing faster than inflation.

If you leave your cash alone without putting it to work, inflation will slowly erode the buying power of your money over time. Doing nothing is risky too.

### Retirement Guides and Calculators:

In the Resources Chapter, you'll find some links to my favourite UK and USA content creators who have created retirement guides and videos. They will talk you through some worked examples of how to calculate your FI number, taking into account the factors I've mentioned above.

A quick search for retirement calculators in an online search engine will give you a plethora of retirement and pension calculators. You can try out some numbers of your own to see how much you need to have invested to retire.

Similarly, you can work backwards and see how much your current savings and investments might be worth by the time you get to retirement. This will help you know if you're on the right track.

One of my favourite free calculators in the UK is the HSBC *'Picture your future lifestyle'* Quiz:

*retirementcalculator.hsbc.co.uk* [289]

This covers many of those questions we asked ourselves earlier, looking at different lifestyle goals. It then helps you to establish your target retirement number. Doing this exercise helps show you whether you're on track or need whether you need to make some adjustments.

The *Gov.UK* website also has some handy information and resources on how to plan for retirement:[290]

*www.gov.uk/plan-for-retirement*

For readers in the USA, you may prefer to work in dollars. *Ramsey Solutions* has a handy free retirement tool to help you know your retirement number, what they refer to as the *'Retire Inspired Quotient' or* R:IQ:[291]

*www.ramseysolutions.com/retirement/riq*

Similarly, *The Money Guy Show* has the *'Know Your Number Course'*.[292] While this isn't a free course, *The Money Guy Show* does provide plenty of free podcast material on related topics which can help you calculate your FI number and what percentage of your income to put into investments depending on your age:

*learn.moneyguy.com/know-your-number-course*

Just keep in mind that you may need a lot more invested than you initially realised so that you can achieve the retirement of your dreams. But don't let that scare you or put you off! It was mind-blowing to me when I first started learning about this topic.

*\*\*\**

I didn't realise that I might need to be a millionaire one day just to retire to the lifestyle I had in mind. I've also learnt that this is achievable, but it will take discipline and can take a while to get there. It also makes working part-time look very appealing and many people choose to transition into retirement over time.

The reality is that most people have no idea what their FI number is and how much they need to invest to successfully retire. You don't need to be one of them. It's up to you how much detail you want to go into when it comes to retirement planning. You may or may not want to include the government's contribution. After all, who knows what these will look like by the time we get to retirement?

Of course, this is just the beginning. Pete Matthew's *Meaningful Money Podcast* is a great place to look up any specific questions you have about retirement planning (see Resources Chapter). There are lots of things we haven't covered, such as 'bucket strategies' and cash buffers, pension drawdown versus annuities.[293] Feel free to explore these yourself.

When things start to get complicated, that's when you might want to involve a financial professional to help you do some expert portfolio design. You can also ask them to stress-test your retirement plan and run various simulations to see what the probability is of your money running out, adjusting for all the variables.

For my medic friends and NHS workers, the *Medics Money Podcast* is a great resource to learn more about *The NHS Pension Scheme.* They can also help pair you up with a specialist medical accountant or financial advisor via their website.

Still don't believe you've got what it takes? I've been saving this, but since we're crunching the numbers, I think it's time to do another Mindful Finance Challenge.

## Mindful Finance Challenge 5: Compound Interest

We keep talking about compound interest. I mentioned it when we looked at *The Principle of Multiplication.* But does it really make sense to you yet? It was new to me once as well.

You may not have given the compounding effect much thought since doing maths at school. I hadn't really either. That's because human minds aren't good with big numbers and we tend to think linearly (in straight lines). This is why the compound effect can feel *mind-blowing.*

As you'll see from this quick example, when it comes to the compound effect, things move *exponentially.* That means instead of a straight line, growth moves in a curve that eventually shoots upwards! Many people struggle to imagine this. But we can use it to our advantage when it comes to wealth-building.

When you start saving or investing you might not feel like you're making much progress when you're starting out. Things go slow at first, but eventually you reach a tipping point where your investments are making more than you're putting in. It's a fascinating thing to see your money multiplying – but it could take 20, 30 or 40 years or more to see your money really take off.

Albert Einstein called compound interest the *'eighth wonder of the world,'* remember? That's really saying something.

Let's crunch some numbers to make this more real for you.

I want to introduce you to one of my favourite tools – the compound interest calculator, from *'The Calculator Site.'* [294]

www.thecalculatorsite.com/finance/calculators/compoundinterest-calculator.php

**Example 1:**

On the opposite page, you'll see I've plugged some numbers into the calculator tool. We're going to start with £100 and invest £100 per month for 30 years, at a compound interest rate of 10%.

Why not have a go at finding the *Calculator Site* webpage and doing this with me? I've chosen 10% to keep the numbers simple for now (I know this is an ambitious rate of return on your investments, but not impossible. It just means we're on the higher end of the risk spectrum).

# Monthly Investing Example

**Compound Interest** | Simple Interest | Daily Compounding | Forex Compounding

Currency:
[ $ ] [ € ] [ **£** ] [ ₹ ] [ ¥ ]

Initial investment:
£ 100

Interest rate:
10 %   yearly

Years: 30   Months: 0

Additional contributions: (optional)
None | **Deposits** | Withdrawals | Both

Deposit amount: (optional)
£ 100   monthly

Deposits made at what point in period?
Beginning | **End**

Annual deposit % increase? (optional)
%

Compound interval:
Monthly (12/yr)   [Calculate]

www.thecalculatorsite.com/finance/calculators/compoundinterestcalculator.php

360 - DR ESTHER J. COLE

# Compound Interest Scenario I

## Projection for 30 years

**Future investment value**
**£228,032.53**

**Total interest earned**
**£191,932.53**

**Initial balance**
**£100.00**

**Additional deposits**
**£36,000.00**

**Interest rate (yearly)**
**10%**

Calculator site

## Compound interest exponential growth curve

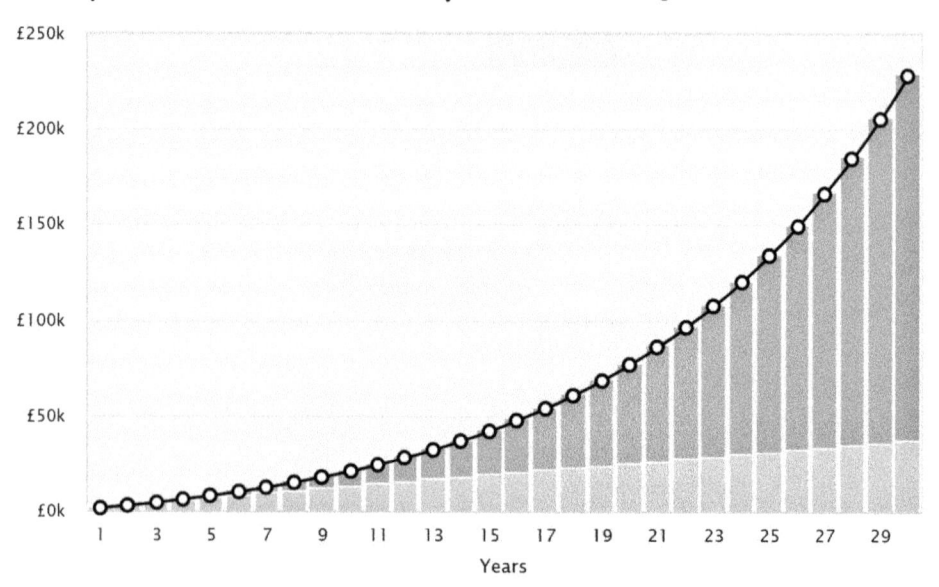

www.thecalculatorsite.com/finance/calculators/compoundinterestcalculator.php

**Example 1: (continued)**

You'll see on the graph how the amount you're investing each month (the lighter coloured bars) appears to grow in a steady line upwards. Over 30 years, you would put in a total of £36,000. But look at the darker bars with the little dots on top. These represent the growth of your money due to compound interest! Notice how it looks quite straight at first, but you can really see the change at 20 years where the curve starts going upwards! That's an exponential growth curve. It starts off slowly and then gets really steep, really quickly.

**Example 2:**

When it comes to exponential curves, the reason why you see the curve shoot up even more steeply over time is because at a 10% interest rate, your money is doubling approximately every 7 years. Imagine if you could invest your money for 40 or 50 years!

Okay, let's change one variable in our calculation. Let's put in the same numbers as before... we're going to start with £100 and invest £100 per month at a compound interest rate of 10%. But this time we'll extend the time to 45 years. Turn over the page to see what happens!

If we carried on our £100 per month investment, we'd put in a total of £54,000. But at 10% compound interest, you'd finally become a millionaire after 45 years! By then your investments would be earning around £100,000 per year in interest!

If you compare the two charts (flip the page back and forth), just look at the difference between our 30 year chart and our 45 year chart! All that crazy exponential growth took place in the last 15 years! And we only put in another £18,000 to get to our £1 million. That's why time is such an important component in the equation.

In reality, most people may not have 45 years to invest. 10% on our investments may be a little too risky. That's why most people need to invest more than £100 per month. It's also why you need to try and start your *mindful finance* journey as early as possible. But we may also need to adjust our end-goal and expectations.

362 - DR ESTHER J. COLE

# Compound Interest Scenario 2

## Projection for 45 years

**Future investment value**
**£1,057,085.59**

**Total interest earned**
**£1,002,985.59**

**Initial balance**
**£100.00**

**Additional deposits**
£54,000.00

**Interest rate (yearly)**
10%

**Time-weighted rate of return**
⬆ 8735.42%

## Compound interest exponential growth curve

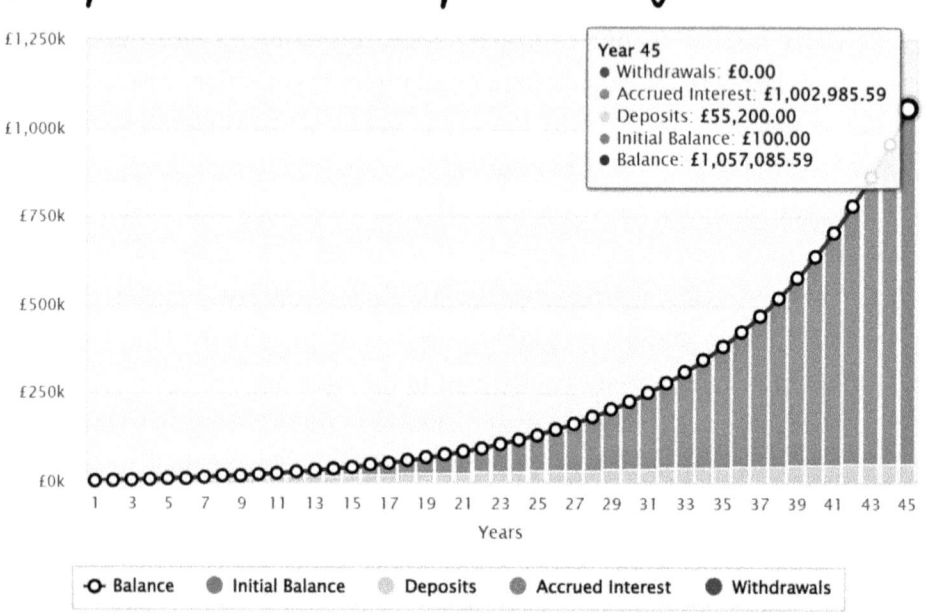

**Year 45**
- Withdrawals: £0.00
- Accrued Interest: £1,002,985.59
- Deposits: £55,200.00
- Initial Balance: £100.00
- Balance: £1,057,085.59

Legend: -O- Balance ● Initial Balance ● Deposits ● Accrued Interest ● Withdrawals

www.thecalculatorsite.com/finance/calculators/compoundinterestcalculator.php

**Example 3:**

Some people already have money invested. The other thing I really like about the compound interest calculator is that it's possible to get a glimpse at what the future might look like. If you have a lump sum to invest, you can play around with the numbers to find out what the growth on your money might look like in 10, 20 or even 40 years' time.

So let's see how much money we'd need to invest as a lump sum at age 30 to reach £1 million by age 65. That gives us 35 years to grow our investment. We'll go for 7% compound interest this time, as that's a little more realistic compared the historic average, but it's still the upper end of the risk spectrum.

Turn over the page to see what happens when we plug the numbers into the compound interest calculator... I've made a graph as well so you can see that lovely exponential growth curve.

**Here's the answer:** According to the compound interest calculator, we'd need to have an investment of £87,000 at age 30, invested at 7% for 35 years to reach £1 million without needing to put in a penny more. Obviously, that may still be a tall order for most 30-year-olds. But in reality, it's likely that you'd still be saving and investing each month on top of this. It's just an example to show you the power of compound interest at work.

## Now it's your turn

Now you've got the compound interest calculator too, why not have a play and put in some numbers of your own? How long do you have to invest? How much can you afford to put in each month or as a lump sum? How much risk are you comfortable taking?

On average, over the long-term you can expect somewhere from 5% to 10% growth on your investment depending on how much risk you're willing to take on. Compound interest works against you too. Things like debt, inflation and fees grow exponentially in the opposite direction!

# Lump Sum Investing Example

**Compound Interest** | Simple Interest | Daily Compound

**Currency:** £

**Initial investment:** £ 87000

**Interest rate:** 7 % yearly

**Years:** 35  **Months:** 0

**Additional contributions:** (optional)
**None** | Deposits | Withdrawals | Both

**Compound interval:** Monthly (12/yr)

[Calculate]

www.thecalculatorsite.com/finance/calculators/compoundinterestcalculator.php

MINDFUL FINANCE - 365

# Compound Interest Scenario 3

## Projection for 35 years

Future investment value
**£1,001,035.21**

Total interest earned
**£914,035.21**

Initial balance
**£87,000.00**

Interest rate (yearly)
**7%**

All-time rate of Return (RoR)
**↑ 1050.62%**

Calculator site

## Compound interest exponential growth curve

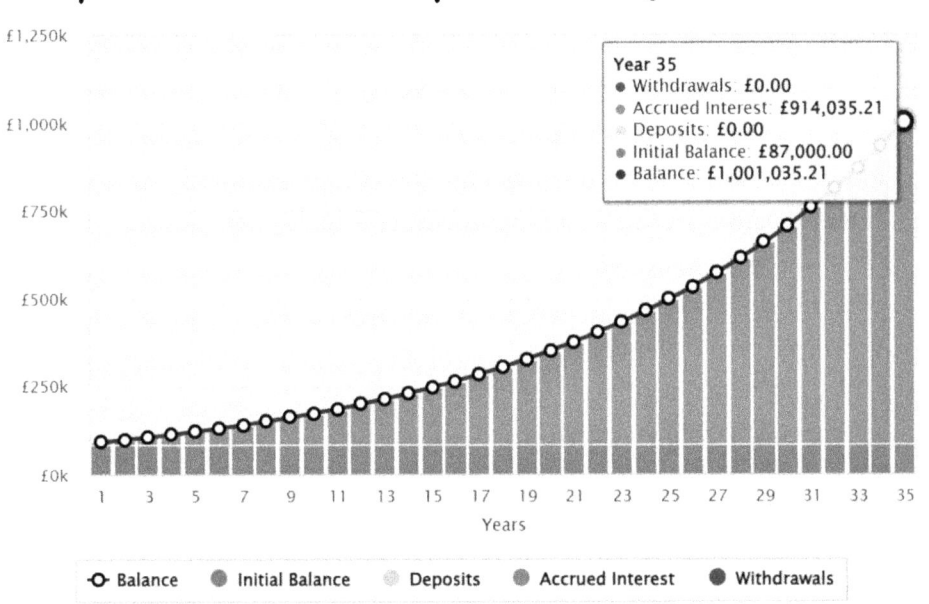

**Year 35**
- Withdrawals: £0.00
- Accrued Interest: £914,035.21
- Deposits: £0.00
- Initial Balance: £87,000.00
- Balance: £1,001,035.21

Legend: Balance, Initial Balance, Deposits, Accrued Interest, Withdrawals

www.thecalculatorsite.com/finance/calculators/compoundinterestcalculator.php

## 3. Plan How To Get There

*'A goal without a plan is just a wish.'*
*~ ANTOINE DE SAINT-EXUPÉRY*

As I said earlier, roadmaps help us to navigate. But we still have to plan our route. There are an infinite number of ways to get from A to B, some more direct than others. So, will you take the scenic route or the motorway (highway)?

There are pros and cons to each. If you go the direct route you may get to your destination quicker. But perhaps you'll miss out on some adventures or life lessons along the way. Of course, this analogy works the other way too. Sometimes we take a detour from the main road and get lost down some country road. You may never reach your destination at all!

That's why it's good to learn from people who are experts in their field or someone who is ahead of us on the journey. If they've been there before, they can act as our guide. They can let us know what challenges to expect and what preparations we need to make. Think of a self-help book, podcast or motivational speaker as being almost like a travel guide for your journey to success.

In the Resources Chapter, you'll find my favourite financial experts, content creators and motivational speakers. I highly recommend you seek some out for yourself.

Learning new skills is good for our mental health and wellbeing. Everything we've already talked about in this book, about building healthy habits and routines, becoming disciplined and developing self-awareness, will help you make a goal and stick to it. But how do we put all this into practice?

It's time to apply what we've been learning. Let's take a look at how some experts approach setting goals and how to achieve them.

## SMART Goals

So, you've been dreaming about what your future retirement might look like. How do we turn that wish into reality? To turn a dream into a goal, as Antoine de Saint-Exupéry puts it, we need to **make a plan.**

Lots of people make New Year's resolutions, but hardly anyone sticks with them. That's because these goals are often very broad, such as *'I want to save more money'* or *'I want to lose weight.'* But how much do you want to save? In what time period? How will you know if you're on track?

That's where **SMART Goals** come in. You've probably heard about these before. But I thought it would be interesting to find out where they came from in the first place.

According to the *Project Smart* website, the idea of SMART goals was developed in 1981 by George T. Doran in a paper entitled *'There's a S.M.A.R.T. Way to Write Management's Goals and Objectives.'*[295, 296] Doran's original S.M.A.R.T. acronym suggests that goals should be:

- **Specific**: target a specific area for improvement
- **Measurable**: quantifiable, so you can measure your progress
- **Assignable**: specify who will do it (although, this later became **Achievable** or **Attainable**)
- **Realistic**: results can realistically be achieved with the resources available (some people use **Relevant**)
- **Time-related**: specify when the result can be achieved (this later became **Time-Bound**)

You'll find plenty of websites and advice on how to set SMART goals, such as a blog post by *DevelopGoodHabits.com*.[297] So I'll stick to the basics and you can do some research if you're interested in learning more.

*The Money Guy Show* team talk about the process of setting goals and following a financial plan on their New Year's show, *'How to win with money in 2023.'*[298] They talk about the importance of writing your goals down and making sure you follow the S.M.A.R.T. framework. Terri Savelle Foy also talks about setting goals on her New Year show.[299]

Jim Rohn had a wonderful way of breaking down goals across different areas of life, by timeframe. If we look at personal finance, for example, you might have a retirement goal but that could be decades away. So it makes sense to set other financial goals to work towards as well. These can act as milestone markers along the way that give you a positive boost of motivation as you achieve them. You may want to set financial goals for the next 1 or 2 years, 5 years and 10 years.

Achieving *Financial Independence* (FI) is a process. Along the journey, you may want to set a goal to become debt-free, build up your emergency fund, get a house deposit together or pay off your mortgage early. You can break a big goal into more manageable chunks.

You may want to set a target of reaching a particular net worth by the age of 30, 40 or 50. You may want to increase your savings rate to a particular percentage of your income. These are just some suggestions. Your financial goals are going to be personal to you, taking into account your specific values and circumstances.

This is why **financial plans**, such as Dave Ramsey's *7 Baby Steps* and *The Money Guy Show's Financial Order of Operations* are so useful.[300, 301] They provide a framework of financial goals, in the right order. They are the inspiration behind Part 1 of this book.

I encourage you to go and look these financial plans up for yourself. While they are primarily aimed at an American audience, there are videos in the Resources Chapter that will help you apply these principles if you live in the UK. We don't have Ramsey Solutions' *Financial Peace University* in the UK (yet), but if you follow Pete Matthew and others, you can do the basics yourself.

Following a financial plan can give you a sense of momentum and control, making sure you're getting your financial priorities right.

An example of a **financial SMART goal** might look like this:

> - **S – specific:** to reach my *Financial Independence* (FI) Number by age 68 (calculated using the 25x / 4% rule)
> - **M – measurable:** to have an amount invested by a certain age or to invest an amount each month for a certain number of years
> - **A – achievable:** based on realistic income / savings rate
> - **R – relevant:** I want to retire one day so it's an appropriate goal
> - **T – time-bound:** the number of years I have left until I'm 68

We could use a retirement calculator, such as *PensionBee* to determine what sort of lifestyle we want in retirement.[302] A moderate retirement income, for example, would need the equivalent of £23,300 per year for one person in today's money (as of 2023). We can then use the 25x (or 4% rule) to calculate that a pension pot of £582,500 is needed to achieve this.

Of course, we'd also have to work out how much we already had invested and how much more we would need. Then you can divide this by the number of years remaining until retirement or use an online retirement calculator to make sure you're on track.

The SMART framework for setting goals is just another tool in your toolkit, but it's a very valuable one. It helps you know if your goal is achievable. If it isn't, then you might need to go back to the drawing board and set a new goal.

\* \* \*

## Dream Books and Vision Boards

*'And the Lord answered me:*
*"Write the vision; make it plain on tablets, so he may run who reads it.*
*For still the vision awaits its appointed time; it hastens to the end--it will not*
*lie. If it seems slow, wait for it; it will surely come; it will not delay."'*
~ HABAKKUK 2:2-3 (ESV: English Standard Version)

When we write down a SMART goal, it's a way of visualising the future and how we're going to get there. We've taken something fluffy and turned it into something solid. We've had to define what we want and we know the daily things we need to do to make it a reality.

Some people decide to create a dream book or vision board to record or remind them of their SMART goals. Having a clear vision of our goals is powerful as it brings clarity and helps focus our minds on what we want to achieve.

So much of what we do is underpinned by thought. If we focus our thoughts on our goal, we're more likely to keep working towards it. After all, *out of sight is out of mind.*

I first heard about dream books and vision boards from Pastor Emma Bryant at Liverpool One Church. She pointed me in the direction of Terri Savelle Foy, a female Christian motivational speaker who had inspired her. I've put links to Terri's work in the References Chapter.

It's hard to say exactly how it works. But there's something special about having a photograph or picturing yourself achieving your goal that draws your attention towards it.

Where your thoughts go, your reality follows. Whatever you want to call it, dream books and vision boards have worked for lots of people. So it's worth a go.

A map is no good unless you can see it in front of you. You need to look at it often to know whether you're on track. So perhaps creating a visual display of your goals is similar to this, focusing you on your destination so that your brain can be working on the questions – *Where am I now? How do I get to where I want to be? Am I on track? What can I do today to move in the direction of the future I desire?*

Some people like to journal. You can make a scrapbook of photos, imagining your dreams and goals becoming real. You can write about goals you've already achieved and dreams that you've already accomplished to encourage you. Writing down and remembering your wins will inspire you by showing you how far you've already come.

Perhaps you can make a vision board, a display that you can hang up and look at every day.

One year I used a cork notice board and pinned photos to it, one for each of my goals. After achieving those goals, I stuck them in my dream book as memories to look back on and celebrate.

I try to take some time every January to reflect on my goals instead of setting New Year's Resolutions. Some years I'm more successful than others - life can get busy and unexpected roadblocks show up.

Some people use Post-it notes. It could be their goals, positive affirmations, motivational quotes or Bible scriptures. You can put them around your mirror, on a wall or wardrobe. You can read them as part of your morning routine.

Maybe you just say out loud every day what your goals are so that they stay at the forefront of your mind.

That's how I wrote this book, visualising it and thinking about it for 2 years. It takes focus and discipline to write a book, to edit it and format it. I can't tell you the number of hours! Even now, writing this, it's exciting to imagine you reading it and I hope you're finding it helpful and transformative.

It's up to you whether you keep your books and vision boards private or not. Just like revealing our goals to someone else, there are pros and cons to doing so. You'll hear some people recommending you share your goals to hold you accountable and other people recommending you keep them secret so nobody can talk you out of them.

Perhaps you decide to have some personal goals and share others as a family. Either way, the key is to remind yourself of them regularly.

You may decide to pray over your goals and dreams. You may ask for spiritual help and guidance to make them a reality.

But don't be surprised if your goals change dramatically over time. You may just find that your goals develop in the same way that you grow and develop. It's an act of faith to step out of your comfort zone and go after the dream that used to seem impossible. Each smaller goal achieved will inspire you to go after the next one.

You can also sow generosity seeds into your goals. We looked at this briefly in the last chapter. Terri Savelle Foy often talks about sowing generosity seeds as a way to make her goals a reality. It's an act of faith, belief and intentionality.

Generosity stretches you, encourages you to imagine big and shows that you're committed to seeing your goal become a reality. It's a way of putting a stake in the ground and saying, *'I believe that I will achieve my goal, so I'm going to bless someone else first., even while I'm waiting for my blessing.'*

This could look like setting a goal to become debt-free and deciding to be generous with your time, talents and treasures along the way. Perhaps you're hoping for a child or family one day, so you offer to babysit for a friend. Perhaps you're dreaming of publishing a book one day, so you help someone else to publish theirs or give books away that encourage others. It's preparing the ground by shifting your mindset.

You can get creative in deciding what generosity seeds to sow. Whatever you're hoping for in your own life, there will be someone you can bless or help along the way. It could be a charity, a good cause, a person or an organisation working in the area of your goal.

You may choose to bless someone who is already successful. Perhaps they have already attained whatever the dream is in your heart. Or maybe they're working towards their dream too.

It may not make any logical sense, but there are numerous stories of people being blessed multiple times over by choosing to plant a seed of generosity first. By stepping out in faith and choosing to bless others in advance, you're committing to making your goal a reality.

If we reach out with generosity, love, compassion and kindness, even though we may feel we're in a place of lack or we're in a season of waiting, we're preparing our hearts to receive.

It will increase our gratitude once we reach our goal. Perhaps it will inspire others to be generous and go after their dreams too. It helps us prepare to carry the weight of responsibility when the success we dreamt of finally arrives.

## 4. How To Course Correct

Your hopes, goals and dreams can feel far off and distant. When the distances are bigger, a small change in trajectory has massive results. Imagine a rocket ship in outer space or a plane travelling off course. How can we avoid ending up in the wrong place, like the poor lorry driver who found himself in Skegness instead of near Spain?

We've got our roadmap. We've made our game plan. Now we need to know if we're on track.

If we break our journey up into smaller goals, we can look for milestones and landmarks, things to celebrate on our way to success. If that's financial independence, well, you can celebrate your first budget and each month you stick to it after that. You can shout for joy when you pay off your consumer debt or do a *debt-free scream* when your mortgage is paid off. You can reward yourself when your emergency fund is complete.

If you're following Dave Ramsey's *7 Baby Steps* or *The Money Guy Show*'s *Financial Order of Operations*, then there are plenty of opportunities to celebrate, especially in those crucial early stages.

As I said before, we can go off course for lots of reasons. Things never go completely to plan. You might get tired of trying, anxious or disheartened. We give up, revert to old habits or make mistakes.

But if you regularly check where you are, if you listen to your internal Sat Nav, you can *'do a U-turn'* or *'turn around when possible.'* This often means adjusting our thinking, expectations, our habits and behaviour. We need to stay vigilant and take action to get us back on course.

So when an unexpected life event happens and you find yourself dipping into your emergency fund, don't despair. It's a setback, usually a temporary one. You'll come back stronger, wiser, better. If you fall off the wagon, you can get back on again. If you have to redo a step of your financial plan, then so be it. You get up and go again. Sometimes you have to go a step back to move forward.

It's later on when you're attacking a big goal - like paying off your house or saving for retirement - that you can lose motivation. That's why I like listening to *The Money Guy Show* when they compare average net worth by age, or averaging retirement account balances for each age group.

We need new milestones to aim for on the longest financial journey of our lives. Maybe doing an annual net worth statement can help you track your progress and give you a boost of motivation. You may not be where you want to be, but you're not where you were. These are all ways of making sure we're still on track.

It's when the goal is very far off that it becomes more useful to focus not just on the distant horizon, but on the day-to-day things you can do to move you in the right direction.

## *Building Healthy Habits*

While I don't go around eating elephants as a general rule, there is a saying that goes, *'How do you eat an elephant? One bite at a time!'*

It means breaking down our huge, almost unimaginable goals into small achievable steps (or even *baby steps* for that matter). This includes things that seem easy to do (which are just as easy not to do) like tracking our spending, being mindful of our emotions, or having important money conversations.

You may have also come across the term *'habit stacking.'* We can start a simple routine or checklist which creates a new habit over time. Starting one small new habit makes it easier to start the next, and so on. That way, you can build more good habits.

Jim Rohn talks about eating an apple a day, walking around the block, working on personal development and intentional giving – each goal accomplished is a psychological uplift that improves self-esteem and leads on to the next.

One habit I do is a 10-point checklist every time I leave the house. That way I can be sure I never go to work without my phone or stethoscope again! It also means I start the day with gratitude for my identity (ID badge), health, keys, purse, my relationships, my faith etc.

Even writing this book involved me setting aside time to write each day. It wasn't something I was able to do every day. There were gaps of weeks and months. Or there were times when I could write for a few hours every day. But over time, a few sentences or paragraphs can become whole chapters. Over weeks, months and years a book can take shape.

What could this look like for our finances? Well, it's the small daily, weekly and monthly habits that stack up over time.

For me, there are a few key habits that I've put in place: I do a monthly budget, setting out my spending before the month begins on the payday I choose. I review my spending at least once a week and check how much is left in my spending categories. I changed my shopping and cooking habits. Generosity has become a rhythm and pattern of my life, as has saving and investing for the future. I've also started doing an annual net worth statement every January to track my progress.

It might even come down to minute-by-minute choices. That's why we need to know our spending habits, our strengths and weaknesses. Are you an impulse buyer? It may seem old fashioned, but I've started writing shopping lists and using coupons. Lots of supermarket apps have these feature built-in and try to make it fun.

It's good to question ourselves in the moment: 'Do I really need this or do I just feel like I want it right now? Is this really a good offer, or do they just want me to buy something because it's got money off? Can I afford this, or should I save up for it another time? If I sleep on it, will I still want it tomorrow or in a week? Will it really make me happy or have I just seen the product in a persuasive advert?'

It's these daily habits and short-term goals that make up the journey towards our long-term goals, including financial independence. Don't worry if you're not there yet. It's a process. As Craig Groeschel puts it, you've got to learn to enjoy the process.

## *Behaviour Change Isn't Easy*

If behaviour change was easy we'd all be running marathons, we'd all be millionaires and have wardrobes full of clothes that actually fit us!

Innate health practitioners, like Dr Giles P. Croft and others, believe that our reality is made up of thought. We all have memories, beliefs and experiences which we rely on to help us interpret the world around us.

Our emotions are feelings in our body that are a direct response to our thoughts. But these are almost always temporary. If we wait long enough we'll get back to a sort of equilibrium of contentment. We don't need to act on our thoughts straight away.

In fact, we can pre-decide how we're going to act in advance irrespective of how we feel. I've heard Pastor Craig Groeschel talk about this often. That's part of how we change our behaviour.

I've also heard Pastor Rick Warren talk about how we can choose which thoughts to hold on to and which ones to let go of and replace with better ones.

Even though this is a book on personal finance, behaviour change and patterns of thinking are a key part of behavioural finance. In the Resources Chapter I've put a list of books and podcasts that I've been learning from in recent years that I hope will help you with these areas of your life.

So what are the thoughts or mindsets that help people become wealthy and stay wealthy? Millionaire studies have shown that there are some consistent factors.[303, 304] For example, the millionaires studied believed that they were in control of their destiny. They didn't allow external circumstances to limit what they could achieve. Instead, they believed that there were things they could do to build wealth that would result in a better future, the same habits we've already mentioned.

There may be even deeper thoughts or beliefs that you have about yourself and your situation that might be holding you back. Maybe you've not thought about it before, but it seems to a universal human condition to feel not good enough, unworthy, not capable or qualified. This may be *'Imposter Syndrome'* or *'negative self-talk.'*

It's all too easy to be hypercritical and overlook the good things about ourselves - remember *negativity bias?* We can look at bad things that have happened or mistakes we've made and let these form a belief structure that we're always going to be a failure. Sometimes we're looking for more evidence to negatively reinforce our beliefs.

But we can also choose to turn our situation around. We can reframe our circumstances: Is it an insurmountable problem or just an obstacle to navigate around? Is it an overwhelming setback or a challenge to overcome? Is it a bad experience or a learning opportunity? Are we stuck, lost and confused or are we just at a crossroads, weighing up our options?

I've heard it said that we can't control which thoughts arrive in our head, but we can choose which ones we allow to stay. Some people use positive affirmations, other people use Bible verses or empowering words of motivation. Whatever your beliefs, you can find uplifting and encouraging truths to speak over yourself and re-wire your thinking.

So much of this process happens on a subconscious level, but if we reflect on our thinking we can notice when a negative or unhelpful thought pops into our heads and call ourselves out: *'Hey, you – negative thought! Stop right there!'*

We can see it for what it is and speak something positive over ourselves instead. In the Bible, 2 Corinthians 10:5 suggests we should take our thoughts captive. It's a form of self-control.

American radio host, Bernard Meltzer, ran an advice call show called *'What's Your Problem'* for over 20 years until the mid-1990s. He is accredited with saying: *"Before you speak, ask yourself if what you are going to say is true, is kind, is necessary, is helpful. If the answer is no, maybe what you are about to say should be left unsaid."*

Well if that's true of our words to others, then it should also be true of the words we speak to ourselves. If our thoughts are overly self-critical, mean, cruel, and not even true, it's important – *imperative* even – to kick them out and show them the door.

Earl Nightingale said: *"Each of us must live off the fruit of his thoughts in the future, because what you think today and tomorrow, next month and next year, you will mould your life and determine your future. You are guided by your mind."*

What we allow to be planted and take root in our minds is what grows. How much better to plant thoughts that bear fruit, rather than a tangle of weeds and briars?

Instead, fill your mind with battles already won. We can remember the things we've already achieved, challenges overcome, things we can be proud of, people we've helped, positive experiences shared and relationships nurtured.

We can do gratitude exercises and think of things every day to be thankful for.

We can look around us at people who have overcome a certain issue and instead of getting jealous we can celebrate their wins, thinking instead: *'If they could do it, then so can I!'*

## 5. Don't Travel Alone

Remember, another key reason why people get lost is that they go it alone when they should be travelling with others. I know I keep repeating it, but it's super important. Just in case you've got this far in the book and still not done it: if you have a spouse or someone you're doing life with, the experts suggest making sure you're travelling together as a couple. So go and have that important money conversation to make sure you're both on the same page!

Going in two different directions will never get you to your destination together. Instead, it'll leave you both feeling frustrated, stressed and disillusioned. But if you're travelling together, instead you can encourage each other and help each other move forward towards your goals, a dream that you both share.

When one of you is struggling, the other can help to pick you up. When one of you loses focus, the other can cheer you on. A good example of this is if you're climbing a mountain as a group, roped together with others, working as a *'rope team'*. Success or failure depends on your ability to work together, helping each other if someone falls into difficulty, aiming for the same mountain summit, otherwise, everyone could be put at risk.[305]

### Find A Community

If you're single or unmarried, then you can still find people to help you reach your goal. This could be a mentor or coach, an accountability partner, a small group of people you trust, or an online community.

Maybe your goal is financial independence, but it could be to get to a healthier bodyweight, running a 10K or marathon, a career goal or relationship, or any other area of life where you want to be successful.

It helps to learn from people more experienced than you, who have gone ahead of you on the journey, and who are willing to share their experience and wisdom. It also helps to surround yourself with positive voices and encouraging people.

You need to find people who are travelling in the same direction that you want to go. The Resources Chapter is full of content creators in the personal finance space who have built up communities of encouraging people. I've joined a few for seasons of my journey. Remember to use wisdom and discernment. Test what you hear and don't follow the herd.

### Working With A Financial Professional

Lastly, there's also the option of a finance coach, financial planner or financial advisor. Each of these different types of finance professionals has a slightly different role and level of regulation. So you need to have a good think about what kind of support you need for your journey and whether you can justify the costs. You might need different types of expert advice at different stages of your journey.[306]

Think of these finance professionals as your navigator or co-pilot. They don't do the driving for you, but they are the word of encouragement in your ear, helping you to read your map and plan your route, looking ahead to bends in the road, guiding you through life's corners and preparing you for what's coming.

They can check your blind spots and alert you to any challenges and obstacles up ahead. Some of them will crunch the numbers with you and let you know when you're off course.

Only *Chartered Financial planners* and *financial advisors* are certified to give financial advice tailored to meet your specific circumstances. *Financial coaches*, on the other hand, are not regulated. You'll find their roles can overlap.

1. **Chartered financial planners** will likely have a holistic approach that includes some behaviour coaching, making sure you can handle the emotions that can come with investing, as well as making sure you're on track towards your goals. They can use computer software to stress-test your financial plans and make sure they're watertight.
2. **Financial advisors** tend to specialise in a particular area and will guide you through the choice of certain financial products to meet your specific needs, such as helping you put together an investment portfolio.
3. **Financial coaches** are unregulated and are more like personal trainers, making sure you're budgeting and saving well, and focusing on your daily habits.

Just like we said in the last chapter, you can learn to grow a few vegetables yourself, but there comes a point where you may want to ask a professional garden designer to help you.

Typically, it makes sense to learn the basics of personal finance and investing for yourself as this is more cost effective. There are lots of content creators, including financial professionals, who have videos and courses for you to learn how to do it yourself. Then you can involve an expert once your investments get to a particular size and complexity.

Just be aware that some financial advisors need you to have a sizable investment portfolio (maybe a few hundred thousand or half a million) before they can help you as a client. But don't worry - it's still possible to get there.

Most of us don't have that sort of money (not yet!). The cost of using a financial professional in the early days doesn't usually make financial sense as they usually take a small percentage of your portfolio to cover their fees. However, eventually it may be worth it if that results in us having better investment returns and tailored advice, helping us stay the course.

So, for now, we're going to go the DIY investing route. There are plenty of excellent YouTube content creators and resources that can help you get started on your financial journey. I'll introduce you to them in *Chapter 10: Way To Invest.*

## Conclusion:

In this chapter, you've learned about setting goals, creating a roadmap and how to navigate your way to financial success. You may find that the path changes course. Even the destination itself may change as you develop and grow along the way. The things we want in our teens, twenties and thirties may not be what we want in later life.

Hopefully this chapter has given you some food for thought. It may have been a challenging read. It can be difficult to come to terms with the reality of where we are now when we realise just how far we are from where we want to be. But we don't need to stay there. We can adjust our course and move forward towards our desired future.

I just wanted to mention one other thing about retirement planning. We've spent this whole chapter just looking at the numbers and maths side of things. But you'll also find lots of retirement planning resources that talk about things that sound a lot like *spiritual wealth*.

Often we find our identity and purpose in our jobs. So when we're working towards financial independence, the point at which we *could* retire, we need to ask ourselves some more questions: *Am I wanting to retire to escape a job I don't like? What would I do in retirement? What would my new purpose be? What am I running away from and what am I running towards?*

Some people put up with a job they hate because they're so focussed on retirement. But the real question might be: *Could I change careers to a job I love now? What am I waiting to do in retirement that I could start doing now? Could I have mini-retirements? What role could I see myself doing which I'm so passionate about and skilled at that it doesn't even feel like work?*

If we don't ask ourselves these questions, you may find yourself faced with a vast emptiness as soon as the job you've put everything into ends suddenly. This happened to me during my multiple phases of un- or under-employment. There has to be more to me than my job!

You hear so many stories of people who've worked so hard to get to retirement, but may not get to enjoy it because of health issues or their lives are sadly cut short. Sometimes work consumes us, but it can also sustain us. There are protective things like regular routine, relationships with colleagues, a sense of purpose and fulfilment.

When work stops, we can be left with feelings of sadness, loss, isolation and loneliness. Some people start volunteering, join classes, go back to education, find a new career, or take the opportunity to travel, start new hobbies or do more of their passions.

This is why some people decide never to stop working, because of the positive effect it can have on our health and wellbeing when we're doing a job we love. Nobody knows what the future holds, so there is a balance between living well now and planning for a future that we only have partial control over.

So while you're planning the financial side of retirement, make sure that you're also thinking about setting some *spiritual wealth* goals as well. Relationships, health, wellbeing, purpose and calling - these are all things that money can't buy. It could be that you end up changing the entire direction of your life in the process. That's certainly what happened to me!

If you're feeling stuck and paralysed with indecision, I've heard lots of motivational speakers suggest that the key is to keep moving anyway. The way will eventually become clear, even if you realise that the decision was the wrong one. At least you'll find out!

If you made the wrong choice, you can turn around and try again. You can learn the ways that have worked for others and follow their roadmap. Stick to the plan, even if it takes longer than you expected.

I love what Simon Sinek writes about in *'The Infinite Game.'*[307] Sometimes, the key to winning is to keep playing the game. We need to become better than who we were yesterday. The trick is to keep going.

## Reflection Questions:

- *Where are you at with your finances at the moment?*
- *Did you do a net worth statement and were you surprised by the result?*
- *Do you have any short-, medium- or long-term financial goals?*
- *Have you dreamed about your ideal retirement?*
- *What will it cost to live that particular lifestyle?*
- *What sorts of spiritual wealth do you want in retirement?*
- *Do you need to adjust your retirement expectations or plan?*
- *Are you following a financial plan?*
- *Where can you go to find help if you need it?*
- *Are there any areas where you need to do more research?*
- *Is there someone ahead of you on the journey who can walk alongside you or help you move forward on your financial journey?*
- *Do you need to employ a personal finance professional?*
- *Could you join an online personal finance community or meet up with some friends to have a conversation about money?*
- *Do you recognise any patterns in your money thoughts and habits?*
- *Are there any negative thoughts that you can reframe and replace with better ones that are more healthy and helpful?*
- *What good money habits can you start today?*
- *What bad money habits can you stop today?*
- *What can you do to make sure you can keep going?*
- *How might you encourage yourself on your journey?*

# A BRIEF HISTORY OF MONEY

# | 9 |

# Chapter 9: A Brief History of Money

*'History repeats her tale unconsciously, and goes off into a mystic rhyme; ages are prototypes of other ages, and the winding course of time brings us round to the same spot again.'*
~ 'THE CHRISTIAN REMEMBRANCER,' *Volume 10, 1845*

This is a bonus chapter for anyone who wants to delve a little bit deeper into definitions and theories of money, currency and assets. I also want to introduce you to the topic of *macroeconomics* (the study of whole economies and how they interact) and *economic cycles*.

It's not essential to know these things to invest your money or plan for retirement. But if you find these topics interesting, I hope this chapter introduces you to some of the financial vocabulary and ideas that you'll hear cropping up again and again in interviews, podcasts or articles by professional economists (people who study economies). I hope it'll save you months or years of confusion!

You'll hear lots of sayings about economists: that they were created to make weather forecasters and astrologists look good; that they try to predict the future, but unlike weather forecasters, they don't get sacked if they get it wrong etc.

Joking aside, financial experts usually give a disclaimer that nobody can precisely predict the future. Nobody can accurately time the markets and nobody has a crystal ball (at least, not one that works – some economists keep one on a shelf as a joke!).

The key thing to remember is that the stock market and the economy are connected, but they often appear to act in completely random ways. Just because the economy looks weak, it doesn't stop the stock market from suddenly melting upwards! Just because the stock market is tanking, it doesn't mean that there's anything wrong with the economy at all.

There are so many moving parts. We're talking about *people* after all – how they think, act and interact. It isn't like the laws of physics. You probably realise the unpredictability of human psychology every time you innocently walk into a supermarket (*"I'm just going in for one thing!"*) and come out with a full trolley.

We'll look specifically at patterns in the stock market in the last chapter. But for now, I just want to focus on the economics. I'll give you a taster of what I've learned about macroeconomics so that you can get a big-picture view before we dive down into the details of investing.

As with the rest of this book, there's more to say than I can cover in this brief introduction. So we'll stick to the basics and you can go find more for yourself if you want to.

I've used *Investopedia.com* to help me define most of the financial terms in this chapter. I've also linked to some key videos (both in the References and the Resources Chapter) which will help explain these ideas better than I can, sometimes with helpful cartoon animations and narrations. They're a lot of fun, so go check them out if you have time!

It's also important to note that there are many different approaches to economics. YouTube content creators often talk about things that aren't taught in schools or universities. Traditional economics failed to predict the 2008 *Great Financial Crash* (GFC). So you may feel like a conspiracy theorist because of the politics involved. Just keep learning and try to weigh up the different opinions if you can.

# What Is Money?

## KEY TAKEAWAYS

- Money is a system of value that helps people make exchanges
- Using money means people don't have to barter for goods or services
- The first forms of money were agricultural e.g. grain or livestock
- Most money systems have currencies controlled by central banks
- Digital cryptocurrencies have some of the same properties as money

As I mentioned in the introduction, money is what we use to buy and sell things. It means we no longer have to barter for goods and services. Instead, smaller alternative commodities were used so that people didn't have to trade with camels or bags of grain![308]

You may be aware that in the past, people sometimes used shells as money. 'Cowrie shell money,' is believed to have been used as early as 1200 BCE. These were traded in parts of the world including Asia, Africa and Oceania. In some places, shells were used as money right up until the 19th and 20th centuries.

Cowrie shells were made from the dried-out shells of marine snails. They were small, durable and difficult to counterfeit. Sometimes they were boiled to bring out their colours and a hole was put through them for use in jewellery.[309, 310]

Imagine making your own money by boiling snails?! Eventually, other types of money were also used, including metal coins of silver and gold, money made of leather, and of course, banknotes.

## What Is Currency?

**KEY TAKEAWAYS**

- Currency is a form of payment usually issued by a government
- The value of any currency fluctuates compared to other currencies
- Currency is a tangible form of money
- (money is an intangible system of value)
- Many countries accept the U.S. dollar for payment
- Some countries 'peg' their currency to the U.S. dollar for stability
- Cryptocurrency is a 21st-century innovation and exists only electronically

Currency is a form of money that you can hold in your hand, like the notes or coins we're currently familiar with. They are standardised by world governments. Having currency makes global trade easier.[311]

So while money is a general term for a system of value with certain key properties, currency is just one form of money. Many things have been used as money in the past including cheques (money substitutes) and cigarettes (used by soldiers in World War II).[4]

Modern *'paper'* currency (even though banknotes are now often made from plastic polymers) takes the form of a promissory note, a bank I.O.U. UK banknotes still have written on them, *"I promise to pay the bearer on demand the sum of five/ten/twenty/fifty pounds."*

Similarly, most coins no longer contain actual gold or silver. That means that they are essentially worthless in themselves. We call this *'fiat money'* as it is backed by the government, rather than by the gold it promises to be worth.[312]

Currencies used to be on the *'Gold Standard,'* backed by gold and sometimes silver. However, this system was slowly abandoned by the UK and USA in the 1930s.

*The Emergency Banking Act* helped stop the outflow of gold during the Great Depression of the 1930s to protect the banking system. It did this by forcing all Americans to convert their gold into U.S. dollars to avoid paying a penalty. Some people see this as a violation of freedom and unconstitutional. If it happened then, they argue, there's no guarantee it won't happen again.

Understandably, countries stopped trusting that America had enough gold to back all the paper dollars that were being printed, leading to a crisis of faith. The USA finally abandoned the remnants of the Gold Standard in 1973. Instead, they introduced *'fiat currency,'* not backed by anything.[313]

Since then, central banks around the world have had free rein to print currency. Central banks were originally set up to help avoid bank runs and to be the lenders of last resort to troubled financial institutions, such as banks and even whole governments.

Before that, it was rich and powerful individuals and their banks, people like J.P. Morgan, that had to step in during a crisis and bail out the banking system. You can look up the collapse of the *Knickerbocker Trust* and the *American banking panic of 1907* if you'd like to learn more about this controversial history.

Central banks, such as the Federal Reserve in the USA (*the 'Fed'*), the Bank of England in the UK (*the 'BoE'*), and the European Central Bank (*the 'ECB'*) have the power to set interest rates. This makes it easier or harder for banks to lend money and is one of the ways central banks can manipulate the monetary system if a financial crisis occurs.[314]

## So Why Do Currencies Fail (or Not Fail)?

What stops central banks or governments from *'printing'* too much currency? We've seen central bank money printing in response to several crises in recent times, such as the aftermath of the 2008 *Great Financial Crisis* and more recently the 2020-22 period following the COVID-19 pandemic. Sometimes this is called *'Quantitative Easing'* or *'QE.'* The reverse is called *'Quantitative Tightening'* or *'QT.'*

One theory is that the majority of world currencies are being devalued at the same time by the coordinated money printing of the world's central banks. As long as they're all doing it, there's not much difference relative to each other. I've heard the US dollar being described as *'a bad apple in a basket of equally bad apples.'*

Ultimately, if countries print more money, it can dilute a currency's purchasing power and lead to inflation. In some cases, it can even result in *'hyperinflation.'*[815] This is where the cost of goods can spiral out of control. There is a mismatch between supply and demand, which makes money almost worthless.

This happened in the Weimar Republic in Germany from 1921 to 1923, Argentina from the 1970s onwards, Zimbabwe from 2007 onwards, and Türkiye since 2021. Many currencies inevitably fail, with some countries having to replace their currency systems with an alternative, like the US Dollar, when things unravel.

Hyperinflation is fascinating and terrifying. Imagine walking into a corner shop. There are no prices on any of the items because the price can change between walking through the front door, picking up your loaf of bread and reaching the checkout. The cashier looks at a database to see what the value of your purchase is at that particular time.

There are photos from history of people with wheelbarrows of money trying to trade in their life savings for a loaf of bread or burning paper notes to keep warm. Hopefully, we'll never have to experience anything like this in our countries in our lifetime. But it can and does happen. Some countries are currently heading that way.

## What Is A Reserve Currency?

**KEY TAKEAWAYS**

> - A reserve currency is a globally-recognized national currency
> - Foreign currency is held *in reserve* in world central banks or institutions
> - A reserve currency makes international trade and global finance possible
> - The official reserve currency changes every century or so
> - British pound was reserve currency until after World War II
> - Today the U.S. dollar (and the Euro) are regarded as a reserve currency
> - Reserve currency status has advantages, like greater buying power &
> - Drawbacks e.g. artificially low interest rates (may cause asset bubbles)

One reason that hyperinflation hasn't happened in America (yet), the biggest economy in the world (at the moment), is because the dollar has *'Reserve Currency status.'* A reserve currency is a foreign currency held by central banks around the world that helps make international commerce possible. It means countries or businesses can buy and sell using the same currency.[316]

However, there is no guarantee that a currency will keep its reserve status. For example, up until recently US dollars were the only way to buy and sell oil, otherwise known as the *'Petrodollar.'* However, since Russia invaded Ukraine in February 2022, some countries have been making arrangements to buy and sell oil in other currencies, not just the US dollar.[317]

## The Eurodollar System

I want to briefly mention the Eurodollar system. This has nothing to do with the Euro or Europe at all. *'Eurodollar'* refers to any US dollars deposited at foreign banks. Imagine how many more dollars are held overseas compared to the USA itself! The answer is that nobody really knows because the number got too big to count.

Eurodollars are essential for countries to borrow money and these debts need to be paid back in US dollars. So a shortage of Eurodollars can make it difficult for world economies to function and can lead to economic instability. A global dollar shortage has potential knock-on effects around the world.[318]

## Investing In Gold

There are several ways to invest in gold – physical gold (e.g. coins, bullion, jewellery), paper gold (e.g. tracking the price of gold through commodity funds on the stock market) and investing in gold production (e.g. gold mining companies and royalty companies.) Gold can also be leased out and interest paid.

Gold has proven itself historically to be a store of value over the centuries. It doesn't always outperform other asset classes. But if fiat currency continues to lose its value, some people like to have a little gold in their investment portfolio, just in case.

Gold tends to do well in a crisis. Some people like to keep some physical gold for this reason, or just as an interesting collectable. Of course, you've then got to think of things like safe storage and avoiding theft. If you've got gold, best not to tell anyone about it or keep it hidden!

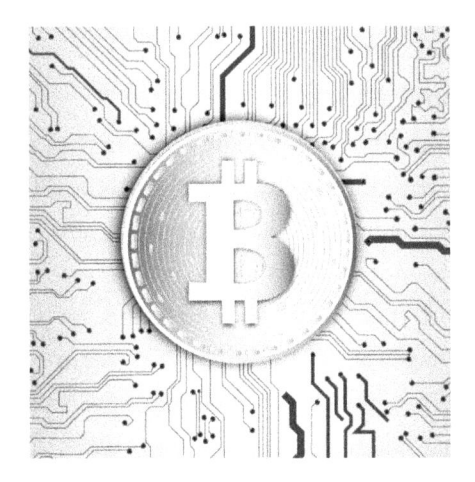

## What About Cryptocurrencies like Bitcoin?

Cryptocurrencies were created in response to the belief that the current system is broken. New forms of electronic currency are being developed based on blockchain technology, a sort of advanced database made out of, yep, you guessed it – chains of blocks (of data).

You'll hear it sometimes called a *'public digital ledger.'* All transactions are recorded and theoretically traceable. However, people have found ways to make their identities hard to trace. Crypto coins can be held in digital wallets (cold storage) or on exchanges (online marketplaces where they can be bought and sold).

Examples include *Bitcoin* (the first and oldest digital currency) and *Altcoins*, such as *Ethereum*. There are thousands of alternative cryptocurrencies being developed, each with different uses and characteristics. There is a lot of speculation as to which will be the winner, if any. That's why prices swing so dramatically. Incidentally, you need stable prices to have an effective currency. So it may take a few more years.

Often people who are involved with cryptocurrency want to establish a new decentralised monetary system (*DeFi*). That means a system outside of the control of banks, governments and central banks. In the same way that gold has historically shown itself to be a store of value against fiat currencies, cryptocurrency is sometimes described as *'digital gold'* and hopes to fulfil a similar role in future.[319]

Some people argue that we already have digital currencies in the form of electronic banking. However, there is a difference between a decentralised digital currency (like Bitcoin) and a centralised digital currency (one that is controlled by governments or central banks).

There are lots of theories about the future of money, including that governments may one day be able to programme money so that it disappears if they don't like your behaviour or if you don't spend it a certain way. Some people think it's a way to control the populace. Only time will tell.

## Speculative Bubbles

I mentioned before how sometimes the stock market and value of investments can seem detached from the reality of how the economy is doing. So why don't we all rush in and invest in cryptocurrencies like Bitcoin or Ethereum? Why do we no longer use tulip bulbs as a form of investment? Will there be a shortage of the materials that make up electronic batteries and should we be buying those?

Throughout history, people have speculated on what the next big thing might be. At the time of writing, artificial intelligence (AI) has been the next craze. In the past, we've seen lots of speculative bubbles, including house prices (the property crash of 2008-9) and the internet (the dot-com bubble of 2000-2002).

When it comes to speculative bubbles, there is usually some sort of narrative, a story that there will be a shortage of something or an amazing new technology that changes the world. Unfortunately, things don't usually pan out this way. But human psychology still kicks in. People get excited, then greedy, then fearful. Bubbles form and dramatically pop. Most people who are in the bubble often don't realise until it's too late.[320]

We're going to look at the ups and downs of the stock market in the next chapter. It's important to know about speculative bubbles because they are an example of how patterns play out through history. Often bubbles form when an economy is booming. They may be a marker that an economic crash is looming. Or not. Who knows? That's why it's important to detach your emotions from investing and take predictions about the future with a pinch of salt.

Looking at history, you'll realise that we've been here before. In Holland in the early 1600s, wealthy people began to collect tulip bulbs as a status symbol. Rare varieties sold for huge prices. You'll hear it referred to as *'tulip mania.'*[17] Of course tulip bulbs became commonplace and prices plummeted. People realised they weren't a good investment (store of value) after all.

Just as the dot-com bubble was blowing up, so did the price of Beanie Babies on the secondary market. You might remember these stuffed toys in the late 1990s. They're still around. People started going crazy and collecting hundreds of them, thinking they'd be worth a fortune one day. Well, this was only perceived scarcity, a clever marketing trick. In reality there was no real scarcity or rareness at all. So prices tanked.[321]

Can you think of some modern examples of speculative bubbles?

You might have heard of NFTs (*'Non-Fungible Tokens'*). These use blockchain technology to make digital assets that some people believe are a good investment. The first NFT was minted in 2014. Since then, it's become possible for almost anyone to create one. NFTs hit bubble-territory around 2021 during the back end of the COVID-19 pandemic. When the bubble popped, prices dropped 50%.

Owning an NFT could mean owning digital art, trading cards, collectables, music, items and real estate in virtual worlds and computer games – the list goes on. Just like the art and collectables market of the real world, these things tend to have a value of whatever someone is willing to pay for them. Who can say if an NFT is worth $1 million or zero? Does it feel like a Beanie Baby or a tulip bulb to you?[322]

## Economic Cycles

Finally I wanted to make you aware of some theories of economic cycles. In the Resources Chapter I've linked to some brilliant animated videos by billionaire investor and hedge fund manager, Ray Dalio. He explains the psychology and mechanics behind why economic cycles occur and how these power dynamics play out on a global scale.

In a 30-minute video, *'How the Economic Machine Works,'* Ray Dalio gives his basic template for how economies work.[323] The economy is made up of transactions (people buying and selling things). The role of central banks is to print money and change interest rates. This in turn effects how easy it is for borrowers to access *'credit'* (another word for *'debt'*).

We have a debt-based economy where more borrowing leads to more spending. This means increased incomes for business owners and employees. This is what underpins the short-term debt cycle (lasting around **5 to 8 years**) and the long-term debt cycle (typically lasting **75 to 100 years**).

There are expansions and recessions, bubbles and sometimes even depressions, cycles of booms and busts. Historically these have played out many times over. Knowing about these cycles can help inform us of where we are now and how to prepare on an individual level. We can reduce the amount of debt we have (to lower our interest payments), increase productivity (maximising or maintaining our income) and make sure we're saving for a rainy day (in case our income drops).

In a 40-minute animated video, *'The Changing World Order,'* Ray Dalio doesn't just look at one economy, but how global economies interact.[324] If you don't have time for the full video, Ray Dalio has created a 5-minute version too.

We've already talked about how central bank *'money printing'* following a crisis can lead to devaluation of the paper currency. Money loses its buying power. This puts financial strain on people, especially if they can't increase their income and things cost more.

Economic debt cycles can lead to internal tensions (between rich and poor, political tensions, civil wars and revolutions) and external tensions (between countries, international wars). This can result in world powers rising up against each other and has happened many times throughout history.

Ray Dalio outlines the rise and fall of empires, which typically occurs in a **250-year cycle**. We've already looked at how America is the current dominant world power. But the US dollar wasn't always the reserve currency of the world. It used to be the Dutch guilder (or florin) when the Netherlands was a global superpower. Eventually, the British Empire rose up and pound sterling became the reserve currency, before giving way to the US dollar after World War II.

Ray Dalio, as a student of history, believes that learning from past cycles can help inform our future and that a new world order might be just beyond the horizon. But nothing is set in stone and it's impossible to know when that new world power will arise or who it might be.

## Conclusion:

As I said at the beginning of the chapter, you don't need to know about macroeconomics to invest successfully. But I find these topics really interesting and I hope you do too.

However, just because we know about history and recognise the patterns of economic cycles, this doesn't mean that we should try to time the stock market. It's still impossible to precisely predict the future. Even the experts get it wrong!

There are things we can do to increase our resilience in the face of these economic cycles, like making sure we don't have excessive debt. We can make sure we're adding value and cutting down on luxuries, making sure we have a financial cushion in case a storm hits.

History has shown that over the very long term the stock market and real-world assets tend to go up over time because of debt cycles and the actions of central banks in response to them. But we shouldn't assume that things will always stay the same. Nor should we get lulled into the false narrative that *'This time it's different.'*

Just because America is the dominant global power and the US dollar is the reserve currency of the world doesn't mean things will stay this way forever. That's why some people choose to diversify their investments across countries as well as asset classes, maybe buying a whole world index fund so that some of their investments are in emerging markets.

## KEY TAKEAWAYS

- Money and currency have evolved over centuries
- We can't rely on the past to accurately predict the future
- But there are often patterns in history we can learn from
- You can choose to diversify your investments across different countries
- Beware of speculative bubbles
- Learn how to determine an asset's true value
- You may not recognise if you're in the middle of a bubble
- Be aware of your emotions (euphoria, greed, fear)
- Macroeconomics is interesting but timing the market is impossible

'No system of government, no economic system, no currency, and no empire lasts forever, yet almost everyone is surprised and ruined when they fail. History has shown that we shouldn't rely on governments to protect us financially.'

~ Ray Dalio, 'Principles for Dealing with the Changing World Order'

# Ways To Invest

# | 10 |

## Chapter 10: Ways To Invest

*'The best time to plant a tree was 30 years ago and the second best time to plant a tree is now.'*
~ ANON.

Okay, you made it! Well done for reaching the investing chapter! You'll find whole books written about this topic. So, while we may have reached the mountain summit of this book, you're only just getting started on your investing journey. Unless you're already an investor, in which case I hope this chapter will still be interesting.

From this height, you can get a really good view of where we've been so far. So let's review: we've looked at building good money habits and getting your financial house in order; we've explored compound interest and the law of multiplication; we've taken some time to plan for the future and set goals; we've got a good overall idea of how economics and the global money system works.

If you've skipped straight here, I encourage you to go back and retrace the route as there are several key principles that it's important to have picked up before you start investing. Remember back in the gardening chapter when we looked at good soil? That's preparing the ground, both practically and in your investing mindset. Hopefully, this will get you ready to start planting some investment seeds.

When I started my *mindful finance* journey I'd only spoken to a handful of people in real life about investing. It seemed very mysterious and exciting. There was nobody that I felt comfortable asking to teach me or show me how to invest. That's probably a good thing, as I later discovered we have to be very careful who gives us financial advice. That's why this book is about education, not advice.

You might still be able to find someone in your world who can talk you through the basics of investing. But make sure it's someone who has already reached the point where you want to be. Don't go getting advice, as Dave Ramsey puts it, *'from TikTok or your broke brother-in-law.'* Remember, personalised financial advice has to come from a financial expert with appropriate qualifications and training.

I learnt to do financial DIY using the online resources I'm passing on to you. They helped demystify investing for me and showed me that investing isn't as exciting as you might think. Be prepared to feel little progress. You may not see any significant growth for a decade. You have to be okay with that. There's always a wait between sowing and reaping.

It's possible to start investing yourself and learn to grow your investment portfolio. One day it may get so large or complicated that it makes sense to get a financial professional to help you. That's the principle behind content creators like Brian Preston's *The Money Guy Show* and Pete Matthew's *Meaningful Money Podcast*. It's their way of sowing seeds of financial education into us so that one day we may be able to work with them as clients.

In this chapter, I'm going to talk you through the main ways to invest. I'll share with you how I currently invest. Then it's up to you to decide how best to apply this knowledge depending on your specific situation. You may even discover that investing isn't the right option for you right now. In which case, there are lots of other things you can do to build wealth.

I hope that you have found this book educational, enjoyable and relatively easy to understand. I know it's long! Tony Robbin's *Money*

*Master The Game* is 688 pages, so I don't feel as bad about it. I hope the pictures and diagrams have been helpful.

As I said before, there are lots of ways to invest. You can invest your time, talents and treasures. It could be starting a business, volunteering or giving to charity, learning new skills, investing in your relationships, spiritual walk, education or health. These things are investments into our *spiritual wealth* that mirror the *NHS 5 pillars of wellbeing*.

I'm sure you can think of lots of other ways to invest – planting a seed and allowing it to multiply. It's good to remind ourselves that it isn't all about the money. I've written this book during busy seasons and slow seasons. Sometimes I had to squeeze in time around my hospital shifts. At other times, I had more time than money. We shouldn't feel guilty about not making financial progress. Success isn't all about seeing our net worth grow year on year, though that would be nice.

Because this is an introduction to investing, I've decided to focus on the stock market. In reality, you can invest in all those asset classes we've mentioned already: cash, bonds, real estate and property, gold, rare earth minerals, oil, bitcoin, fine art, collectables and antiques etc.

But investing in the stock market is where the core of most people's wealth building will be, usually in tax-efficient retirement accounts like an ISA or pension in the UK (or a Roth IRA or 401K in the USA). So it make sense to start there.

Like the rest of the book, this is an information-dense chapter. So I want you to think of it as a guided walking tour of the investing world. We'll wander around, I'll point out some interesting landmarks and give you some information about them. But don't expect to remember it all!

It's just a starting place to help you understand the basics. Hopefully, it'll get you interested so you can go find out more if you want to. Take your time. You don't need to read it all in one go! It's just not that kind of book. Your wealth-building journey can take a lifetime. So there's no rush. We live *unhurried*, remember? Start when you're ready. But ultimately, you just need to start. I hope you enjoy the tour!

## Should I invest in the stock market?

Just like we explored in the gardening chapter, you need to prepare the ground before you invest. If you look at any expert advice, it's generally accepted wisdom that you shouldn't invest in the stock market unless you meet some very specific criteria. If you're in the UK, you can learn more about these in Pete Matthew's *Meaningful Money Podcast,* 'Season 14: New Accumulators.'

These steps mirror Dave Ramsey's *7 Baby Steps* and *The Money Guy Show*'s *Financial Order of Operations.* If you haven't got familiar with these yet, then you can look them up online or go to the Chapter 8 Resources on how to translate these to a UK setting.

### 1. You need to have your financial house in order

These are the foundational principles we went through in the first half of this book. Have you developed financial discipline? Are you on a budget or spending plan? Are you able to save regularly, living on less than you make? Have you got your 4 walls covered – can you pay for your utility bills, clothes, food, shelter and transport? Are you covered with a roof of protection – your insurance policies, if you need them?

### 2. You need to pay off your high-interest debt

Typically you'll hear people say that the average return of the stock market is somewhere from 5 to 10% per year over the long-term.[325] So if you have 29.9% APR on your credit card debt, it makes sense to go pay that off before you invest as it's unlikely you'll make that much on your investments.

### 3. You need to have a 3 to 6-month emergency fund

Some people will suggest a smaller or bigger emergency fund depending on your job stability, dependants, age and other personal factors. Ultimately, you need a cushion between you and life so that you're not forced to pull out your investments at the wrong time.

### 4. You need to understand your risk tolerance

It's good to get to know yourself and see how likely you are to act on your emotions if the stock market suddenly drops. This is your *'risk tolerance.'* There are investing risk tolerance quizzes available online to help you get an idea of how you will act under pressure.

The stock market is one of the riskiest ways to invest but can have the greatest returns if you have a long time horizon. For some people, they may want to invest in more stable assets like bonds or cash. If you think you might act on your emotions, you may need a financial professional to keep you on track and make sure you don't jump off the rollercoaster at the wrong time.

### 5. You understand what you are investing in

It was Warren Buffet who is attributed with the saying, *"investment must be rational; if you can't understand it, don't do it."* Ultimately, you shouldn't invest in what you don't understand.

If you don't understand what you're investing in, then you're more likely to do the wrong thing at the wrong time, acting on your emotions rather than sticking to the process.

Whether it's the stock market, the underlying business or the style of investing, you need to know how it works. Or you need to work with a finance professional who does, one who is working in your best interests (who has a *'fiduciary duty'*).

There are also Robo-advisers, computer programs that can invest for you. It was Arthur Weasley in *'Harry Potter and the Chamber of Secrets'* who said, *"Never trust anything that can think for itself if you can't see where it keeps its brain!"* The same is true if you're relying on Robo-advisers to tell you how to invest your money or if you're just copying what other people are doing.

If you understand the process, then you're less likely to panic, sell at a loss and quit investing forever. As Simon Sinek puts it in his book *'The Infinite Game,'* the objective is to keep playing.[326]

## 6. You have a time horizon of at least 3 to 5 years

How long you've got to reach your investment goal matters. The stock market makes money most of the time and there is a gradual upward trend. But there can be wild swings up and down. The typical advice is that you shouldn't invest money you need in the next 3 years. So short-term investing, where you need the money in the next 3 to 5 years, needs to be invested conservatively.

If you've got 30+ years until you need your money, then you can take more risk as you've got time for your investments to recover if there is a market downturn.

An example would be saving for a house deposit. Sometimes house prices crash at the same time as the stock market. So if the economy goes into recession and people lose their jobs, you might have a buying opportunity but no money.

You don't want your money tied up in risky stocks. Instead, short-term money should stay in cash or equivalents. It may decline in value due to inflation, but at least you know you won't be losing money if you need it soon. Time horizon matters.

*\*\**

Of course, this means that for some people it may never be the right time to invest. I've got a friend who used to work in the finance industry. He believes the system is rigged to make money from retail investors (I agree, from what I've read, there's a lot of truth to this). His risk tolerance for stock market investing is low. He realises that investing is not for him.

For some people, a better option may be paying into a workplace pension (which is still investing) or building up cash savings, starting a business or buying real estate. There are lots of ways to build wealth that don't involve the stock market.

Perhaps you're still in the process of getting your financial house in order. Your priority may be paying off debt or building an emergency fund. This will improve your chances of being a successful investor in future. I hope this chapter inspires you to keep going.

## How Stock Market Investing Works

In Part 1 of the book, we focussed on points 1 to 3 which lay the groundwork. In this chapter, we'll tackle points 4 and 5 to help you understand what you're investing in and what your risk tolerance is. This will help you decide which investment style suits you best.

I'm going to use the terms *'trading'* and *'investing'* interchangeably for now to keep things simple. But, as you'll see later, there's a big difference between the two. Firstly, let's take a look at the stock market. I'm sure you've heard of it. But you might not know what it is.

### What Is The Stock Market?

A *'stock market'* or *'stock exchange'* refers to the same thing. There are many stock exchanges around the world which ultimately make up the entire stock market including the *New York Stock Exchange* (USA), the *London Stock Exchange* (UK) and *Shanghai Stock Exchange* (China) to name but a few.[327]

The first stock market was in Amsterdam in 1602. *The Dutch East India Company* was the first publicly traded company. Shares of the company were sold to the public in exchange for a share of future profits.[328]

You can think of stocks and shares as owning a small piece of a business. A company *'goes public'* and is listed on a stock exchange. You can own a small slice of a very large pizza. As a part-owner of that business, you get to benefit from future **growth** (as stock price goes up) and **income** (some companies pay a dividend, rewarding investors by paying them profits).

You'll also hear some companies doing *'stock buybacks.'* This is where they *'buy back'* their own shares, reducing the overall number available, and so the value of your share goes up. Imagine that there are now fewer pizza slices available, so your slice is worth more.[329]

## Why Does The Stock Market Go Up And Down?

In the same way that Ray Dalio describes the economy as being made up of *'zillions of transactions,'* the stock market is made up of lots of people buying and selling stocks and shares throughout the trading day. Stock exchanges in different countries operate across different time zones. Traditionally the stock market would open and close with the ringing of a bell (this is mostly symbolic, but still happens in some stock exchanges, sometimes virtually).

For every buyer, there must also be a seller. There are sometimes individuals or companies who act in the middle called *'market makers.'* They provide *'liquidity'* (they make it easier for transactions to happen) a bit like an auction house, allowing offers and bids to be made, whilst trying to make a profit themselves.

The price of a stock is whatever anyone is willing to pay for it. If people are willing to pay a higher price for a share in a company, then the share price goes up. If someone decides to sell at a lower price, then the price goes down. So share price is based on supply and demand.

It doesn't change the underlying value of a stock (what the company is worth). Sometimes share price can be different from its underlying value. It might be *'under'* or *'over-valued'* at a particular time. It's possible to calculate what a business is worth using formulas that look at company's earnings, debt, assets and their cash buffer. An *economic moat* is a business's ability to maintain a competitive edge over its competitors.

It's the interactions between all these stock market participants that result in the ups and downs in the price of the stock market, the characteristic jagged up and down lines on the stock charts.

You'll sometimes hear people refer to *'Mr Market.'* This comes from Benjamin Graham's 1949 book, *'The Intelligent Investor.'* [330] It describes why the stock market can sometimes appear irrational or contradictory. He imagined that Mr Market was a character with bipolar affective disorder, whose mood swung between euphoric highs and overwhelming pessimism without an obvious reason.

I like to think of the stock market as a rollercoaster, with ups and downs, twists and turns. Sometimes this is because of a news event or a story that economists are telling. Sometimes it seems to be for no reason at all. It's important not to jump off the rollercoaster at the wrong time. Remember, while the stock market and the economy are separate, the two are closely linked.

Stock markets in the USA and around the world tend to go up gradually over time. This is partly due to inflation and the devaluation of currency. It's also based on the assumption that businesses add value over time; countries are growing and getting better into the future.

## Who Are The People Who Buy Stocks And Shares?

There are two main groups of people who buy and sell stocks and shares – let's call them the little fish and the big fish.

Firstly, there are the average **retail investors**, like you and me. Sometimes we are referred to as *'Main Street'* or by the unfortunate term *'dumb money.'*

You can think of retail investors as little fish in a big ocean. Unfortunately, many new retail investors tend to fall into predictable patterns of behaviour, making them easy targets for the bigger fish.

Retail investors are unable to make much of a splash on their own, but as proved by the *'meme stocks'* of 2020 to 2021, by working together in a coordinated way, they can dramatically push up a stock price and move markets.[331]

Remember the scene in *'Finding Nemo'* where all the fish are caught in a net? Dory, Marlin and Nemo get the fish to swim in the same direction – *"Just keep swimming!"* Together they almost capsized the boat and were able to make their escape. Well, that's what happens when the little retail investors work together. They can fight back.

So who are the big fish? These are **professional stock market traders** and **institutional investors**. They manage hedge funds (where wealthy individuals pool their money together), pension funds, mutual funds and insurance companies.

You'll hear them sometimes referred to as *'Wall Street'* or *'smart money.'* Richard Wyckoff thought of them as a single entity, the *'Composite Man,'* to explain how they tend to work together to outsmart retail investors.

Professional investors are generally regarded as more sophisticated than the average retail investor. They have tools such as *Bloomberg Terminals* (to get the latest stock market news and analytics).

Sometimes they use trading bots (computer programs that analyse data to look for buying and selling opportunities). Stock market investing may be an area where we see more *Artificial Intelligence* (AI) used in future to analyse stock market patterns and trends.

Some stock market commentators like to track the direction that retail traders are moving in compared to professional investors. If the little fish and big fish are swimming in the opposite direction there could be a reason. Retail traders tend to move in the same direction, like shoals of fish, due to herd mentality. That's why it's important not to follow the crowd. You could be swimming into a trap.

Large-scale investors who operate funds in the billions of dollars are sometimes referred to as *'stock market whales.'*[332] They can cause big splashes in the stock market when they buy or sell stocks. They like to eat up small fish and take all their money.

## Ways To Buy Stocks And Shares As A Retail Investor

Digital technology and the internet have opened up the stock market to more retail investors than ever before. In the old days, you'd need a stockbroker. You might have been issued with paper stock certificates or have to do it over the telephone.

These days, trading and investing in stocks and shares can be done on an investment platform via an app or website within minutes or hours. Technology has democratised investing in many ways, allowing pretty much anyone to invest using a smartphone. You don't need to be wealthy or pay someone to manage your money for you.

Some people choose to buy single stocks and shares of an individual company. This is one of the riskiest ways to invest as the price of a single stock can be very volatile with big swings up and down.

You can also buy *'fractional shares'* where you can own part of a share, rather than a whole one. It's a bit like getting a bite of a pizza rather than an entire slice, which may be too expensive.

Other people choose to diversify and spread their investments over many companies and countries. The easiest way to do this is to buy a basket of stocks in an *'investment fund.'* A fund pools investors' money together, meaning you can get opportunities that might not be available on your own.

There are different types of investment funds. You may come across different funds, including index funds, mutual funds and Exchange-Traded Funds (ETFs), money market funds and target date funds. Some contain stocks, bonds or a mixture of the two.

Some funds aim to track or outperform a stock market index. An **index** is a basket of companies selected to fulfil certain criteria – including quality, profitability and size. You may have heard of some of these already. The S&P 500 (*The Standard and Poor's 500*) tracks 500 of the largest companies listed on stock exchanges in the USA. The FTSE 100 (*The Financial Times Stock Exchange 100 index*) tracks 100 of the largest companies listed on the London Stock Exchange. There are many indices around the world.

Buying a fund enables you to hold hundreds or thousands of stocks at a time in a single product. Index funds are an example of *'passive management'* as the funds are automatically selected, keeping costs low. You may also come across *'actively managed'* funds, where a manager selects stocks into a portfolio, aiming to beat the stock market index. But you usually pay more for these as the fund manager needs paying.

Investment funds can cover different sectors (like finance, technology, healthcare or energy production), whole countries or regions (like emerging markets), or even the entire world in one go.

## Patterns In The Stock Market

As I said before, the stock market is a bit like a rollercoaster. It can form patterns over years, weeks or even minutes.

One way of visualising the stock market is using a *'candlestick chart.'* These have little boxes, green for up and red for down, showing the highest and lowest stock price for that particular time frame. Over time, these can form trends and patterns.

Some traders try to analyse and profit from these short-term movements using *'technical analysis.'* Websites, like *TradingView,* let you look at stock charts for free. You can search for stocks, shares and funds by their *ticker symbols*.[333]

So far we've been talking about trading. Investing, on the other hand, is over a longer time frame. In general, the stock market goes up over decades. Of course, there are always exceptions, such as Japan which experienced a big stock market crash in 1991 followed by a *'lost decade'* until 2001 from which it still hasn't fully recovered.[334] After *The Great Depression* of 1929, the US stock market didn't return to its former high until 1954.[335]

Could you stay the course for a quarter of a century? If you stick to a proven investing plan, taking dividends into account, it's still possible to make money in these circumstances. Some styles of investing ignore the crazy ups and downs of the daily stock market. When you step back and look at the bigger picture, even dramatic crashes look like tiny dips over a gradual climb higher.

Stock market charts always go up and down, irrespective of their timeframe. But long-term investing looks very different to short-term trading. To take the fish analogy to another level, you can imagine the stock market as if you were watching the ocean in a David Attenborough nature documentary.

We start off with an aerial view. The ocean looks flat and calm with distant waves. This is the stock market over years or decades. You can barely see the whales and fish, but you know they're there, underneath the waves. As you zoom in, the waves get bigger.

But it's only when you're in the water, up close and personal, that you see the interaction between the big fish and shoals of little fish as stock market traders try to outsmart each other. This could be an hourly or even 5-minute stock chart. It's why trading is exciting and full of drama.

While these fishy interactions make up the stock market and may cause a splash at times, there are bigger forces at play, just like the effects of gravity on the tide, the *'macroeconomics'* we talked about in the last chapter. The stock market is also driven by *'market sentiment'*. This is what causes the ocean waves.

## What is Market Sentiment?

*'The stock market is the story of cycles and of the human behaviour that is responsible for overreactions in both directions.'*
~ SETH KLARMAN

### The Battle between the 'Bulls' and the 'Bears'

As well as the game being played out between the big fish (professional investors) and little fish (retail investors), there's also another tug-of-war at play: the battle between the bulls and the bears.

This is called *'market sentiment.'* It's the emotions that set the tone of a market. It's a sort of crowd psychology that pushes stock prices up or down. You can think of it as the waves of the stock market ocean.

Market sentiment is *'bullish'* when prices are driven upwards (*think of a bull with the horns going upwards*). Market sentiment is *'bearish'* when prices are pushed downwards (*think of the bear pouncing downwards with its claws*).[336] These stock market movements up or down can last for hours, days, weeks or longer. This is called *'momentum'*.

I've included a photo of the bull and bear statue in front of the *Frankfurt Stock Exchange* to help you remember.[337] You'll hear someone described as a *'bull'* if they think the stock market will go up in future. You'll hear someone described as a *'bear'* if they think the stock market will go down in future. It took me ages to work out what these terms meant, so hopefully this makes sense to you now!

In crowd psychology, just like Ray Dalio described in his short- and long-term debt cycles, a cycle occurs when stock market bubbles form. It's driven by market sentiment. Underneath the bear and bull, I've included a graphic that shows the stages of a bubble.[338]

You can see how investors get sucked into a story that feeds on their emotions – euphoria and greed, followed by fear. It could be the stock market, bitcoin or tulip bulbs - the same sort of pattern occurs.

# Market Sentiment

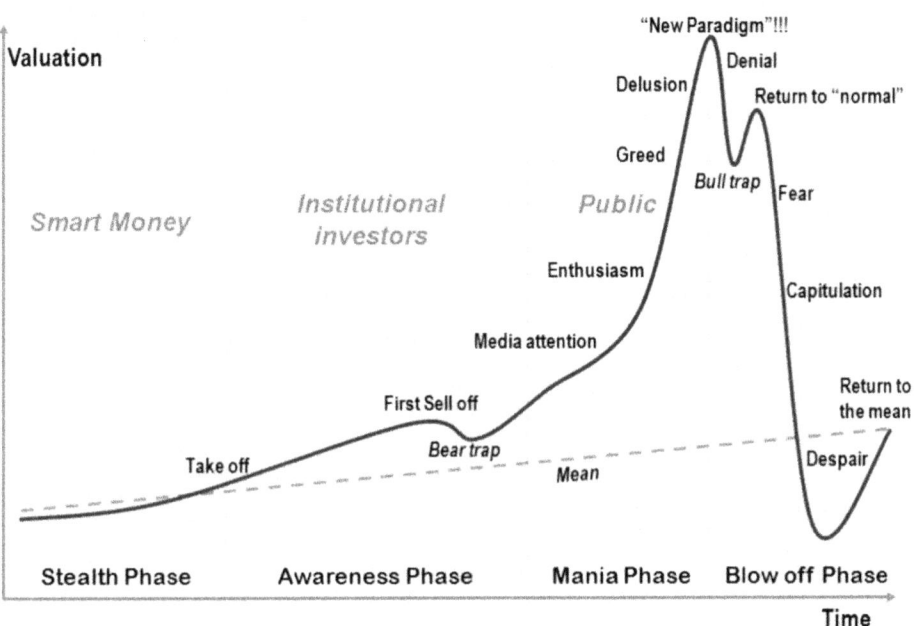

Eva K., CC BY-SA 2.5, 'Bull and bear in front of the Frankfurt Stock Exchange by the sculptor Reinhard Dachlauer' (top).
Jean-Paul Rodrigue, 'Stages of a bubble' (bottom).

When things are going good and the stock price is gradually going up, people start to pay attention. They think, 'Hey, I can get rich doing this! All my friends are making lots of money from it. I'd better jump in too.' You'll probably recognise this as FOMO (*Fear Of Missing Out*).

Eventually, the stock price skyrockets upwards, sometimes almost vertically, based on greed and delusions that *'things will always be this way'* – it's a new paradigm. But guess what – when someone says, *"This time it's different!"* it probably isn't and the cycle starts again. That straight-up exponential growth curve just isn't sustainable and a stock market crash could be just around the corner.

The little dip that follows marked *'bull trap'* is where there is a sudden drop and reversal back up again. This is sometimes called a *'dead cat bounce'* (sorry animal lovers, but there's an unfortunate saying that *'even a dead cat can bounce'*). This rally sucks in people who believe the upward move is back on. But it isn't. The fall is harder and more painful.

As people panic, the stock market *'capitulates'* and crashes into despair, with some people deciding never to invest again. The key is to avoid being one of them.

It's this pattern of emotions that explains why people get hurt riding the rollercoaster. They are *'all-in'* on the way up because everything looks great and they're making money. But they can't handle the rapid fall and despair when things go back down. So they jump off, usually at the bottom and lose money. Until the pattern repeats.

It's precisely because of these waves of emotions up and down that different investing styles exist. There are things you can learn about the psychology of investing, including types of *'bias'* and *'behavioural finance,'* which can help you avoid common traps and pitfalls.[339]

What's more, the YouTube and news algorithms don't help because they amplify emotion. Fear sells. Catchy titles about an imminent stock market crash and pictures of the apocalypse are great clickbait.

Going further into this fascinating topic is beyond the scope of my book, but I've put some useful videos in the Resources Chapter that will explain market sentiment better than I can. Go check these out if you'd like to learn more about the psychology of investing.

When it comes to investing, some people use the waves of the stock market to make money, while other styles of investing simply rise above the waves and focus on the bigger picture.

For passive index fund investing in particular, the waves no longer matter very much if you have a time horizon of several decades. This is why you'll often hear it said that *'time in* the market is more important than *timing* the market.'

### *Is Investing In The Stock Market Like Gambling?*

Well, no, not exactly. When you gamble in a casino the odds are stacked against you. The house always wins in the long run and lots of gamblers end up losing money. When it comes to investing, it's the other way round. The stock market generally goes up over time, but you can lose out if you jump off at the wrong time. If you stick to a proven plan, then you greatly increase your chance of winning, especially if you give the process enough time. We'll explore this idea further when we look at the different styles of investing.

**KEY POINTS: THE STOCK MARKET**

- The stock market tends to go steadily upwards over time
- Market cycles are based on fear and greed
- Just because something has done well in the past, doesn't mean it'll do well in future
- What goes up must come down (*'reversion to the mean'*)
- Be aware of all the doom and gloom headlines
- Get to know yourself and your risk tolerance
- Be aware of bias and traps (*'behavioural finance'*)

# Investing Myths and Pitfalls

## Here are some common misconceptions

### 1. INVESTING IS JUST LIKE GAMBLING
Not if you don't try to time the market. Studies show that the stock market tends to go up in the long run, so you could use a buy-and-hold index fund strategy over decades.

### 2. INVESTING IS RISKY
You DO need to take some risk if you want to build wealth. You need to get to know your risk tolerance as some types of investing are more risky than others. Choosing NOT to invest is ALSO risky as your money will be eroded by inflation. Some people forget that sitting on the side-lines is risky too as you'll watch the stock market go up without you and panic!

### 3. INVESTING IS FOR RICH PEOPLE
Not true! Because of online educational resources, technology and fractional investing, more people than ever have access to investing. You no longer need a physical stock broker because you can have an app, online platform or robo-advisor instead.

### 4. I DON'T HAVE TIME TO INVEST
Again, not true! Some investment styles e.g. passive investing into index funds, don't need much research. You don't always need to follow investing news. You can even automate your investment account to invest every month, just like regular savings.

### 5. I NEED TO KNOW THE RIGHT TIME TO INVEST IN STOCKS
Trying to time the stock market is actually one of the worst things you can do. We have a habit of listening to our emotions, which means buying and selling at exactly the wrong time! Buying consistently, no matter what the stock market is doing, can help us avoid investing mistakes (such as jumping off the rollercoaster at the wrong time).

### 6. INVESTING IS A QUICK WAY TO MAKE MONEY
Trying to get rich quick is a sure way to take on too much risk and lose money. Investing is a great way to grow wealth over the long term. But just like an acorn becoming an oak tree, it can take decades to get there. Compound interest is very powerful but you need to give it 20 or 30 years to work. You may not feel any growth in the early days. But be patient and stay the course. Plant seeds now and wait.

## An Introduction To Different Styles Of Investing

When it comes to mindfulness some people like to connect with nature. Back in *Chapter 7: Make Your Garden Grow*, I gave you your *'Green Prescription'* when we designed your dream garden and investment portfolio. Now it's time for your *'Blue Prescription.'* we're going to take a trip along the seashore.

There are many different investing strategies out there. A useful article by *Investopedia.com* explains what preparations you need to make before you start investing. It also gives you the pros and cons of different investing styles.[340]

For now, I'm going to stick to the **4 main investing styles** that I hear financial experts talk about:

1. **Trading**
2. **Value Investing**
3. **Global Macro Investing**
4. **Passive Investing**

Only a qualified finance professional can advise which strategy will suit you best. I can only tell you my own experience and what I've learned. It may be that you start off with one strategy and progress to others as you learn more. You may find that this is more information than you need right now. That's okay - you can revisit it later.

So, let's start our tour of different investment styles. If you're new to investing and want to skip ahead to the easiest way to invest for beginners, the style that takes the least amount of time and energy, then you can go to **Number 4: Passive Investing**. I'll join you over there.

I hope you enjoy the walk. Don't forget to grab an ice cream!

## 1. Trading (Fish In The Ocean)

*'The man who begins to speculate in stocks
with the intention of making a fortune usually goes broke,
whereas the man who trades with a view of getting
good interest on his money sometimes gets rich.'*
~ CHARLES HENRY DOW

**EXAMPLES OF SUCCESSFUL TRADERS:**

- **Ross Cameron** (Day Trader, *'Warrior Trading'* – YouTube)
- **Brett N. Steenbarger** (Trading Coach, *'TraderFeed'* – Blog)
- **Sasha Evdakov** (Options Trader, *'Tradersfly'* – YouTube)
- **Rayner Teo** (Trader, *'TradingWithRayner'*, YouTube)

I don't trade myself. I mention these traders because they are also educators. Trading isn't the same as investing, but often the words 'trading' and 'investing' are used interchangeably. It means buying and selling stocks to make short-term gains, usually anywhere from minutes to 18 months.

When you think of a professional investor, you'll probably think of men in suits on the trading floor, surrounded by computer screens with charts, yelling *"buy, buy, buy!"* or *"sell, sell, sell!"* over a telephone. Yeah, that's trading. It's exciting and scrappy, with fortunes sometimes made or lost in moments. Investing is usually dull by comparison.[341]

To make a trade, traders must take a *'position.'* There are two types: a *'long'* position is where you make money if the stock price goes up; a *'short'* position is where you make money if the price goes down.[342]

Styles of trading are named after timeframe:[15]

- *'Position trading'* – positions held for months to years
- *'Swing trading'* – positions held for days to weeks
- *'Day trading'* – positions held during a day
- *'Scalp trading'* – positions held for minutes to seconds

In fact, when we invest, we are actually taking a *'long'* position as we're hoping to make money from the stock market going up in future. But we're using a timeframe of years to decades.

The COVID-19 pandemic saw huge numbers of people become retail traders. At that time, stock markets were going up and lots of people got lucky or greedy. But eventually, market sentiment turned and a lot of people inevitably lost money. Some of them may decide never to trade or invest in the stock market again.

Trading is one of the riskiest ways to participate in the stock market and many people lose money doing it, with some articles quoting 90% or more.[343] Just think about that - if 100 people were to trade, less than 10 of them would make any money! The big fish can swallow you whole and take your money.

It's possible to trade all sorts of things, including single stocks and index funds. Some traders use *Technical Analysis* to look for patterns that indicate if the stock market will go up or down. Other people trade based on *'fundamentals'* - what they think a business is worth, with price movements affected by news events or market sentiment.

While the aim is to buy low and sell high, it's almost impossible to time the stock market. So traders need a successful strategy that protects them from falling into emotion traps and being victims of investment bias. It's about maximising profits and minimising losses. As long as you make more than you lose, then you can be a successful trader. But it's easier said than done.

I don't do any trading in my core portfolio, but I like to listen to YouTube channels about trading so that I can understand how the stock market works. I enjoy watching the interactions between the little fish (retail investors) and big fish (professional investors) in the stock market ocean without getting caught up in it.

To be a successful trader you have to switch off your emotions. It's easy to lose money, especially if you don't know what you're doing. When you jump into the ocean unprepared you'll definitely get wet! This is a warning, especially for those of you with a taste for adventure – will you sink or swim? Maybe stay out of the ocean, full stop.

One of my favourite channels is called *FX Evolution*. Tom, from Australia, has a great community and does regular livestreams. Back in February 2022, Tom was talking about the difference between trading and investing. I liked it so much, I wrote it down. He said:

*"...if you're trading, remember: a trader will have an entry, a stop loss and a take profit. An investor tends to have an entry and a time frame. Okay? So I think that's really important or a thesis as well. This is an important delineation. If you're buying and trading you really shouldn't be taking massive losses. You should be taking the loss that you have specified with your stop loss etc."*

You'll notice that Tom speaks in trading language. A *'stop loss'* is an order to sell if the stock you're trading drops below a certain price point. This protects you from losing more money if the stock market drops further.

Meanwhile, *'taking profit'* means selling when a certain price target is reached, so you can collect your gains before the market drops again. Sometimes traders have to *'cut their losses'* which means getting out of a trade early when they realise it's not profitable.

It's too complicated for me to go into what *'options trading'* is here, mainly because I don't fully understand it myself, no matter how often I read about it. You can think of options trading as placing timed bets on whether the stock market will go up or down. Some hedge funds and global macro investors use these too, but it's usually as a *'hedge,'* to protect their wealth like an insurance policy should their investment not go the way they hoped.

Retail investors, on the other hand, sometimes use options to gamble. It can be very dangerous, especially if they use leverage (borrow money) to do it. Not only are their gains amplified but so are their losses.

If you'd like to know more, *Investopedia.com* has an article explaining how options trading works.[344]

## KEY POINTS: TRADING

- Trading is one of the riskiest ways to 'play' the stock market.
- Around 90 to 95% of traders lose money day trading, so only risk what you can afford to lose.
- While investing isn't gambling, sometimes trading is.
- Be careful when using leverage or borrowing money to trade.
- Always use a trading plan (know when to enter and exit a trade).
- If the trading plan isn't working, it's okay to bail out and start over.
- Remember to protect your downside risk with a stop loss.
- Watch out for adverts trying to sell you a winning trading strategy. They may be salesmen trying to make money from you. If it sounds too good to be true, then it probably is.

## 2. Value Investing (Hidden Treasure In Rock Pools)

*'All intelligent investing is value investing
– acquiring more than you are paying for.
You must value the business in order to value the stock.'*
~ CHARLIE MUNGER

**NOTABLE VALUE INVESTORS:**

- **Benjamin Graham** (Creator of Value Investing, *'The Intelligent Investor,'* published 1949)
- **Warren Buffet** (Chairman/CEO of *Berkshire Hathaway*)
- **Charlie Munger** (Vice Chairman of *Berkshire Hathaway*)
- **Mohnish Pabrai** (Hedge fund manager)
- **Phil Town** (Hedge fund manager, *'Rule #1 investing'* – YouTube)
- **Peter Lynch** (Hedge Fund Manager, *'One Up on Wall Street'* – book)

Value investing is interesting, but not exciting. Paul Samuelson said, "*Investing should be more like watching paint dry or watching grass grow. If you want excitement, take $800 and go to Las Vegas.*"

Value investors can go for months or years without finding a stock that is *good value*. It's a strategy that made Warren Buffet one of the wealthiest people on the planet and most successful investors of all time, still working into his 90s. He pens an annual letter to *Berkshire Hathaway* shareholders. He shares his pearls of wisdom and explains his methods. He has certainly benefited from the compound effect and is a *buy-and-hold* investor, acquiring stocks like Coca Cola and Apple, and holding onto them for decades.

To continue our seaside analogy, you can imagine a value investor searching around the rock pools for something of value that everyone else has missed. What looks a useless shell could in fact be a mussel or oyster with a pearl inside. That's how value investing works. It's taking time to analyse stocks to find good quality businesses that the rest of the market has missed, stocks which are under-priced and under-valued. Essentially, it's finding a bargain - buying stocks when they are on sale.

I like this rock pool analogy as it links in to some of Warren Buffet's other famous sayings, such as '*only when the tide goes out do you discover who's been swimming naked.*' Some companies borrow too much or take too much risk. They look great when circumstances are perfect, but as soon as the tide goes out everything is exposed.

To be a successful value investor, you have to be prepared to do some homework. So if you don't have time, this style of investing probably isn't for you. There are ways to analyse individual companies to determine whether they are cheap or not. Here are some pitfalls:

**Scenario 1:** *You hear a friend in the pub, or a family member, or even a shop assistant, bragging about how they made a fortune in Amazon, Bitcoin or X (formerly Twitter). You rush out and buy the stock! The price drops soon after! You panic, sell and lose a pile of money. You never invest again.*

So, why does that happen? Well, it's market sentiment again. This was an overvalued asset that formed a bubble which burst.

Warren Buffet also famously said, *"be fearful when others are greedy, and greedy when others are fearful."* That means you want to try and buy stocks when the tide goes out, at the bottom of the drop, when everyone is rushing for the exit. That's when the oysters with the pearls will be hiding in rock pools, waiting for you to find them. It's not the business that has changed, after all, just the price.

I'll give you a personal example. A little while ago, even my mum asked me if she should invest in Bitcoin! That's how I knew we were in a bubble. Even my mum who knows very little about investing was asking about cryptocurrency! This is why you have to watch out for FOMO and ignore the guy talking about how big his catch was. Wait for him to say he's terrified of fishing and will never do it again – that's probably the time to invest. It's not timing the market, as such. It's looking for a bargain and being aware of market sentiment.

**Scenario 2:** *You see a stock that looks like it's on sale. The price looks way cheaper than what you think the underlying business is worth. Why is nobody else buying it? It's a bargain! So you buy in. And the price goes down a bit more. It's still a bargain! So you buy a bit more... wait a minute, how low can this thing go? The company goes bankrupt and you lose everything. You never invest again.*

Okay, a bit over-dramatic maybe. This scenario is based on a story told by Peter Lynch on how to deal with a falling stock. Stock price can fall for lots of reason – market sentiment; a bad news story; a problem with the underlying business; or even random chance. That's why it's important to know about the business if you're picking individual stocks.

There's a principle in statistics called *'regression'* or *'reversion to the mean.'* [345] This is where a price can go up or down but eventually it will return back to the long-term average. So what goes up will usually come down. Unfortunately, what goes down can keep going down, and down, and down…

There are several styles of value investing. There's Warren Buffet's pearls in a rock pool approach. But his mentor and creator of value investing, Benjamin Graham, used a *'cigar butt'* approach. Imagine a cigar on the street with one last puff in it. It might be a rubbish stock, *'trash'* as Buffet calls it, a business on the way out – but it's possible to pick it up for next to nothing and make a tiny profit before it goes down completely. One last hurrah.

Later value investors like to own quality businesses. They buy them when they represent good value: bought at a discount, with a *'moat of protection'* around them, such as not having too much debt. Sometimes they buy and hold them for a very long time.

Phil Town likes to buy stocks when they're cheap and sell them when they are overvalued. Mohnish Pabrai likes to look for undervalued stocks that are *'spawners,'* businesses that generate other businesses (a bit like Amazon, which started as a bookseller, but has now branched out into selling everything, streaming music, videos and even cloud storage.)

So if you want to be a value investor, prepare to do some homework and prepare to wait a long time. You have to enjoy watching paint dry, grass grow and exploring rock pools!

## KEY POINTS: VALUE INVESTING

- Value investors look for good quality undervalued stocks
- Value investors aim to buy low and sell high, through some – like Warren Buffet – like to buy and hold forever.
- You need to do your homework and analyse stocks to know whether they are truly undervalued
- But remember, some stock prices are low for a reason

## 3. Global Macro Investing (Surfing The Waves)

*'Most active investors fail to realize that they are part of the crowd themselves. They are trying to beat the crowd while being the crowd.'*
~NAVED ABDALI

### NOTABLE GLOBAL MACRO INVESTORS:

- Ray Dalio
- George Soros
- Jim Rogers
- Paul Tudor Jones
- Stanley Druckenmiller
- Bruce Kovner

The first 3 styles of investing we're looking at are all examples of *'active investing.'* This is where someone is aiming to do better than simply buying the whole stock market. Active investors try to pick stocks that they think will do better (*'outperform'*) and dump stocks that they think won't, trying to buy low and sell high for a profit.

In reality, active investors use a mixture of asset classes and investing styles. Sometimes they try to take a bigger picture view and invest based on global trends that affect the world's stock markets. This is called '*Global Macro Investing.*'

If you've read the last chapter, '*A Brief History of Money,*' then you may remember the term '*macroeconomics.*' This is the study of how different world economies interact with each other. Macroeconomists build a story of what the stock market will do based on the actions of governments and central banks, news stories, wars, pandemics, the weather etc. They then invest based on these theories.

There are patterns and trends from history that help predict what might happen in future. Certain months perform better than others. There's usually a '*Santa Clause rally*' in the run up to Christmas. There are principles based on stock market performance in January or election years. Stock prices behave a certain way based on interest rates or inflation. This helps them know when to buy, sell, or stay in cash, waiting for an opportunity.

They can also '*hedge*' their investments so that they can make money or protect themselves from too much loss if they turn out to be wrong. Ultimately, global macro investors are trying to ride waves of momentum in the stock market, a bit like a surfer.

I found a beginner's guide to surfing that says '*no matter what size of wave, catching the wave is all about timing and positioning on the wave.*' [346] If they get it wrong, then guess what – they're in the water! The same is true of macro investing: stock market timing and positioning are crucial.

I've heard lots of active investors admit to not being able to time the stock market perfectly. But if they catch a few more waves than the average stock market index fund, there's a chance they'll still be able to outperform. It's risky and research shows very few active investors are able to beat the market.

You may also have heard of something called a '*Black Swan Event.*' The phrase was made popular by Nassim Nicholas Taleb in his 2007 book, *'The Black Swan.'* He talks about statistical improbabilities – to expect the unexpected and prepare for the unpredictable.[347]

The book title is based on a story where at one point in history everyone believed the same truth – that all swans were white. This formed their entire worldview. All it took was one black swan to prove them wrong. A swan with black plumage was discovered in Australia in 1697 by a Dutch explorer. This forced everyone to adjust to a new truth or way of thinking, known as a paradigm shift. These are rare occurrences but can cause significant upheaval.

Throughout history, there are lots of events that seemed impossible at the time and nobody predicted them, or if they did they were made fun of. Very few people saw the 1929 *Wall Street Crash* coming or *The Great Depression* of 1929-1939. People thought the booming stock market of the *'Roaring Twenties'* would last forever.

However, an economist called Roger Babson was one of the few people who predicted it correctly. He said, "S*ooner or later a crash is coming [...] then there will immediately be a stampede to save what paper profits then exist.*"[348]

A similar story occurred around the time of the 2008 *Great Financial Crisis* where Michael Bury famously predicted the stock market would crash as depicted in the movie *'The Big Short.'*[349] His theory seemed so strange that nobody took him seriously. When you swim against the current you are being a *'contrarian.'*

Bury made a lot of money for himself and his clients by predicting the subprime mortgage crisis. He positioned his investments to take advantage of this. Timing and positioning are crucial, but almost impossible to predict accurately. Incidentally, there have also been many times when Michael Bury has predicted a crash and nothing happened.

It can be tempting to copy other investors, follow the herd or move with the mainstream. This works just fine when the stock market is going up. However, unpredictable things do happen that the stock market hasn't priced in. There may be an opportunity for active investors to make profits on these occasions when the stock market is still catching up with reality.

It's impossible to time the market perfectly. *'Black Swan Events'* are impossible to predict – that's what defines them. If you listen to too many economists, you may hear them predicting a black swan event every week! They'll make you believe that the sky is always about to fall in or that the end of the world is nigh!

At some point, an economist will be right and a crash will be right on cue. But what about all those times when the stock market went up? If you listen to too much of the doom and gloom you may be too scared to invest at all! So it's important to be aware of your emotions.

## Active vs. Passive Investing

You'll hear arguments on both sides as to which is better – active or passive investing. I've linked to some videos in the Resources Chapter if you want to find out more.

I think the statistics of randomness is very interesting. Some studies have even shown that monkeys can be better stock pickers than the professionals![350] But this doesn't mean that you should just pick stocks with a pin or let an animal do it for you.

Just because someone has been successful as an active investor doesn't mean that they can keep outperforming the stock market indefinitely. That's because of *'reversion to the mean'* again, that statistical effect we talked about before. This applies to all investors.

How do we know if active investors have been skilful or just lucky? It's hard to say. Active fund managers who have done the best one year are likely to underperform in future years. This is because performance moves back to the average. What goes up usually has to come down.

But it's almost impossible to say if a fund manager having a down year is going to outperform next year. They could just be really bad at stock picking! Sometimes their portfolio can just keep going down… and down… and down…

That's what you need to ask yourself if choosing an actively managed fund or portfolio manager. Will they be able to outperform for decades? What happens if they leave the fund?

There are a few things to keep in mind. Actively managed funds are often heavily marketed products. Sometimes there can be a lot of hype surrounding a fund that is thought to be doing well and people rush in, which pushes the price up, causing more people to rush in. Recognise that bubble psychology again?

So if a fund is doing well, it might be that it contains good outperforming stocks, but it could also mean that it's just very popular and there's a lot of demand right now. This is called *'fund flow.'*[351]

It works in the other direction too. As people pull out of a fund, the price can also go down disproportionately. Active managers sometimes need to liquidate the stocks they hold to return money to people who want to exit the fund. This can happen at the worst possible time, such as when there's panic in the markets (which is usually the best time to be buying stocks on sale!)

There are many things stacked against a fund manager to make life difficult. They have performance targets to hit and a reputation to protect which means that sometimes they have to do some window dressing to make things appear better than they are.

Active fund managers can also be a victim of their own success. As the fund size increases, opportunities to outperform the markets are harder to find. Sometimes it can be easier for retail investors to make money as they can invest in smaller high-growth companies that the big funds no longer have access to.[352]

There are also higher fees for actively managed funds as they have to pay their manager. These can compound and add up to a substantial amount over time. So if you've got a portfolio manager you need to ask yourself if they're value for money.

I don't want to seem too biased against active investing. There are some pros as well, but that involves finding an active investment strategy that you know will work, that can outperform the markets and protect your wealth over the long term. In practice, it can be quite hard to find a trusted advisor whose values match your own.

I still find it interesting to learn about active investing and macroeconomics, even though it's not an approach I use personally, at least, not in my main portfolio. That's what satellite portfolios are for - to experiment and learn.

Everyone has a bias and unfortunately the active fund management industry seems well-positioned to make money from unsuspecting retail investors who haven't done their research and end up paying high fees as a result. If stock picking is hard, then picking a successful active fund manager out of the pile is also going to be hard. That's why so many people opt for a passive investing approach.

An episode of *'The Money Guy Show'* addressing this topic concludes that ultimately, it doesn't matter if active or passive investing achieves the best returns in the long run. The key is your investing behaviour. Are you investing regularly? What is your savings rate? Are you investing enough? Are you avoiding the investment pitfalls? Those are the things that *really* matter.

## KEY POINTS: GLOBAL MACRO INVESTING

- *'Active investors'* try to beat a *'benchmark'* by picking stocks that outperform the stock market index
- *Global Macro Investing* takes into account world events and geopolitical trends to try to pick stocks that they think will do well
- It's hard to predict the future
- A *'Black Swan Event'* is something nobody saw coming, meaning the price hasn't been factored into the stock market yet. This may be the trigger for a stock market crash or buying opportunity
- Active Fund Managers and financial advisors make money from fees. So make sure you're getting value for money if you use one.

## 4. Passive Investing (Aerial Flight)

*'Don't look for the needle in the haystack. Just buy the haystack!'*
~ JOHN C. "JACK" BOGLE

**NOTABLE PASSIVE INVESTORS:**

- **Burton Malkiel** ~ Economist, author of *'A Random Walk Down Wall Street'*, 1973
- **John C. 'Jack' Bogle** ~ Founder of the Vanguard Group, creator of the first index fund
- **Pete Matthew** ~ Chartered Financial Planner, *'Meaningful Money'*
- **Brian Preston** ~ CPA, CFP®, PFS. USA. *'The Money Guy Show'*
- **JL Collins** ~ Blog writer, author of *'The Simple Path To Wealth'*
- **Lars Kroijer** ~ Author of *'Investing Demystified'*

I've spent a lot of time outlining the different styles of active investing because they're interesting and grab the headlines. You'll hear about hedge fund managers and famous billionaire investors, people who got wealthy by predicting stock market crashes or correctly picking stocks that did disproportionately well over time.

But what can ordinary retail investors do if most active investors rarely outperform the stock market in the long run and if 90% of traders lose money?

If it's impossible to accurately time the market or predict the future, even with all the research and expertise that the professionals have, then what chance do we have as ordinary retail investors?

This is where *passive investing* comes in. It can help us avoid many of the traps and cognitive biases that come with active investing by taking emotion out of the process. The fees associated with it are also usually much lower. Passive investing is a simple approach that has worked well for many people, especially if they have a time horizon of decades. These things make it great for retirement investing.

I describe passive investing as riding above the waves of the stock market because the ups and downs no longer matter. It's about that upwards drift of stock market prices over the long-term.

If you invest regularly and consistently in diversified index funds, no matter what the ups and downs of the stock market are doing, then you can achieve an average stock market return. That's better than a lot of active managers!

You don't need to feel the emotion of a crashing economy or the FOMO of a rising stock you missed out on. You don't need to worry about whether the stock market is going down tomorrow. You just buy the index and aim to hold it forever.

A stock market index tracks the top companies in a particular country or sector using pre-defined criteria. So if some companies are not doing so well, they automatically drop out of the index and a better one takes its place. If a company is doing well, then it may get added to the index. These means you're investing in quality companies that will hopefully add value over time.

By investing in this way, you can stay emotionally detached like the aerial camera shots of a nature documentary, looking down on the waves but not even touching the water. The only way to get wet is if you panic and sell at the wrong time. Like I said before, you only get hurt if you jump off the rollercoaster. So stay the course!

## A Brief History Of Index Fund Investing

Burton Malkiel is sometimes referred to as the father of passive investing. His famous investing book, *'A Random Walk Down Wall Street'* published in 1973, inspired many of those who pioneered index funds, including Jack Bogle, founder of Vanguard and creator of the first index fund.

However, many people at the time ridiculed both Malkiel and Bogle's ideas. They laughed off the suggestion that investors are better off buying a broad basket of stocks while keeping fees to a minimum. The alternative is paying an active manager who may not even be able to beat the market. So of course the idea was met with resistance from active managers who didn't want to see outflows of fee-paying customers from their funds.[353]

Jack Bogle was pivotal in making index fund investing a reality. He founded the Vanguard Group in 1975 with a very different structure from what had been seen in the investment industry before. Investors in Vanguard's funds became the company's shareholders.

In 1976, Vanguard launched an S&P 500 index fund, the world's first index fund. This made index investing available to individual investors when previously only the big institutional investors had been able to benefit from this approach. Passive index investing still took a few years to catch on with a rival index fund only launching in 1984.[354,355]

Jack Bogle died in 2019 aged 89, leaving behind an incredible legacy of helping ordinary investors become wealthy, not just rich people or institutional investors.[356] Vanguard has always prioritised keeping the cost of investing low which completely changed the investing landscape.

The popularity of index funds has exploded over the last 20 years. As of May 2022, for the first time in history, retail investors hold more money in index funds than actively managed funds.[357]

In *'The Little Book of Common Sense Investing'* first published in 2007, you'll find among other pearls of wisdom Jack Bogle's famous quote,

*'Don't look for the needle in the haystack. Just buy the haystack!'* The idea is that if you can't decide which stocks are going to outperform, you can just buy them all using an index fund.

Another proponent of passive index fund investing is Warren Buffet, the famous value investor we looked at before. He has recommended index fund investing to people who don't have the time and expertise to do the detailed research needed to be a value investor.

In fact, Buffet wrote in his 2013 letter to Berkshire Hathaway shareholders that if he were to pass away, he wanted the majority of his wife's inheritance to go into an S&P index fund.[358]

Buffet also made a million-dollar bet against the hedge funds by saying that an S&P index fund would beat a selection of actively managed hedge funds over a 10-year period (taking fees, costs and expenses into account). He was proved right.[359] He won the bet in spectacular style and gave the money away to charity.

## Concerns About Index Fund Investing

If passive index fund investing is simple, low-cost, it doesn't require much research or skill, why do certain people critical of it? One of the main concerns is whether index funds and ETFs could be in a bubble with money being concentrated in a few overweight stocks.

Some people think that indexing on a mass scale could take away the process of *'price discovery'* (the process where the market decides how expensive a stock should be).

With a growing number of retail investors opting for a passive index fund approach, is this a problem? Research suggests that passive funds account for less than 5% of trading volume, so perhaps not yet.[360]

Index funds are often *'cap-weighted,'* meaning the bigger the company, the bigger its representation in the index. So money tends to flow into the big companies of an index rather than smaller companies which have the most potential for growth.

The very fact that a company is included in an index could theoretically push up the price of a stock as all index fund holders are forced to buy it. Similarly, if one of those big companies does badly, it may disproportionately pull down the value of the entire index.

Take Tesla, for example. The electric vehicle manufacturer only entered the S&P 500 index in December 2020 when it met the strict inclusion criteria. Before that time it wasn't profitable. Tesla stock did well in 2021, in part boosted by its index fund inclusion. But Tesla stock performed poorly in 2022, pulling down the value of the index. S&P 500 index fund investors have no choice but to own Tesla, irrespective of how well the company is doing or how expensive it is, until it is dropped from the index.[361]

Michael Burry, who predicted the 2008 subprime mortgage crisis, thinks there may be a bubble caused by index fund investing, according to Bloomberg News. The same effects of *'herd behaviour'* and *'mania'* that caused inflows of money into index funds in the first place could arguably go in the other direction if people were to lose confidence in index fund investing.[362]

Burry is reported to have said: *"Trillions of dollars in assets globally are indexed to these stocks. The theater keeps getting more crowded, but the exit door is the same as it always was. All this gets worse as you get into even less liquid equity and bond markets globally."*[37]

The counter-argument to this would be to look at the type of investors who tend to follow a passive investment approach. Many of them are *buy-and-hold* retirement investors, not speculators. It's a *set-it-and-forget-it* approach. You don't need to worry about prices for decades.

If stock prices were to drop and not recover for several years, some of these investors would still have a long enough timeframe for short-term price changes not to matter too much. So the *'rush to the exit'* may be less likely. In fact, many long-term investors are looking for opportunities to buy stocks at a discount!

## How To Invest Passively

I'm not going to go into all the details of how to open an investment account, what platform to pick, what index funds to buy, all those things. You can research those steps for yourself in the Resources Chapter.

Pete Matthew has created a beginner's guide to investing. People like JL Collins (author of *The Simple Path to Wealth*) and Lars Kroijer (author of *Investing Demystified*) were great people to listen to when I was starting out. They'll help you answer the question, *"How should I invest?"*

Now might be a good time to go back through that check-list from the beginning of the chapter and ask yourself:

- Am I in the financial position to start investing?
- What are my investing goals and time horizon?
- What is my risk tolerance?
- Have I used an online calculator to check?
- Should I invest in stocks or something else?
- Do I understand what I'm investing my money into?
- Do I need someone to help me or can I go it alone?

For some people, passive investing may look like automatically putting money away each month directly from their paycheque into an index fund, or perhaps a multi-asset fund (with stocks and bonds).

Most financial experts advise not to look at your investments very often as it will only freak you out. Maybe once a year or every quarter, then rebalance your stocks and bonds if necessary.

For other people, it will be paying into a workplace pension. But be sure to find out what kind of funds your money is being invested into.

It could be a core portfolio of globally-diversified index funds and a satellite portfolio of fun investments (money that you are prepared to lose, just for you to learn and play with).

If you watch the stock market too closely, if you're tempted to buy out and sell in again, there's a danger that you'll panic, sell or meddle. You could lose out on the good days of the stock market, which usually come straight after the bad days. It might cost you in fees as well.

If you understand how passive index fund investing works, then you'll feel more confident about putting money in and waiting, letting compound interest work for you. It's okay to do a little checking and course-correcting with your investments, but it's also okay to do absolutely nothing.

In an interview, Jack Bogle said to Tom Gardener of *The Motley Fool*: *"...you should have a serious money account, I might even call it a boring money account, where you put money in the stock market index fund and balance it out a little bit with some bonds, depending on age and so on and don't look at it for 50 years, don't peek, but when you retire open the envelope, be sure a doctor is nearby to revive you, you will go into a dead faint you can't believe there is that much money in the world and that's where we fool ourselves."* [363]

I admit to looking at the stock market too much. Something in me is very interested in those ups and downs, the stock market news and world events, people telling me to buy into a story of how the future might be, the idea that I might find the next Amazon or Google, a stock on sale that nobody else has discovered yet.

That's why I have a core portfolio of index funds and a satellite portfolio where I invest in fun things like alternative assets. But it's money that I'm willing to lose. It means I keep my core portfolio alone.

When I'm tempted to gamble or speculate, when I think maybe I can be better than average, I keep reminding myself of Jack Bogle's words and advice. Keep investing for the long term. Don't worry about the ups and downs. Don't jump off the rollercoaster.

## Pound (Dollar) Cost Averaging vs. Lump Sum Investing

Here's another clever psychological trick that can help us stay the course while navigating a choppy stock market ocean. In the UK, it's called *'pound cost averaging.'* In the USA, it's called *'dollar cost averaging.'* Just switch the name of the currency for whatever you're investing in. The principle is the same.

*'Pound cost averaging'* is the process of drip-feeding your money into the stock market, maybe monthly or weekly, irrespective of whether the stock market is up or down. Over the years, it should theoretically average out. You don't get all the highs, but you don't get all the lows either.

If you decide that passive investing is for you, then there's usually a question that pops up – should I put in all my money in one go or invest it gradually?

In reality, most people will be investing from their pay cheque each month which means they will probably be pound cost averaging by default. But every now and again you may get a windfall, like a tax refund, gift, inheritance or (though I don't recommend gambling) a lottery win!

There is research that suggests that *'lump sum investing'* – investing all your money in one go – tends to do better mathematically in the long term because the stock market generally goes up over time, so it's good to get exposure as early as possible.[364]

But psychologically, there is a benefit to drip-feeding your investments into the stock market. You're more likely to keep going over the long term and build good investing habits. If you invest and then the stock market crashes soon afterwards, you can be left with an overwhelming feeling of regret which makes you too scared to invest again.

Similarly, it can be tempting to try to time the market and buy in at a low point. But it's almost impossible to know when that will be. You could be left waiting on the sidelines in a state of inertia while the stock market climbs higher and higher without you. Many people have missed out on a stock market rally waiting for the right time to invest that never comes.

Pound cost averaging is a behaviour hack. It means pre-deciding to invest a certain amount of money consistently over time, no matter what the stock market is doing. It takes away the emotion from investing and removes a lot of those biases in behavioural psychology that make investors do the wrong thing at the wrong time.[365]

Instead of getting you to imagine ocean waves, I've included a picture from one of my investment accounts from 2022. It looks just like the ocean! In this case, pound cost averaging allowed me to consistently buy into the stock market each month. I didn't hit all the stock market bottoms but I didn't hit all the peaks either. I'm probably somewhere in the middle. That's how pound cost averaging works.

I felt no panic or euphoria. I just set my account to buy each month and let the stock market do whatever it wants. If it crashes, then stocks are on sale and I keep buying (perhaps I even decide to buy a bit more). If it goes up, then that's great too – I'll benefit from dividends and compound interest over time.

### KEY POINTS: PASSIVE INVESTING

- Passive investors are content with an average performance, by owning a whole stock market index
- Some index funds are targeted to a particular sector, country or the whole world
- Passive investing typically keeps fees as low as possible
- Some funds are only traded once a day, while others, like ETFs, can be traded on the stock market at any time.
- Some people choose to invest a lump sum, while other people do 'pound cost-averaging,' drip-feeding money into the stock market, to avoid feelings of regret if the stock market drops suddenly after they've invested.

MINDFUL FINANCE - 447

# Pound Cost Averaging

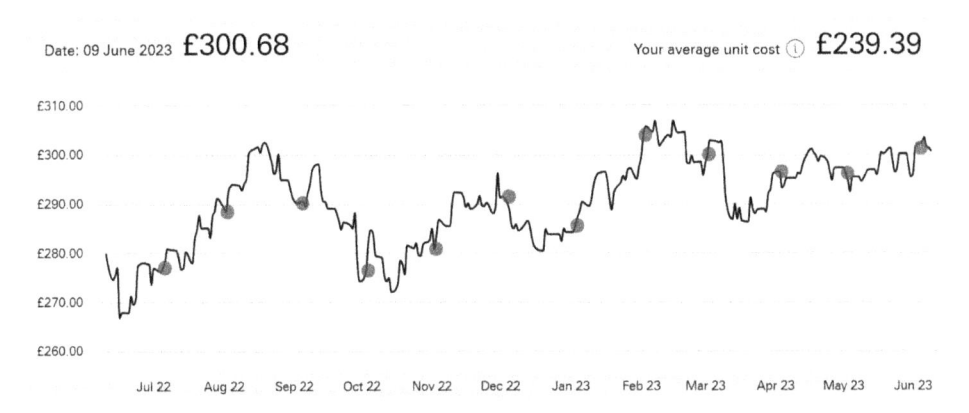

Date: 09 June 2023  £300.68     Your average unit cost  £239.39

Here's an example of 'pound cost averaging' from my stocks and shares ISA. This is a global index fund. (Not a recommendation, just an example).

1. Notice how the stock market was very choppy, like waves of the ocean. Some years it can go dramatically up or down. In 2022-23, it went sideways - either way, it can be an emotional rollercoaster!

2. See how difficult it is to time the market! Don't give in to emotion.

3. Notice the dots? Each one represents an investment in the stock market and shows you what price I paid at that time.

4. Some investment accounts let you automate your investments. So I have a certain amount set to invest every month, no matter what the stock market is doing. You set-it-and-forget-it. Then you just wait.

5. So I don't get the bottoms or the highs - I just get the average.

## Conclusion:

So that's the end of this brief introductory guide on how to invest. It was a whistle-stop tour but I hope you enjoyed your trip to the seaside. There's so much more for you to learn and apply. I hope you will continue your journey by checking out the Resources Chapter and finding some links to my favourite finance experts. They will be your guide from now on.

I hope this chapter has given you some food for thought, as well as hope and confidence that investing is something that you can do when the time is right. There's a process to go through before you start and techniques to help you stay the course. The important thing is to keep going, even if you make mistakes. It's okay to get up and go again.

If you're in the early stages of your mindful finance journey, I hope that this chapter has inspired you to get your financial house in order and keep building those good money habits. Hopefully one day you'll get to a place where you can start planning for retirement and growing your wealth, or whatever goal you choose to set.

I hope I've debunked some investing myths for you and helped you avoid some pitfalls. Stick to the proven path. It's okay to get wealthy slowly, just like it's okay to go the long way around and take a scenic route. Success is something you get to define for yourself. Gratitude is the key to living an abundant life.

Whether it's your *material wealth* or *spiritual wealth* (relationships, physical and mental health, identity, purpose, calling and wellbeing), I hope this book has helped you on your journey towards flourishing, to become who you were created to be.

Remember to enjoy the journey. Take a moment to pause, reflect and look around.

Stewardship will take a lifetime and I hope your legacy of generosity will go further still. The seeds you plant now will grow into trees that will last for generations to come.

# Resources for your JOURNEY

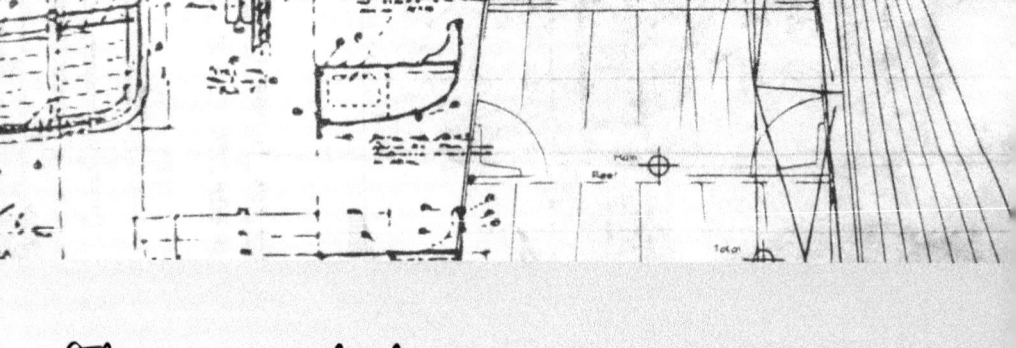

*It's just the beginning...*

| 11 |

## Chapter 11: Resources

In this chapter, I've put together some of my favourite resources for you: YouTube videos, books, blogs, podcasts and resources. I've tried to keep it brief as you've probably noticed I've already mentioned many pages of helpful websites and resources in the references. So I'll try not to duplicate too much.

The world of personal finance education is vast. One of the best things you can do is '**Like**, **Subscribe** and **Follow**' the content creators that you most enjoy and the YouTube algorithm will bring more helpful videos your way. That's pretty much how I learnt how to do it.

Remember, these resources are for your education and entertainment only. They are not personal recommendations for what to do with your money, so do your own research and don't take on more risk than you're comfortable with.

This book was written and edited from January 2022 to October 2023. I may update the resources in future editions. There will always be new and archived content out there. So have fun exploring.

Instead of typing in a website URL or YouTube link, you might want to do an internet search or YouTube search for a particular keyword of content creator. Most of the books will be available to purchase at your favourite bookstore. You might even find the out-of-print books in eBook form or as free audio versions online. Some people have even made video summaries that give you an overview in minutes.

Have fun exploring the world of personal finance education. Find your own content creators. Find your tribe. Find what works for you. And don't forget to tell a friend! We're all on this journey together. I wish you well and hope you become successful with money, whatever that means for you. Good luck!

## Introduction to Mindful Finance:

**Big Think** on YouTube, *'Personal finance: How to save, spend, and think rationally about money,'* 23 Sept 2020, accessed 1 Aug 2022 <youtu.be/0uYnj1i1EQw>

**Christians Against Poverty**, YouTube Playlist, *'Debt advice UK – tips for dealing with debt,'* accessed 5 Apr 2022 <youtube.com/playlist?list=PLXkFADMbm9pIBZLA1-mZ_KBAplAoaBHoe>

**Amy Roberts**, MoneySavingExpert.com, 'Debt problems: What to do & where to get help,' 5 Apr 2022, accessed 19 July 2023 <www.moneysavingexpert.com/loans/debt-help-plan/>

## Chapter 1: Building A Firm Foundation

**Pete Matthew**, MeaningfulMoney.tv, *'The Ultimate Guide to Budgeting',* 14 Oct 2020, accessed 19 July 2023 <meaningfulmoney.tv/2020/10/14/the-ultimate-guide-to-budgeting/>

**Craig Groeschel**, Life.Church Media, *'Financial Margin,'* accessed 6 Feb 2023 <www.life.church/media/margin/financial-margin/>

**George Kamel** on YouTube, *'5 Side Hustles I Used to Build Wealth,'* 19 Jun 2023, accessed 15 Aug 2023 <youtu.be/XmOGg_OR-hA>

**Jenifer Thomson** on YouTube, *'NEW TO Additional Incomes & Business? START HERE,'* 12 Jan 2023, accessed 19 July 2023 <youtube.com/playlist?list=PLzRnZ7Iu5bTYh4JhMvLm2STmg_zuvuw9R>

**Ali Abdaal** on YouTube, *'7 Side Hustles You Can Start in 2023,'* 26 Jan 2023, accessed 15 Aug 2023 <youtu.be/I-dlPuqFguo>

**Graham Stephan** on YouTube, *'The 7 BEST Side Hustles That Make $100+ Per day,'* 22 Nov 2021, accessed 15 Aug 2023 <youtu.be/XoPX0G8GnwI>

## Careers and Finding Your Purpose:

**Ken Coleman**, *'The Ken Coleman Show'* on YouTube, radio show and podcast (USA), accessed 19 July 2023 <www.ramseysolutions.com/shows/the-ken-coleman-show>

**Rick Warren**, *'Purpose Driven Life: What on Earth Am I Here For?'* Zondervan, USA, 10th Anniversary Edition, published 1 Dec 2013.

## Key Books for Building a Firm Financial Foundation:

**John Mark Comer**, *'The Ruthless Elimination of Hurry: How to stay emotionally healthy and spiritually alive in the chaos of the modern world,'* Oct 2019, John Murray Press, London, UK.

**David Swenson**, *'Margin: Restoring Emotional, Physical, Financial, and Time Reserves to Overloaded Lives,'* NavPress, Colorado Springs, 25 Oct 2004.

**George S. Clason**, *'The Richest Man in Babylon,'* 1926, accessed 12 Feb 2022 (full text available at the Internet Archive) <archive.org/details/RichestManInBabylon_650/page/n3/mode/2up>

**Robert T. Kiyosaki**, *'Rich Dad Poor Dad: What the Rich Teach their Kids About Money That the Poor and Middle Class Do Not!"* Plata Publishing, 2007.

**David Bach**, *'The Automatic Millionaire: a powerful one-step plan to live and finish rich,'* New York, Broadway Books, 2004.

**Thomas J. Stanley, William D. Danko**, *'The Millionaire Next Door: The Surprising Secrets of America's Wealthy,'* Taylor Trade Publishing; Reissue edition, 2010.

**Morgan Housel**, *'The Psychology of Money: Timeless lessons on wealth, greed, and happiness,'* Harriman House, Petersfield, UK, 2020.

## Chapter 2: The 4 Walls

### *Financial Minimalism and the FIRE Movement:*

**Matt D'Avella** on YouTube, *'A Minimalist Approach to Personal Finance,'* 26 June 2018, accessed 27 July 2023 <youtu.be/zVcwvCL2C2c>

**Exploring Alternatives** on YouTube, *'Family Man Retires at 39 – Extreme Early Retirement | FIRE,'* 25 January 2020, accessed 21 July 2023 <youtu.be/8yNsKxbq0Ak>

**Next Level Life** on YouTube, *'Why I LOVE Coasting Financial Independence,'* 9 Mar 2020, accessed 21 July 2023 <youtu.be/0Ydt9u6Iljk>

**Erin Talks Money** on YouTube, *'Barista FIRE - Financial Independence Retire Early,'* 17 Aug 2020, accessed 21 July 2023 <youtu.be/xrPxGztAltg>

**Marko – Whiteboard Finance** on YouTube, *'What is Coast FIRE? (Financial Independence Retire Early),'* 21 Feb 2022, accessed 21 July 2023 <youtu.be/6OX5SmWFrE8>

**Rob Berger** on YouTube, *'A Beginner's Guide to FIRE (Financial Independence Retire Early),'* 15 Jan 2021, accessed 21 July 2023 <youtu.be/31Q7-jeH9Pc>

### *Some websites and blogs from the FIRE movement:*

**Sam Swenson**, CFA, CPA, *'Financial Independence, Retire Early (FIRE),'* updated 17 July 2023, accessed 21 July 2023 <www.fool.com/retirement/strategies/fire/>

**Mr Money Moustache** (blog)     <www.mrmoneymustache.com/>
**Playing With Fire** (film)     <www.playingwithfire.co/>
**Mad Fientist** (blog)     <www.madfientist.com/>
**Financial Samurai** (blog)     <www.financialsamurai.com/>
**Choose FI** (podcast)     <www.choosefi.com/>

## Mindful Eating and recipes:

**Zoe Health & Nutrition Podcast,** accessed 8 Nov 2023 <zoe.com/learn/category/podcasts>

**Culinary Medicine UK**, 'Teaching health practitioners the foundations of clinical nutrition and how to cook,' accessed 23 Sept 2023 <culinarymedicineuk.org/>

**Planet Nourish** (App), 'Ethnically-focused Digital Healthcare: We help you manage your diet and lifestyle in a way that's relevant to you and your cultural background,' accessed 23 Sept 2023 <planetnourish.com/>

**My Fitness Pal** (App), 'Good health starts with what you eat. Want to eat more mindfully? Track meals, learn about your habits, and reach your goals with MyFitnessPal,' accessed 23 Sept 2023 <www.myfitnesspal.com/>

**Dlife**, 'India Low Carb High Fat – LCHF & Keto – Diet Plan & Recipes For Diabetes Reversal & Weight Loss,' accessed 23 Sept 2023 <www.dlife.in/category/indian-lchf-keto-diet-recipes/>

## Food Minimalism:

**The Minimal Mom** on YouTube, 'The Minimalist Pantry (waste less, cook more),' 7 Dec 2021, accessed 27 July 2023 <youtu.be/EMf2xLP_3Ts> <www.youtube.com/@TheMinimalMom>

**Freezer Meals 101** on YouTube, accessed 27 July 2023 <www.youtube.com/@FreezerMeals101>

**Clara Cannucciari** (Clara's Kitchen), **Great Depression Cooking** on YouTube, filmed 2007-2012, accessed 27 July 2023 <www.youtube.com/c/GreatDepressionCooking/>

**Chef Grandma Cooking** on YouTube, accessed 27 July 2023 <www.youtube.com/@chefgrandmacooking>

**Honeyjubu** on YouTube, 'How to separate and store Costco bulk ingredients,' 19 Feb 2021, accessed 19 Mar 2022 <www.youtube.com/watch?v=soTIHvQ3IXs&t=517s>

## Clothing Minimalism:

**Cynthia Ajayi** on YouTube, accessed 21 Mar 2022 <www.youtube.com/@CynthiaAjayi/>

**A Small Wardrobe** on YouTube, accessed 27 July 2023 <www.youtube.com/@ASmallWardrobe/>

**The Minimal Mom** on YouTube, 'What I Wear in a Week (Minimalist Mom),' 9 Aug 2022, accessed 27 July 2023 <youtu.be/MZeSgMmYeSI>

## Shelter & Utilities:

**Graham Stephan** on YouTube, 'Why You'll Regret Buying A Home In 2022,' 18 Mar 2022, accessed 28 July 2023 <youtu.be/WHy96Qn1bOk>

**James Shack** on YouTube, 'Renting Vs Buying a Home | The 4% Rule,' 27 Jun 2021, accessed 28 July 2023 <youtu.be/KlsArhE_IwQ>

**Rule #1 Investing** on YouTube, 'Why You Should Rent vs Own | Phil Town,' 12 Sept 2018, accessed 28 July 2023 <youtu.be/ErjqwvXJAGg>

**PensionCraft** on YouTube, 'Buy vs Rent House - Which Is Best?,' 29 Oct 2019, accessed 28 July 2023 <youtu.be/HQk6aD2AHXE>

## Transportation:

**The Ramsey Show** on YouTube, 'How Do I Get Rid Of A Car That's Worth Less Than What I Owe?,' 17 Feb 2022, accessed 31 July 2023 <youtu.be/R7Kgf2WM_N4>

**The Money Guy Show** on YouTube, 'How to Buy a Car the RIGHT Way!' 27 Dec 2022, accessed 31 July 2023 <youtu.be/BJnkKkhkDP0>

**Marko – WhiteBoard Finance** on YouTube, 'DON'T PAY CASH AT CAR DEALERSHIPS! (Here's Why),' 11 Aug 2020, accessed 31 July 2023 <youtu.be/MleR3FFaKMU>

## Chapter 3: Roof of Protection

**Pete Matthew**, MeaningfulMoney.tv, '*The Ultimate Guide to Wealth Protection*', 28 Oct 2020, accessed 8 Aug 2023 <meaningfulmoney.tv/2020/10/28/the-ultimate-guide-to-wealth-protection/>

**The Rachel Cruze Show** on YouTube, '*Dave Ramsey Shares How to Rebuild an Emergency Fund,*' 1 Jul 2020, accessed 8 Aug 2023 <youtu.be/zxfiEeia5EM>

**Brian Preston, Bo Hanson,** The Money Guy Show on YouTube, '*Do You ALWAYS Need an Emergency Fund?*' 3 Jul 2023, accessed 8 Aug 2023 <youtu.be/yJCQxcECUGw>

**Marko – WhiteBoard Finance** on YouTube, '*Term Vs. Whole Life Insurance (Life Insurance Explained)* 21 Aug 2019, accessed 8 Aug 2023 <youtu.be/ZFLAsu97C9M>

## Chapter 4: Possessions and Debt

**Grandma Dina,** Living Lchaim (Kosher Money Podcast) on YouTube, '*Jewish Grandma's 19 Brilliant Pieces of Advice | KOSHER MONEY Episode 53,*' 15 June 2023, accessed 15 Aug 2023 <youtu.be/Vjmelj3GQxg>

**The Rachel Cruze Show** on YouTube, '*Things Minimalists Never Buy,*' 19 Jul 2023, accessed 10 Aug 2023 <youtu.be/CSHPX4fCDQI>

**Slave Free Alliance** on YouTube, '*Slave-Free Alliance and Hope for Justice - Our role in Operation Fort,*' 17 Dec 2020, accessed 10 Aug 2023 <youtu.be/AJe5gHlkvXE>

**TEDx Talks** on YouTube, '*The carbon footprint of consumption | Diana Ivanova | TEDxTrondheim,*' 21 Dec 2016, accessed 10 Aug 2023 <youtu.be/jXCZ9MFBBp4>

**Dave Ramsey & George Kamel,** The Ramsey Show – Highlights on YouTube, '*The 7 Baby Steps Explained – Dave Ramsey*', 20 Sept 2021, accessed 12 Aug 2023 <youtu.be/OO25TrVo_dU>

**Pete Matthew,** Meaningful Money on YouTube, '*Dave Ramsey's Baby Steps - For the UK*,' 15 Mar 2019, accessed 12 Aug 2023 <youtu.be/MBfd-NdRQVDc>

**Jennifer Thomson** on YouTube, '*Dave Ramsey Baby Steps Explained UK*,' 4 Oct 2019, accessed 12 Aug 2023 <youtu.be/77Glhx6FLpg>

**Brian Preston, Bo Hanson,** Money Guy Show on YouTube, '*Average Debt by Age! (How Do You Compare Against Other Americans?)*' 11 Aug 2023, accessed 12 Aug 2023 <youtu.be/o1j6qt_gJbM>

**Tommy Perkins,** Medics Money on YouTube, '*You will hate this book, but it will make you rich,*' 12 Aug 2023, accessed 12 Aug 2023 <youtu.be/MsN0aycSbUg>

## Student Loans in the UK and USA:

**Martin Lewis,** Money Saving Expert.com on YouTube, '*Martin Lewis, Good Debt, Bad Debt,*' 19 Nov 2007, accessed 12 Aug 2023 <youtu.be/DLkxA53qWts>

**Martin Lewis,** MoneySavingExpert.com on YouTube, '*Martin Lewis: How to teach your kids about debt (& why financial education matters),*' 28 Nov 2017, accessed 12 Aug 2023 <youtu.be/Ja5iJcE9Gz8>

**Martin Lewis,** MoneySavingExpert.com on YouTube, '*Martin Lewis: Student Loans Decoded*', 1 Oct 2019, accessed 12 Aug 2023 <youtu.be/mO_rAsMuAIM>

**Ramsey Solutions,** '*Borrowed future' podcast,* Sept-Nov 2021, accessed 12 Aug 2023
<www.ramseysolutions.com/shows/borrowed-future>

**Anthony O'Neal**, '*Debt-Free Degree : The Step-By-Step Guide to Getting Your Kid Through College without student loans,*' Ramsey Press, 2019.

## How To Pay Off Debt:

**George Kamel** on YouTube, *'Best Way to Pay Off Debt Fast (That Actually Works),'* 14 Aug 2023, accessed 15 Aug 2023 <youtu.be/w4Kbq0VJEhY>

**Brian Preston, Bo Hanson,** Money Guy Show on YouTube, *'Debt Snowball vs. Debt Avalanche: Which is the BEST Way to Pay Off Debt?,'* 11 Jun 2021, accessed 15 Aug 2023 <youtu.be/IYKAwumnVm4>

**Next Level Life** on YouTube, *'How to Pay off Debt With the Debt Snowflake Method,'* 2 Feb 2018, accessed 15 Aug 2023 <youtu.be/ecT6ULg3Yxw>

**Jennifer Thomson** on YouTube, *'How to Pay Off Debt FAST (even on a Low income),'* 5 Nov 2019, accessed 15 Aug 2023 <youtu.be/0ceAqUe_lOo>

## Debt Myths Busted:

**StepChange.org**, *'Busting common debt myths: The facts,'* accessed 12 Aug 2023 <www.stepchange.org/debt-info/debt-myths-true-or-false.aspx>

**Bill Fay**, Debt.org, *'Debt Myths,'* 29 Apr 2021, accessed 12 Aug 2023 <www.debt.org/advice/myths/>

**Rhiannon Philps**, Nerdwallet, *'Five Common Debt Myths Debunked,'* 20 July 2023, accessed 12 Aug 2023 <www.nerdwallet.com/uk/personal-finance/debt-help-myths-debunked/>

# Chapter 5: Family

## The Myth Of Work-Life Balance

**Craig Groeschel**, Life.Church on YouTube, *'Best Way to Avoid an Overwhelming Life,'* 10 Jul 2022, accessed 15 Aug 2023 <youtu.be/hWAGVKkKlmo>

## Breaking Generational Chains:

**James Allen**, *'As A Man Thinketh,'* originally published in 1903. Modern reprints available by various publishers, audio available read by Earl Nightingale.

**Earl Nightingale**, *'The Strangest Secret,'* originally published in 1956, based on a spoken word record. Modern reprints available by various publishers, audio available read by Earl Nightingale.

## Some of my favourite motivational channels on YouTube:

| | |
|---|---|
| Above Inspiration | @aboveinspiration |
| Motiversity | @motiversity |
| Mind Motivation Coaching | @mindmotivationcoaching |
| Craig Groeschel Leadership Podcast | @craiggroeschel |

## My favourite meditation channels on YouTube:

| | |
|---|---|
| Calm | @calm |
| The Mindful Movement | @TheMindfulMovement |
| Christian Thomas | @MeditationVacation |
| Abide | @AbideSleepMeditation |
| Headspace | @headspace |

## Teaching Kids About Money:

**Dave Ramsey, Rachel Cruze**, *'Smart Money Smart Kids: Raising the Next Generation to Win with Money,'* published 2014, Thomas Nelson, Nashville, USA.

**Will Rainey**, *'Grandpa's Fortune Fables: Fun stories to teach kids about money,'* Independently Published, 2021.

**Pete Matthew, Will Rainey**, Meaningful Money Podcast, *'Teaching Kids About Money,'* 18 Aug 2021, accessed 12 Aug 2023 <meaningfulmoney.tv/2021/08/18/teaching-kids-about-money/>

**Pete Matthew**, Meaningful Money Podcast, *'Tag: Children'* (various dates and podcast episodes) <meaningfulmoney.tv/tag/children/>

## *Legacy and Generational Wealth:*

**Brian Preston, Bo Hanson,** The Money Guy Show on YouTube, *'The Dark Side of Being a Millionaire! (The Truth About Being Wealthy),'* 27 May 2022, accessed 28 May 2022 <youtu.be/blLaDWYZgLo>

## *Wills and Estate Planning:*

**Dave Ramsey**, The Ramsey Show – Highlights on YouTube, *'How To Talk To My Family About My Will,'* 26 Apr 2018, accessed 24 Aug 2023 <youtu.be/fS0PAN80hzw?si=OHd6mQ1NY9lDZkDT>

**Ramsey Solutions**, *'How to talk about your legacy guide,'* accessed 24 Aug 2023 <www.ramseysolutions.com/retirement/how-to-talk-about-your-legacy-guide>

**Ramsey Solutions**, *'What Is Estate Planning? 6 Steps to Get Started,'* 3 Aug 2023, accessed 24 Aug 2023 <www.ramseysolutions.com/retirement/what-is-estate-planning>

**Pete Matthew**, Meaningful Money Podcast, *'The Ultimate Guide to ESTATE PLANNING,'* 20 Jan 2021, accessed 12 Aug 2023 <meaningfulmoney.tv/2021/01/20/the-ultimate-guide-to-estate-planning/>

**Age UK**, *'Wills and Estate Planning,'* published August 2023, accessed 12 Aug 2023 <www.ageuk.org.uk/globalassets/age-uk/documents/information-guides/ageukig31_wills_and_estate_planning_inf.pdf>

## Chapter 6: Generosity

> **Craig Groeschel**, Life.church on Youtube, 'When You Stop Holding Back,' 6 Feb 2022, accessed 25 Aug 2023 <youtu.be/Kkk21wZLWL4>
>
> **Tim Mackie, Jon Collins**, BibleProject on YouTube, 'Does A Good Christian Tithe 10%? (It's Not That Simple),' 29 Mar 2023, accessed 12 Apr 2023 <youtu.be/RN3wYVRkmno>

### *Some Of My Favourite Scam-Baiting Channels (YouTube):*

| | |
|---|---|
| **Scammer Payback** | @ScammerPayback |
| **Triology Media** | @TrilogyMedia |
| **Kitboga** | @KitbogaShow |
| **Jim Browning** | @JimBrowning |
| **Karl Rock** | @KarlRock |
| **IRL Rosie** | @irlrosie |
| **DEYOCLUB** | @DEYOCLUB |

### *Generosity and Giving:*

> **Pastor Levi Lusko**, Red Rocks Church YouTube, 'A Morning Routine That Could Change Your Life,' 17 Jul 2022, accessed 2 Aug 2022 <youtu.be/JHhXhU2b0mI>
>
> **Dave Ramsey**, 'The Legacy Journey: A Radical View of Biblical Wealth and Generosity,' 1 Oct 2014, Ramsey Press.
>
> **Bobby Gruenewald**, Life.Church on YouTube, '3 Mindset Shifts for a Heart of Generosity,' 2 Oct 2022, accessed 29 Oct 2022 <youtu.be/UXZtGsBjjD4/>
>
> **Shawn Johnson**, Life.Church on YouTube, 'A $50 Check Changed the Course of My Life,' 9 Oct 2022, accessed 29 Oct 2022 <youtu.be/5xtLa4ViWVo>

**Rick Warren**, Pastor Rick's Daily Hope, *'Financial Fitness,'* July 2022, accessed 18 July 2022 <pastorrick.com/series/financial-fitness-2022/>

**Luke Bryant**, Liverpool One Church on YouTube, *'Legacy Sunday – Liverpool One Church,'* 30 Oct 2022, accessed 31 Oct 2022 <youtu.be/wuCjo8m7Zac>

**Craig Groeschel**, Life.church Media, *'Sowing and Reaping (Multiply),'* 2013, accessed 06 Feb 2023 <www.life.church/media/multiply-2013/sowing-and-reaping/>

### *Leaving A Legacy:*

**Pete Matthew**, Meaningful Money Podcast, *'The Ultimate Guide to ESTATE PLANNING,'* 20 Jan 2021, accessed 12 Aug 2023 <meaningfulmoney.tv/2021/01/20/the-ultimate-guide-to-estate-planning/>

**Pete Matthew,** Meaningful Money Podcast, *'Strategies for Impactful Giving,'* 5 Oct 2022, accessed 18 Jan 2023 <meaningfulmoney.tv/2022/10/05/strategies-for-impactful-giving/>

## Chapter 7: Make your Garden Grow

### *Investor Gardeners:*

**Investing in Stocks for the Longterm** on YouTube, *'Why I don't Day Trade...How investing is like gardening,'* 22 Jul 2020, accessed 7 Jan 2023 <youtu.be/9ULR2Lh25tw>

**Grow Family Network** on YouTube, *'Gardening vs Investing| Week 8,'* 26 Feb 2021, accessed 7 Jan 2023 <youtu.be/JVQwyPmjPyU>

## Preparing The Ground Ready To Start Investing:

**Pete Matthew**, Meaningful Money, *'Season 14: New Accumulators,'* accessed 1 Sept 2023 <meaningfulmoney.tv/season-14-new-accumulators/>

## Where to invest (for UK audience):

**Pete Matthew**, Meaningful Money Podcast, *'The Ultimate Guide to PLATFORMS, PENSIONS & ISAs,'* 25 Nov 2020, accessed 16 Jan 2023 <meaningfulmoney.tv/2020/11/25/the-ultimate-guide-to-platforms-pensions-isas/>

**Pete Matthew**, Meaningful Money Podcast, *'Pension or ISA?'* 23 Mar 2022, accessed 16 Jan 2023 <meaningfulmoney.tv/2022/03/23/pension-or-isa/>

**Chris Bourne** on YouTube, *'ISA vs Pension - The Winner FINALLY Revealed!'* 28 Jan 2022, accessed 1 Sept 2023 <youtu.be/g6kCpoyisfY?si=8S6Ip2NfzCwwljtN>

**Ramin Nakisa,** PensionCraft on YouTube, *'UK Investment For Beginners: SIPP vs ISA Which Is Best?'* 1 Apr 2019, accessed 1 Sept 2023 <youtu.be/aYhGjewV_LA?si=9UDwifCwTtghTzwl>

**Charlotte Gifford**, Which.co.uk, *'Best investment platforms,'* updated 7 Dec 2022, accessed 14 Jan 2023 <www.which.co.uk/money/investing/investment-platforms-and-fund-supermarkets/investment-platforms-reviewed/best-and-worst-investment-platforms-a2Rra4r9bgT8>

**Gov.UK**, *'Capital Gains Tax: what you pay it on, rates and allowances,'* accessed 13 Jan 2023 <www.gov.uk/capital-gains-tax/what-you-pay-it-on>

**Gov.UK**, *'Individual Savings Accounts (ISAs),'* accessed 16 Jan 2023 <www.gov.uk/individual-savings-accounts/how-isas-work>

## The Multiplication Principle:

**Brian Preston, Bo Hanson**, The Money Guy Show, *'The Most Valuable Asset in Building Wealth!'* 10 Feb 2023, accessed 11 Feb 2023 <youtu.be/fDXIUruuVQU>

**Brian Preston, Bo Hanson**, The Money Guy Show, *"Watch This Before Rebalancing Your Investment Portfolio!'* 3 March 2023, accessed 3 March 2023 <youtu.be/2_4A-2fJ25Y>

# Chapter 8: Roadmap To Your Financial Future

## A good place to start (UK):

**Gov.uk,** *'Plan Your Retirement Income,'* accessed 20 Nov 2023 <www.gov.uk/plan-retirement-income/get-financial-advice>

**Pete Matthew,** Meaningful Money Podcast, *'Season 17: Retirement Planning,'* accessed 20 Nov 2023 <meaningfulmoney.tv/season-17-retirement-planning/>

## For Medical Health Professionals:

**Tommy Perkins, Ed Cantelo,** *Medics Money Podcast*, accessed 20 Nov 2023 <www.medicsmoney.co.uk/>

## YouTube Videos on retirement planning:

**James Shack on YouTube,** *'All good retirement plans start here - Step 1,'* 10 Oct 2021, accessed 2 Apr 2023 <youtu.be/9NGajZhp-C0>

**James Shack on YouTube**, *'How Much do You Need to Retire in 2023? (Less than you think)'* 20 Dec 2022, accessed 2 Apr 2023 <youtu.be/h7WIV4WspL0>

**James Shack on YouTube**, *'How much do I need to retire with £20k/£40k/£60k per year?'* 2 May 2022, accessed 2 Apr 2023 <youtu.be/Jm6d7UdSCsk>

**Pete Matthew,** Meaningful Money on YouTube, *'How Much Is Enough To Retire Comfortably?'* 10 June 2021, accessed 2 Apr 2023 <youtu.be/0JjBgzJd4z8>

**Brian Preston, Bo Hanson,** Money Guy Show on YouTube, *'How to Retire Early By Age! (What FIRE Gets Wrong)'* 2 July 2021, accessed 2 Apr 2023 <youtu.be/zy-WToA1v_4>

**Chris Bourne** on YouTube, *'How Much Will My Pension Pay Me? (Different Fund Sizes),'* 16 Sept 2022, accessed 2 Apr 2023 <youtu.be/sJbur8zJi_8>

## *Book on Longevity:*

**Lynda Gratton & Andrew Scott,** 'The 100-Year Life: Living and Working in an Age of Longevity,' 2017, Bloomsbury, UK.

## *My Favourite Motivational Speakers:*

Jim Rohn, Brian Tracy, Earl Nightingale, Nick Vujicic, Zig Ziglar, Dave Ramsey, Les Brown, Steve Harvey, Tony Robbins, Terri Savelle Foy and others.

## How to set SMART Goals:

**Brian Preston, Bo Hanson,** The Money Guy Show on YouTube, *'How to Win With Money in 2023!'* 27 Jan 2023, accessed 30 Jan 2023 <youtu.be/XwMNYBDqvUQ>

**Terri Savelle Foy** on YouTube, *'My 7 Step Goal Setting Process That Works! | how to set goals!'* 24 Jan 2022, accessed 20 Apr 2023 <youtu.be/ku4rO9ANvbg>

## Vision Boards and Planting Seeds:

**Terri Savelle Foy,** '*Imagine Big: Unlock the Secret to Living Out Your Dreams*,' 15 March 2013, Regal Books.

**Terri Savelle Foy** on YouTube, *'Making your 2023 Vision Board,'* 9 Jan 2023, accessed 20 Apr 2023 <youtu.be/7ytYDonanDU>

## How To Build Healthy Habits and Routines:

**Craig Groeschel**, *'Power to Change: Mastering the Habits That Matter Most,'* Zondervan Books, 16 Feb 2023.

**James Clear,** *'Atomic habits: tiny changes, remarkable results: an easy & proven way to build good habits & break bad ones,'* New York, Avery, an imprint of Penguin Random House, 2018.

Penguin Random House, *'Books to Read After "Atomic Habits,"* accessed 6 Sept 2023. <www.penguinrandomhouse.com/the-read-down/books-to-read-after-atomic-habits/>

**Life.Church on YouTube**, *'Making Change: Part 1 - "Less is More" with Craig Groeschel,'* 11 Sept 2016, accessed 18 Apr 2023 <youtu.be/SPD7aVR_1hw>

**Life.Church on YouTube**, *'Making Change: Part 2 - "Stress Is Bad" with Craig Groeschel,'* 18 Sept 2016, accessed 18 Apr 2023 <youtu.be/Wm5PI77HJ_Y>

Life.Church on YouTube, 'Making Change: Part 3 - "Giving is Good" with Craig Groeschel,' 25 Sept 2016, accessed 18 Apr 2023 <youtu.be/jc1nAE2SEJ0>

Life.Church on YouTube, 'Making Change: Part 4 - "Tomorrow Matters" with Craig Groeschel,' 2 Oct 2016, accessed 18 Apr 2023 <youtu.be/fhIP4H3iYGQ>

Principles by Ray Dalio on YouTube, 'Principles For Success by Ray Dalio (In 30 Minutes),' 21 May 2018, accessed 11 May 2023 <youtu.be/B9XGUpQZY38>

## Chapter 9: A Brief History of Money

Heresy Financial on YouTube, 'How Currencies Start - and Why they Always Fail,' 23 Apr 2023, accessed 11 May 2023 <youtu.be/BRbIW-dx7jw>

Wealthion on YouTube, '**Jeff Snider:** Recession Will Worsen The Bear Market & The Fed Is Powerless To Stop It,' 14 Jul 2022, accessed 23 May 2023 <youtu.be/g1ll7kxkun0>

The Royal Mint, 'Investment Guide', accessed 7 Jan 2023 <www.royalmint.com/invest/investing-in-precious-metals/investment-guide/>

2 is 1 on YouTube, '14 Years of Buying Gold and Silver - Here's What I've Learned,' 24 Mar 2022, accessed 11 May 2023 <youtu.be/Zf2OWk1ielo>

Wealthion on YouTube, 'How To Buy Gold and Silver: Everything You Need To Know with Adam Taggart,' 9 Jun 2021, accessed 23 May 2023 <youtu.be/RdeZUIMVfeE>

Principles by Ray Dalio on YouTube, 'How The Economic Machine Works by Ray Dalio,' 22 Sept 2013, accessed 11 May 2023 <youtu.be/PHe0bX-Aluk0>

Principles by Ray Dalio on YouTube, 'Principles for Dealing with the Changing World Order by Ray Dalio,' 2 Mar 2022, accessed 11 May 2023 <youtu.be/xguam0TKMw8>

Principles by Ray Dalio on YouTube, 'Principles for Dealing with the Changing World Order (5-minute Version) by Ray Dalio,' 23 May 2023, accessed 25 May 2023 <youtu.be/BB2r_eOjsPw>

# Chapter 10: Ways To Invest

## *Market Sentiment:*

**James Shack on YouTube,** 'Why a Stock Market Crash Always Seems Imminent,' 12 Sept 2021, accessed 11 May 2023 <youtu.be/pEFd1C2sw6M>

**One Minute Economics on YouTube,** 'Fear and Greed... in One Minute: Emotional vs. Rational Economic Thinking and Investment Decisions,' 5 Dec 2019, accessed 11 May 2023 <youtu.be/741WQ8y9sB0>

**Pete Matthew,** Meaningful Money on YouTube, 'Behavioural Finance for New Accumulators - Part 1,' 5 Jun 2019, accessed 30 May 2023 <youtu.be/SCQeBaRTu-M>

## *1. Trading: (YouTube Videos)*

| | |
|---|---|
| **FX Empire** | @Fxempirenetwork |
| **FX Evolution** | @fxevolutionvideo/ |
| **My Strategic Forecast** | @msforecasting |
| **Game of Trades** | @GameofTrades |
| **The Kendall Report** | @TheKendallReport |

**Explore The Shore**     @ExploreTheShore

Want to know more about rock pools? Whilst researching this value investing section, I found a wonderful YouTube channel about marine biology in South Africa – here you go!

## *2. Value Investing: (YouTube Videos)*

| | |
|---|---|
| **Rule #1 Investing** | @PhilTownRule1Investing |
| **Sven Carlin, Ph.D** | @Value-Investing |
| **Learn to Invest** | @LearntoInvest |

**Phil Town,** Rule #1 Investing on YouTube, *'How Fear Impacts the Stock Market | Phil Town,'* 2 May 2019, accessed 11 May 2023 <youtu.be/WvFlJkH_Lmw>

**Sven Carlin,** Value Investing with Sven Carlin, Ph.D on YouTube, *'Value Investing Proper Definition - Is Value Investing For You?'* 14 Nov 2020, accessed 2 June 2023 <youtu.be/2GFwfNOKWJM>

**Jimmy Copell,** Learn to Invest – Investors Grow on YouTube, *'8 Steps to Research a Company to Invest in - Best Investment Series,'* 14 Nov 2018, accessed 7 June 2023 <youtu.be/fGVtypWv04Y>

## 3. Global Macro Investing: (YouTube Videos)

| | |
|---|---|
| **Wealthion** | @Wealthion |
| **Adam Taggart** | @adam.taggart (Thoughtful Money) |
| **Eurodollar University** | @eurodollaruniversity |
| **Steven Van Metre** | @stevenvanmetre5087 |
| **Blockworks Macro** | @BlockworksHQ |
| **The Macro Trading Floor** | @TheMacroTradingFloor |
| **The David Lin Report** | @TheDavidLinReport |
| **Kitco News** | @kitco |
| **Danielle DiMartino Booth** | @DanielleDiMartinoBoothQI |
| **Economics Explained** | @EconomicsExplained |

## 4. Passive (Index Fund) Investing: (YouTube Videos)

| | |
|---|---|
| **Graham Stephan** (USA) | @GrahamStephan |
| **Andrei Jikh** (USA) | @AndreiJikh |
| **Meaningful Money** (UK) | @MeaningfulMoney |
| **The Money Guy Show** (USA) | @MoneyGuyShow |
| **PensionCraft** (UK) | @Pensioncraft |
| **Ben Felix** (Canada) | @BenFelixCSI |
| **James Shack** (UK) | @jamesshack |

## *How to invest (passive / index fund investing):*

**The Motley Fool** on YouTube, *'Jack Bogle on Index Funds, Vanguard, and Investing Advice,'* 17 Jan 2019, accessed 7 June 2023 <youtu.be/MLgn_kVKjCE>

**Pete Matthew,** Meaningful Money on YouTube, *'The Ultimate Guide To INVESTING - Part One,'* 11 Nov 2020, accessed 11 May 2023 <youtu.be/SStg4QsivZw>

**Pete Matthew,** Meaningful Money on YouTube, *'How I Invest (I'm a financial adviser),'* 26 Aug 2021, accessed 7 June 2023 <youtu.be/bp5R3dIQzhU>

**Graham Stephan** on YouTube, *'How To Become A Millionaire: Index Fund Investing For Beginners,'* 8 Mar 2019, accessed 7 June 2023 <youtu.be/fwe-PjrX23o>

**James Shack** on YouTube, *'Vanguard Lifestrategy Funds Explained | The only fund you will ever need (Investing for beginners),'* 22 Jan 2021, accessed 7 June 2023 <youtu.be/lGQ9KyQq8Jw>

**Talks at Google** on YouTube, *'The Simple Path to Wealth | JL Collins | Talks at Google,'* 20 Feb 2018, accessed 7 June 2023 <youtu.be/T71ibcZAX3I>

**Lars Kroijer** on YouTube, *'Investing Demystified - (How to Invest if you can't beat the markets - Part 1 of 5),'* 15 July 2016, accessed 7 June 2023 <youtu.be/_chiIlxMGI0>

## *Active v. Passive Investing: Pros and Cons*

**Brian Preston, Bo Hanson,** The Money Guy Show on YouTube, *'Popular Investing Strategies That Are Actually LOSING You Money!'* 31 Mar 2023, accessed 6 June 2023 <youtu.be/khIAZ7afMe8>

**Ramin Nakisa,** PensionCraft on YouTube, *'Active vs Passive Performance: S&P's Andrew Innes On His Index vs Active Report,'* 19 Oct 2018, accessed 6 June 2023 <youtu.be/HbqnnKpRO7c>

**Morningstar Europe** on YouTube, *'Active and Passive Strategies Within a Retirement Portfolio,'* 19 Jun 2015, accessed 6 June 2023 <youtu.be/o0BAVybNREE>

**Ben Felix** on YouTube, *'Who Should NOT Invest in Total Market Index Funds?,'* 11 May 2023, accessed 7 June 2023 <youtu.be/4hSFzVoZkiA>

**Sven Carlin,** Value Investing with Sven Carlin, Ph.D on YouTube, 'THE INDEX FUNDS BUBBLE NOBODY TALKS ABOUT,' 25 Jul 2022, accessed 7 June 2023 <youtu.be/0bRXTCJ1-lc>

## Other useful resources to learn about investing

| | |
|---|---|
| **Killik Explains** with Tim Bennett | @KillikFinanceVideos> |
| **Killik & Co** knowledge hub | <www.killik.com/learn/> |
| **Hargreaves Lansdown** | <www.hl.co.uk/learn> |

**Gavin Shepherd and Sam Dunn,** MoneySavingExpert.com, *'Investing for beginners: 10 key need to knows to get you started,'* updated 3 May 2023, accessed 21 July 2023 <www.moneysavingexpert.com/savings/investment-beginners/>

**Matthew Frankel, CFP,** The Motley Fool, 'How to Invest in Stocks: A Beginner's Guide for Getting Started,' updated 26 June 2023, accessed 21 July 2023 <www.fool.com/investing/how-to-invest/stocks/>

# REFERENCES

# References

1. The World Bank, *'Nearly Half the World Lives on Less than $5.50 a Day,'* 17 Oct 2018, accessed 25 Sept 2023 <www.worldbank.org/en/news/press-release/2018/10/17/nearly-half-the-world-lives-on-less-than-550-a-day>
2. Bankrate.com, *'Living paycheck to paycheck statistics,'* 18 Sept 2023, accessed 25 Sept 2023 <www.bankrate.com/finance/credit-cards/living-paycheck-to-paycheck-statistics/>
3. British Society of Lifestyle Medicine, *'What Is Lifestyle Medicine?'* accessed 22 Sept 2023 <bslm.org.uk/lifestyle-medicine/what-is-lifestyle-medicine/>
4. NHS, *'5 steps to mental wellbeing,'* accessed 22 Sept 2023 <www.nhs.uk/mental-health/self-help/guides-tools-and-activities/five-steps-to-mental-wellbeing/>
5. Social Prescribing Academy, *'Finding Practical Support,'* accessed 23 Sept 2023 <socialprescribingacademy.org.uk/socialprescribingandme/finding-practical-support/>
6. Burton WN, Schultz A, Edington DW, *'Health and Wealth: The Importance for Lifestyle Medicine,'* Am J Lifestyle Med. 2021 Apr 3;15(4):407-412.
7. British Society of Lifestyle Medicine, *'Socioeconomic Determinants of Health,'* accessed 22 Sept 2023 <bslm.org.uk/socioeconomic-determinants-of-health/>
8. Clare Casalis, MoneySavingExpert.com, *'Debt problems & help available: what to do & where to get support,'* 30 May 2023, accessed 13 June 2023 <www.moneysavingexpert.com/loans/debt-help-plan/>
9. John C. Maxwell, *'Today Matters: 12 Daily Practices to Guarantee Tomorrow's Success,'* published 2004, Warner Faith, New York: USA
10. Dave Ramsey, Rachel Cruze, *'Smart Money Smart Kids: Raising the Next Generation to Win with Money,'* published 2014, Thomas Nelson, Nashville, USA.
11. Will Buckingham, LookingForWisdom.com, *'Aristotle on Flourishing,'* 19 Aug 2021, accessed 18 July 2023 <www.lookingforwisdom.com/aristotle-on-flourishing/>

12. John Mark Comer, *'The Ruthless Elimination of Hurry: How to stay emotionally healthy and spiritually alive in the chaos of the modern world,'* Oct 2019, John Murray Press, London, UK.
13. Ramsey Solutions, *'The 7 Baby Steps,'* 2022, accessed 29 Jan 2022 <www.ramseysolutions.com/dave-ramsey-7-baby-steps>
14. The Money Guy Show, *'Resources,'* 2022, accessed 29 Jan 2022 <www.moneyguy.com/resources/>
15. Jessica Dickler, CNBC.com, *'With inflation stubbornly high, 58% of Americans are living paycheck to paycheck: CNBC survey,'* Apr 11 2023, accessed 23 June 2023 <www.cnbc.com/2023/04/11/58percent-of-americans-are-living-paycheck-to-paycheck-cnbc-survey-reveals.html>
16. Craig Groeschel, Life Church Resources, *'Margin,'* 26 Jan 2016, accessed 24 Feb 2022 <open.life.church/resources/1447-margin>
17. David Swenson, *'Margin: Restoring Emotional, Physical, Financial, and Time Reserves to Overloaded Lives,'* NavPress, Colorado Springs, 25 Oct 2004.
18. Craig Groeschel, Life.Church Open Network, *'Margin 3 Message,'* YouTube, 26 Jan 2016, accessed 25 Feb 2022 <youtu.be/a_DbdfTof6E>
19. MoneyHelper.org, *'Understanding Your Payslip,'* accessed 29 Jan 2022 <www.moneyhelper.org.uk/en/work/employment/understanding-your-payslip>
20. GOV.UK, *'Check your Income Tax for the current year,'* accessed 29 Jan 2023 <www.gov.uk/check-income-tax-current-year>
21. GOV.UK, *'Income Tax Rates and Personal Allowances,'* accessed 1 Mar 2022 <www.gov.uk/income-tax-rates>
22. Indeed Editorial Team, Indeed.com, *'What salary increase should I expect when changing jobs in the UK?'* 14 June 2023, accessed 24 June 2023 <uk.indeed.com/career-advice/pay-salary/salary-increase-changing-jobs-uk>
23. Ken Coleman, Fremont News Messenger, *'Ask for a raise with humility and grace,'* 06 Aug 2018, accessed 12 Feb 2022 <eu.thenews-messenger.com/story/news/2018/08/06/ken-coleman-start-humility-and-gratitude-when-asking-raise/887819002/>
24. Zoe Wickens, EmployeeBenefits.co.uk, *'65% of remote working UK staff are less likely to take sick leave,'* 16 June 2022, accessed 24 June 2023 <employeebenefits.co.uk/65-of-remote-working-uk-staff-are-less-likely-to-take-sick-leave/>
25. Indeed Editorial Team, Indeed.com, *'Side hustle ideas: 15 clever ways to earn money on the side,'* 11 May 2023, accessed 24 June 2023 <uk.indeed.com/career-advice/finding-a-job/side-hustle-ideas>
26. MyFitnessPal.com, accessed 24 June 2023 <www.myfitnesspal.com/>

27. Ramsey Solutions, Ramseysolutions.net, *'Dave Ramsey's Nerd or Free Spirit Quiz,'* 1 Dec 2016, viewed 9 Feb 2022 <cdn.ramseysolutions.net/media/pdf/NerdFreeSpiritQuiz.pdf>
28. Cyril Northcote Parkinson, The Economist, *'Parkinson's Law,'* 19 November 1955, accessed 20 July 2023 (made available by Berglas.org) <www.berglas.org/Articles/parkinsons_law.pdf>
29. Wikipedia contributors, Wikipedia, The Free Encyclopedia, *'Parkinson's Law,'* 28 June 2023, accessed 20 July 2023 <en.wikipedia.org/w/index.php?title=Parkinson%27s_law&oldid=1162268038>
30. This is a joke. I have not published my theory that *'no matter how big your freezer is, you will always fill it,'* though I have observed that this is often the case. We're going to talk about the importance of knowing what food you already have in your cupboards and freezer in the next chapter. I call it *'mindful storage.'*
31. George S. Clason, *'The Richest Man in Babylon,'* 1926, accessed 12 Feb 2022 (full text available at the Internet Archive) <archive.org/details/RichestManInBabylon_650/page/n3/mode/2up>
32. Malachi 3:10, The Bible: New International Version (NIV), *'Bring the whole tithe into the storehouse, that there may be food in my house. Test me in this," says the Lord Almighty, "and see if I will not throw open the floodgates of heaven and pour out so much blessing that there will not be room enough to store it.'*
33. Ramsey Solutions, Ramsey Solutions.com, *'Tithes and Offerings: Your Questions Answered,'* 31 May 2023, accessed 20 July 2023 <www.ramseysolutions.com/budgeting/daves-advice-on-tithing-and-giving>
34. Robert T. Kiyosaki, *'Rich Dad Poor Dad: What the Rich Teach their Kids About Money That the Poor and Middle Class Do Not!* Plata Publishing, 2007.
35. Jim Rohn, Success.com, *'Jim Rohn Says These Are the 3 Money Habits of a Rich Mindset,'* updated 26 March 2022, accessed 20 July 2023 <www.success.com/jim-rohn-says-these-are-the-3-money-habits-of-a-rich-mindset/>
36. Ramsey Solutions, RamseySolutions.com, *'The 7 Baby Steps,'* accessed 29 Jan 2022 <www.ramseysolutions.com/dave-ramsey-7-baby-steps>
37. The Money Guy Show, moneyguy.com, *'Resources,'* accessed 29 Jan 2022 <www.moneyguy.com/resources/>
38. Daniel May (CFP), moneyguy.com, *'FYI by FTE: How Much Should I Be Saving For Retirement,'* 8 Jul 2021, accessed 10 Mar 2022 <fyi.moneyguy.com/p/how-much-should-i-be-saving-for-retirement>
39. Luke Bryant, Liverpool One Church YouTube, *'How to Sabotage Your Family's Finances,'* 25 June 2023, accessed 20 July 2023 <www.youtube.com/live/vVU9Z0jlu00?feature=share>

40. Christians Against Poverty, capuk.org, 'How to start saving money,' 2 Nov 2022, accessed 20 July 2023 <capuk.org/news-and-blog/how-to-start-saving-money>
41. David Bach, 'The Automatic Millionaire: a powerful one-step plan to live and finish rich,' New York, Broadway Books, 2004.
42. Kristin Stoller, Forbes.com, 'The 5 Best Round-Up Apps For Saving Money,' 13 May 2020, accessed 12 Feb 2022 <www.forbes.com/advisor/personal-finance/the-5-best-round-up-apps-for-saving-money/>
43. Chris Owen, Money Saving Expert, 'Automatic Savings Apps: What they are, how they work & our top picks,' 20 January 2022, accessed 12 Feb 2022 <www.moneysavingexpert.com/savings/auto-saving-apps/>
44. Martin Lewis, MoneySavingExpert.com, 'Home Page,' March 2022, accessed 12 Mar 2022 <www.moneysavingexpert.com/>
45. Esther Cole, Western_Spiral_Art on Instagram, March 7 2020, accessed 12 Feb 2022 <www.instagram.com/p/B9css66lNCH/>
46. Dr Saul McLeod, SimplePsychology.org, 'Maslow's Hierarchy of Needs,' first published 2007, updated 29 Dec 2020, accessed 15 Mar 2022 <www.simplypsychology.org/maslow.html>
47. Poverty and Social Exclusion (PSE), 'What do we think we need?,' 28 Mar 2013, accessed 31 July 2023 <www.poverty.ac.uk/pse-research/what-do-we-think-we-need>
48. CitizensAdvice.org, 'Work out which debts to deal with first,' 22 Feb 2019, accessed 15 Mar 2022 <www.citizensadvice.org.uk/debt-and-money/help-with-debt/dealing-with-your-debts/work-out-which-debts-to-deal-with-first/>
49. MoneyGuy.com, 'Wealth Multiplier: How Much Do You Need to Save Each Month to Reach $1 Million?' 2022, accessed 20 July 2023 <moneyguy.com/resources/how-powerful-are-your-dollars/>
50. Katie Brockman, The Motley Fool, 'How $200 per Month Could Make You A Stock Market Millionaire,' 16 Feb 2022, accessed 21 Mar 2022 <www.fool.com/investing/2022/02/16/how-200-month-make-you-stock-market-millionaire/>
51. BarefootMinimalists.com, 'How Minimalism Can Improve Your Finances,' 2023, accessed 27 July 2023 <barefootminimalists.com/how-minimalism-can-improve-your-finances/>
52. Alexandra Kerr, Investopedia.com, 'Financial Independence, Retire Early (FIRE) Explained: How It Works,' 27 March 2023, accessed 27 July 2023 <www.investopedia.com/terms/f/financial-independence-retire-early-fire.asp>
53. Elliot Smith, CNBC.com, 'UK inflation exceeds expectations in May, piling pressure on the government and Bank of England,' 21 June 2023, accessed 27 July 2023 <www.cnbc.com/2023/06/21/uk-inflation-exceeds-expectations-in-may-piling-pressure-on-the-government-and-bank-of-england.html>

54. Nadia Rocha & Alvaro Espitia, The Trade Post, *'One year after Ukraine invasion, food export curbs have subsided, but concerns remain,'* 22 Feb 2023, accessed 27 July 2023 <blogs.worldbank.org/trade/one-year-after-ukraine-invasion-food-export-curbs-have-subsided-concerns-remain>
55. James Walton, BackDoorSurvival.com, *'Preparedness: Tasty Survival Recipes with rice and beans,'* 25 Apr 2020, accessed 27 July 2023 <www.backdoorsurvival.com/tasty-survival-recipes-with-rice-and-beans/>
56. Jo Bruni, ConsumerReports.org, *'Is Rice & Beans Good For You?,'* 22 Aug 2019, accessed 17 Mar 2022 <www.consumerreports.org/healthy-eating/is-rice-and-beans-good-for-you-a1152368032/>
57. GHI team, GoodHouseKeeping.com, *'Why you can ignore 'best before' labels,'* 27 Mar 2023, accessed 27 July 2023 <www.goodhousekeeping.com/uk/house-and-home/household-advice/a665683/confused-by-food-labelling-the-ghi-is-here-to-help/>
58. Jen Schmidt, Balancing Beauty & Bedlam, *'My No Spend Pantry Challenge & Meal Ideas,'* 18 Sept 2013, accessed 19 Mar 2022 <beautyandbedlam.com/saving-on-the-food-budget/>
59. MyFitnessPal.com, accessed 27 July 2023 <www.myfitnesspal.com/>
60. Graeme Tomlinson (Thefitnesschef_) on Instagram, accessed 27 July 2023 <www.instagram.com/thefitnesschef_/>
61. Rebecca Smithers, GoodHouseKeeping.com, *'The 5 best apps for food waste,'* 1 Feb 2023, accessed 27 July 2023 <www.goodhousekeeping.com/uk/consumer-advice/consumer-rights/a37768393/food-waste-apps/>
62. Cynthia Ajayi, *Cynthersizer* on Instagram, accessed 21 Mar 2022 <www.instagram.com/cynthersizer/>
63. Cynthia Ajayi on YouTube, accessed 21 Mar 2022 <www.youtube.com/c/CynthiaAjayi>
64. Imperial War Museums, IWM.org, *'10 Top Tips for Winning at 'Make Do and Mend,'* accessed 23 Mar 2022 <www.iwm.org.uk/history/10-top-tips-for-winning-at-make-do-and-mend>
65. Andrew Fennell, Job Description Library, *'Average Cost of Living in the UK,'* Jan 2022, accessed 23 Mar 2022 <jobdescription-library.com/cost-of-living-uk>
66. Rachel Cruze, RamseySolutions.com, *'How Much House Can I Afford?,'* 14 Jan 2022, accessed 23 Mar 2022 <www.ramseysolutions.com/real-estate/how-much-house-can-i-afford/>
67. Joe Wright, Which?, *'How much can you borrow for a mortgage?'* 21 June 2023, accessed 28 July 2023 < <www.which.co.uk/money/mortgages-and-property/mortgages/getting-a-mortgage/how-much-can-you-borrow-aUysL0V7VCXK>

68. BankofEngland.co.uk 'Why have interest rates in the UK gone up?' 22 June 2023, accessed 28 July 2023 <www.bankofengland.co.uk/explainers/why-are-interest-rates-in-the-uk-going-up>
69. MoneyHelper.org, 'How to check your credit report,' accessed 28 July 2023 <www.moneyhelper.org.uk/en/everyday-money/credit-and-purchases/how-to-check-your-credit-report>
70. Elizabeth Scott, PhD, VeryWellMind.com, 'Hedonic Adaptation: Why You Are Not Happier,' 16 Jul 2020, accessed 23 Mar 2022 <www.verywellmind.com/hedonic-adaptation-4156926>
71. Dan Base, Money.co.uk, 'Should you rent or buy a home?' 15 Mar 2022, accessed 28 July 2023 <www.money.co.uk/mortgages/should-you-rent-or-buy-a-home>
72. Meaghan Hunt, Bankrate.com, 'How long should you live in a house before selling?' 21 Oct 2022, accessed 28 July 2023 <www.bankrate.com/real-estate/how-long-should-you-live-in-your-home-before-selling/>
73. Sajni Shah, Comparethemarket.com, 'What to do if you can't afford your energy bills,' 25 May 2023, accessed 28 July 2023 <www.comparethemarket.com/energy/content/cant-pay-energy-bills/>
74. Martin Lewis, MoneySavingExpert.com, *Energy Articles* (various), accessed 28 July 2023 <www.moneysavingexpert.com/energy/>
75. Andrew Capstick, MoneySavingExpert.com, 'What to do if you're struggling to pay your energy bills,' 11 July 2023, accessed 28 July 2023 <www.moneysavingexpert.com/utilities/how-to-get-help-if-you-re-struggling-with-your-energy-bills-/>
76. Citizens Advice, 'How to read your energy meter,' accessed 25 Mar 2022 <www.citizensadvice.org.uk/consumer/energy/energy-supply/your-energy-meter/how-to-read-your-energy-meter/>
77. EcoMasteryProject.com, 'Top 8 eco-friendly ways of alternative transport,' 5 Mar 2020, accessed 31 Mar 2022 <www.ecomasteryproject.com/alternative-transportation/>
78. John Ellmore, Nerdwallet.com, 'What is the cost of owning a car in the UK?,' 19 July 2021, accessed 31 July 2023 <www.nerdwallet.com/uk/personal-finance/cost-of-car-ownership/>
79. Moneyhelper.org.uk, 'Car tax bands explained,' accessed 2 Apr 2022 <www.moneyhelper.org.uk/en/everyday-money/buying-and-running-a-car/car-tax-bands-explained>
80. Tom Sasse, instituteforgovernment.org.uk, 'Electric vehicle switch is a test of the government's net zero approach,' 8 June 2022, accessed 31 July 2023 <www.instituteforgovernment.org.uk/comment/electric-vehicle-switch-government-net-zero>

81. Direct Line, 'Cheapest cars to repair,' 6 Mar 2020, accessed 2 Apr 2022 <www.directline.com/car-cover/magazine/cheapest-cars-to-repair>
82. Moneyhelper.org.uk, 'Best way to finance buying a car,' accessed 1 Apr 2022 <www.moneyhelper.org.uk/en/everyday-money/buying-and-running-a-car/whats-the-best-way-to-finance-buying-a-car>
83. Motorway.co.uk, 'Car Depreciation – The Ultimate Guide,' accessed 1 Apr 2022 <motorway.co.uk/sell-my-car/guides/car-depreciation-guide>
84. Citizens Advice, 'Buying a used car,' accessed 1 Apr 2022 <www.citizensadvice.org.uk/consumer/buying-or-repairing-a-car/buying-a-used-car/>
85. Harriet Meyer, MoneySavingExpert.com, '20+ tips on buying a new car,' updated 16 Sept 2021, accessed 1 Apr 2022 <www.moneysavingexpert.com/loans/buying-new-car/>
86. Harriet Meyer, MoneySavingExpert.com, '19 tips for buying a used car,' updated 1 Mar 2018, accessed 1 Apr 2022 <www.moneysavingexpert.com/loans/buying-used-car/>
87. Ramsey Solutions, 'How to get out of a car loan,' 30 May 2023, accessed 31 July 2023 <www.ramseysolutions.com/debt/dont-let-your-car-loan-own-you>
88. RamseySolutions, 'Should I buy a new or used car?,' 20 July 2023, accessed 31 July 2023 <www.ramseysolutions.com/insurance/new-car-vs-used-car>
89. Brian Preston, Moneyguy.com, 'How to buy a new (or used) car,' 6 Nov 2020, accessed 2 Apr 2022, <moneyguy.com/2020/11/how-to-buy-a-new-or-used-car/>
90. Ramsey Solutions, 'What if Your Emergency Fund Can't Cover Your Emergency?' 12 Apr 2023, accessed 8 Aug 2023 <www.ramseysolutions.com/saving/what-to-do-if-emergency-is-more-than-emergency-fund>
91. Matthew Goldberg, Bankrate.com, 'How to start (and build) an emergency fund,' 24 March 2022, accessed 2 Apr 2022 <www.bankrate.com/banking/savings/starting-an-emergency-fund/>
92. Pete Matthew, MeaningfulMoney.tv, *The Ultimate Guide to Wealth Protection*, 28 Oct 2020, accessed 4 Apr 2022 <meaningfulmoney.tv/2020/10/28/the-ultimate-guide-to-wealth-protection/>
93. Citizens Advice, 'Check if you can get sick pay,' accessed 8 Aug 2023 <www.citizensadvice.org.uk/work/sick-leave-and-sick-pay/check-if-you-can-get-sick-pay/>
94. Money Helper, 'What disability and sickness benefits can I claim?' accessed 8 Aug 2023 <www.moneyhelper.org.uk/en/benefits/benefits-if-youre-sick-disabled-or-a-carer/what-disability-and-sickness-benefits-can-i-claim>
95. Citizens Advice, 'Income Protection Insurance,' accessed 4 Apr 2022 <www.citizensadvice.org.uk/consumer/insurance/isnsurance/income-protection-insurance/>

96. Citizens Advice, 'Critical Illness Insurance,' accessed 4 Apr 2022 <www.citizensadvice.org.uk/consumer/insurance/insurance/what-critical-illness-insurance-is/>
97. Which? Money Team, 'What is term life insurance?' 8 June 2023, accessed 9 Aug 2023 <www.which.co.uk/money/insurance/life-insurance-and-protection/term-life-insurance-explained-aphsw2r4aAtd>
98. Andrew Beattie, Investopedia.com, 'How much life insurance should you carry?' Jan 26 2022, accessed 4 Apr 2022 <www.investopedia.com/articles/pf/06/insureneeds.asp>
99. Julia Kagan, Investopedia.com, 'Cash Value Life Insurance,' 11 Oct 2021, accessed 4 Apr 2022 <www.investopedia.com/terms/c/cash-value-life-insurance.asp>
100. Daniel Goldstein, Marketwatch.com, '10 things life insurance agents won't say,' 4 May 2015, accessed 4 Apr 2022 <www.marketwatch.com/story/10-things-your-life-insurance-agent-wont-say-2014-07-11>
101. Thom Tracy, Investopedia.com, 'When Should You Get Life Insurance? When it comes to buying life insurance, younger is usually better,' 6 Aug 2023, accessed 9 Aug 2023 <www.investopedia.com/articles/investing/072816/what-best-age-get-life-insurance.asp>
102. Amy Roberts, MoneySavingExpert.com, 'Debt problems: What to do & where to get help', 5 Apr 2022, accessed 18 Apr 2022 <www.moneysavingexpert.com/loans/debt-help-plan/>
103. Alcoholics Anonymous, 'The Twelve Steps,' accessed 10 Aug 2023 <www.aa.org/the-twelve-steps>
104. Celebrate Recovery UK, 'Twelve Steps,' accessed 10 Aug 2023 <www.celebraterecovery.co.uk/the-12-steps/>
105. Dave Ramsey, 'The Legacy Journey: A Radical View of Biblical Wealth and Generosity,' published 1 Oct 2014, Thomas Nelson, Nashville, Tennessee, USA.
106. Lost in the Pond on YouTube, Laurence M. Brown, 'Why Do Americans Have So Much Stuff?' 12 Apr 2023, accessed 10 Aug 2023 <youtu.be/OGElT2bYMLY>
107. Gov.UK, 'Capital Gains Tax on personal possessions,' accessed 10 Aug 2023 <www.gov.uk/capital-gains-tax-personal-possessions>
108. 1 Timothy 6: 10, New International Version (NIV)
109. James Chen, Investopedia.com, 'What is Debt?' 13 Jan 2022, accessed 13 Apr 2022 <www.investopedia.com/terms/d/debt.asp>
110. The Investopedia Team, Investopedia.com, 'What are the main categories of debt?,' 17 Feb 2023, accessed 12 Aug 2023 <www.investopedia.com/ask/answers/110614/what-are-main-categories-debt.asp>

111. Citizens Advice, *'Hire purchase and conditional sale,'* accessed 13 Apr 2022 <www.citizensadvice.org.uk/debt-and-money/borrowing-money/types-of-borrowing/hire-purchase-and-conditional-sale/>
112. Money Helper, *'Payday loans – what you need to know,'* accessed 13 Apr 2022 <www.moneyhelper.org.uk/en/everyday-money/types-of-credit/payday-loans-what-you-need-to-know>
113. Citizens Advice, *'Payday loans,'* accessed 13 Apr 2022 <www.citizensadvice.org.uk/debt-and-money/borrowing-money/types-of-borrowing/loans/payday-loans/taking-out-a-payday-loan/>
114. Holly Bennett, nerdwallet, *'What are mortgage terms and how do they work?'* 4 Apr 2022, accessed 13 Apr 2022 <www.nerdwallet.com/uk/mortgages/what-is-a-mortgage-term/>
115. Stephen Maunder, Which?, *'Mortgage types explained,'* 3 Aug 2023, accessed 12 Aug 2023 <www.which.co.uk/money/mortgages-and-property/mortgages/types-of-mortgage/mortgage-types-explained-af1319h2cmck>
116. Amy Roberts, MoneySavingExpert.com, *'Debt problems: What to do & where to get help',* updated 5 Apr 2022, accessed 18 Apr 2022 <www.moneysavingexpert.com/loans/debt-help-plan/>
117. Chris Dorrell, City A.M., *'Banks to avoid surge in delinquency even as average interest rate on credit card hits highest level this millennium,'* 19 July 2023, accessed 12 Aug 2023 <www.cityam.com/banks-to-avoid-surge-in-delinquency-even-as-average-interest-rate-on-credit-card-hits-highest-level-this-millennium/>
118. Proverbs 6:1-5, New International Version (NIV) also warns against co-signing on loans and describes how to get away from entrapment and the slavery of debt. *'My son, if you have put up security for your neighbor, if you have shaken hands in pledge for a stranger, you have been trapped by what you said, ensnared by the words of your mouth. So do this, my son, to free yourself, since you have fallen into your neighbor's hands: Go—to the point of exhaustion— and give your neighbor no rest! Allow no sleep to your eyes, no slumber to your eyelids. Free yourself, like a gazelle from the hand of the hunter, like a bird from the snare of the fowler.'*
119. MoneyGuy.com, *'Resources: Learn How to Manage Your Money Better,'* accessed 12 Aug 2023 <moneyguy.com/resources/>
120. Robert Kiyosaki, Richdad.com, *'What is bad debt?'* 1 Oct 2019, accessed 23 Apr 2022, <www.richdad.com/what-is-bad-debt>
121. Paul Kosakowski, Investopedia.com, *'The fall of the market in the Fall of 2008,'* updated 30 June 2023, accessed 12 Aug 2023 <www.investopedia.com/articles/economics/09/subprime-market-2008.asp>

122. Martin Lewis and Clare Casalis, Money Saving Expert, 'Student loan repayment: Is it better to save or pay it off?' 21 July 2023, accessed 12 Aug 2023 <www.moneysavingexpert.com/students/student-loans-repay/>
123. Martin Lewis and Clare Casalis, Money Saving Expert, 'Student loan interest is at 7.1% - should I panic or pay it off?,' 1 June 2023, accessed 19 Aug 2023 <www.moneysavingexpert.com/students/repay-post-2012-student-loan/>
124. Ramsey Solutions, 'Borrowed future' podcast, Sept-Nov 2021 (9 episodes), accessed 12 Aug 2023 <www.ramseysolutions.com/shows/borrowed-future>
125. StepChange Debt Charity, 'Priority debts and bills. Find out which debts to pay first,' accessed 13 Aug 2023 <www.stepchange.org/debt-info/dealing-with-debt-problems/what-debts-to-pay-first.aspx>
126. CitizensAdvice.org.uk, 'Work out which debts to deal with first,' 22 Feb 2019, accessed 10 May 2022 <www.citizensadvice.org.uk/debt-and-money/help-with-debt/dealing-with-your-debts/work-out-which-debts-to-deal-with-first/>
127. Citizens Advice, 'Collecting information about your debts,' accessed 13 Aug 2023 <www.citizensadvice.org.uk/debt-and-money/help-with-debt/dealing-with-your-debts/collecting-information-about-your-debts/>
128. StepChange Debt Charity, 'How companies collect debt,' accessed 13 Aug 2023 <www.stepchange.org/debt-info/debt-collection.aspx>
129. Citizens Advice, 'Dealing with a letter saying bailiffs will visit,' accessed 13 Aug 2023 <www.citizensadvice.org.uk/debt-and-money/action-your-creditor-can-take/bailiffs/stopping-bailiffs/dealing-with-a-letter-saying-bailiffs-will-visit/>
130. Citizens Advice, 'Action your creditor can take,' accessed 13 Aug 2023 <www.citizensadvice.org.uk/debt-and-money/action-your-creditor-can-take/>
131. Ramsey Solutions, 'How to Deal With Debt Collectors When You Can't Pay,' 23 Aug 2022, accessed 13 Aug 2023 <www.ramseysolutions.com/debt/how-to-deal-with-debt-collectors>
132. Citizens Advice, 'Debt solutions,' accessed 13 Aug 2023 <www.citizensadvice.org.uk/debt-and-money/debt-solutions/>
133. Kiah Treece, Lindsay VanSomeren, Forbes Advisor, 'Pros And Cons Of Debt Consolidation,' 7 Aug 2023, accessed 15 Aug 2023 <www.forbes.com/advisor/personal-loans/pros-and-cons-of-debt-consolidation/>
134. Ramsey Solutions, 'How the Debt Snowball Method Works,' 3 May 2023, accessed 13 Aug 2023, <www.ramseysolutions.com/debt/how-the-debt-snowball-method-works>
135. Pete Matthew, MeaningfulMoney.TV, 'Ultimate guide to paying off debt – debt snowball or debt avalanche,' 31 Jan 2022, accessed 10 May 2022 <meaningfulmoney.tv/2022/01/31/ultimate-guide-to-paying-off-debt-debt-snowball-or-debt-avalanche/>

136. Julia Kagan, Investopedia.com, 'Debt Snowball: Overview, Pros and Cons, Application ,' 31 May 2023, accessed 15 Aug 2023 <www.investopedia.com/terms/s/snowball.asp>
137. Bev O'Shea, Sean Pyles, nerdwallet, 'How To Use The Debt Snowball To Pay Off Debt,' 22 Feb 2023, accessed 15 Aug 2023 <www.nerdwallet.com/article/finance/what-is-a-debt-snowball>
138. Brian Preston, MoneyGuy.com, 'Debt Snowball vs. Debt Avalanche: Which is the BEST way to pay off debt?' 11 June 2021, accessed 10 May 2022 <moneyguy.com/2021/06/debt-snowball-vs-debt-avalanche-best-way-to-pay-off-debt/>
139. Carla Tardi, Investopedia.com, 'Debt Avalanche: Meaning, Pros and Cons, Example,' 27 Apr 2023, accessed 15 Aug 2023 <www.investopedia.com/terms/d/debt-avalanche.asp>
140. Jennifer Thomson, MamaFurFur.com, 'How to pay off debt faster', 21 May 2018, accessed 11 May 2022, <mamafurfur.com/blog/payoffdebtfaster/>
141. Jennifer Thomson, MammaFurFur.com, 'How we paid off $28k/£22k debt within 3 years using the AutoPilot Money Strategy', 15 Sept 2017, accessed 11 May 2022 <mamafurfur.com/vlogs/how-we-paid-off-debt/>
142. Bev O'Shea, nerdwallet, 'How To Snowflake Your Debt,' 31 Jan 2022, accessed 15 Aug 2023 <www.nerdwallet.com/article/finance/paying-off-debt/debt-snowflake>
143. Jim Rohn, Success.com, 'Rohn: 5 Money Principles You Need to Know,' 10 July 2016, accessed 12 Aug 2023 <www.success.com/rohn-5-money-principles-you-need-to-know/>
144. Brean Horne, nerdwallet.com, 'What is the average credit score in the UK?', 27 Aug 2021, accessed 12 May 2022, <www.nerdwallet.com/uk/personal-finance/average-credit-score-uk/>
145. myFICO.com, 'What's in my credit scores?' accessed 12 May 2022, <www.myfico.com/credit-education/whats-in-your-credit-score>
146. Karen Axelton, Experian.com, 'Do Parking Tickets Affect Your Credit Score?' 3 Jul 2021, accessed 12 Aug 2023 <www.experian.com/blogs/ask-experian/do-parking-tickets-affect-credit-score/>
147. Experian.co.uk, 'What affects your credit score,' accessed 12 Aug 2023 <www.experian.co.uk/consumer/guides/what-affects-score.html>
148. Ramsey Solutions, 'Living Without a Credit Score,' 27 Oct 2022, accessed 12 Aug 2023 <www.ramseysolutions.com/debt/living-without-credit-score>
149. Experian.co.uk, '10 tips to improve your credit score,' accessed 12 May 2022 <www.experian.co.uk/consumer/guides/improve-credit-score.html>
150. HSBC.co.uk, 'Financial fitness score,' accessed 12 Aug 2023 <www.hsbc.co.uk/financial-fitness/fitness-score/>

151. Ecclesiastes 7:12, New International Version (NIV)
152. TheIdioms.com, *'HOME IS WHERE THE HEART IS,'* accessed 22 Aug 2023 <www.theidioms.com/home-is-where-the-heart-is/>
153. David Pullinger, Single Friendly Church, *'40% of adults in UK are single,'* May 2019, accessed 21 Aug 2023 <www.singlefriendlychurch.com/further-resources/40-of-adults-in-uk-are-single>
154. Nick Stripe, ONS, *'Whatever happened to 2 Point 4 children?'* 2 Aug 2019, accessed 21 Aug 2023 <blog.ons.gov.uk/2019/08/02/whatever-happened-to-2-point-4-children/>
155. Clea Skopeliti, The Guardian, *"Socially stunted': how Covid pandemic aggravated young people's loneliness,'* 19 June 2023, accessed 15 Aug 2023 <www.theguardian.com/society/2023/jun/19/socially-stunted-how-covid-pandemic-aggravated-young-peoples-loneliness>
156. Rachel Cruze, Ramsey Solutions, *'7 Steps to Stop Fighting Over Money,'* 4 Oct 2022, accessed 15 Aug 2023 <www.ramseysolutions.com/relationships/how-to-put-an-end-to-money-arguments>
157. Craig Groeschel, Life.Church on YouTube, *'Best Way to Avoid an Overwhelming Life,'* 10 Jul 2022, accessed 15 Aug 2023 <youtu.be/hWAGVKkKlmo>
158. John Mark Comer, *'The Ruthless Elimination of Hurry: How to stay emotionally healthy and spiritually alive in the chaos of the modern world,'* Oct 2019, John Murray Press, London, UK.
159. Elizabeth Scott, PhD, VeryWellMind.com, *'What Is the Law of Attraction? How Your Thoughts Can Influence Outcomes in Your Life,'* 7 Nov 2022, accessed 22 Aug 2023 <www.verywellmind.com/understanding-and-using-the-law-of-attraction-3144808>
160. Earl Nightingale, *'The Strangest Secret,'* originally published in 1956, based on a spoken word record. Modern reprints available by various publishers.
161. James Allen, *'As A Man Thinketh,'* originally published in 1903. Modern reprints available by various publishers.
162. Proverbs 23:7, King James Version (KJV): *'For as he thinketh in his heart, so is he: Eat and drink, saith he to thee; but his heart is not with thee.'*
163. Wikipedia contributors, Wikipedia, The Free Encyclopedia, *'Frequency illusion,'* 14 August 2023, accessed 16 Aug 2023 <en.wikipedia.org/w/index.php?title=Frequency_illusion&oldid=1170278106>
164. Romans 12:2, New International Version (NIV): *'Do not conform to the pattern of this world, but be transformed by the renewing of your mind. Then you will be able to test and approve what God's will is—his good, pleasing and perfect will.'*

165. Amanda Jane Modaragamage, RPN, HealthNews.com, *'The Science of Manifestation,'* 14 Mar 2023, accessed 22 Aug 2023 <healthnews.com/mental-health/self-care-and-therapy/the-science-of-manifestation/>
166. Kendra Cherry, Very Well Mind, *What Is the Negativity Bias?'* 14 Nov 2022, accessed 17 Aug 2023 <www.verywellmind.com/negative-bias-4589618>
167. Aimee Groth, BusinessInsider.com, *'You're The Average Of The Five People You Spend The Most Time With,'* 24 Jul 2012, accessed 26 May 2022 <www.businessinsider.com/jim-rohn-youre-the-average-of-the-five-people-you-spend-the-most-time-with-2012-7>
168. Mark 6:4, New International Version (NIV) *'Then Jesus told them, "A prophet is honoured everywhere except in his own hometown and among his relatives and his own family."'*
169. BibleStudy.org, *'Why Didn't Jesus Do Miracles in Nazareth?'* accessed 16 Aug 2023 <www.biblestudy.org/maturart/miracles-in-nazareth.html>
170. Clarence L Haynes Jr. Christianity.com, *'Why Was Jesus Being from Nazareth Derogatory?'* 25 Oct 2022, accessed 22 Aug 2023 <www.christianity.com/wiki/jesus-christ/why-was-jesus-being-from-nazareth-derogatory.html>
171. Luke 4:22, New International Version (NIV) *'All spoke well of him and were amazed at the gracious words that came from his lips. "Isn't this Joseph's son?" they asked.'*
172. Joshua 5:6, English Standard Version (ESV) *'For the people of Israel walked forty years in the wilderness, until all the nation, the men of war who came out of Egypt, perished, because they did not obey the voice of the Lord; the Lord swore to them that he would not let them see the land that the Lord had sworn to their fathers to give to us, a land flowing with milk and honey.'*
173. Sandra Lee Dennis, PhD, *'Betrayal: Did You Choose Your Reality?'* 26 Sept 2014, accessed 22 Aug 2023 <www.sandraleedennis.com/2014/09/26/choose-reality/>
174. Madhuleena Roy Chowdhury, BA, *'ACT Theory: Acceptance and Commitment Therapy Explained'* 30 Jun 2019, accessed 22 Aug 2023 <positivepsychology.com/act-therapy/>
175. The Compassionate Mind Foundation, *Homepage*, accessed 22 Aug 2023 <www.compassionatemind.co.uk/>
176. GoodTherapy.org, *'Compassion-Focused Therapy (CFT),'* 3 Aug 2018, accessed 22 Aug 2023 <www.goodtherapy.org/learn-about-therapy/types/compassion-focused-therapy>
177. Headspace, *Homepage*, accessed 22 Aug 2023 <www.headspace.com/>

178. Rachel Gillett, Inc. *'Icons & Innovators: How Walt Disney, Oprah Winfrey, and 19 Other Successful People Rebounded After Getting Fired,'* 7 Oct 2015, accessed 16 Aug 2023 <www.inc.com/business-insider/21-successful-people-who-rebounded-after-getting-fired.html>
179. Rachel Cruze, Ramsey Solutions, *'How To Talk To Your Parents About Money,'* 17 Jan 2022, accessed 24 Aug 2023 <www.ramseysolutions.com/relationships/talk-to-your-parents-about-money>
180. Dave Ramsey, Rachel Cruze, *'Smart Money Smart Kids: Raising the Next Generation to Win with Money,'* Nashville: Thomas Nelson, 2014.
181. Will Rainey, *'Grandpa's Fortune Fables: Fun stories to teach kids about money,'* Independently Published, 2021.
182. David Kleinhandler, Nasdaq.com, *'Generational Wealth: Why do 70% of Families Lose Their Wealth in the 2nd Generation?'* 19 Oct 2018, accessed 28 May 2022 <www.nasdaq.com/articles/generational-wealth%3A-why-do-70-of-families-lose-their-wealth-in-the-2nd-generation-2018-10>
183. Fran Ivens, ThisIsMoney.co.uk, *'What happens when you win really big on the lottery?'* updated 25 May 2022, accessed 14 Jul 2022 <www.thisismoney.co.uk/money/investing/article-10848695/What-happens-win-big-lottery>
184. Brian Preston, Bo Hanson, The Money Guy Show on YouTube, *'The Dark Side of Being a Millionaire! (The Truth About Being Wealthy),'* 27 May 2022, accessed 28 May 2022 <youtu.be/blLaDWYZgLo>
185. Thomas Stanley, William Danko, *'The Millionaire Next Door: The Surprising Secrets of America's Wealthy,'* New York: Pocket Books, 1996.
186. Proverbs 22:6, English Standard Version (ESV)
187. Dave Ramsey, The Ramsey Show – Highlights on YouTube, *'How To Talk To My Family About My Will,'* 26 Apr 2018, accessed 24 Aug 2023 <youtu.be/fS0PAN80hzw?si=OHd6mQ1NY9lDZkDT>
188. Age UK, *'Wills and Estate Planning,'* published August 2023, accessed 12 Aug 2023 <www.ageuk.org.uk/globalassets/age-uk/documents/information-guides/ageukig31_wills_and_estate_planning_inf.pdf>
189. DigitalLegacyAssociation.org, *Homepage*, accessed 15 Jul 2022 <digitallegacyassociation.org/>
190. CitizensAdvice.org.uk, *'Managing affairs for someone else'*, 2022, accessed 15 Jul 2022 <www.citizensadvice.org.uk/family/looking-after-people/managing-affairs-for-someone-else>
191. Pete Matthew, Meaningful Money Podcast, *'The Ultimate Guide to ESTATE PLANNING,'* 20 Jan 2021, accessed 31 May 2022 <meaningfulmoney.tv/2021/01/20/the-ultimate-guide-to-estate-planning/>

192. Kathleen Elkins, CNBC.com, 'Here's how much money it takes to be among the richest 50 percent of people worldwide,' 19 Nov 2018, accessed 30 Aug 2023 <www.cnbc.com/2018/11/19/how-much-money-it-takes-to-be-among-the-richest-50-percent-worldwide.html>
193. Khanyi Mlaba, Global Citizen, 'The Richest 1% Own Almost Half the World's Wealth & 9 Other Mind-Blowing Facts on Wealth Inequality,' 19 Jan 2023, accessed 30 Aug 2023 <www.globalcitizen.org/en/content/wealth-inequality-oxfam-billionaires-elon-musk/>
194. Proverbs 21: 20, NIV 'The wise store up choice food and olive oil, but fools gulp theirs down.'
195. Craig Groescel, Life.Church on YouTube, 'When You Stop Holding Back,' 6 Feb 2023, accessed 25 Aug 2023 <youtu.be/Kkk21wZLWL4>
196. Acts 20:35, New Living Translation (NLT), 'And I have been a constant example of how you can help those in need by working hard. You should remember the words of the Lord Jesus: 'It is more blessed to give than to receive.''
197. Luke 21: 1-4, New Living Translation (NLT) 'The Widow's Offering: While Jesus was in the Temple, he watched the rich people dropping their gifts in the collection box. Then a poor widow came by and dropped in two small coins. "I tell you the truth," Jesus said, "this poor widow has given more than all the rest of them. For they have given a tiny part of their surplus, but she, poor as she is, has given everything she has."
198. Ramsey Solutions, '5 Simple Habits of the Average Millionaire,' 15 Aug 2023, accessed 29 Aug 2023 <www.ramseysolutions.com/retirement/habits-of-millionaires-and-billionaires>
199. Deuteronomy 12:10-12, Holy Bible, New International Version (NIV)
200. Peter Haas, 'The Truth About Tithes And First-Fruits – The Jewish Practice Of Tzedakah,' Aug 19 2023, accessed 25 Sept 2023 <www.peterhaas.org/the-truth-about-tithes-and-first-fruits-the-jewish-practice-of-tzedakah/>
201. My Jewish Learning, MyJewishLarning.com, 'Tzedakah: Tithing,' accessed 12 Apr 2023 <www.myjewishlearning.com/article/tithing/>
202. Matthew 23:23, New Living Translation (NLT)
203. Acts 4:32, Holy Bible, New International Version (NIV): 'All the believers were one in heart and mind. No one claimed that any of their possessions was their own, but they shared everything they had.'
204. BibleProject on YouTube, 'Does A Good Christian Tithe 10%? (It's Not That Simple),' 29 Mar 2023, accessed 12 Apr 2023 <youtu.be/RN3wYVRkmno>
205. Shelter.org.uk, 'Legal definition of homelessness and threatened homelessness,' accessed 29 Aug 2023 <england.shelter.org.uk/professional_resources/legal/homelessness_applications/homelessness_and_threatened_homelessness/legal_definition_of_homelessness_and_threatened_homelessness>

206. Shelter.org.uk, *'What causes homelessness?'* accessed 24 Aug 2022 <england.shelter.org.uk/support_us/campaigns/what_causes_homelessness>
207. Direct Relief, WikiHow.com, *'How to Help Improve the Lives of the Poor,'* 22 Apr 2021, accessed 24 Aug 2022 <www.wikihow.com/Help-Improve-the-Lives-of-the-Poor>
208. Together Liverpool, *'Network of Kindness: Supporting you to take the next step in your social action,'* accessed 29 Aug 2023 <togetherliverpool.org.uk/>
209. Facebook Group, *'Hope for Justice - Liverpool & Wirral Abolition Group,'* accessed 29 Aug 2023 <www.facebook.com/groups/312958469062961/>
210. Emma Turner, Barclays.com, *'Barriers to giving'*, 15 Nov 2019, accessed 24 Aug 2022 <privatebank.barclays.com/news-and-insights/2019/november/barriers-to-giving/>
211. Nonprofit Tech For Good, *'6 reasons why people do not give to charity,'* 10 Oct 2018, accessed 24 Aug 2022 <www.nptechforgood.com/2018/10/10/6-reasons-why-people-do-not-give-to-charity/>
212. Health Poverty Action, *'Social Determinants,'* 2018, accessed 3 Sept 2023 <www.healthpovertyaction.org/how-poverty-is-created/power-and-politics/social-and-political-determinats/>
213. Rachel Cruze, Ramsey Solutions, *'Should You Ever Loan Money To Family?'* 24 Sept 2021, accessed 3 Sept 2023 <www.ramseysolutions.com/debt/should-you-ever-loan-money-to-family>
214. Pastor John Lindell, James River Church YouTube, *'A Heart For The Poor,'* 26 Nov 2018, accessed 24 Aug 2022 <youtu.be/dFzFKUvzwLM>
215. Robert Murray McCheyne, springsofgrace.church Blog, *'Giving to the poor,'* 30 July 2014, accessed 24 Aug 2022 <springsofgrace.church/2014/07/giving-to-the-poor-robert-murray-mccheyne/>
216. Triology Media on YouTube, *'GLITTERBOMBING a Scam Call Center w/ Mark Rober,'* 8 May 2022, accessed 30 Aug 2023 <youtu.be/YfQU_Qf_uTI?si=SMd2rma9at6f81Ov>
217. Age UK, *'Avoiding Scams Information Guide,'* Aug 2021, accessed 25 Aug 2022 <www.ageuk.org.uk/globalassets/age-uk/documents/information-guides/ageukig05_avoiding_scams_inf.pdf>
218. CitizensAdvice.org, *'Check if something might be a scam,'* 30 May 2019, accessed 25 Aug 2022 <www.citizensadvice.org.uk/consumer/scams/check-if-something-might-be-a-scam/>
219. Scammer Payback on YouTube, *'We created the First Ever **ANTI-SCAM** call Center,'* 20 Aug 2022, accessed 25 Aug 2022 <youtu.be/_u_JTddAYes>
220. Dave Ramsey, *'The Legacy Journey: A Radical View of Biblical Wealth and Generosity,'* 1 Oct 2014, Ramsey Press, Franklin, Tennessee, USA.

221. Jason Cabler, Celebrating Financial Freedom, 'Havdalah - How to Have an Overflowing Cup of Financial Abundance,' 9 Jan 2015, accessed 29 Oct 2022 <www.cfinancialfreedom.com/havdalah-how-to-overflowing-cup-financial-abundance/>
222. The Ramsey Show on YouTube, 'The Ramsey Giving Show 2021,' 22 Dec 2021, accessed 25 Aug 2022 <youtu.be/8cT_cAHfSPc>
223. Kathleen Elkins, CNBC, 'A janitor secretly amassed an $8 million fortune and left most of it to his library and hospital,' 29 Aug 2016, accessed 30 Aug 2023 <www.cnbc.com/2016/08/29/janitor-secretly-amassed-an-8-million-fortune.html>
224. Morgan Housel, 'The Psychology of Money: Timeless lessons on wealth, greed, and happiness,' Harriman House, Petersfield, UK, 2020.
225. Wikipedia contributors, Wikipedia, The Free Encyclopedia, 'William Roscoe,' 20 Mar 2023, accessed 30 Aug 2023 <en.wikipedia.org/wiki/William_Roscoe>
226. Wikipedia, 'Survivalism,' accessed 14 Jan 2023 <en.wikipedia.org/wiki/Survivalism>
227. Marta Teegen, 'Homegrown: a growing guide for creating a cook's garden,' (New York: Rodale, 2010)
228. Jean Folger, Investopedia.com, 'Why is social security running out of money?' updated 18 July 2022, accessed 6 Dec 2022 <www.investopedia.com/ask/answers/071514/why-social-security-running-out-money.asp>
229. Alexandra Kerr, 'Financial Independence, Retire Early (FIRE) Explained: How It Works,' Investopedia.com, updated 1 Sept 2022, accessed 7 Jan 2023 <www.investopedia.com/terms/f/financial-independence-retire-early-fire.asp>
230. Kelly Anne Smith, 'How To Retire Early With FIRE,' Forbes.com, updated 7 Dec 2022, accessed 7 Jan 2023 <www.forbes.com/advisor/retirement/the-forbes-guide-to-fire/>
231. Catherine Brock, The Motley Fool, 'All About Asset Classes and Investment Diversification,' updated 2 Nov 2022, accessed 7 Jan 2023 <www.fool.com/investing/stock-market/basics/asset-classes/>
232. Zaven Boyrazian, The Motley Fool, 'What to Invest In: 7 Types of Investments to Make Money,' updated 13 Dec 2022, accessed 14 Jan 2023 <www.fool.co.uk/investing-basics/getting-started-in-investing/what-are-your-options/>
233. Royal Horticultural Society, RHS.org.uk, 'Beetroot,' accessed 06 Jan 2023 <www.rhs.org.uk/vegetables/beetroot/grow-your-own>
234. Ryan Pannell, Forbes.com, 'Retail Traders: It's Discipline That Slays Markets,' 20 Dec 2022, accessed 07 Jan 2023 <www.forbes.com/sites/forbesfinancecouncil/2022/12/20/retail-traders-its-discipline-that-slays-markets/>

235. Adam Hayes, Investopedia.com, *'What Are Meme Stocks, and Are They Real Investments?'* updated 12 Sept 2022, accessed 12 Jan 2023 <www.investopedia.com/meme-stock-5206762>
236. Greg Iacurci, CNBC, *'2022 was the worst-ever year for U.S. bonds. How to position your portfolio for 2023,'* 7 Jan 2023, accessed 31 Aug 2023 <www.cnbc.com/2023/01/07/2022-was-the-worst-ever-year-for-us-bonds-how-to-position-for-2023.html>
237. Megan Schaltegger, Better Homes & Gardens, *'Why Lettuce Is Harder to Find (and Pricier) at Grocery Stores Right Now,'* 22 Feb 2023, accessed 31 Aug 2023 <www.bhg.com/lettuce-shortage-2023-7110763>
238. James Chen, Investopedia.com, *'Growth Company: Definition, Characteristics, and Examples,'* 23 Feb 2021, accessed 31 Aug 2023 <www.investopedia.com/terms/g/growthcompany.asp>
239. James Chen, Investopedia.com, *'Income Stock: What it is, How it Works, Example,'* 25 Apr 2022, accessed 31 Aug 2023 <www.investopedia.com/terms/i/incomestock.asp>
240. The Royal Mint, *'Get Into Gold,'* accessed 7 Jan 2023 <www.royalmint.com/invest/get-into-gold/>
241. Wikipedia Contributors, Wikipedia, The Free Encyclopedia, *'Soil,'* accessed 2 Dec 2022 <en.wikipedia.org/wiki/Soil>
242. Matthew 13: 1-23, New International Version (NIV) – The parable of the sower
243. Pete Matthew, Meaningful Money, *'Season 14: New Accumulators,'* accessed 1 Sept 2023 <meaningfulmoney.tv/season-14-new-accumulators/>
244. Bob Pisani, CNBC, *'One year ago stocks dropped 12% in a single day. What investors have learned since then,'* 16 Mar 2021, accessed 1 Sept 2023 <www.cnbc.com/2021/03/16/one-year-ago-stocks-dropped-12percent-in-a-single-day-what-investors-have-learned-since-then.html>
245. James Royal, Arielle O'Shea, nerdwallet.com, *'What Is the Average Stock Market Return?'* 8 Dec 2022, accessed 14 Jan 2023 <www.nerdwallet.com/article/investing/average-stock-market-return>
246. MoneySavingExpert.com, *'Pensions & Investing,'* accessed 14 Jan 2023 <www.moneysavingexpert.com/investments/>
247. Richard Best, Seeking Alpha, *'4 Types of Investment Accounts,'* 18 Apr 2022, accessed 14 Jan 2023 <seekingalpha.com/article/4459087-investment-account-types>
248. Pete Matthew, Meaningful Money Podcast, *'Platforms, Wrappers and Funds – The building blocks of a portfolio,'* 21 May 2013, accessed 14 Jan 2023 <meaningful-

money.tv/2013/05/21/mmp011-platforms-wrappers-and-funds-the-building-blocks-of-a-portfolio-podcast/>
249. Rick Warren, Pastor Rick's Daily Hope, *'Financial Fitness'*, July 2022, accessed 18 July 2022 <pastorrick.com/series/financial-fitness-2022/>
250. Terri.com, *'Terri Savelle Foy Ministries Home Page,'* accessed 19 Jan 2023 <www.terri.com>
251. Brian Preston, Bo Hanson, Money Guy Show on YouTube, *'Are You Taking Advantage of the Abundance Cycle?'* 25 Nov 2021, accessed 20 Jan 2023 <youtu.be/aiiY3XPDb4Q>
252. Ripple Effect on YouTube, *'Ripple Effect: what we do,'* 6 June 2022, accessed 20 Jan 2023 <youtu.be/gqJc4552cjQ>
253. Maurie Backman, The Motley Fool – The Ascent, *'Dave Ramsey Says '79% of Millionaires Inherited $0.' Here's How They Got Where They Are,'* 28 May 2022, accessed 25 Jan 2023 <www.fool.com/the-ascent/buying-stocks/articles/dave-ramsey-says-79-of-millionaires-inherited-0-heres-how-they-got-where-they-are/>
254. Mark P. Cussen, Investopedia.com, *'Why a 60/40 Portfolio Is No Longer Good Enough,'* 30 Oct 2022, accessed 25 Jan 2023 <www.investopedia.com/articles/financial-advisors/011916/why-6040-portfolio-no-longer-good-enough.asp>
255. Jason Fernando, Investopedia.com, *'The Power of Compound Interest: Calculations and Examples,'* updated 19 Jul 2022, accessed 3 Feb 2023 <www.investopedia.com/terms/c/compoundinterest.asp>
256. Ramsey Solutions, *'Why should I invest 15% of my income for retirement,'* 2 Dec 2022, accessed 9 Feb 2023 <www.ramseysolutions.com/retirement/why-should-i-invest-15-of-my-income-for-retirement>
257. The Money Guy Show, *'3 signs you're saving TOO MUCH for retirement!'* 1 Oct 2021, accessed 9 Feb 2023 <moneyguy.com/2021/10/3-signs-youre-saving-too-much-for-retirement/>
258. Gov.UK, *'Workplace Pensions,'* accessed 9 Feb 2023 <www.gov.uk/workplace-pensions/joining-a-workplace-pension>
259. Carmen Reinicke, CNBC.com, 'You might start hearing about capitulation in the markets. Here's why you should invest anyway,' 17 May 2022, accessed 22 Feb 2023 <www.cnbc.com/2022/05/17/what-market-capitulation-means-and-what-investors-should-do-.html>
260. Leslie Kramer, Investopedia.com, *'What caused the stock market crash of 1929?'* 31 Dec 2021, accessed 14 Feb 2023 <www.investopedia.com/ask/answers/042115/what-caused-stock-market-crash-1929-preceded-great-depression.asp>
261. Royal Horticultural Society, RHS.org.uk, *'Crop Rotation,'* 2023, accessed 23 Feb 2023 <www.rhs.org.uk/vegetables/crop-rotation>

262. Philip Ryland, Investors' Chronicle, 'An All-Weather Portfolio,' 15 Sept 2022, accesse 14 Feb 2023 <www.investorschronicle.co.uk/ideas/2022/09/15/an-all-weather-portfolio/>
263. Adam Hayes, Investopedia.com, 'Portfolio Management: Definition, Types and Strategies,' 27 Nov 2022, accessed 14 Feb 2023 <www.investopedia.com/terms/p/portfoliomanagement.asp>
264. Michael Schmidt, Investopedia.com, 'Buy-and-Hold Investing vs. Market Timing: What's the Difference?' 7 Jul 2022, accessed 24 Feb 2023 <www.investopedia.com/articles/stocks/08/passive-active-investing.asp>
265. Adam Hayes, Investopedia.com, 'Dollar-Cost Averaging (DCA) Explained With Examples and Considerations,' 19 Aug 2022, accessed 23 Feb 2023 <www.investopedia.com/terms/d/dollarcostaveraging.asp>
266. Royal Horticultural Society, RHS.org.uk, 'Pruning,' 2023, accessed 23 Feb 2023 <www.rhs.org.uk/pruning>
267. Liz Manning, Investopedia.com, 'Rebalancing: Definition, Why It's Important, Types and Examples,' updated 12 July 2022, accessed 24 Feb 2023 <www.investopedia.com/terms/r/rebalancing.asp>
268. Brian Preston, Bo Hanson, Money Guy Show on YouTube, 'Watch This Before Rebalancing Your Investment Portfolio!' 3 March 2023, accessed 3 March 2023 <youtu.be/2_4A-2fJ25Y>
269. Ramin Nakisa, PensionCraft.com, 'Blackrock MyMap or Vanguard LifeStrategy: Which is best?' 21 Jun 2019, accessed 24 Feb 2023 <www.pensioncraft.com/blackrock-mymap-vs-vanguard-lifestrategy/>
270. DavisFunds.com, 'Wisdom of Great Investors,' accessed 27 Feb 2023 <davisfunds.com/wisdom/quotes.php>
271. Brian J Bloch, Investopedia.com, 'Risk Warnings and Investment Disclaimers,' 26 Jan 2022, accessed 22 May 2023 <www.investopedia.com/articles/fundamental-analysis/08/risk-warnings.asp>
272. The Investopedia Team, Investopedia.com, 'Investing Fads,' 1 Nov 2022, accessed 28 Feb 2023 <www.investopedia.com/terms/i/investing-fads.asp>
273. Money Helper, 'Choosing a financial advisor,' accessed 28 Feb 2023 <www.moneyhelper.org.uk/en/getting-help-and-advice/financial-advisers/choosing-a-financial-adviser>
274. Morgan Housel, Collaborative Fund, 'Everyone is still Learning,' 2017, accessed 25 Jan 2022, <www.collaborativefund.com/blog/everyone-is-still-learning/>
275. Tim Macwelch, Outdoor Life, '10 reasons people get lost in the wild,' 20 Apr 2021, accessed 02 Mar 2023 <www.outdoorlife.com/10-reasons-people-get-lost-in-wild/>

276. Aislinn Simpson, Telegraph.co.uk, *'Syrian lorry driver takes a 1,600 mile detour to Gibraltar via Skegness thanks to sat nav,'* 21 July 2008, accessed 2 Mar 2023 <www.telegraph.co.uk/news/newstopics/howaboutthat/2440539/Syrian-lorry-driver-takes-a-1600-mile-detour-to-Gibraltar-via-Skegness-thanks-to-sat-nav.html>

277. MoneyGuy.com, *'Net Worth Template,'* 2022, accessed 26 Mar 2023 <moneyguy.com/resources/net-worth-template/>

278. The Money Guy Show on YouTube, *'Average Net Worth By Age in 2023!'* 6 Jan 2023, accessed 26 Mar 2023 <youtu.be/wof7NIgbnis>

279. Jean Folger, Investopedia.com, *'Assets That Increase Your Net Worth,'* 8 Mar 2022, accessed 5 Sept 2023 <www.investopedia.com/articles/pf/12/assets-that-increase-net-worth.asp>

280. Ella Jukwey, MoneySuperMarket.com, *'Dormant bank accounts: A complete guide,'* 24 Mar 2023, accessed 17 Apr 2023 <www.moneysupermarket.com/savings/dormant-account-guide/>

281. Money Helper, MoneyHelper.org.uk, *'Finding your lost pension: tracing and finding lost pensions,'* 2023, accessed 28 Mar 2023 <www.moneyhelper.org.uk/en/pensions-and-retirement/pension-problems/tracing-and-finding-lost-pensions>

282. Financial Services Compensation Scheme, FSCS.org, *'Homepage,'* 2023, accessed 17 Apr 2023 <www.fscs.org.uk/>

283. Federal Deposit Insurance Corporation, FDIC.gov, *'Homepage,'* 2023, accessed 17 Apr 2023 <www.fdic.gov/>

284. Erin Gobler, Investopedia.com, *'What Happened to Silicon Valley Bank?'* 1 May 2023, accessed 5 Sept 2023 <www.investopedia.com/what-happened-to-silicon-valley-bank-7368676>

285. Jean Folger, Investopedia.com, *'Will Your Retirement Income Be Enough? Start by estimating your future expenses,'* updated 28 Mar 2023, accessed 13 Apr 2023 <www.investopedia.com/retirement/retirement-income-planning/>

286. Rob Berger, Forbes Advisor, *'How the 25x Rule Can Help You Save for Retirement,'* updated Jan 12 2021, accessed 13 Apr 2023 <www.forbes.com/advisor/retirement/25x-rule-retirement/>

287. Sun Life, *'History of house prices in Britain,'* updated 12 July 2022, accessed 13 Apr 2023 <www.sunlife.co.uk/articles-guides/your-money/the-price-of-a-home-in-britain-then-and-now/>

288. Bank of England, *'Inflation Calculator,'* updated 24 Mar 2023, accessed 17 Apr 2023 <www.bankofengland.co.uk/monetary-policy/inflation/inflation-calculator>

289. HSBC, 'Retirement Calculator,' accessed 17 Apr 2023 <retirementcalculator.hsbc.co.uk/>
290. Gov.UK, 'Plan your retirement income: step by step,' accessed 17 Apr 2023, <www.gov.uk/plan-for-retirement>
291. Ramsey Solutions, Ramsey Solutions.com, 'How Much Money Do I Need to Retire?' 2023, accessed 17 Apr 2023 <www.ramseysolutions.com/retirement/riq>
292. The Money Guy Show, MoneyGuy.com, 'Know Your Number and How to Reach It!' 2023, accessed 17 Apr 2023 <learn.moneyguy.com/know-your-number-course>
293. Frank Armstrong, Investopedia.com, 'How to Create a Retirement Portfolio Strategy,' 22 Aug 2021, accessed 6 Sept 2023 <www.investopedia.com/articles/retirement/11/implement-effective-retirement-income-strategy.asp>
294. TheCalculatorSite.com, 'Compound Interest Calculator,' 2023, accessed 11 June 2023 <www.thecalculatorsite.com/finance/calculators/compoundinterestcalculator.php>
295. Duncan Haughey, Project Smart, 'A Brief History of SMART Goals,' 13 Dec 2014, accessed 19 Apr 2023 <www.projectsmart.co.uk/smart-goals/brief-history-of-smart-goals.php>
296. George T. Doran, Management Review, 'There's a S.M.A.R.T. Way to Write Management's Goals and Objectives,' (1981), Vol. 70, Issue 11, pp. 35-36.
297. DevelopGoodHabits.com, 'The Ultimate Guide to SMART Goals,' 2023, accessed 19 Apr 2023 <www.developgoodhabits.com/smartgoals/>
298. Brian Preston, Bo Hanson, The Money Guy Show on YouTube, 'How to Win With Money in 2023!' 27 Jan 2023, accessed 30 Jan 2023 <youtu.be/XwMNYBDqvUQ>
299. Terri Savelle Foy on YouTube, 'My 7 Step Goal Setting Process That Works!| how to set goals!' 24 Jan 2022, accessed 20 Apr 2023 <youtu.be/ku4rO9ANvbg>
300. Ramsey Solutions, 'The 7 Baby Steps,' 2023, accessed 19 Apr 2023 <www.ramseysolutions.com/dave-ramsey-7-baby-steps>
301. The Money Guy Show, 'Resources,' 2023, accessed 19 Apr 2023 <www.moneyguy.com/resources/>
302. PensionBee.com, 'Inflation Calculator: How far will your savings go in retirement?' 2023, accessed 19 Apr 2023 <www.pensionbee.com/inflation-calculator>
303. Thomas Stanley, William Danko, 'The Millionaire Next Door: The Surprising Secrets of America's Wealthy,' New York: Pocket Books, 1996.
304. Ramsey Solutions, RamseySolutions.com, 'The National Study of Millionaires,' 12 Apr 2023, accessed 2 May 2023 <www.ramseysolutions.com/retirement/the-national-study-of-millionaires-research>

305. Wikipedia, 'Rope Team,' 2 Mar 2023 <en.wikipedia.org/wiki/Rope_team>
306. Angharad Carrick, ThisIsMoney.co.uk, 'What is the difference between a financial adviser and a coach? Why you should consider asking for money help regardless of your situation,' 26 Aug 2021, accessed 27 Mar 2023 <www.thisismoney.co.uk/money/investing/article-9912531/What-difference-financial-adviser-coach.html>
307. Simon Sinek, 'The Infinite Game,' London: England, Portfolio Penguin, 2020
308. The Investopedia team, Investopedia.com, 'Understanding Money: Its Properties, Types, and Uses,' 4 July 2022, accessed 22 May 2023 <www.investopedia.com/terms/m/money.asp>
309. Wu Mingren ('Dhwty'), Ancient-origins.net, 'Paying With Shells: Cowrie Shell Money Is One of the Oldest Currencies Still Collected Today,' 26 Apr 2019, accessed 23 May 2023 <www.ancient-origins.net/history-ancient-traditions/shell-money-0011793>
310. Amy Tikkanen, Encyclopedia Britannica, 'A Brief (and Fascinating) History of Money,' 31 Jan 2020, accessed 23 May 2023, <www.britannica.com/story/a-brief-and-fascinating-history-of-money>
311. Jake Frankenfield, Investopedia.com, 'Currency: What It Is, How It Works, and How It Relates to Money,' 22 July 2022, accessed 22 May 2023 <www.investopedia.com/terms/c/currency.asp>
312. James Chen, Investopedia.com, 'Fiat Money: What It Is, How It Works, Example, Pros & Cons,' 28 Mar 2023, accessed 22 May 2023 <www.investopedia.com/terms/f/fiatmoney.asp>
313. Nick Lioudis, Investopedia.com, 'What Is the Gold Standard? Advantages, Alternatives, and History,' 30 Apr 2023, accessed 22 May 2023 <www.investopedia.com/ask/answers/09/gold-standard.asp>
314. Troy Segal, Investopedia.com, 'What Is a Central Bank, and Does the U.S. Have One?' 6 Apr 2022, accessed 22 May 2023 <www.investopedia.com/terms/c/centralbank.asp>
315. Will Kenton, Investopedia.com, 'What Is Hyperinflation? Causes, Effects, Examples, and How to Prepare,' 9 Apr 2023, accessed 22 May 2023 <www.investopedia.com/terms/h/hyperinflation.asp>
316. Brent Radcliffe, Investopedia.com, 'A Primer On Reserve Currencies,' 23 Feb 2021, accessed 23 May 2023 <www.investopedia.com/articles/economics/13/reserve-currencies.asp>
317. James Chen, Investopedia.com, 'Petrodollars: Definition, History, Uses,' 19 July 2022, accessed 23 May 2023 <www.investopedia.com/terms/p/petrodollars.asp>

318. James Chen, Investopedia.com, 'Eurodollar: Definition, Why It's Important, and Example,' 31 Jan 2021, accessed 23 May 2023 <www.investopedia.com/terms/e/eurodollar.asp>
319. Jake Frankenfield, Investopedia.com, 'Cryptocurrency Explained With Pros and Cons for Investment,' 21 Apr 2023, accessed 22 May 2023 <www.investopedia.com/terms/c/cryptocurrency.asp>
320. Will Kenton, Investopedia.com, 'What Is an Economic Bubble and How Does It Work, With Examples,' 3 Apr 2022, accessed 23 may 2023 <www.investopedia.com/terms/b/bubble.asp>
321. Wikipedia.org, 'Beanie Babies,' accessed 23 May 2023 <en.wikipedia.org/wiki/Beanie_Babies>
322. Rakesh Sharma, Investopedia.com, 'Non-Fungible Token (NFT): What It Means and How It Works,' 6 Apr 2023, accessed 22 May 2023 <www.investopedia.com/non-fungible-tokens-nft-5115211>
323. Principles by Ray Dalio on YouTube, 'How The Economic Machine Works by Ray Dalio,' 22 Sept 2013, accessed 11 May 2023 <youtu.be/PHe0bXAIuk0>
324. Principles by Ray Dalio on YouTube, 'Principles for Dealing with the Changing World Order by Ray Dalio,' 2 Mar 2022, accessed 11 May 2023 <youtu.be/xguam0TKMw8>
325. James Royal, Arielle O'Shea, Nerwallet.com, 'What Is the Average Stock Market Return?' 13 Feb 2023, accessed 24 May 2023 <www.nerdwallet.com/article/investing/average-stock-market-return>
326. SimonSinek.com, 'The Infinite Game – Home Page,' accessed 25 Sept 2023 <simonsinek.com/books/the-infinite-game>
327. James Chen, Investopedia.com, 'What Is the Stock Market, What Does It Do, and How Does It Work?' 22 Apr 2023, accessed 24 May 2023 <www.investopedia.com/terms/s/stockmarket.asp>
328. AMSA Network, 'History of the World's Oldest Stock Exchange,' 16 Apr 2023, accessed 25 May 2023 <amsa-network.com/amsanews/search/2019/4/16/history-of-the-worlds-oldest-stock-exchange>
329. Troy Segal, Investopedia.com, 'Stock Buybacks: Why Do Companies Buy Back Shares?' 30 Mar 2023, accessed 25 May 2023 <www.investopedia.com/ask/answers/042015/why-would-company-buyback-its-own-shares.asp>
330. Graham, Benjamin, 'The Intelligent Investor: a Book of Practical Counsel,' New York: Harper, 1959.
331. Adam Hayes, Investopedia.com, 'What Are Meme Stocks, and Are They Real Investments?' 12 Sept 2022, accessed 25 May 2023 <www.investopedia.com/meme-stock-5206762>

332. P.S. I know a whale isn't technically a fish, but you'll have to bear with me here! It's just a picture to help you understand better.
333. TradingView.com, *Home Page*, 2023, accessed 30 May 2023 <www.tradingview.com/
334. Barry Nielson, Investopedia.com, *'The Lost Decade: Lessons From Japan's Real Estate Crisis,'* 14 Jan 2022, accessed 30 May 2023 <www.investopedia.com/articles/economics/08/japan-1990s-credit-crunch-liquidity-trap.asp>
335. Will Kenton, Investopedia.com, *'Stock Market Crash of 1929: Definition, Causes, Effects,'* 16 Mar 2023, accesse 30 May 2023 <www.investopedia.com/terms/s/stock-market-crash-1929.asp>
336. Tim Smith, Investopedia.com, *'What Is Market Sentiment? Definition, Indicator Types, and Example,'* 13 May 2022, accessed 30 May 2023 <www.investopedia.com/terms/m/marketsentiment.asp>
337. Eva K., CC BY-SA 2.5, via Wikimedia Commons, *'Bull and bear in front of the Frankfurt Stock Exchange by the sculptor Reinhard Dachlauer,'* dated 4 September 2007, accessed 30 May 2023 <creativecommons.org/licenses/by-sa/2.5> The image has been changed to greyscale.
338. Jean-Paul Rodrigue, via Wikimedia Commons, *'Stages of a bubble,'* accessed 30 May 2023 <commons.wikimedia.org/wiki/File:Stages_of_a_bubble.png> The image has been changed to greyscale.
339. Ben McClure, Investopedia.com, *'An Introduction to Behavioral Finance,'* 26 Jan 2022, accesse 30 May 2023 <www.investopedia.com/articles/02/112502.asp>
340. Ben Taylor, Investopedia.com, *'4 Key Investment Strategies to Learn Before Trading,'* 19 Jul 2022, accessed 31 May 2023 <www.investopedia.com/investing/investing-strategies/>
341. Jean Folger, Investopedia.com, *'Investing vs. Trading: What's the Difference?'* 29 Nov 2021, accessed 31 May 2023 <www.investopedia.com/ask/answers/12/difference-investing-trading.asp>
342. Adam Hayes, Investopedia.com, *'Position Definition—Short and Long Positions in Financial Markets,'* 1 Dec 2021, accessed 31 May 2023 <www.investopedia.com/terms/p/position.asp>
343. Benzinga, Markets Insider, *'If You're Day Trading, You Will Probably Lose Money: Here's Why,'* 30 Jul 2021, accessed 31 May 2023 <markets.businessinsider.com/news/stocks/if-you-re-day-trading-you-will-probably-lose-money-here-s-why-1030667770>
344. Elvin Mirzayev, Investopedia.com, *'Options Trading For Beginners,'* 5 Apr 2023, accessed 31 May 2023 <www.investopedia.com/articles/active-trading/040915/guide-option-trading-strategies-beginners.asp>

345. James Chen, Investopedia.com, 'What Is Mean Reversion, and How Do Investors Use It?' 18 Aug 2021, accessed 1 June 2023 <www.investopedia.com/terms/m/meanreversion.asp>
346. Wavehuggers.com, 'Beginners guide to surfing: how to catch waves,' accessed 6 June 2023 <wavehuggers.com/beginners-guide-surfing-catch-waves/>
347. Nassim Nicholas Taleb, 'The Black Swan: The Impact of the Highly Improbable,' 2008, Harlow, England, Penguin Books.
348. Dave Roos, History.com, 'Here Are Warning Signs Investors Missed Before the 1929 Crash,' 27 Mar 2023, accessed 6 June 2023 <www.history.com/news/1929-stock-market-crash-warning-signs>
349. Michelle Lodge, Investopedia.com, 'Who is Michael Burry?' 27 Feb 2023, accessed 6 June 2023 <www.investopedia.com/who-is-michael-burry-5235600>
350. Thomas McMahon, Trustnet.com, 'Why do monkeys outperform fund managers?' 11 June 2014, accessed 6 June 2023 <www.trustnet.com/news/515389/why-do-monkeys-outperform-fund-managers>
351. Zacks, nasdaq.com, 'How Do Fund Flows Affect Fund Performance?' 23 Sept 2015, accessed 6 June 2023 <www.nasdaq.com/articles/how-do-fund-flows-affect-fund-performance-2015-09-23>
352. Ronald Fink, Chicago Booth Review, 'Why Active Managers Have Trouble Keeping Up with the Pack,' 3 July 2014, accessed 6 June 2023 <www.chicagobooth.edu/review/why-active-managers-have-trouble-keeping-up-with-the-pack>
353. Jesse Pound, CNBC.com, 'The father of the passive investing revolution on Wall Street says his idea was called 'garbage", 2 Jan 2020, accessed 7 June 2023 <www.cnbc.com/2020/01/02/burton-malkiel-says-his-passive-investing-idea-was-called-garbage.html>
354. Vanguard.com, 'Our History Serving investors for nearly five decades,' 2023, accessed 7 June 2023 <corporate.vanguard.com/content/corporatesite/us/en/corp/who-we-are/sets-us-apart/our-history.html>
355. Michael Batnick, theirrelevantinvestor.com, 'Today in Market History, The First Index Fund,' 31 Aug 2017, accessed 7 June 2023 <theirrelevantinvestor.com/2017/08/31/today-in-market-history-the-first-index-fund/>
356. Elizabeth MacBride, CNBC, 'Jack Bogle's last warning to the investment industry: "Don't forget the little guy you serve"', 19 Jan 2019, accessed 7 June 2023 <www.cnbc.com/2019/01/17/jack-bogles-last-warning-to-the-investment-industry-dont-forget-the-little-guy-you-serve---.html>
357. Allan Sloan, Yahoo!Finance, 'The democratization of investing': Index funds officially overtake active managers,' 22 May 2022, accessed 7 June 2023

&lt;uk.news.yahoo.com/index-fund-assets-exceed-active-fund-assets-120639243.html&gt;

358. Daniel Kurt, Investopedia.com, *'Is Warren Buffett's 90/10 Asset Allocation Sound?'* 27 Dec 2022, accessed 7 June 2023 &lt;www.investopedia.com/articles/personal-finance/121815/buffetts-9010-asset-allocation-sound.asp&gt;

359. David Floyd, Investopedia.com, *'Buffett's Bet with the Hedge Funds: And the Winner Is...'* 25 June 2019, accessed 7 June 2023 &lt;www.investopedia.com/articles/investing/030916/buffetts-bet-hedge-funds-year-eight-brka-brkb.asp&gt;

360. Patrick Cairns, The Evidence-Based Investor, *'IS THE GROWTH OF PASSIVE INVESTING MESSING WITH THE MARKETS?'* 17 Nov 2022, accessed 7 June 2023 &lt;www.evidenceinvestor.com/is-the-growth-of-passive-investing-messing-with-markets/&gt;

361. Dan Caplinger, The Motley Fool, *'S&P 500 Investors Have Lost Billions on Tesla Stock,'* 23 Nov 2022, accessed 7 June 2023 &lt;www.fool.com/investing/2022/11/23/sp-500-investors-have-lost-billions-on-tesla-stock/&gt;

362. Yun Li, CNBC.com, *'Michael Burry of 'The Big Short' says he has found the next market bubble,'* 4 Sept 2019, accessed 7 June 2023 &lt;www.cnbc.com/2019/09/04/the-big-shorts-michael-burry-says-he-has-found-the-next-market-bubble.html&gt;

363. The Motley Fool, Nasdaq.com, *'Jack Bogle on Index Funds, Vanguard, and Investing Advice,'* 17 Jan 2019, accessed 9 June 2023 &lt;www.nasdaq.com/articles/jack-bogle-index-funds-vanguard-and-investing-advice-2019-01-17&gt;

364. Vanguard.com, *'How to invest a lump sum of money,'* accessed 10 June 2023 &lt;investor.vanguard.com/investor-resources-education/online-trading/dollar-cost-averaging-vs-lump-sum&gt;

365. Adam Hayes, Investopedia.com, *'Dollar-Cost Averaging (DCA) Explained With Examples and Considerations,'* 26 Apr 2023, accessed 9 June 2023 &lt;www.investopedia.com/terms/d/dollarcostaveraging.asp&gt;

WHAT

WE

THINK

WE

BECOME

# Glossary (Phrasebook)

**Artificial scarcity** – pretending you have less money so you spend less
**Assets** – positively valued items on the balance sheet e.g. investments (opposite of liability)
**Asset allocation** – proportion of your investment portfolio in different asset classes
**Asset class** – different types of investments e.g. cash, stocks, bonds, gold
**Balance sheet** – a financial statement that shows the balance of your assets and liabilities at a particular moment in time
**Bears** – people who trade and invest as if the stock market is going down over time
**Bulls** – people who trade and invest as if the stock market is going up over time
**Black Hole** – a heavy collapsed star, the gravity of which is so strong that nothing escapes, not even light. A great metaphor for debt.
**Budget** – in personal finance, a spending plan (usually monthly), often divided up into categories (e.g. bills, food, housing, transportation, entertainment etc.)
**Candlestick chart** – chart used by traders and investors. Candlesticks are bars that show the opening and closing balance of the stock market. They can be over different time frames, weekly, daily and even 5-minute candles. They are green when positive and red when negative.
**Compound interest** – cash made on your money (e.g. in an investing account) not only on the original amount, but also on your interest. Your money grows in an upwards curve.
**Day trading** – people who buy and sell investments quickly, sometimes only holding them for minutes or hours
**Deflation** – when money gains its buying power over time, stuff costs less
**Diversification** – spreading your investments over different types of assets
**Fiat currency** – paper money, not backed by gold
**Fiduciary duty** – someone acting in your best interests, used to describe the relationship between a certified financial advisor and a client. Fiduciary duties include duty of care, loyalty, good faith, confidentiality, prudence, and disclosure.

**Financial Independence** – when your investments make enough for you to replace your income without having to work a traditional job

**Financial minimalism** – people who try to live well on less, who simplify their lives

**Headwind** – when things are working against the stock market (like going head-first into the wind)

**Hedonic adaptation** – when we no longer find pleasure in something that used to be new and exciting

**Index** (stock market) – measures the performance of part of the stock market, companies selected by certain criteria e.g. size, profitability, etc.

**Index fund** – a basket of stocks and shares that tracks a particular index

**Inflation** – when money loses its buying power over time, stuff costs more

**Investing** – buying things of value; using your time, talent and treasures to have a positive effect, e.g relationships, career progression, spiritual walk etc.

**Liabilities** – negatively valued items on the balance sheet e.g. debt (opposite of assets)

**Liquidity** – how easy it is to buy and sell a particular investment

**Macroeconomics** – the study of whole economies and how they interact

**Margin** – has several different meanings. In personal development, it's creating room in your budget and your life; in business terms, it's the difference between what something is sold for and what it costs to make; in trading terms, it's money borrowed from a broker to purchase an investment

**Market sentiment** – the mood of the stock market (fear or greed)

**Material wealth** – accumulation of things money can buy, e.g. possessions and stuff

**Mindful Finance** – mindfulness techniques applied to money, being aware of your financial situation, your thoughts and emotions, being intentional about how you manage money, stewardship

**Net worth statement** – a financial statement showing how much wealth you have, calculated by working out how much you own and how much you owe; can be positive or negative.

**Options trading** – a special type of trading where bets can be put on whether the stock market will go up and down in a particular time frame (by buying put and call options)

**Rebalancing** – adjusting the proportion your assets when they get out of balance e.g. bonds vs stocks

**Reversion to the mean** – in statistics there is a tendency for what goes up to come back down. Like an elastic band, the stock market goes up and down, but always likes to go back to the average.

**Rich** – looking the way people imagine wealthy people should look, even if they're broke

**Risk tolerance** – your ability to withstand up and down movements of investments e.g. the stock market

**Simple interest** – cash made on your money (e.g. in a savings account) but only on the original amount. Your money grows in a straight line.

**Spiritual wealth** – blessings in different areas of your life, often things that money can't buy

**Stagflation** – when there's inflation (stuff costs more) but the economy is stagnant

**Stewardship** – doing the best we can with the resources we have been given

**Stocks and shares** – publically traded slices of a company; also known as equities

**Stock buybacks** – when companies buy their own stocks and shares. Reduces the number available and raises the price overall.

**Tailwind** – when things are working in favour of the stock market (like having the wind at your back)

**Technical analysis** – using stock market trends and patterns to predict future price movements. Sometimes these use maths and statistics, clever tools like fractals and Fibonacci retracement levels. Some peple study momentum or look for shapes within the chart (e.g. *'head and shoulders pattern'*).

**Ticker symbol** – unique abbreviation used to identify a particular stock on a particular stock market, used to originally be on ticker tape (e.g. AAPL = Apple, GOOGL = Alphabet Inc, MSFT = Microsoft Corporation, AMZN = Amazon.com).

**Tithe** – a special type of percentage giving. For modern day Christians it is usually taken to mean giving 10% of their increase to the local church.

**Volatility** – the up and down movements of investments e.g. of the stock market

**Wealth effect** – people feel richer when the economy is doing well, their house price is up, they spend more

CARPE DIEM

# ABOUT THE AUTHOR

Dr Esther J. Cole is a hospital doctor, based in Liverpool, UK. She grew up in Staffordshire where her family currently live. She moved to Liverpool in 2005 to study Medicine at the University of Liverpool. She trained as a physician, before embarking on a creative portfolio career. This alternative career path has allowed her to write this book alongside working as a doctor.

Her medical interests include geriatric medicine (care of older people), health and wellbeing (including Lifestyle Medicine and healthy aging). She is a co-director of Beatitude, a social enterprise that promotes mental health by providing training in resilience, personal happiness and wellbeing.

Esther has always had a passion for writing. She attained an Intercalated BA in Medical Humanities at The University of Bristol during her medical undergraduate training, which included English Literature, History of Medicine and Philosophy of Science. Her study of medical narratives has been a mixed blessing - it has certainly influenced her NHS work (but means she has a tendency to write long stories in case notes).

She has a particular interest in the history of The Liverpool Medical Students' Society (LMSS). She has written several brief histories for student publications outlining the society's 1874 origins and occasionally bizarre traditions. She has served two terms as an LMSS charity trustee and is an Honorary Life Member.

Alongside her medical career, Esther has a variety of interests. She started a side-hustle in 2016 called Western Spiral Art, a creative business that uses sci-fi and fantasy to encourage people to get into arts and crafts. She has run maker workshops at Makefests and Comic Cons along with a trusty crew of friends and volunteers. She also sells products online on her Etsy shop.

Esther also attends and volunteers regularly at Liverpool One Church. Much of her worldview and life-direction has been influenced by her Christian faith with the support and encouragement of the local church.

*Mindful Finance: How To Be Successful With Money* is her debut non-fiction book, bringing together her passion for financial stewardship, personal development, health and wellbeing. She hopes it helps you on your mindful finance journey.